Lately, I hear about manga being drawn using computers. I don't know much about it, but the tones are supposed to be better, and a lot of details can be added easily, allowing the artist to complete the project more quickly. It sounds wonderful. I'd like to learn how to do that, too, little by little... but, on the other hand, looking at a monitor non-stop doesn't sound so easy... Oh, well. As I contemplate the possibilities, my next deadline is approaching rapidly...
— Koji Inada

Author Riku Sanjo and artist Koji Inada were both born in Tokyo in 1964. Sanjo began his career writing a radio-controlled car manga for the comic **Bonbon**. Inada debuted with **Kussotare Daze!!** in **Weekly Shonen Jump**. Sanjo and Inada first worked together on the highly successful **Dragon Quest–Dai's Big Adventure**. **Beet the Vandel Buster**, their latest collaboration, debuted in **Monthly Shonen Jump** in 2002 and was an immediate hit, inspiring an action-packed video game and an animated series on Japanese TV.

BEET THE VANDEL BUSTER
VOL. 3
The SHONEN JUMP Graphic Novel Edition

STORY BY RIKU SANJO
ART BY KOJI INADA

English Adaptation/Shaenon K. Garrity
Translation/Naomi Kokubo
Touch-Up & Lettering/Mark McMurray
Cover Design/Sean Lee
Interior Design/Andrea Rice
Editor/Pancha Diaz

Managing Editor/Elizabeth Kawasaki
Director of Production/Noboru Watanabe
Editorial Director/Alvin Lu
Executive Vice President & Editor in Chief/Hyoe Narita
Sr. Director of Acquisitions/Rika Inouye
Vice President of Sales & Marketing/Liza Coppola
Vice President of Strategic Development/Yumi Hoashi
Publisher/Seiji Horibuchi

BOUKEN OH BEET –BEET THE VANDEL BUSTER–
©2002 by RIKU SANJO, KOJI INADA. All rights
reserved. First published in Japan in 2002 by SHUEISHA
Inc., Tokyo. English translation rights in the United States
of America and Canada arranged by SHUEISHA Inc. The
stories, characters and incidents mentioned in this publi-
cation are entirely fictional.

No portion of this book may be reproduced or trans-
mitted in any form or by any means without written
permission from the copyright holders.

Printed in the U.S.A.

Published by VIZ, LLC
P.O. Box 77064
San Francisco, CA 94107

SHONEN JUMP Graphic Novel Edition
10 9 8 7 6 5 4 3 2 1
First printing, January 2005

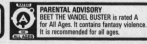

PARENTAL ADVISORY
BEET THE VANDEL BUSTER is rated A
for All Ages. It contains fantasy violence.
It is recommended for all ages.

THE WORLD'S
MOST POPULAR MANGA

www.viz.com

www.shonenjump.com

SHONEN JUMP GRAPHIC NOVEL

Beet
THE VANDEL BUSTER

Volume 3

Story by **Riku Sanjo**
Art by **Koji Inada**

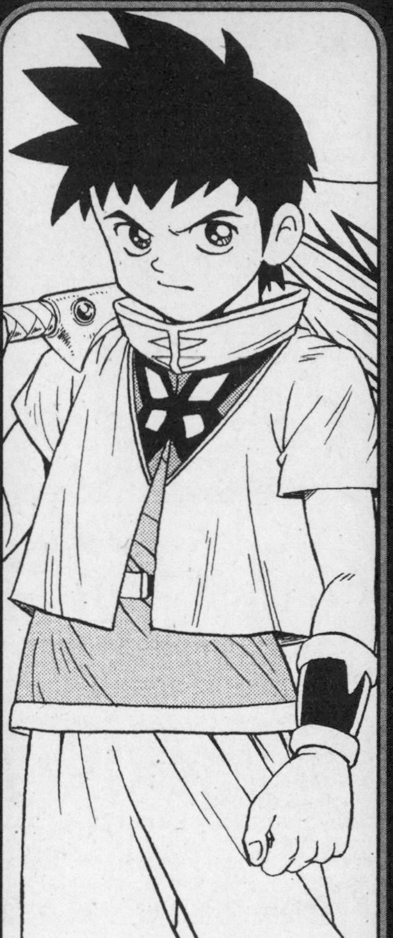

BEET

The hero of this story.
Believing in justice, he sets out on a journey to save the world. He received five Saiga weapons from the Zenon Warriors.

STORY

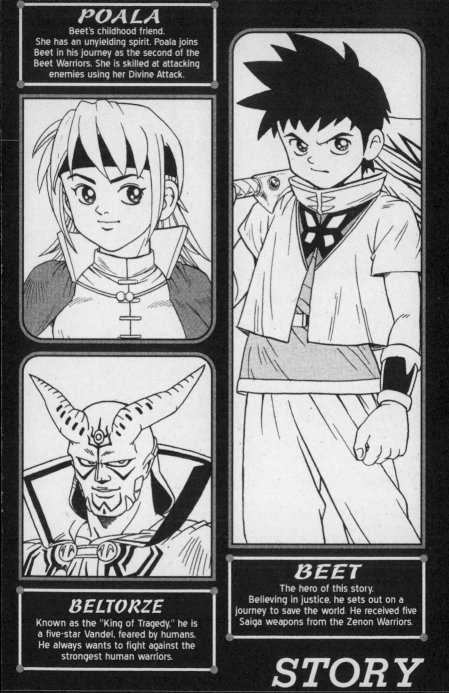

POALA

Beet's childhood friend.
She has an unyielding spirit. Poala joins Beet in his journey as the second of the Beet Warriors. She is skilled at attacking enemies using her Divine Attack.

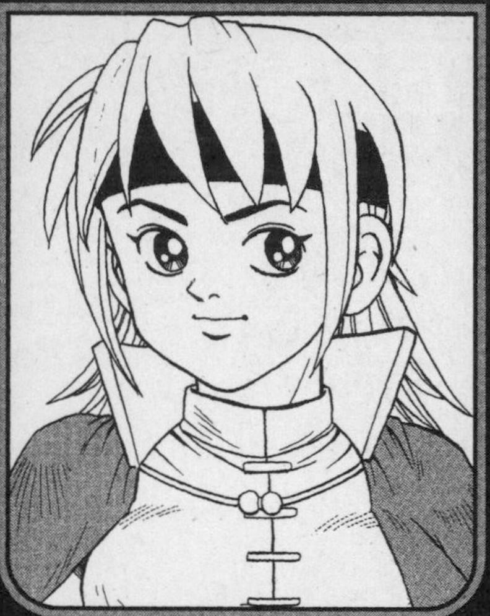

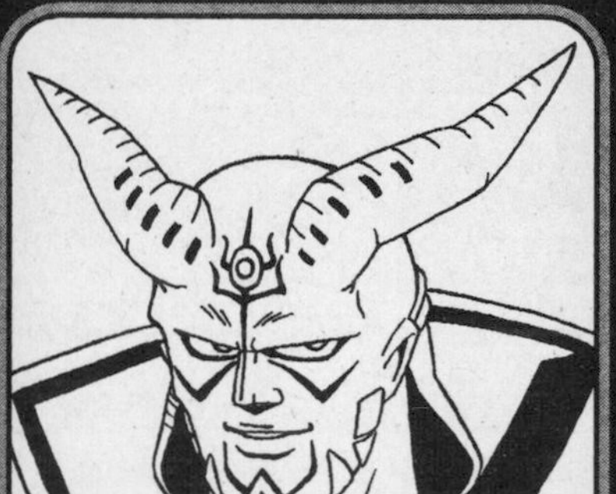

BELTORZE

Known as the "King of Tragedy," he is a five-star Vandel, feared by humans. He always wants to fight against the strongest human warriors.

Beet THE VANDEL BUSTER

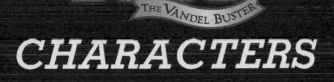

CHARACTERS

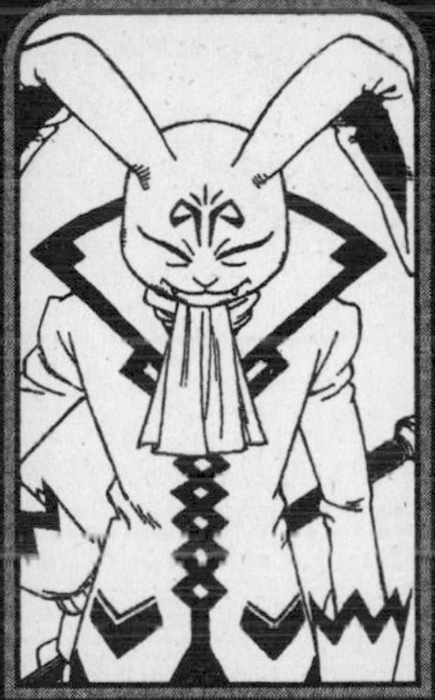

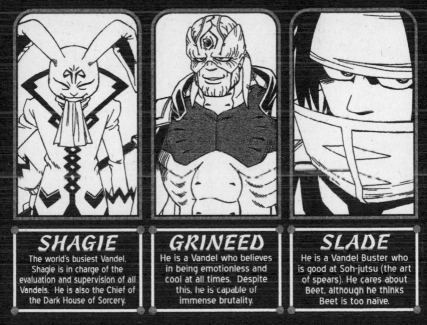

SHAGIE

The world's busiest Vandel. Shagie is in charge of the evaluation and supervision of all Vandels. He is also the Chief of the Dark House of Sorcery.

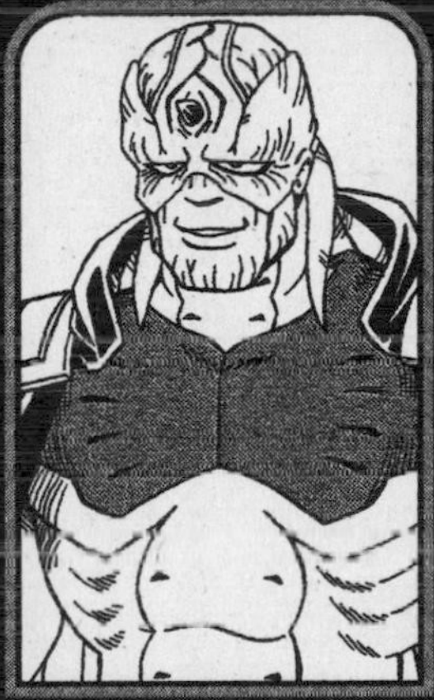

GRINEED

He is a Vandel who believes in being emotionless and cool at all times. Despite this, he is capable of immense brutality.

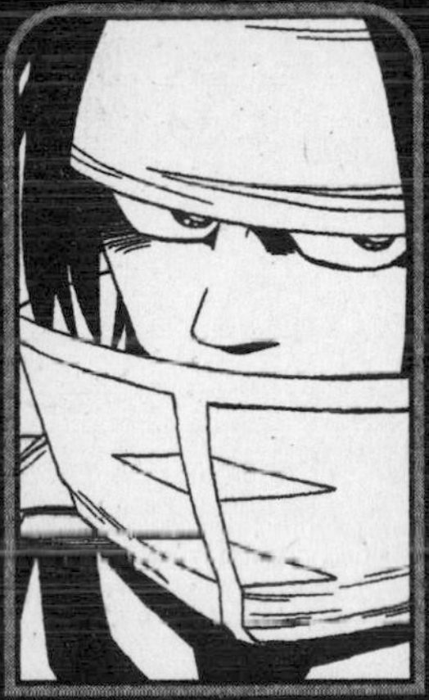

SLADE

He is a Vandel Buster who is good at Soh-jutsu (the art of spears). He cares about Beet, although he thinks Beet is too naïve.

"Vandels"... In this story, that's what we call evil creatures with magical powers. One day they appeared on the surface of the Earth, releasing monsters and destroying the peace and order of nations. People called this seemingly endless era "The Dark Age."

Beet, a young boy who believes in justice, binds himself with a contract to become a Vandel Buster, and conquer Vandels for a living. However, Beet stumbles into the middle of a battle between Beltorze and the Zenon Warriors, where he suffers a fatal injury. He miraculously survives by receiving the Saiga of the Zenon Warriors.

Three years later, Beet sets out on a journey with Poala to carry on the Zenon Warriors' mission in the world beyond. However, as soon as they reach the port city of Ledeux, they're ambushed by Grineed -- a Vandel known as the "Clever Honcho of Deep Green" -- and Poala is poisoned. Then Beltorze shows up, hoping to provoke Grineed. In his battle against Beltorze, Beet uses every power he has, finally resorting to his special deathblow. However...

Beet
THE VANDEL BUSTER

③

Chapter 7: The Clash with Beltorze!

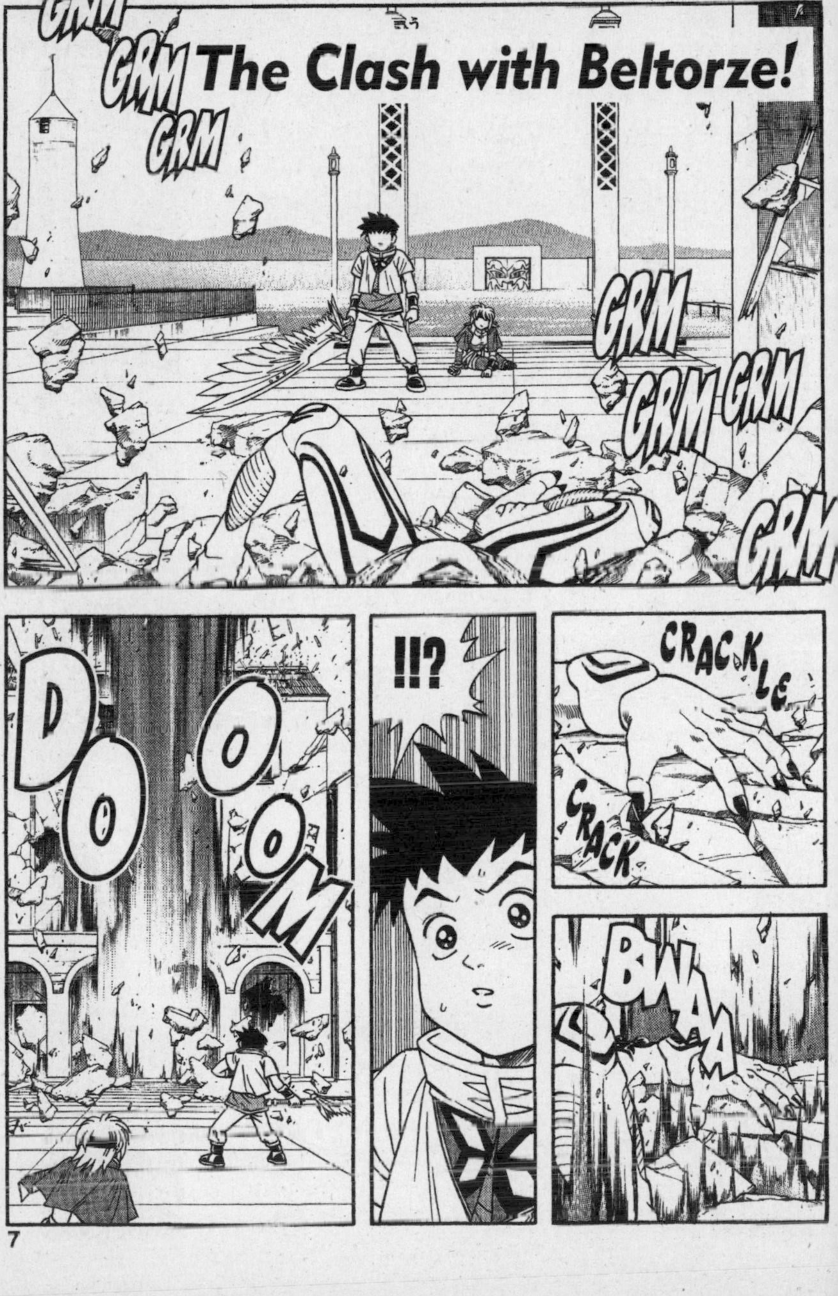
GRM
GRM
GRM
GRM
GRM GRM
GRM
CRACKLE
CRACK
BWAAA
!!?
DOOOOM

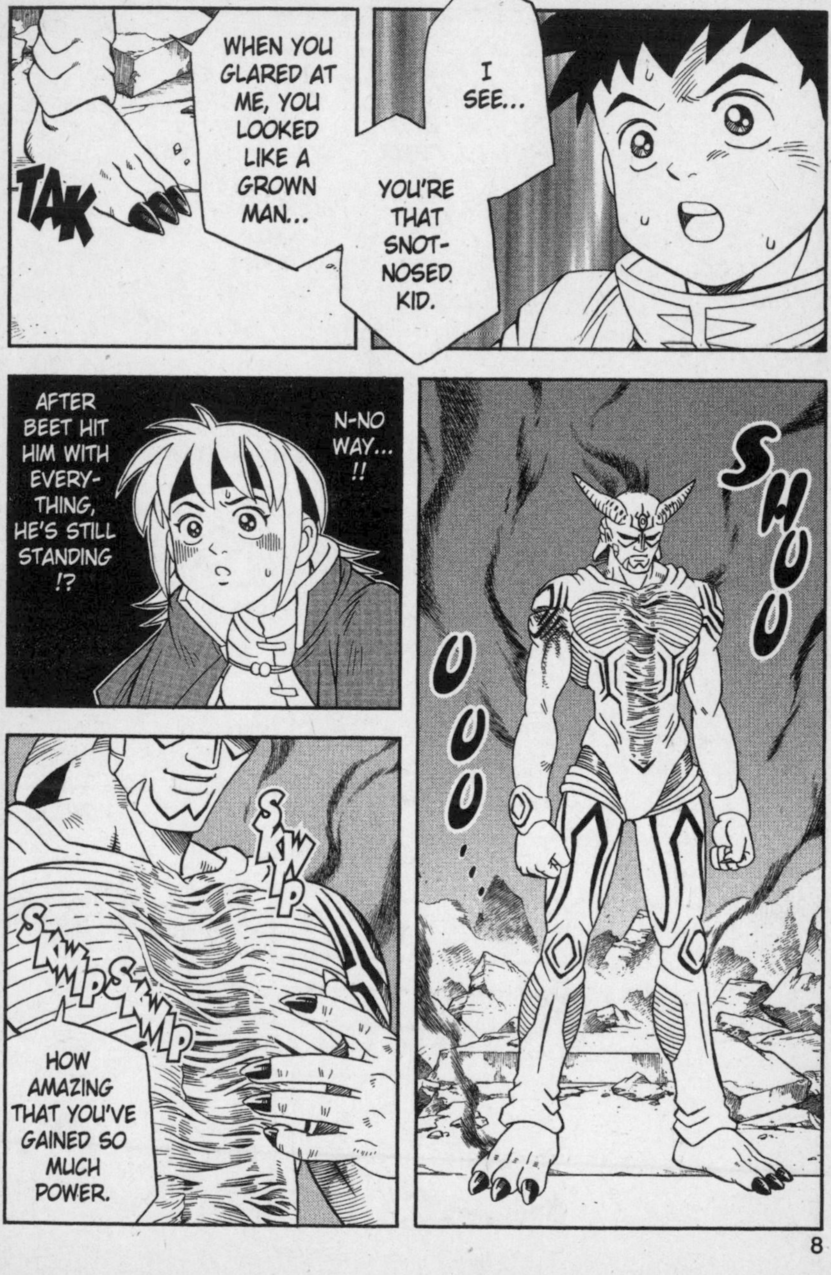
I SEE...
YOU'RE THAT SNOT-NOSED KID.
WHEN YOU GLARED AT ME, YOU LOOKED LIKE A GROWN MAN...
TAK
SHOUUUUU...
N-NO WAY...!!
AFTER BEET HIT HIM WITH EVERY-THING, HE'S STILL STANDING!?
SKWIP
SKWIP SKWIP
HOW AMAZING THAT YOU'VE GAINED SO MUCH POWER.

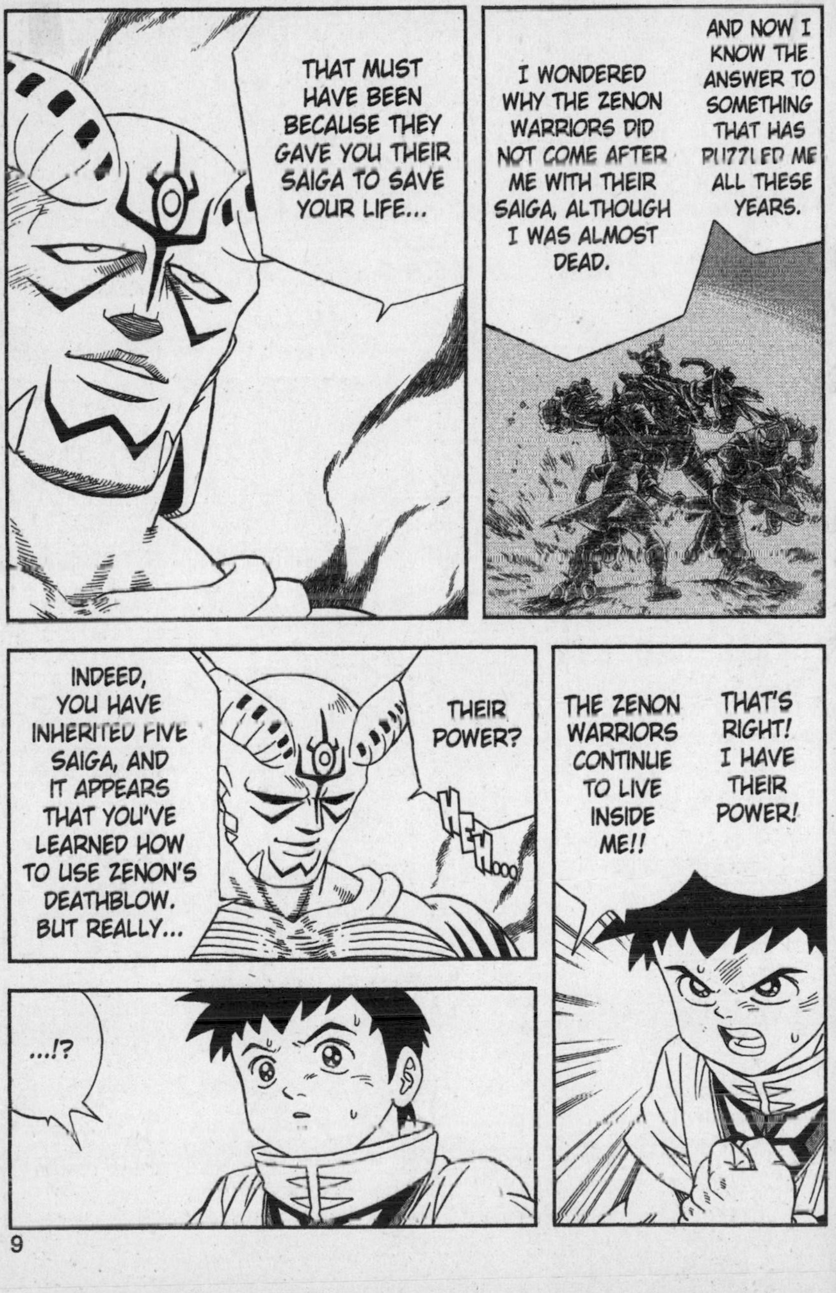
AND NOW I KNOW THE ANSWER TO SOMETHING THAT HAS PUZZLED ME ALL THESE YEARS.
I WONDERED WHY THE ZENON WARRIORS DID NOT COME AFTER ME WITH THEIR SAIGA, ALTHOUGH I WAS ALMOST DEAD.
THAT MUST HAVE BEEN BECAUSE THEY GAVE YOU THEIR SAIGA TO SAVE YOUR LIFE...
THAT'S RIGHT! I HAVE THEIR POWER!
THE ZENON WARRIORS CONTINUE TO LIVE INSIDE ME!!
THEIR POWER?
HEH...
INDEED, YOU HAVE INHERITED FIVE SAIGA, AND IT APPEARS THAT YOU'VE LEARNED HOW TO USE ZENON'S DEATHBLOW. BUT REALLY...
...!?

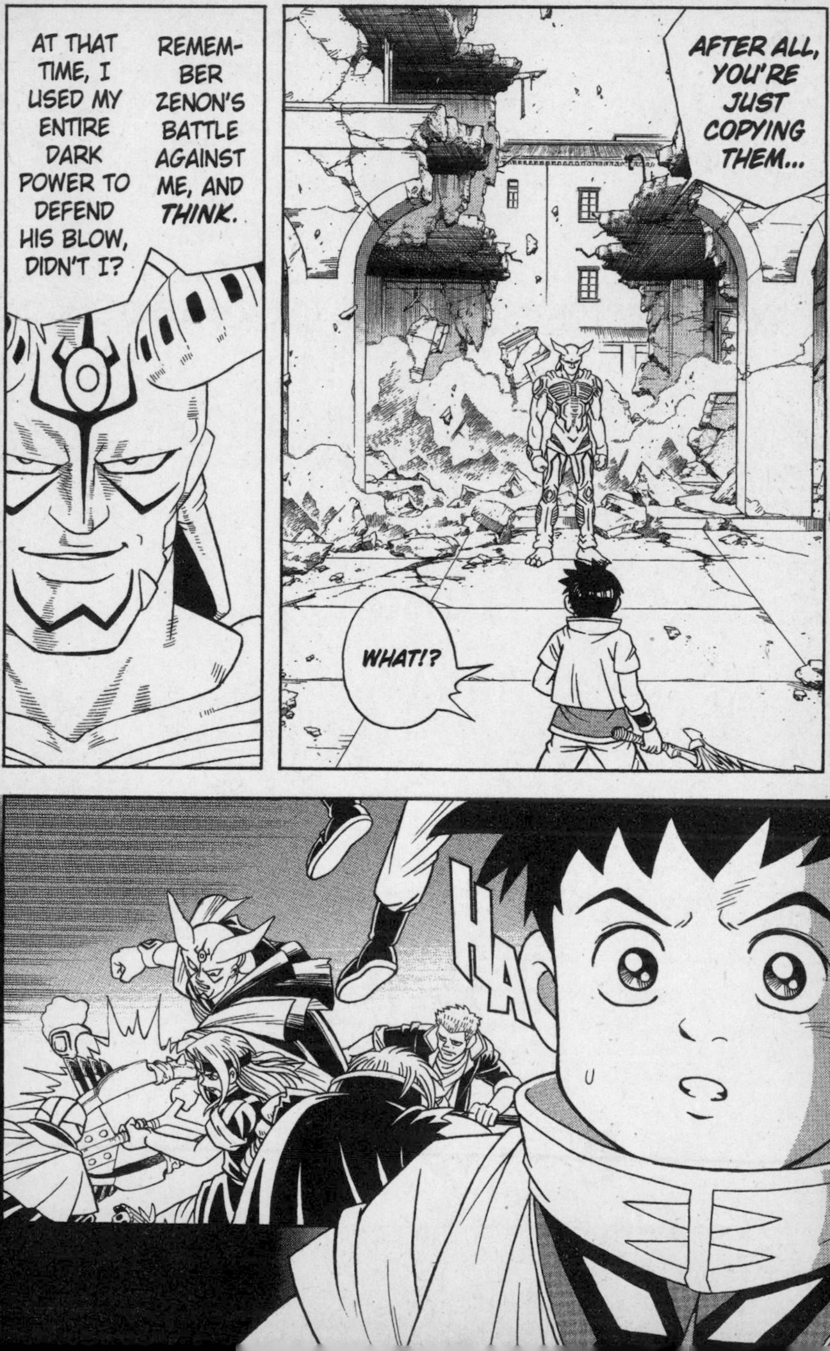
AFTER ALL, YOU'RE JUST COPYING THEM...
WHAT!?
REMEMBER ZENON'S BATTLE AGAINST ME, AND *THINK*.
AT THAT TIME, I USED MY ENTIRE DARK POWER TO DEFEND HIS BLOW, DIDN'T I?
HA

READ THIS WAY

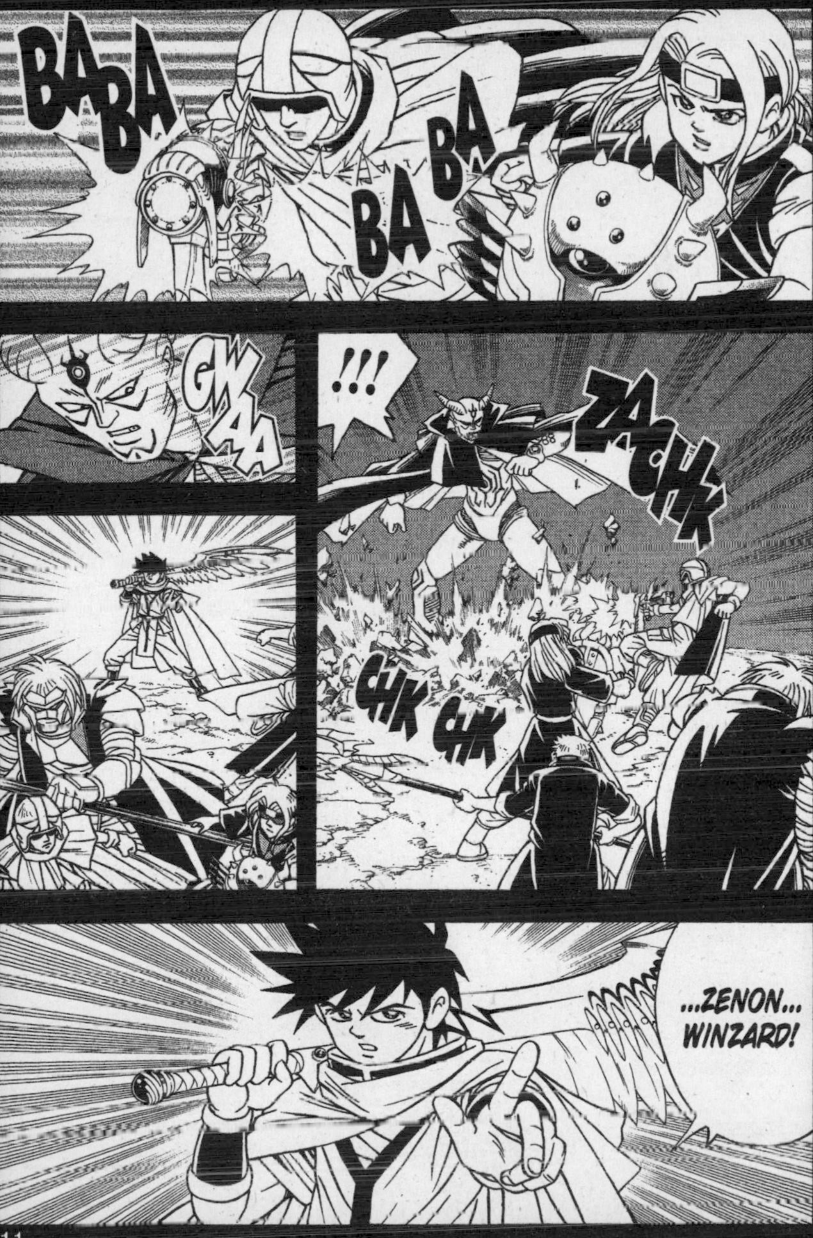
BA BA
BABA
!!!
ZACHK
CHK CHK
GWAA
...ZENON... WINZARD!

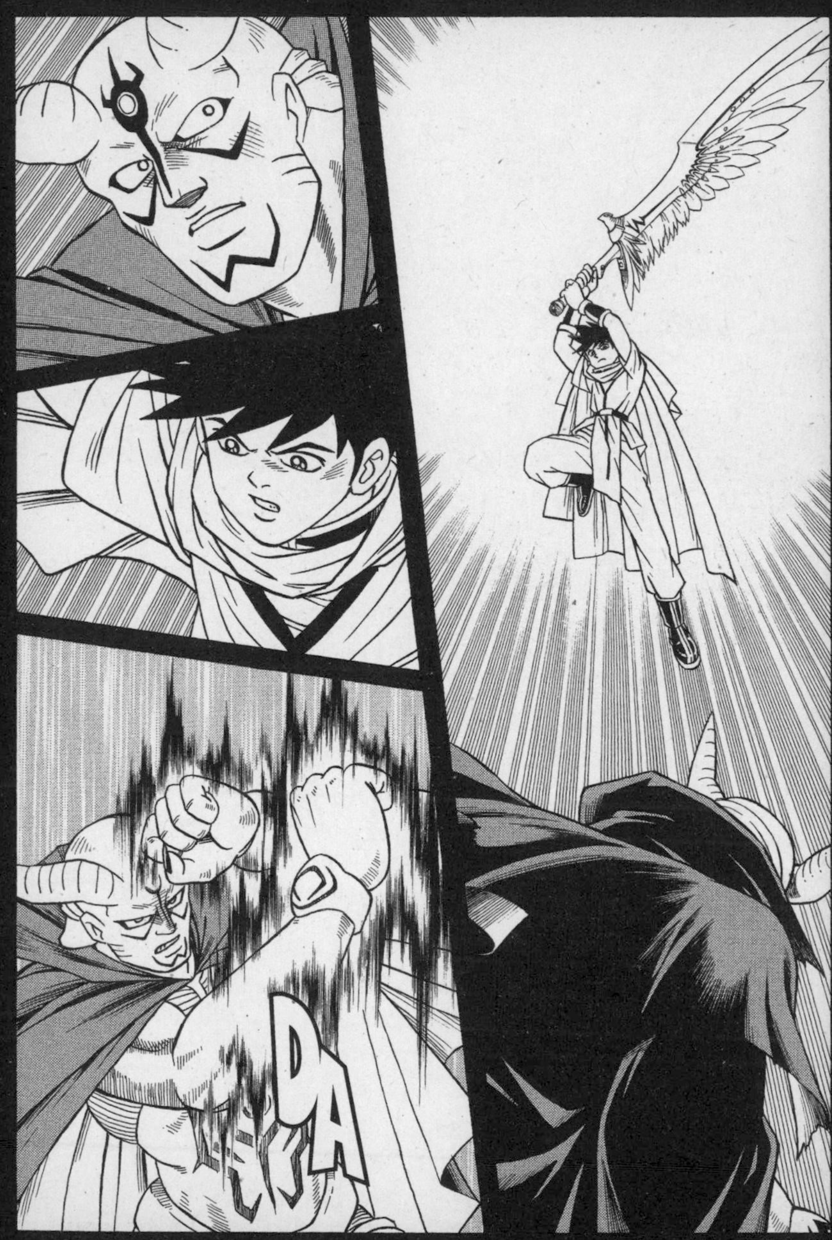
DA

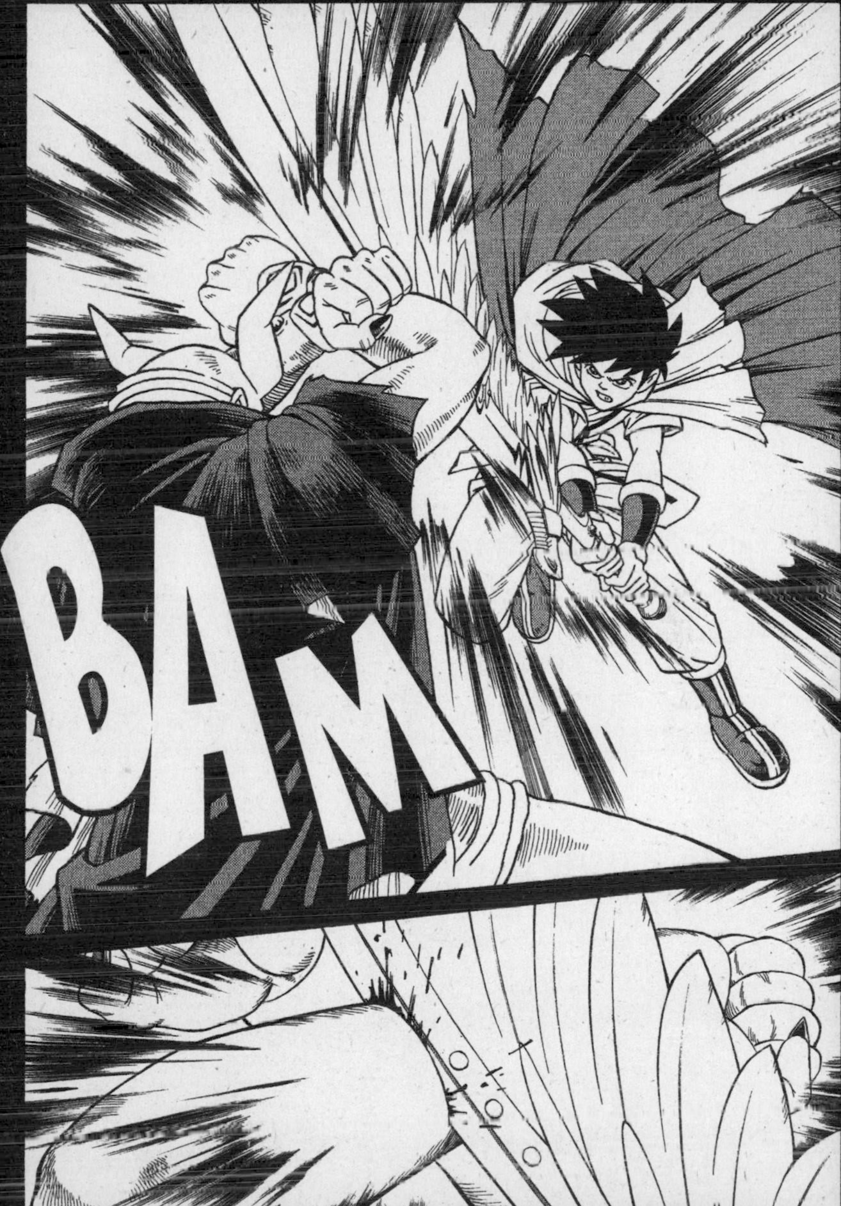
BAM

BLUP
BLUP
BLUP

CHAK

SH
OO

TH...
THAT'S...
TRUE...
!!

14

READ THIS WAY

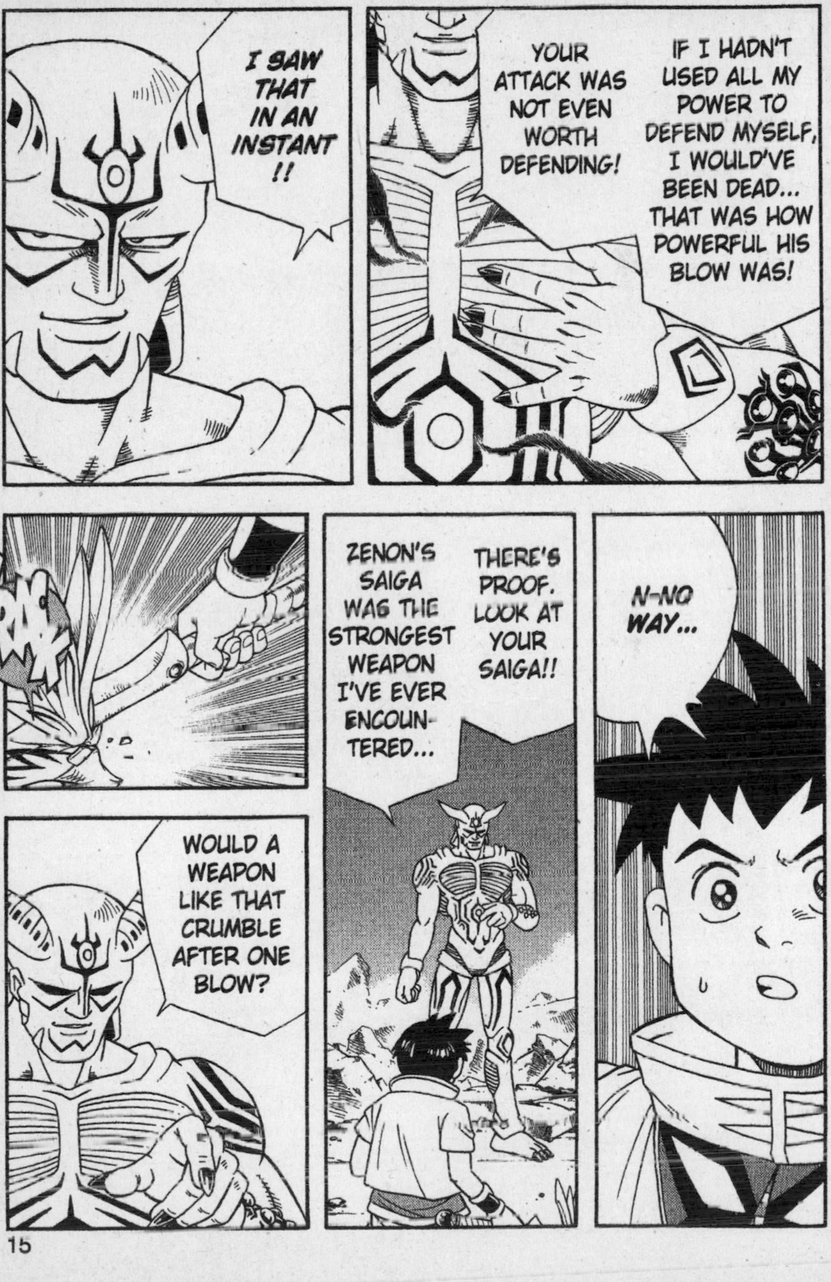

IF I HADN'T USED ALL MY POWER TO DEFEND MYSELF, I WOULD'VE BEEN DEAD... THAT WAS HOW POWERFUL HIS BLOW WAS!
YOUR ATTACK WAS NOT EVEN WORTH DEFENDING!
I SAW THAT IN AN INSTANT !!
N-NO WAY...
THERE'S PROOF. LOOK AT YOUR SAIGA!!
ZENON'S SAIGA WAS THE STRONGEST WEAPON I'VE EVER ENCOUNTERED...
WOULD A WEAPON LIKE THAT CRUMBLE AFTER ONE BLOW?

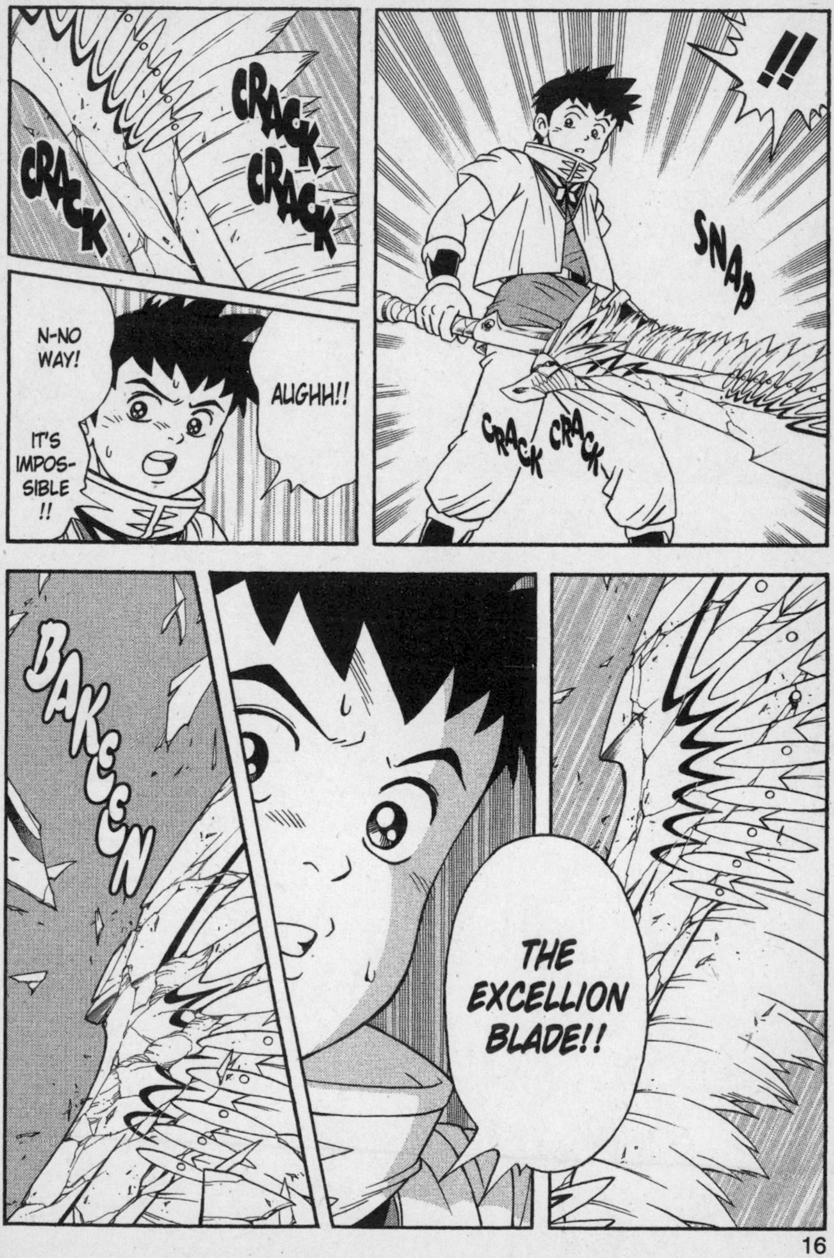
!!
SNAP
CRACK
CRACK
CRACK
CRACK
CRACK
N-NO WAY!
AUGHH!!
IT'S IMPOSSIBLE!!
THE EXCELLION BLADE!!
BAKEEN

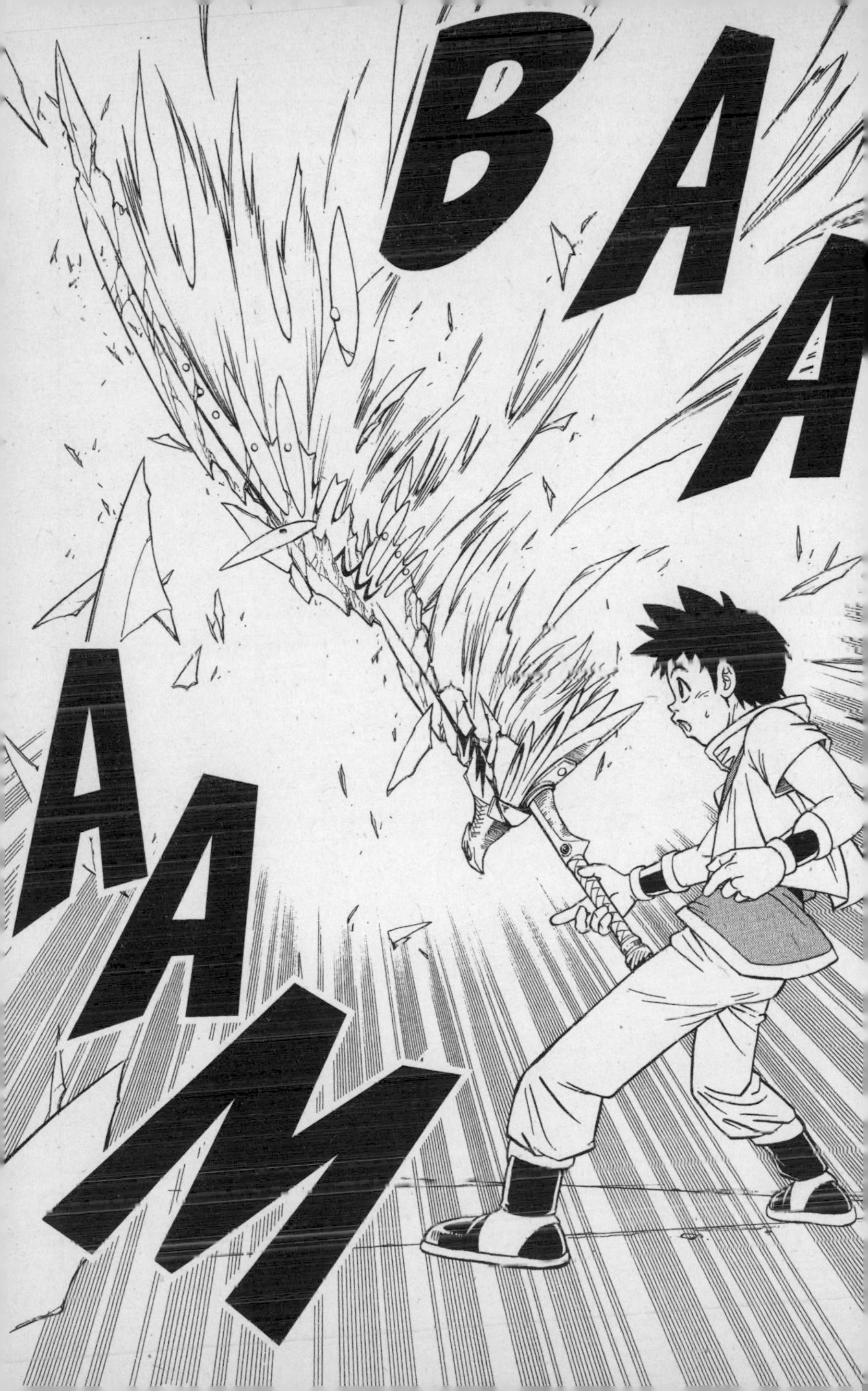
BAAAAAM

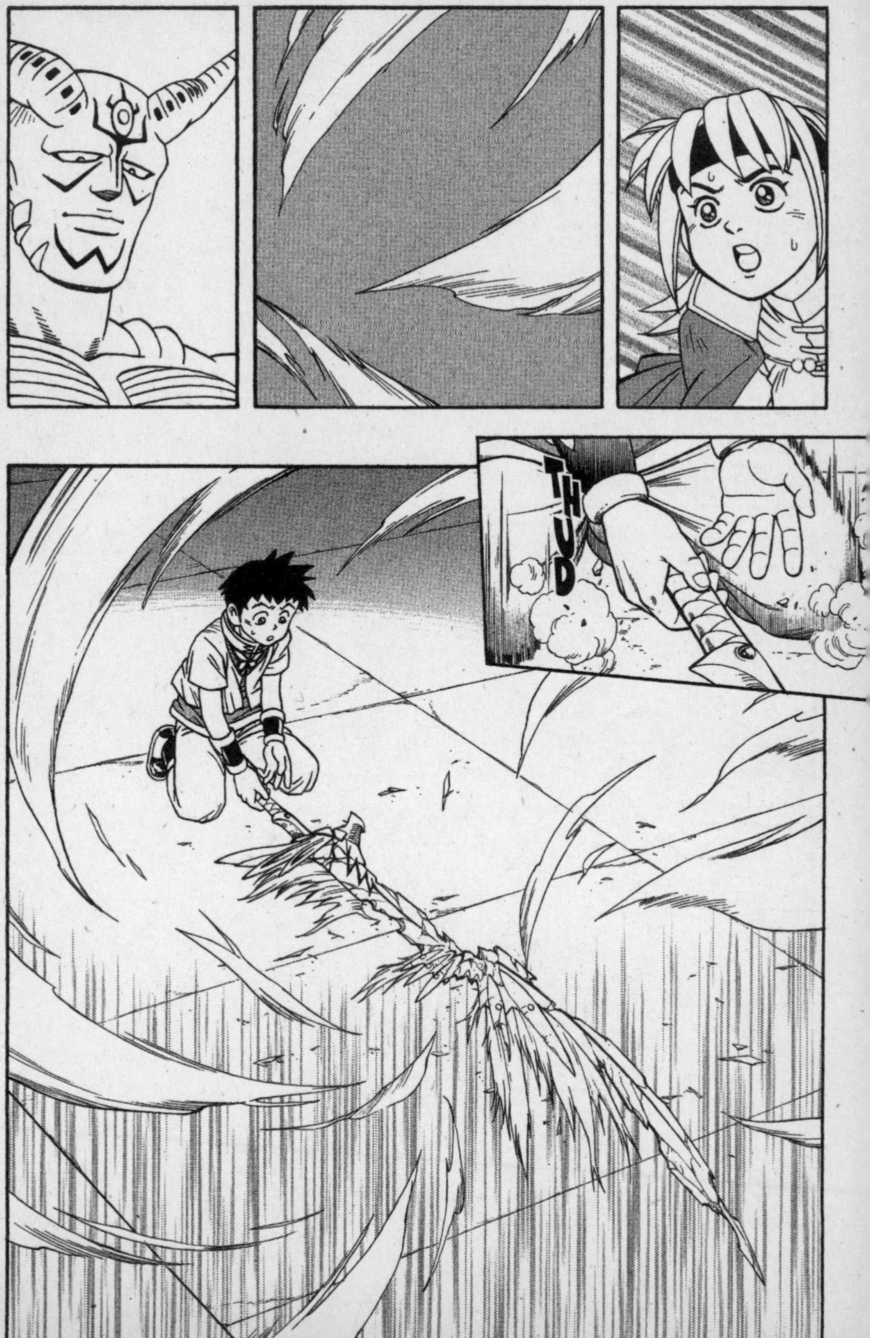
THUD

READ THIS WAY

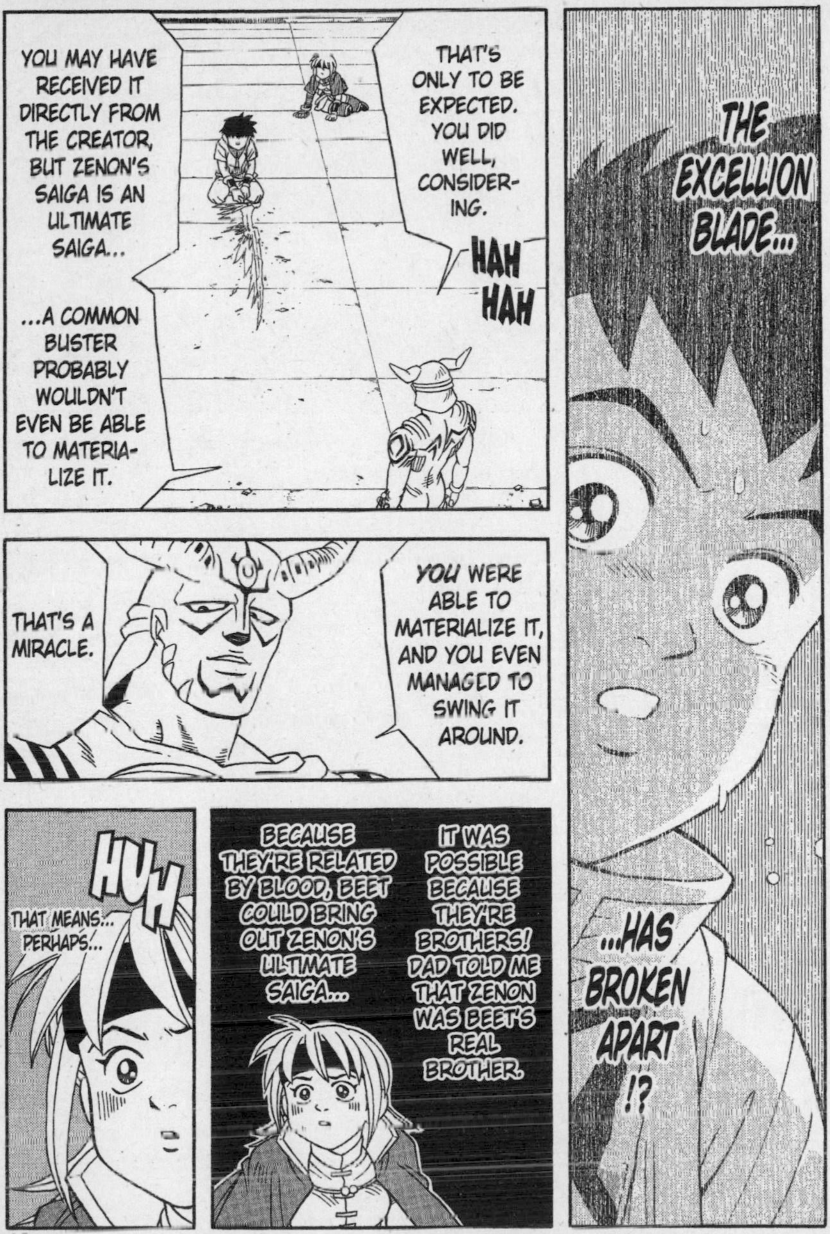

THE EXCELLION BLADE...
...HAS BROKEN APART !?
THAT'S ONLY TO BE EXPECTED. YOU DID WELL, CONSIDERING.
HAH HAH
YOU MAY HAVE RECEIVED IT DIRECTLY FROM THE CREATOR, BUT ZENON'S SAIGA IS AN ULTIMATE SAIGA...
...A COMMON BUSTER PROBABLY WOULDN'T EVEN BE ABLE TO MATERIALIZE IT.
YOU WERE ABLE TO MATERIALIZE IT, AND YOU EVEN MANAGED TO SWING IT AROUND.
THAT'S A MIRACLE.
IT WAS POSSIBLE BECAUSE THEY'RE BROTHERS! DAD TOLD ME THAT ZENON WAS BEET'S REAL BROTHER.
BECAUSE THEY'RE RELATED BY BLOOD, BEET COULD BRING OUT ZENON'S ULTIMATE SAIGA...
HUH
THAT MEANS... PERHAPS...

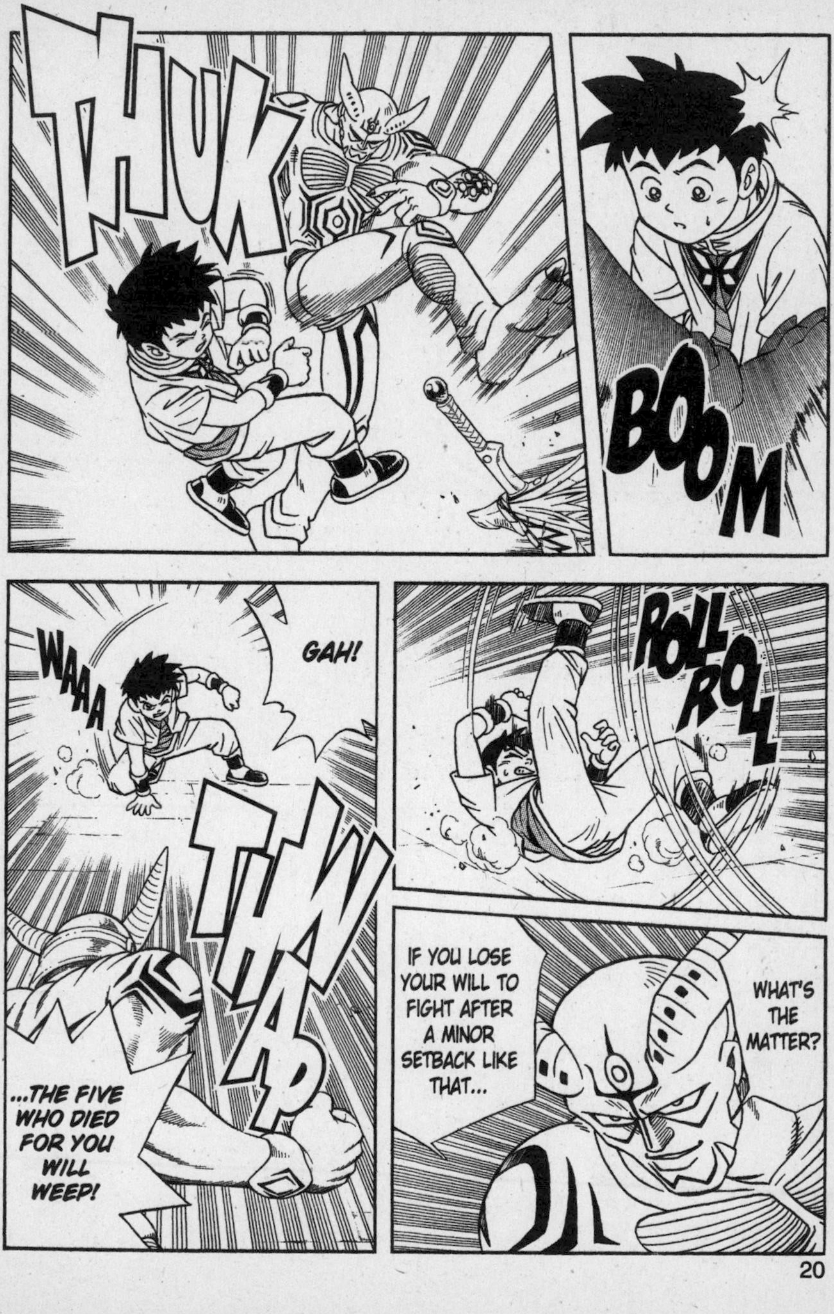
BOOOM
THUK
ROLL ROLL
WHAT'S THE MATTER?
IF YOU LOSE YOUR WILL TO FIGHT AFTER A MINOR SETBACK LIKE THAT...
GAH!
WAAAA
THWAP
...THE FIVE WHO DIED FOR YOU WILL WEEP!

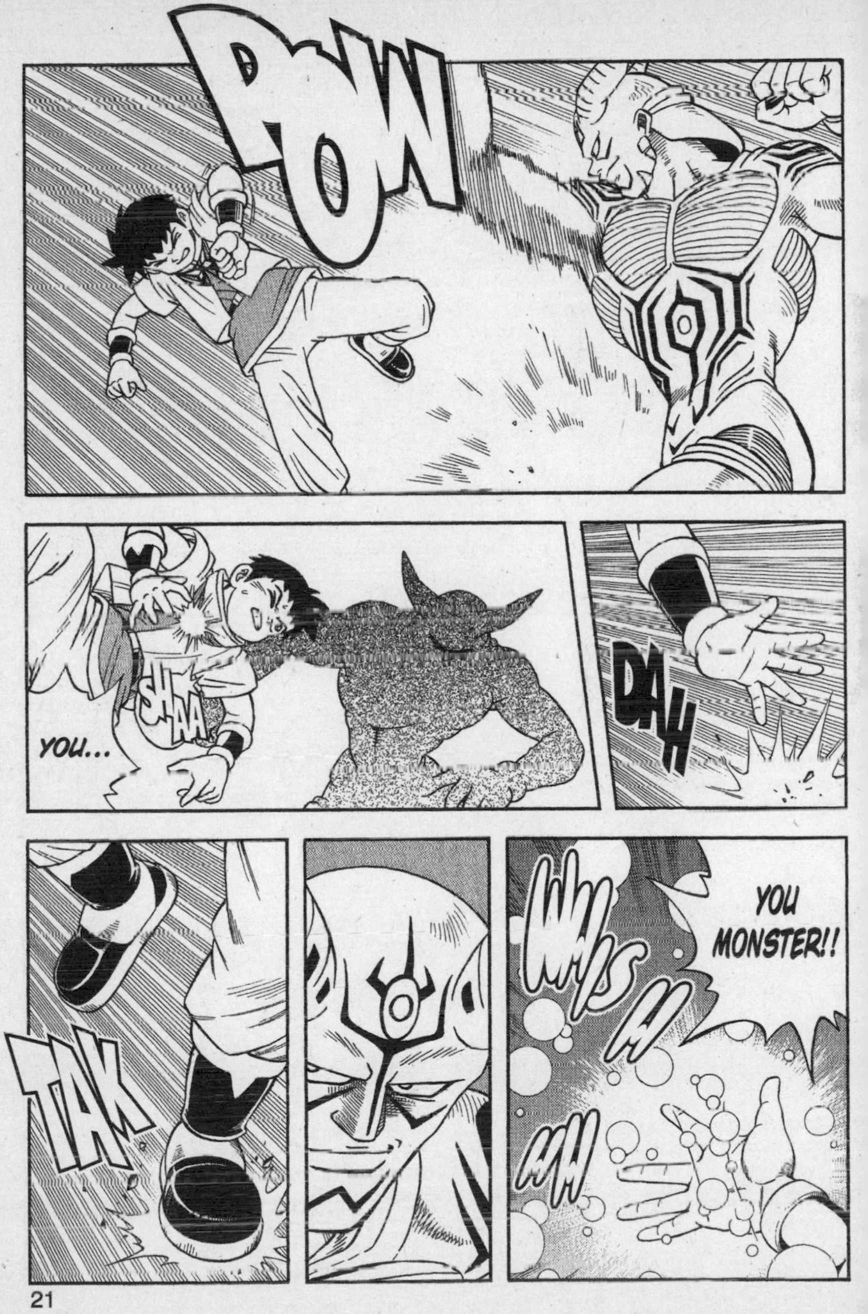
POW
DAH
SHAA
YOU...
YOU MONSTER!!
TAK

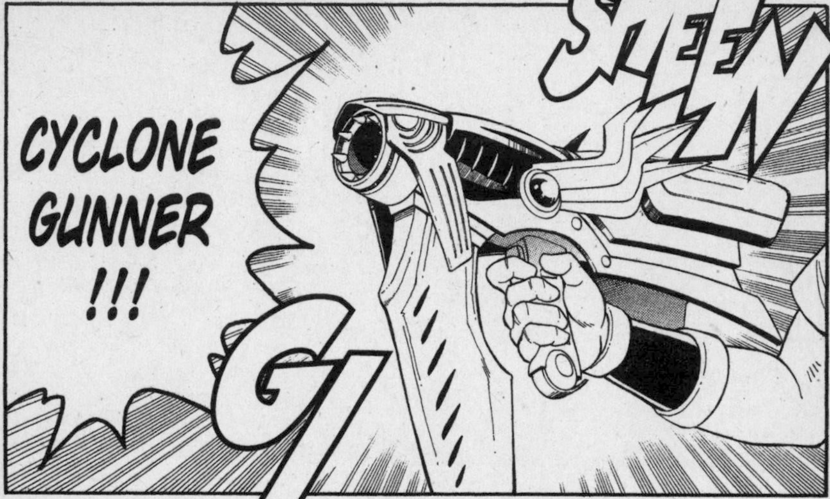
SHEEN
CYCLONE GUNNER !!!
GI

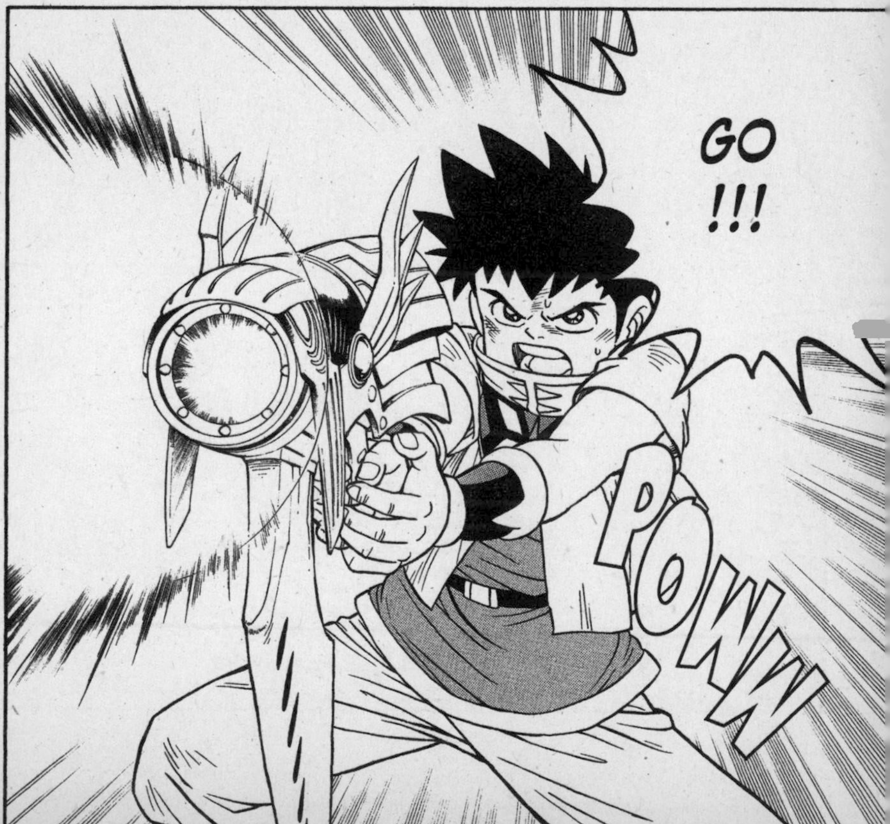
GO !!!
POWN

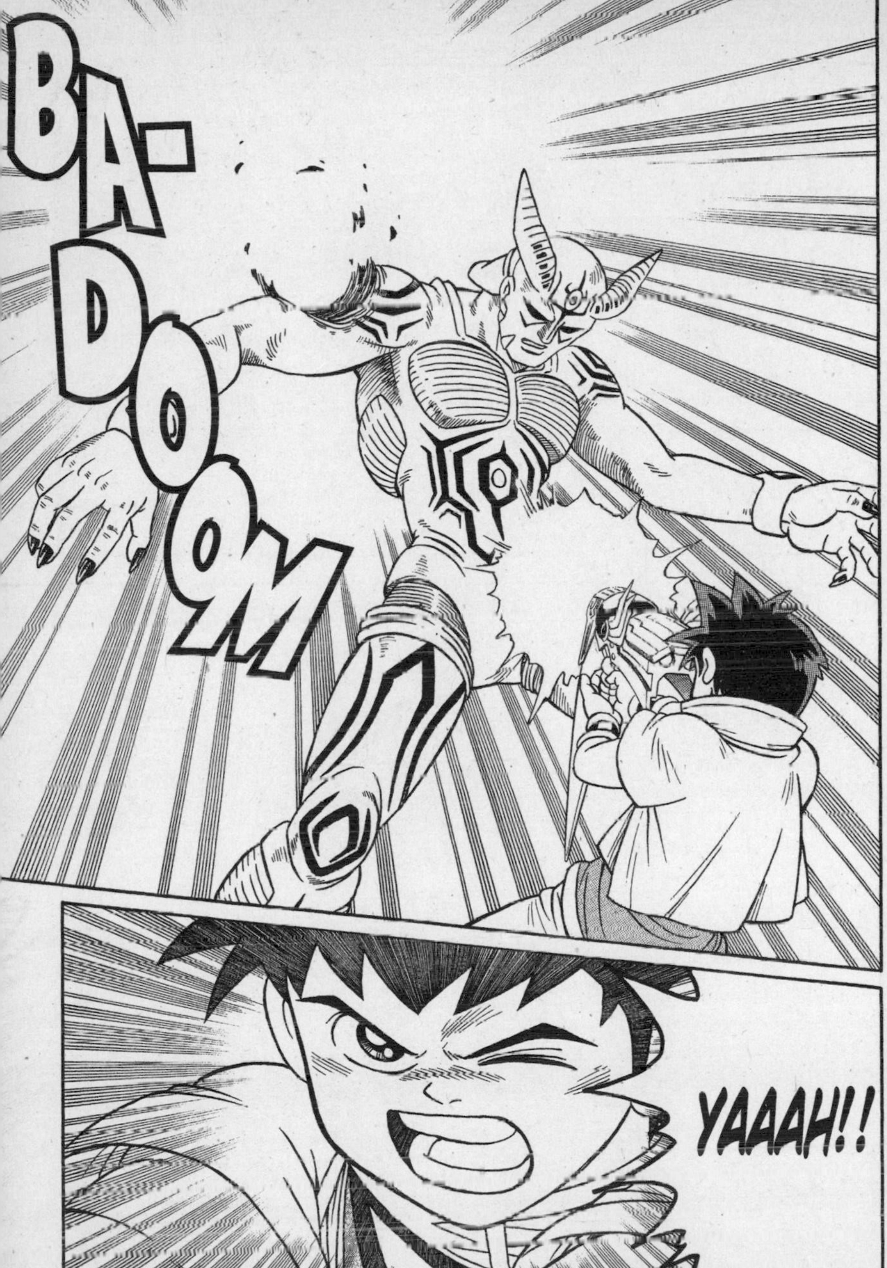
BA-DOOM
YAAAH!!

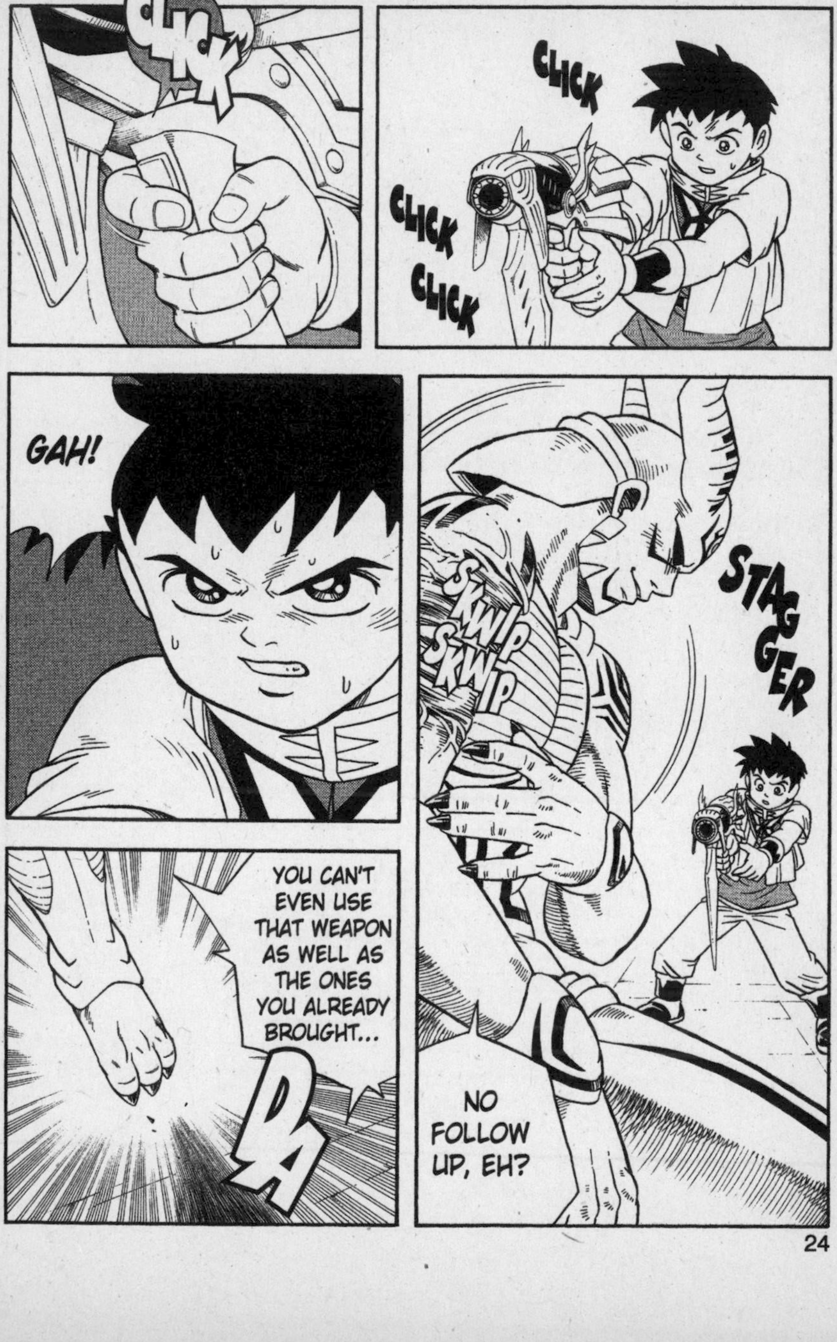
CLICK
CLICK
CLICK
CLICK
STAGGER
SKWIP
SKWIP
NO FOLLOW UP, EH?
GAH!
YOU CAN'T EVEN USE THAT WEAPON AS WELL AS THE ONES YOU ALREADY BROUGHT...
DA

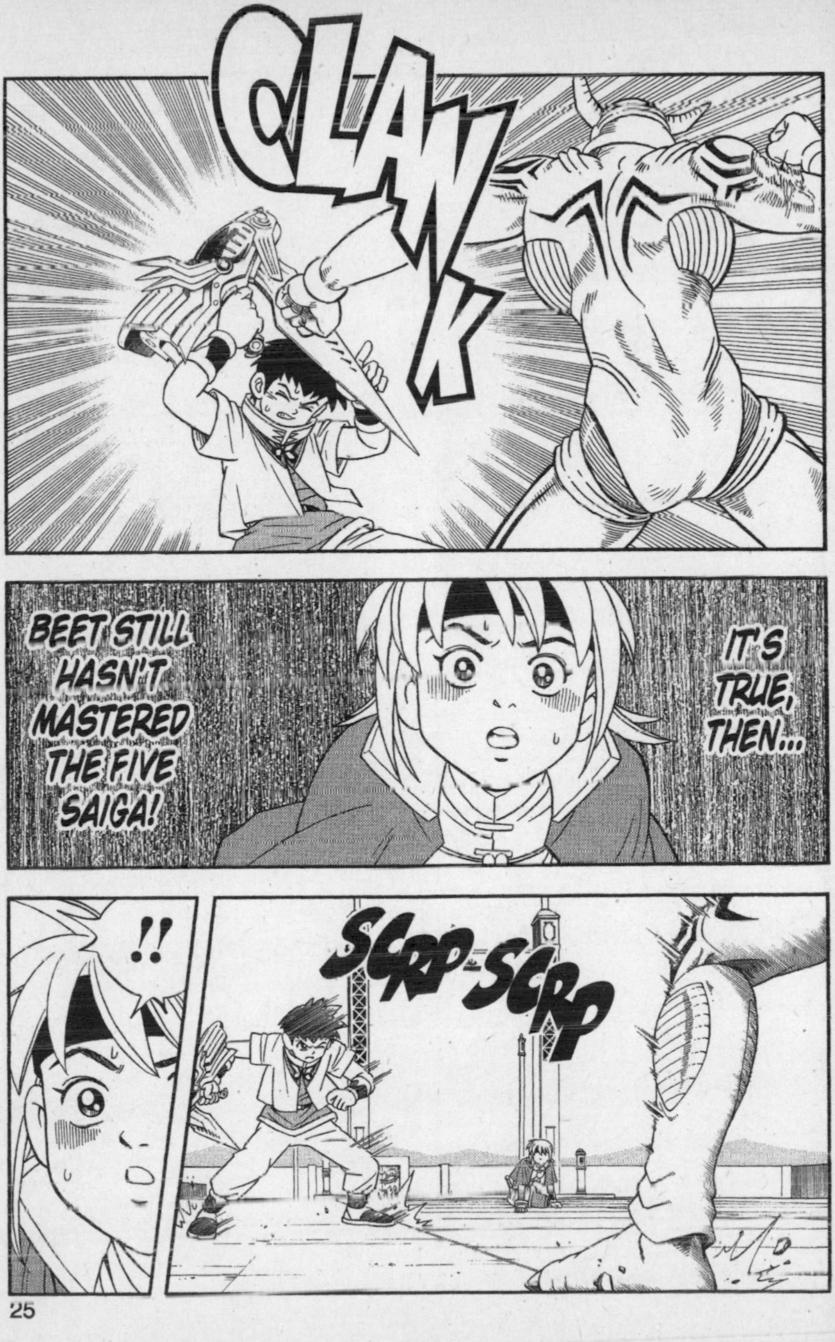
CLANK
IT'S TRUE, THEN...
BEET STILL HASN'T MASTERED THE FIVE SAIGA!
SCRP SCRP
!!

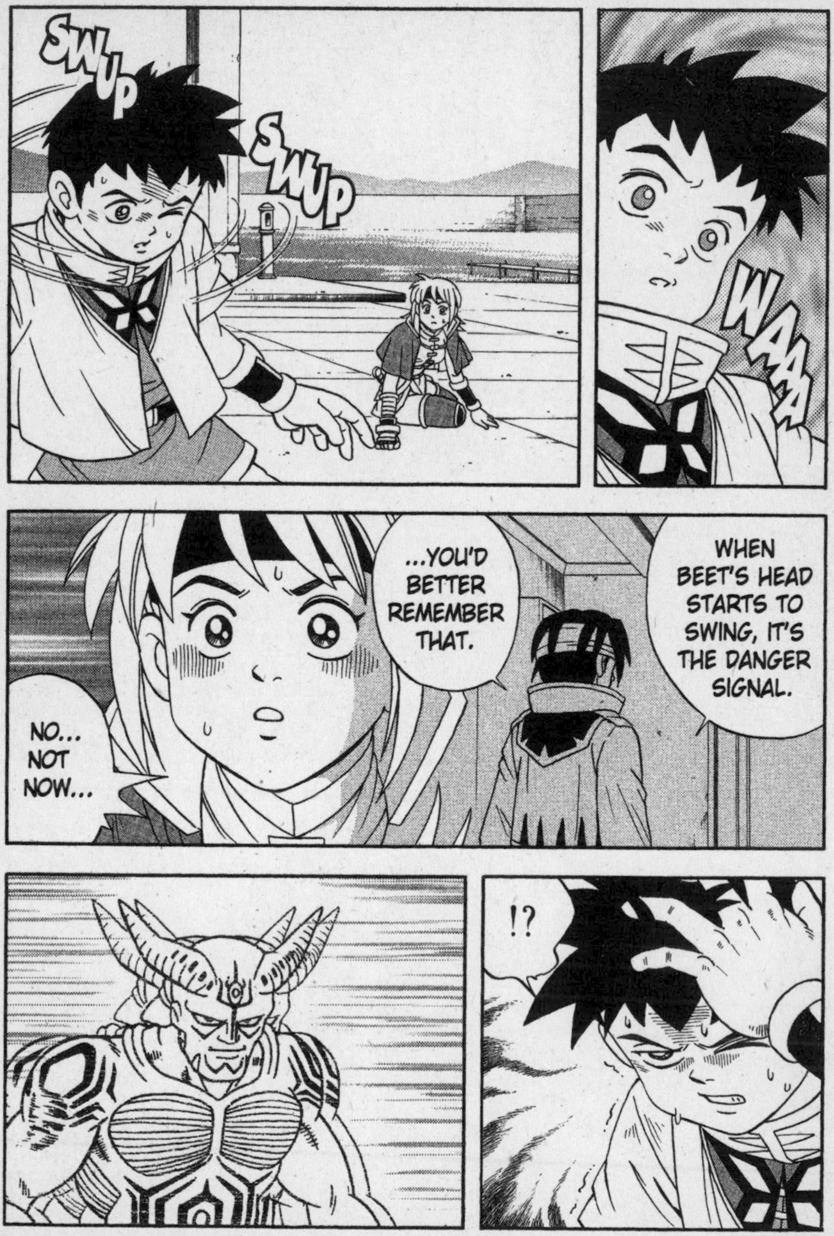
WAAA
SWUP
SWUP
WHEN BEET'S HEAD STARTS TO SWING, IT'S THE DANGER SIGNAL.
...YOU'D BETTER REMEMBER THAT.
NO... NOT NOW...
!?

READ THIS WAY

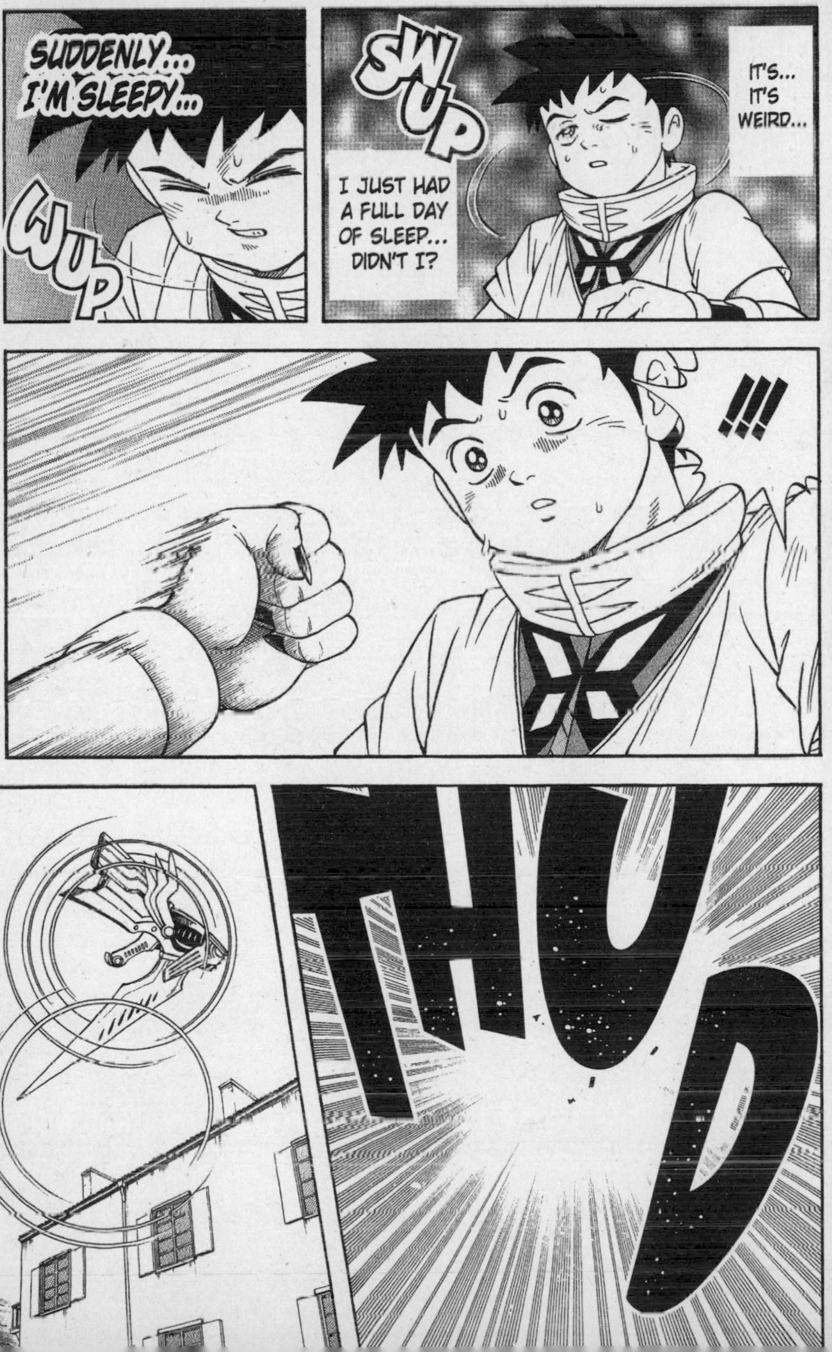
SWUP
IT'S... IT'S WEIRD...
I JUST HAD A FULL DAY OF SLEEP... DIDN'T I?
SUDDENLY... I'M SLEEPY...
WUP
!!!!
THUD

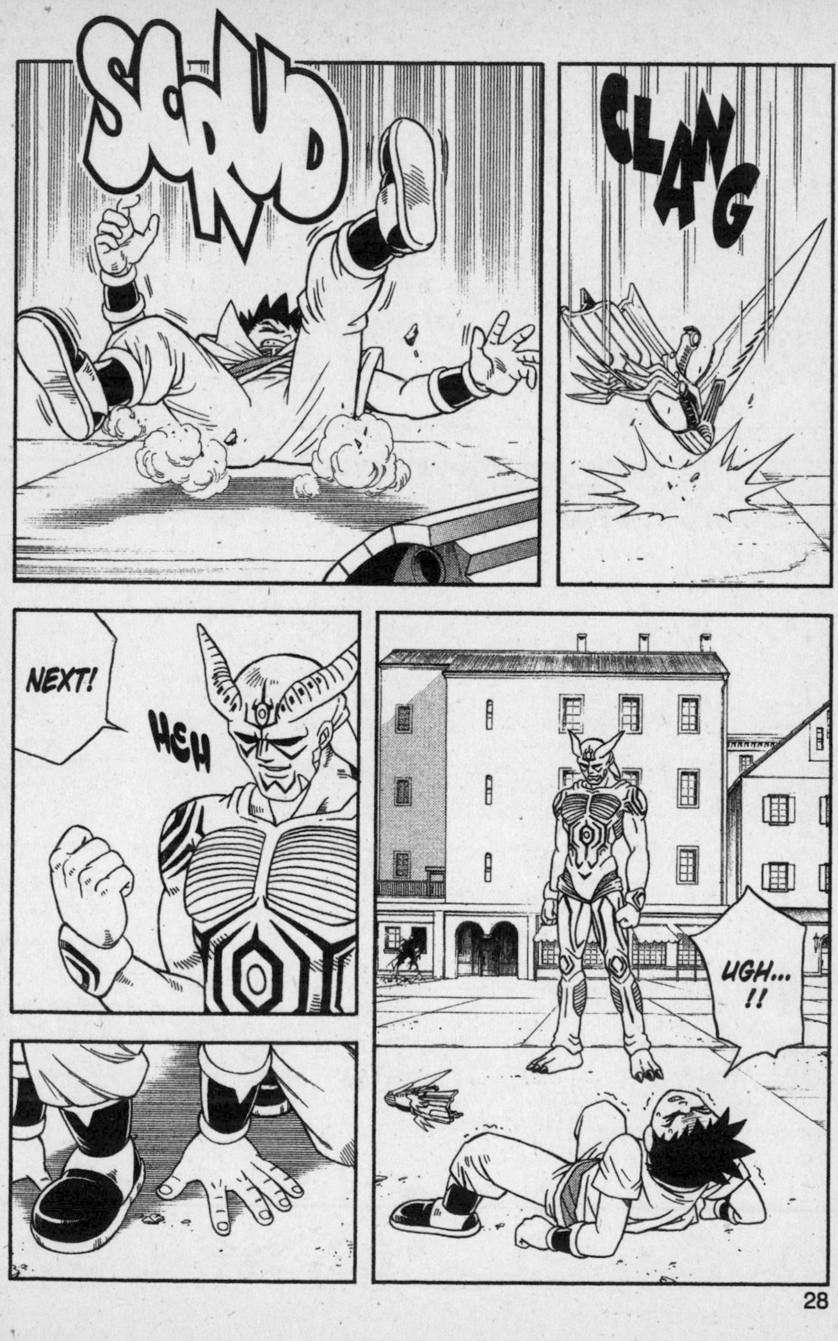
CLANG
SCRUD
UGH... !!
NEXT!
HEH

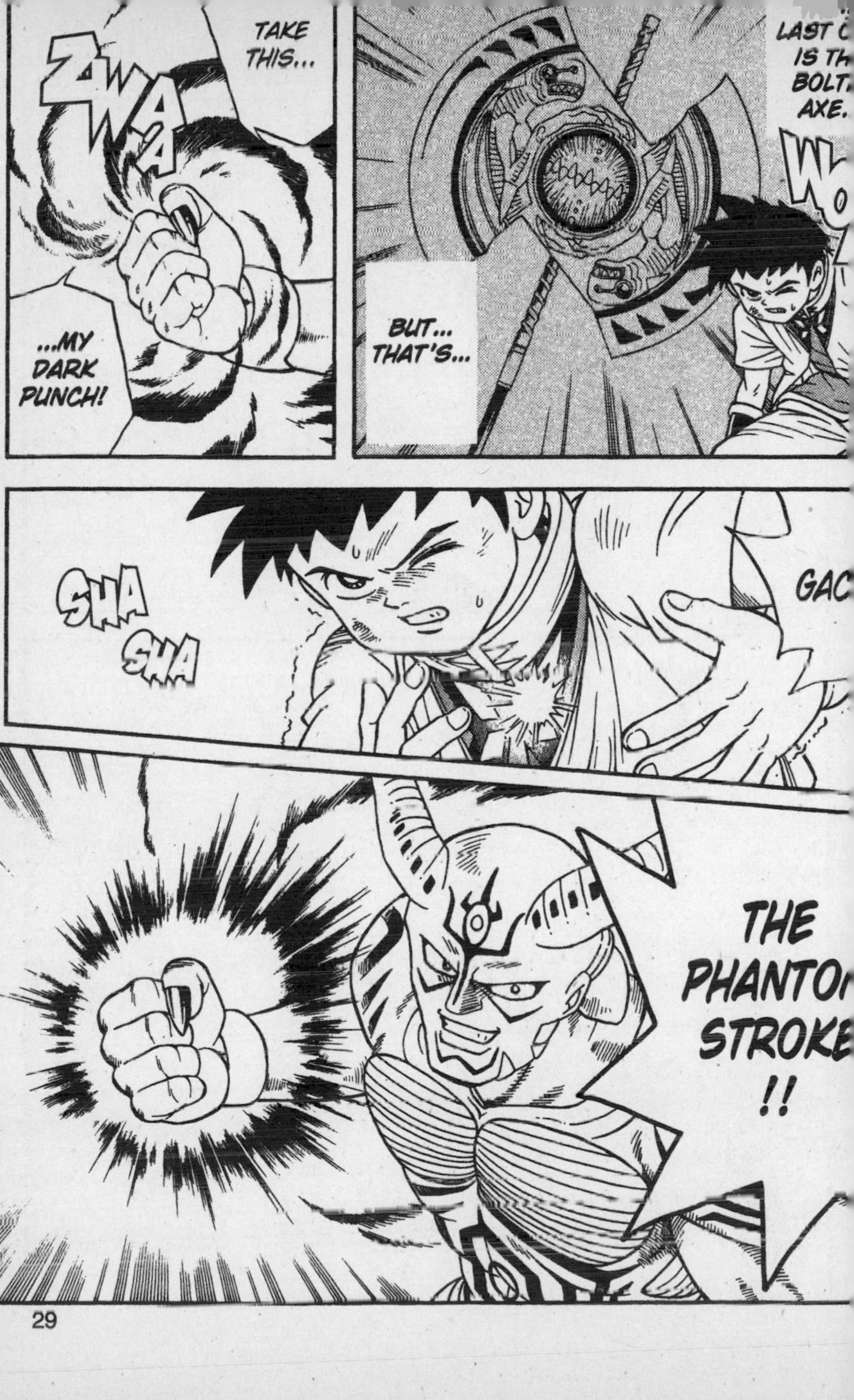
LAST C
IS TH
BOLT
AXE...
WO
BUT... THAT'S...
TAKE THIS...
ZWAA
...MY DARK PUNCH!
GAC
SHA
SHA
THE PHANTO
STROKE
!!

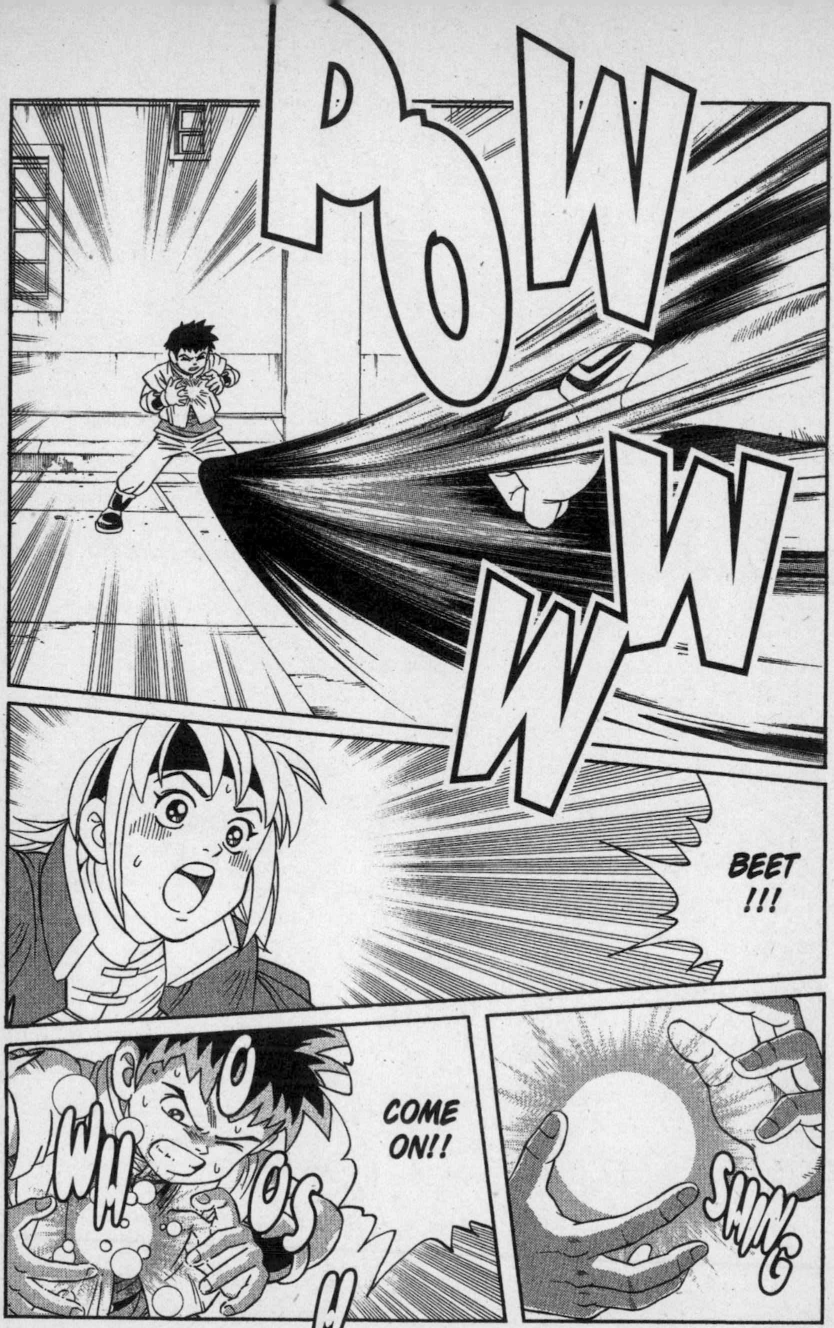
POWWW
BEET !!!
SHING
COME ON!!
WHOOSH

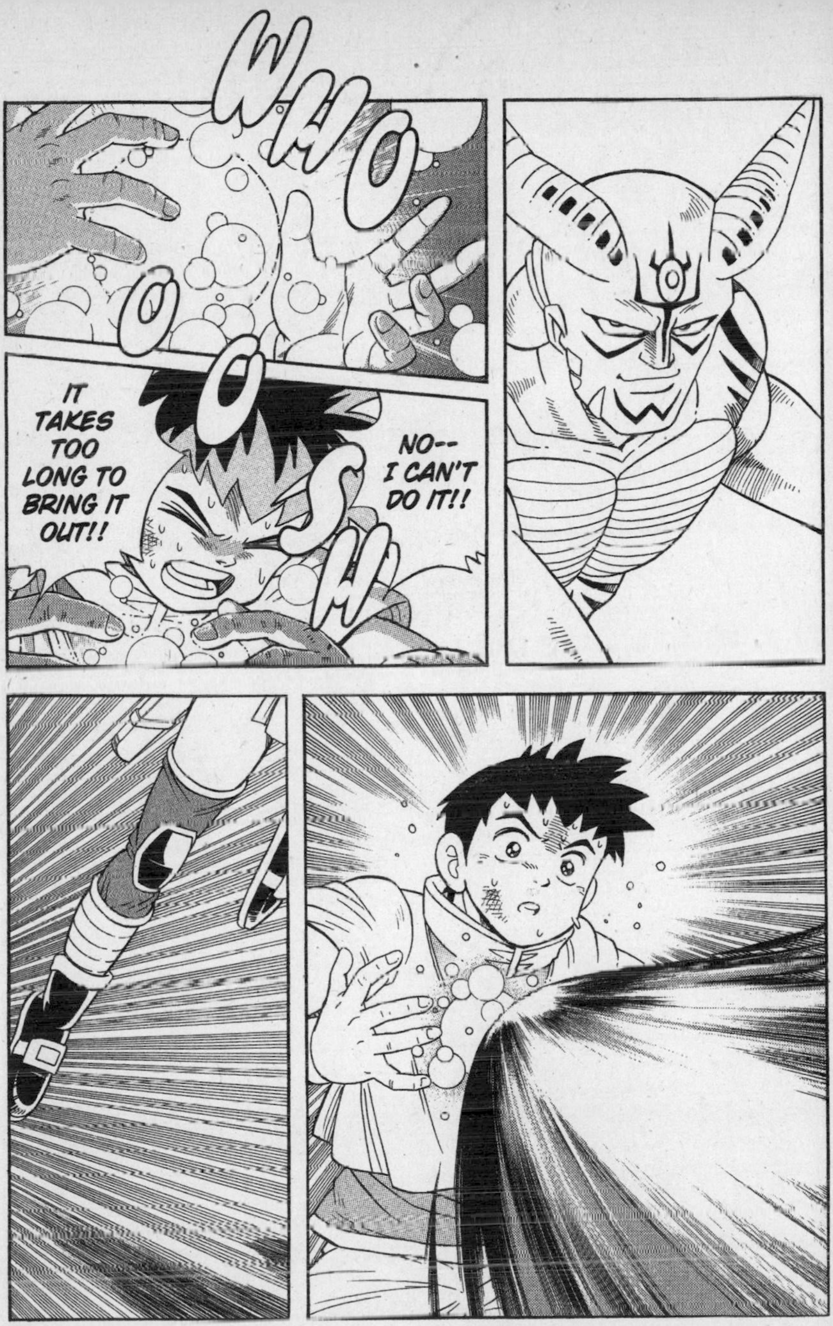
WHOOOSH
NO-- I CAN'T DO IT!!
IT TAKES TOO LONG TO BRING IT OUT!!

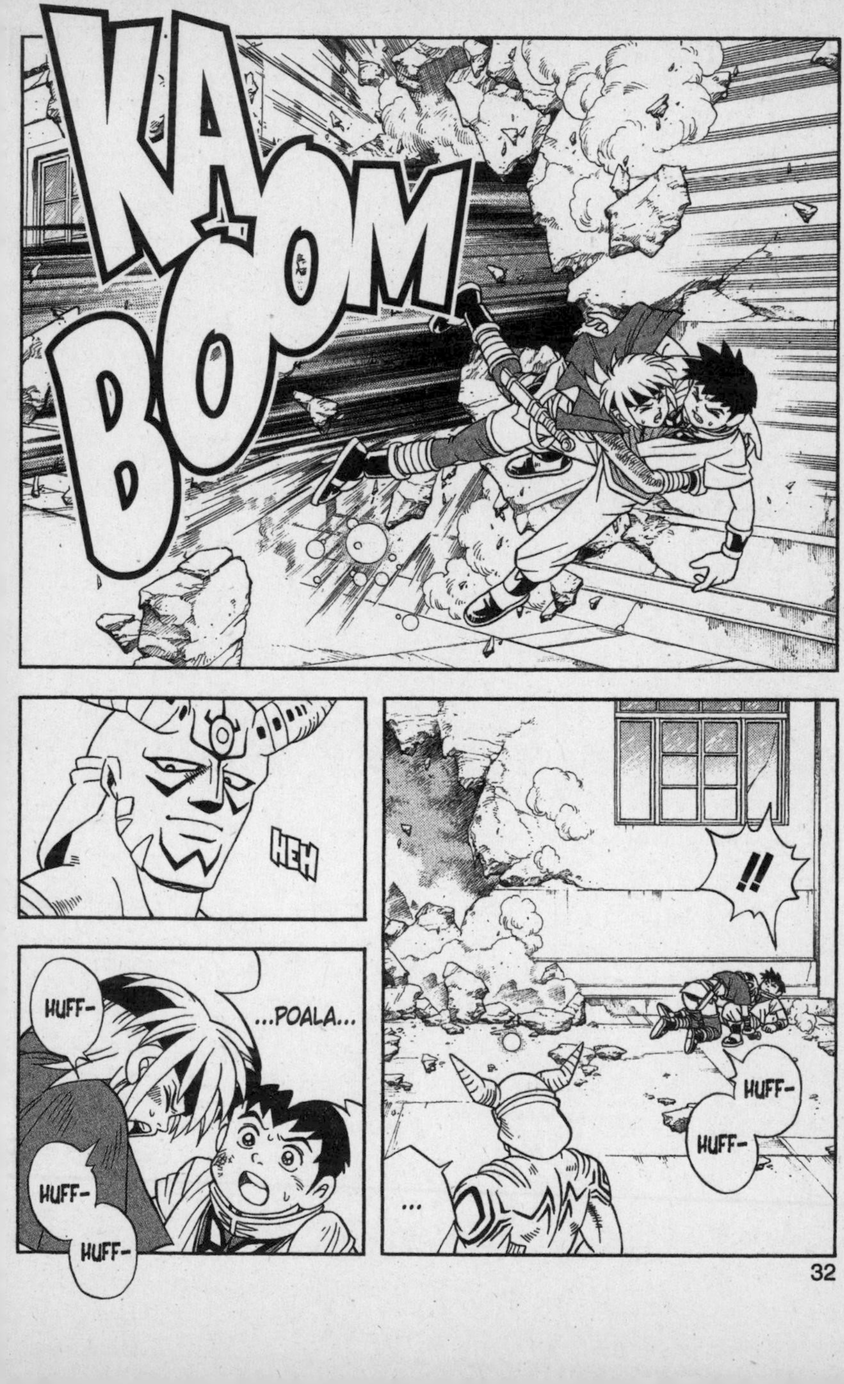
KA-BOOM
!!
HUFF-
HUFF-
...
HEH
...POALA...
HUFF-
HUFF-
HUFF-

READ THIS WAY

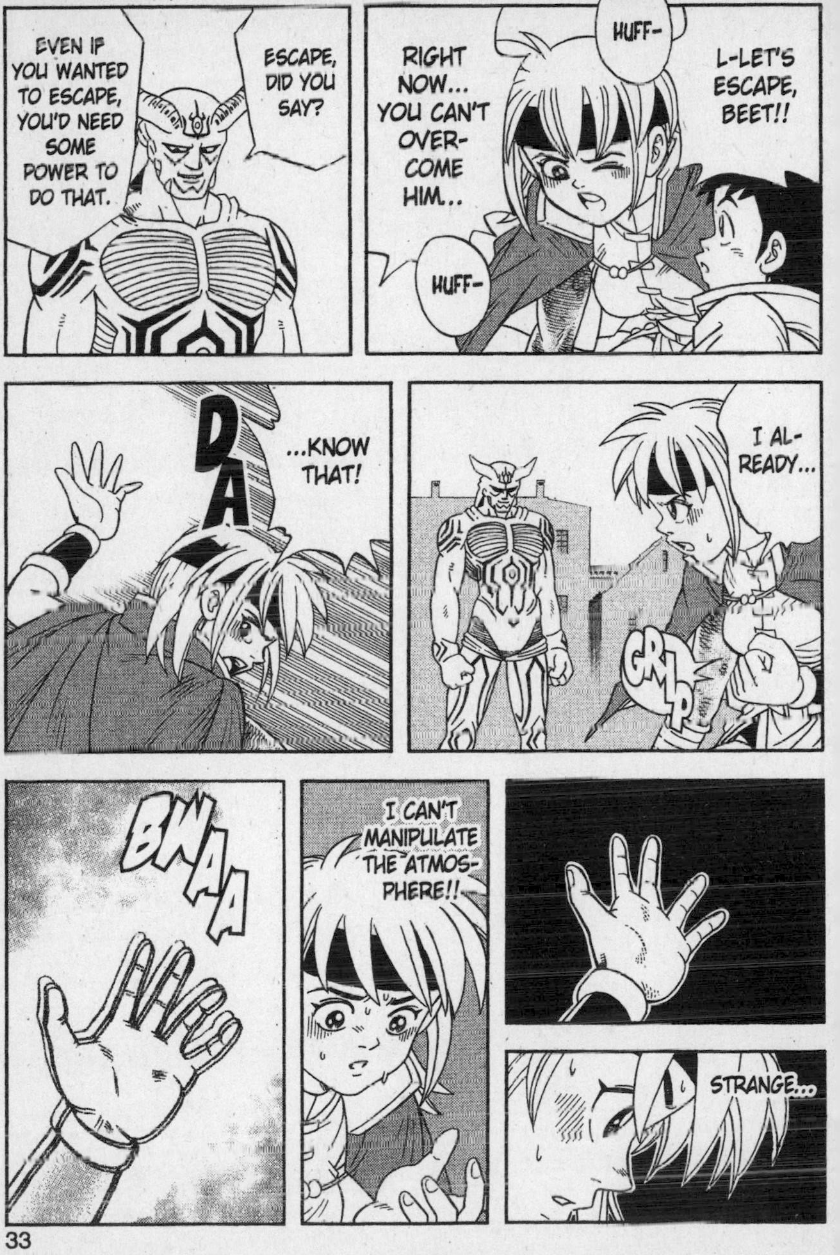
L-LET'S ESCAPE, BEET!!
HUFF-
RIGHT NOW... YOU CAN'T OVER-COME HIM...
HUFF-
ESCAPE, DID YOU SAY?
EVEN IF YOU WANTED TO ESCAPE, YOU'D NEED SOME POWER TO DO THAT.
I AL-READY...
GRIP
DA
...KNOW THAT!
STRANGE...
I CAN'T MANIPULATE THE ATMOS-PHERE!!
BWAAA

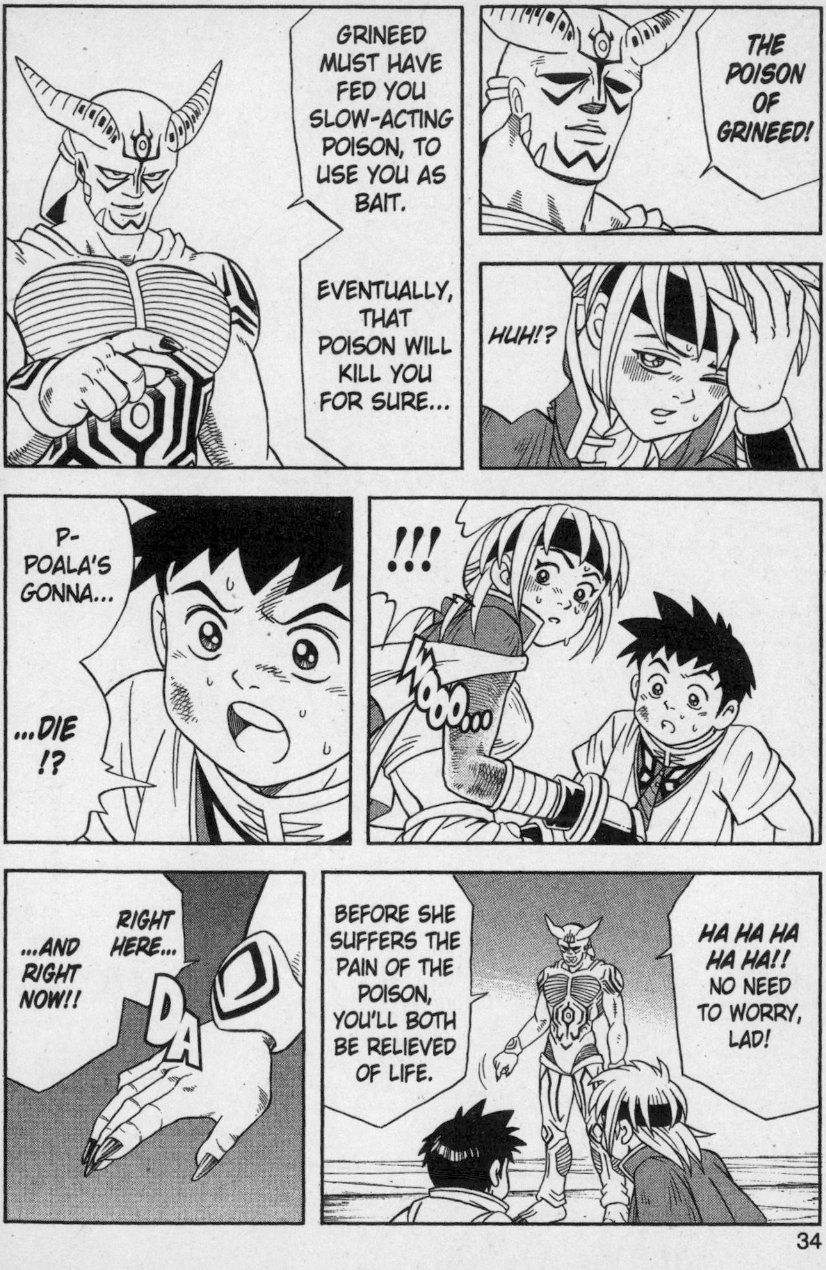
THE POISON OF GRINEED!
HUH!?
GRINEED MUST HAVE FED YOU SLOW-ACTING POISON, TO USE YOU AS BAIT.
EVENTUALLY, THAT POISON WILL KILL YOU FOR SURE...
!!!
WOOO...
P-POALA'S GONNA...
...DIE!?
HA HA HA HA HA!! NO NEED TO WORRY, LAD!
BEFORE SHE SUFFERS THE PAIN OF THE POISON, YOU'LL BOTH BE RELIEVED OF LIFE.
RIGHT HERE...
...AND RIGHT NOW!!
DA

READ THIS WAY

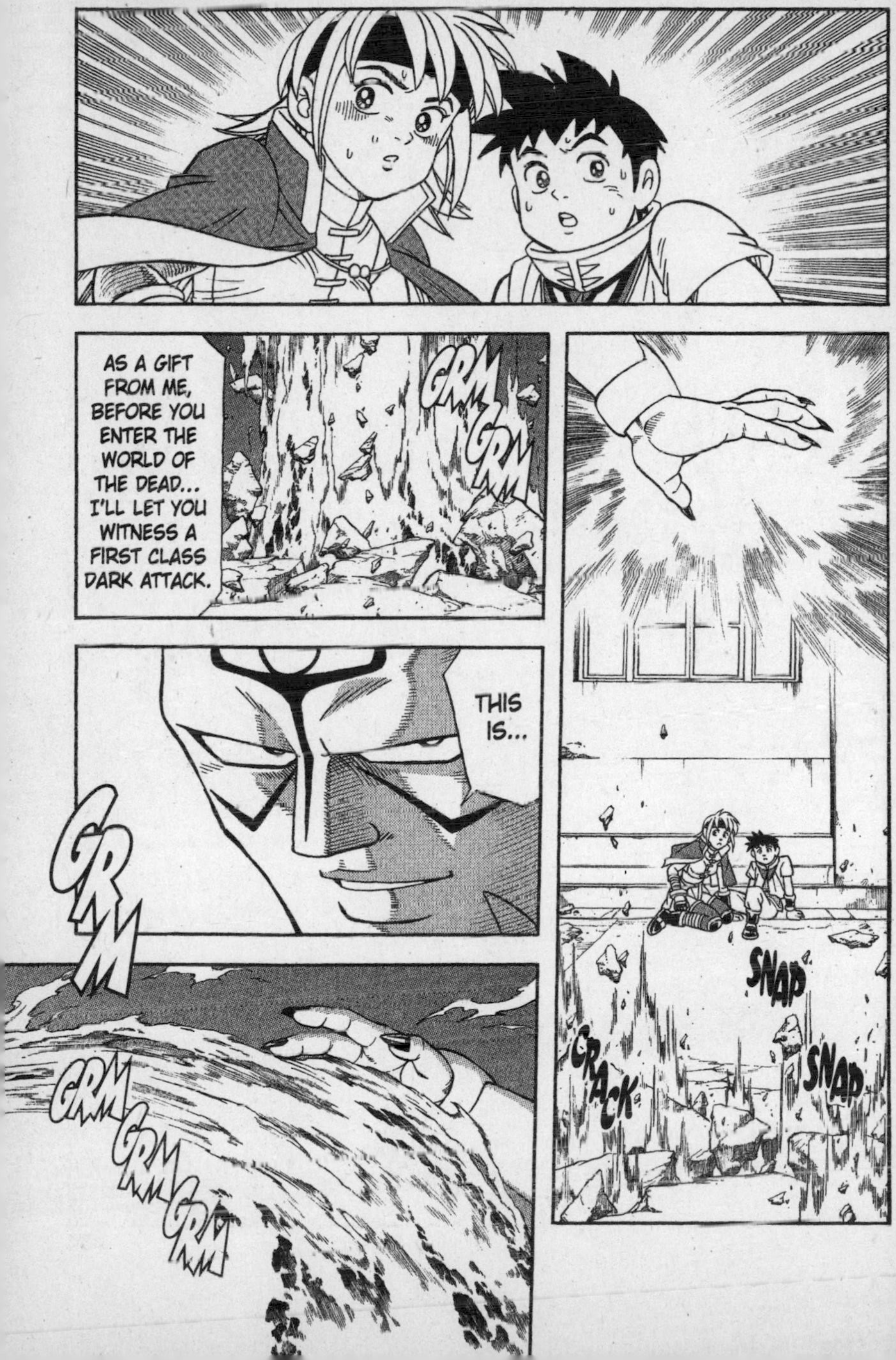
SNAP
SNAP
CRACK
GRM GRM
AS A GIFT FROM ME, BEFORE YOU ENTER THE WORLD OF THE DEAD... I'LL LET YOU WITNESS A FIRST CLASS DARK ATTACK.
THIS IS...
GRM
GRM GRM GRM

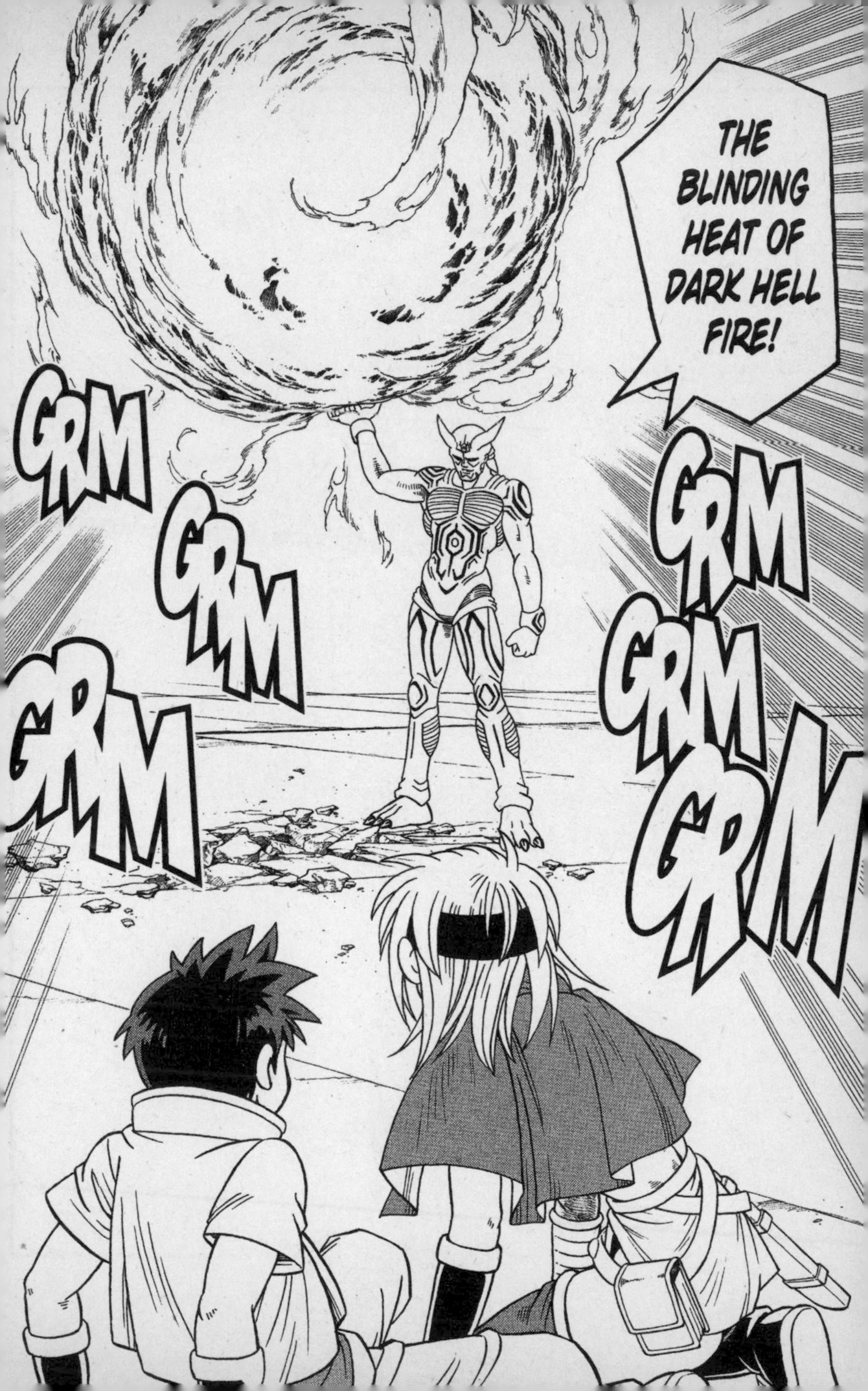

THE BLINDING HEAT OF DARK HELL FIRE!
GRM GRM GRM
GRM GRM GRM

READ THIS WAY

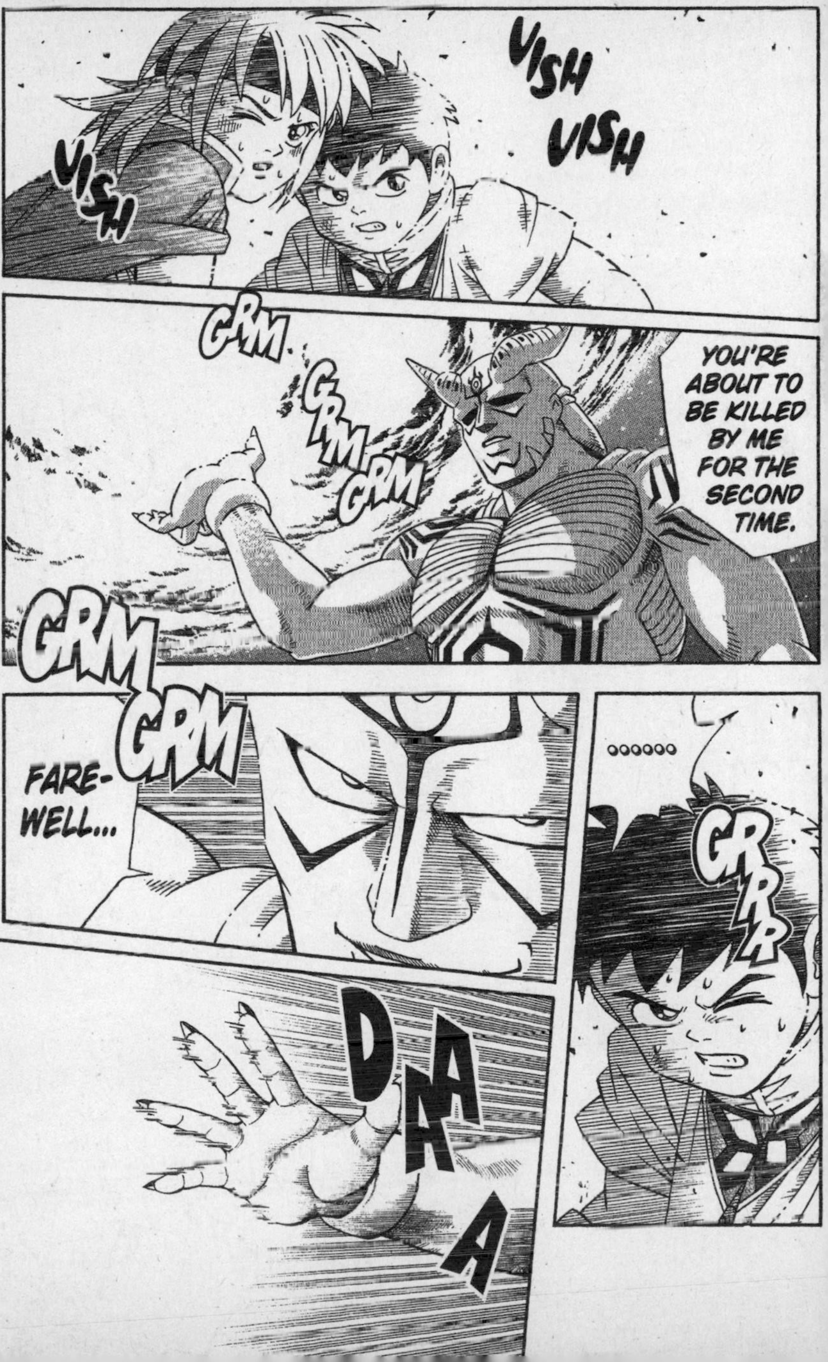
VISH
VISH
VISH
YOU'RE ABOUT TO BE KILLED BY ME FOR THE SECOND TIME.
GRM
GRM
GRM
GRM
......
GRRR
GRM
FARE-WELL...
DAAAA

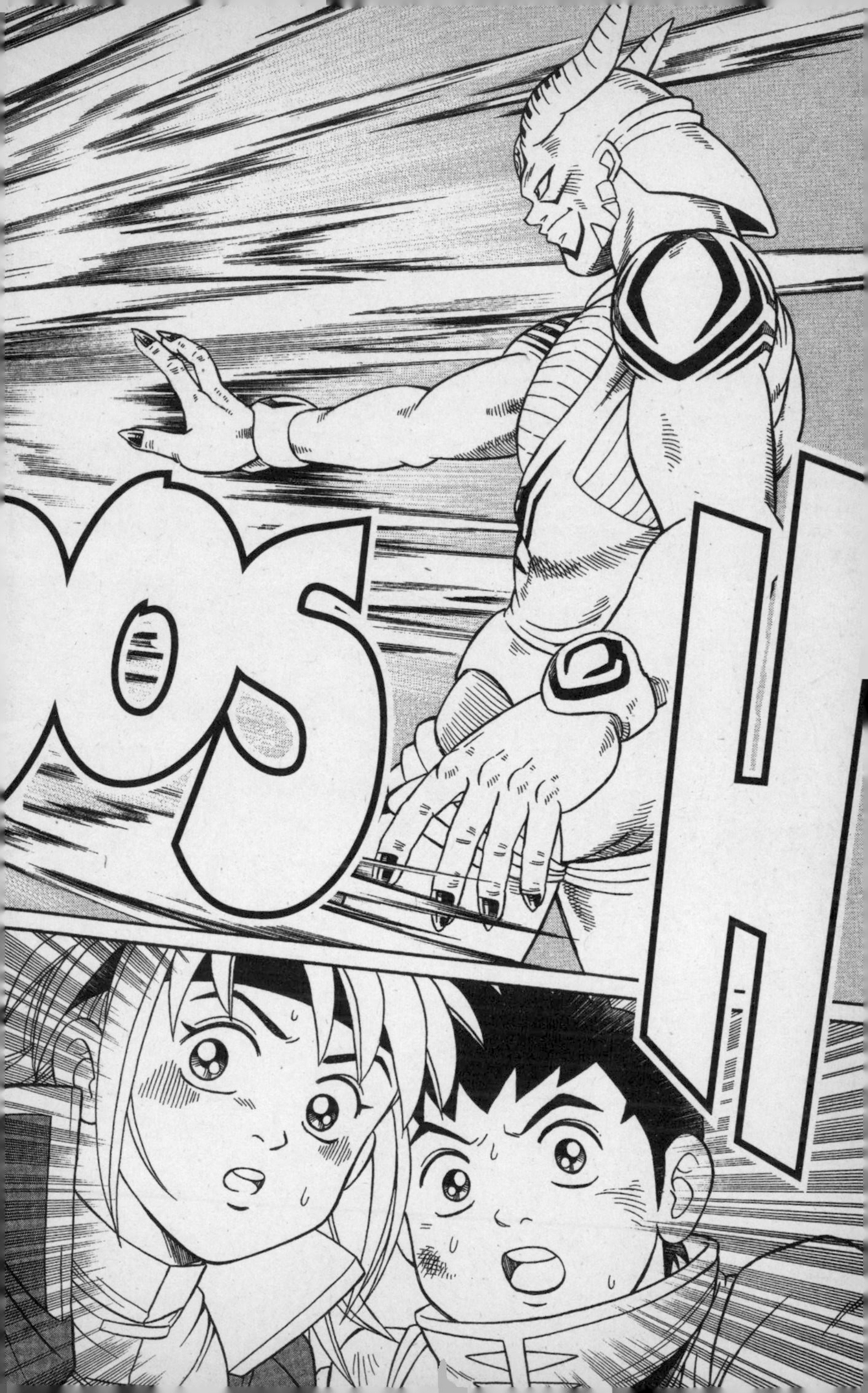

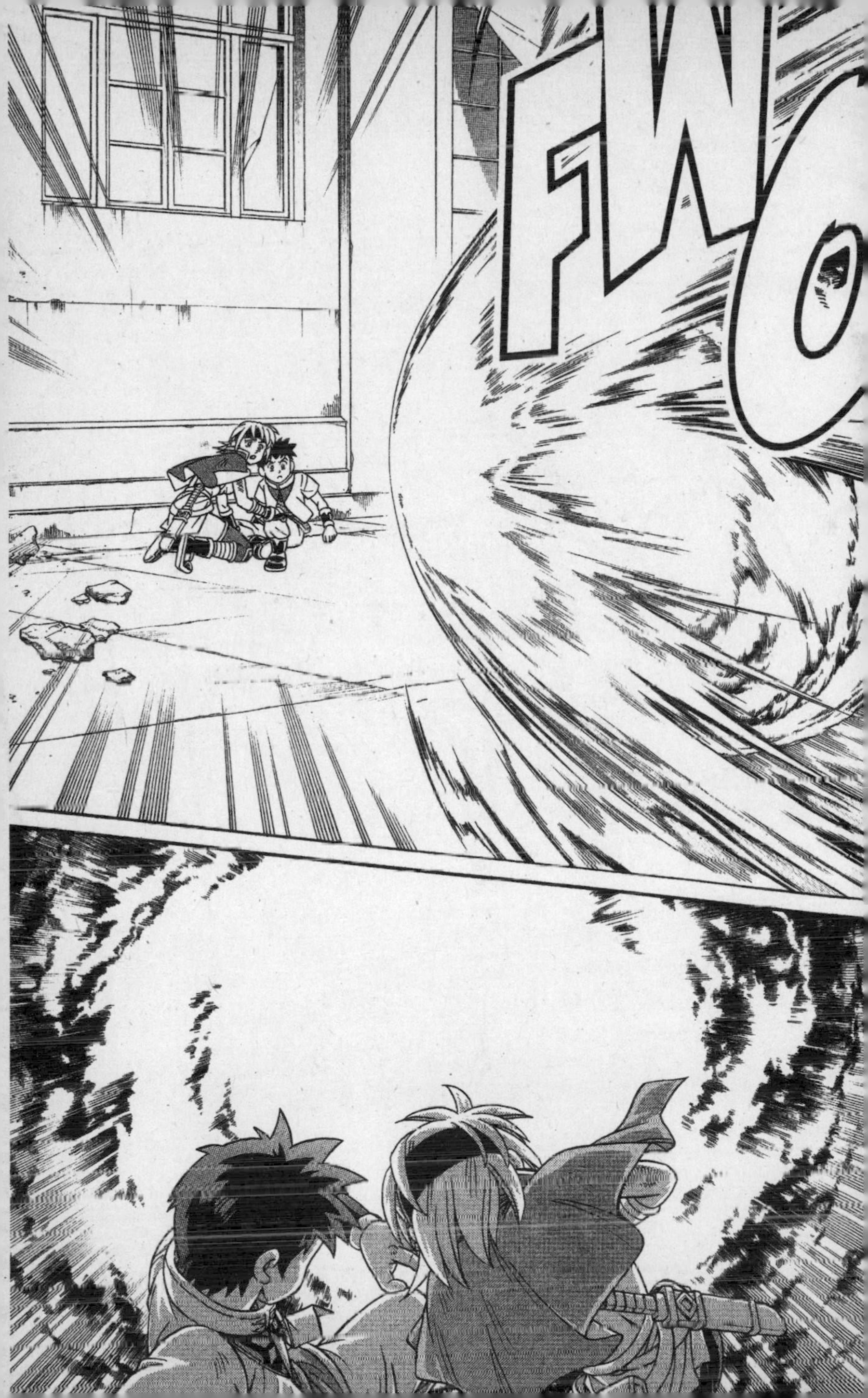
FWO

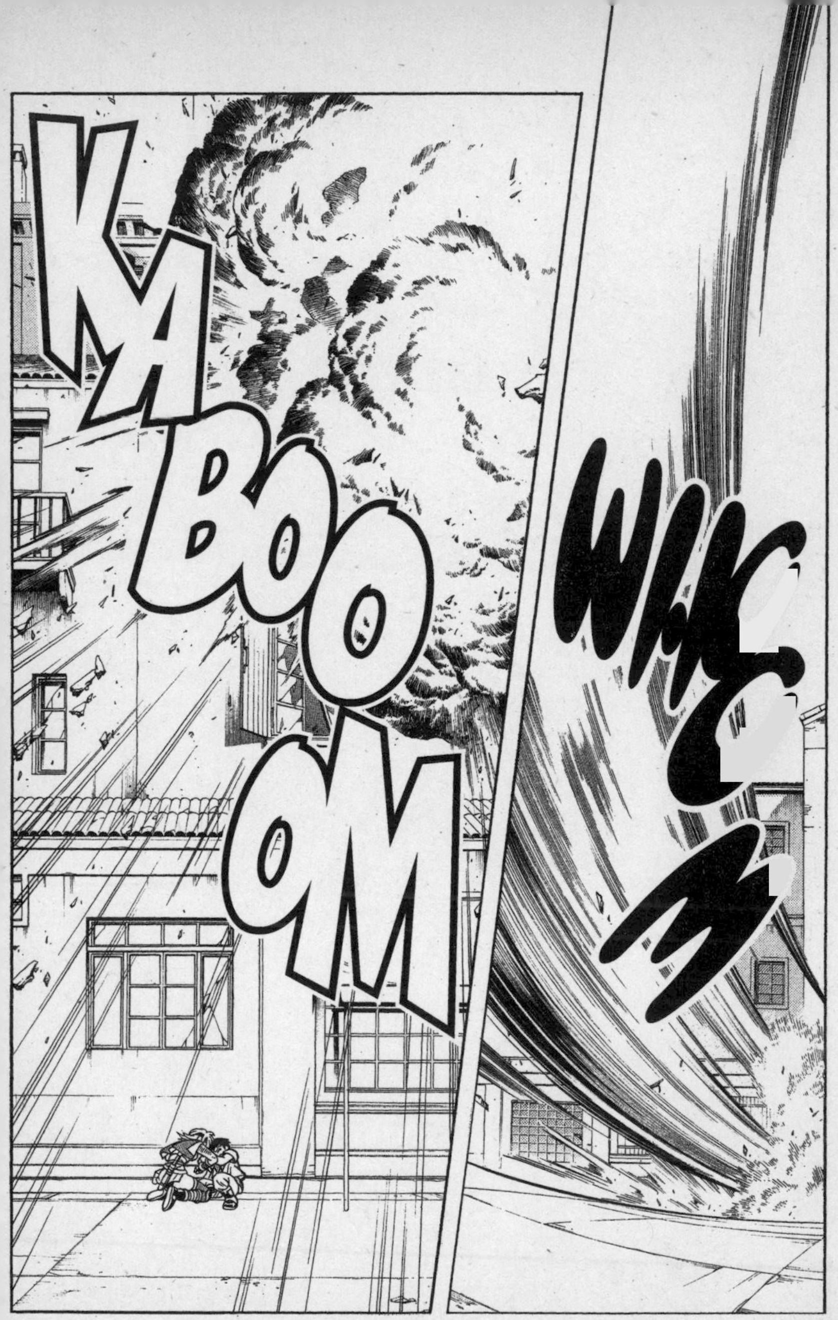
KABOOOM

READ THIS WAY

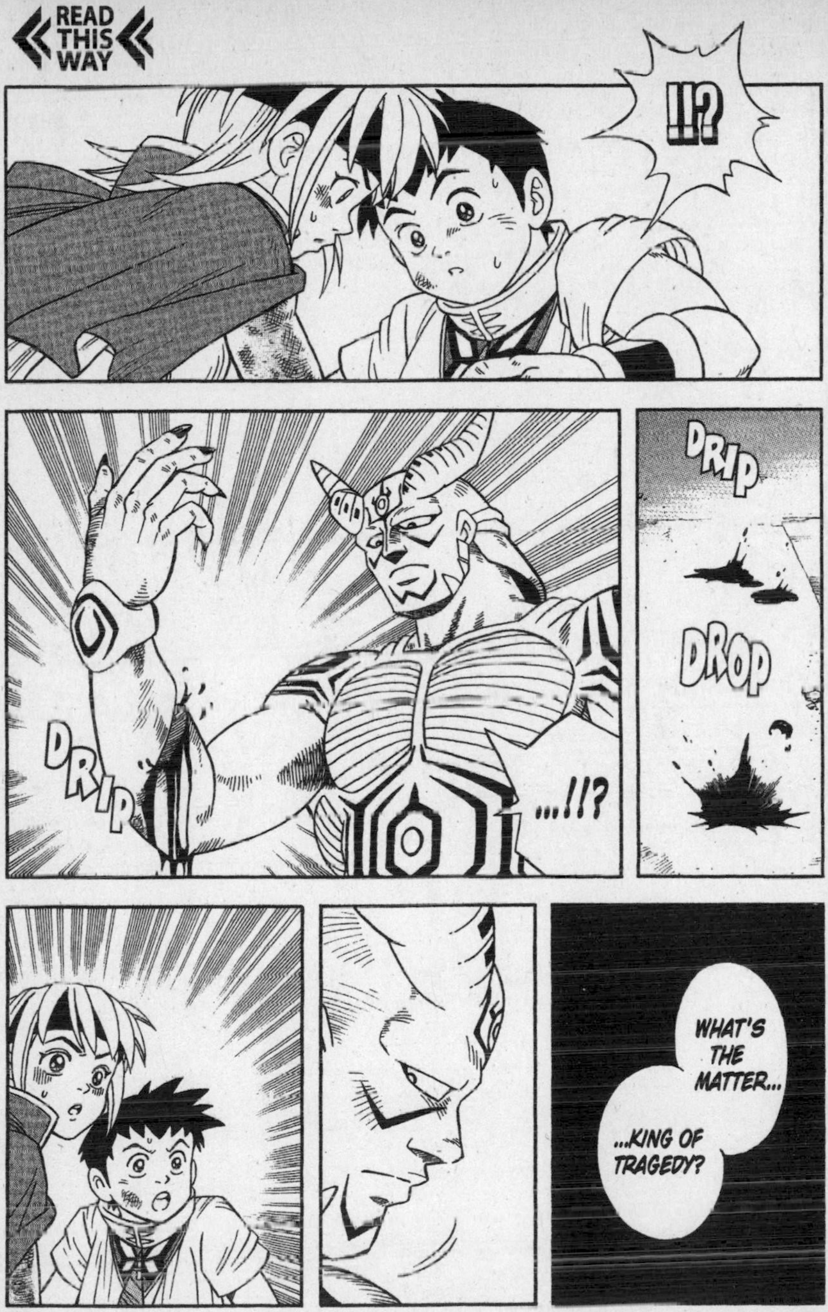

!!?
DRIP
DROP
DRIP
...!!?
WHAT'S THE MATTER...
...KING OF TRAGEDY?

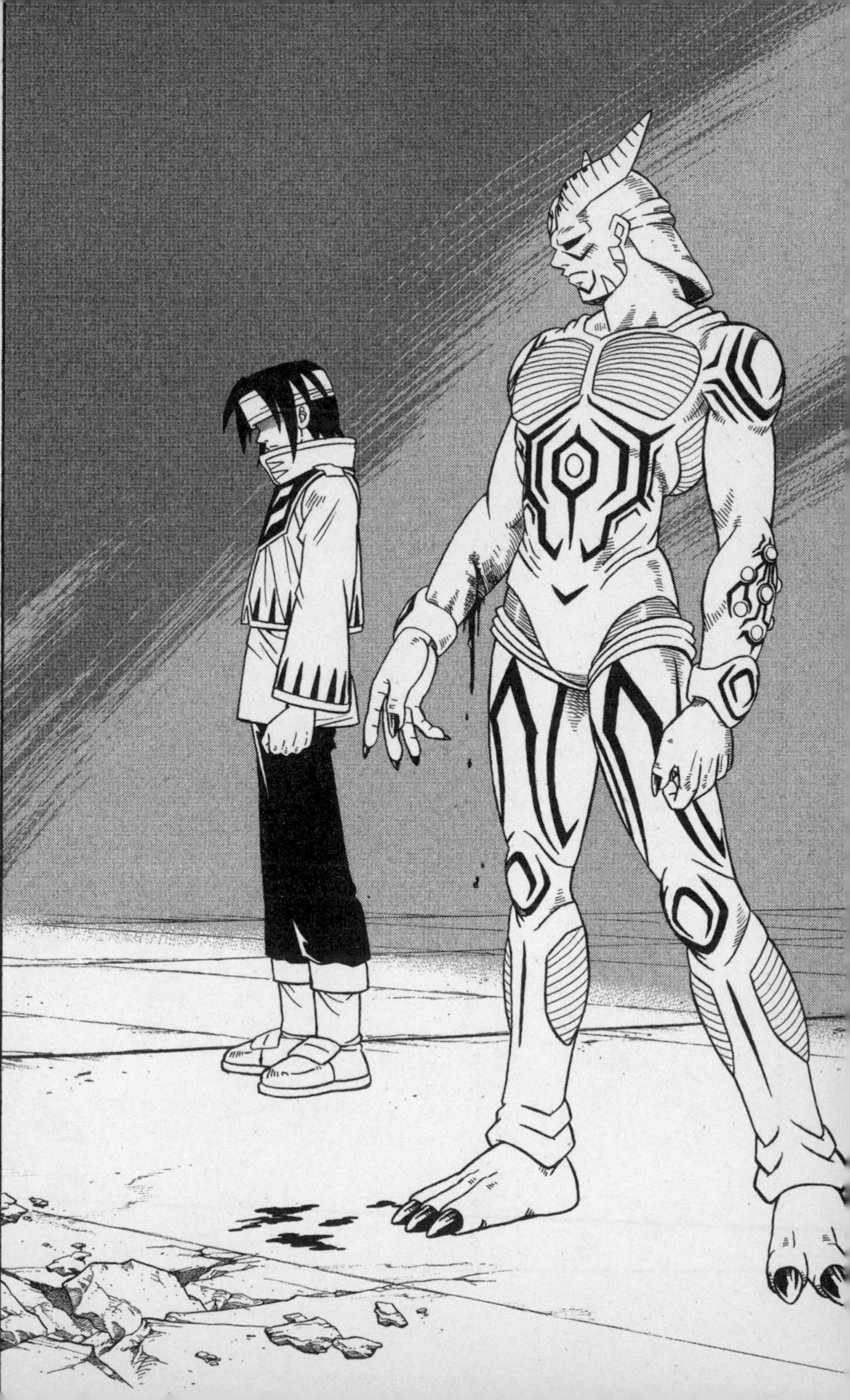

READ THIS WAY

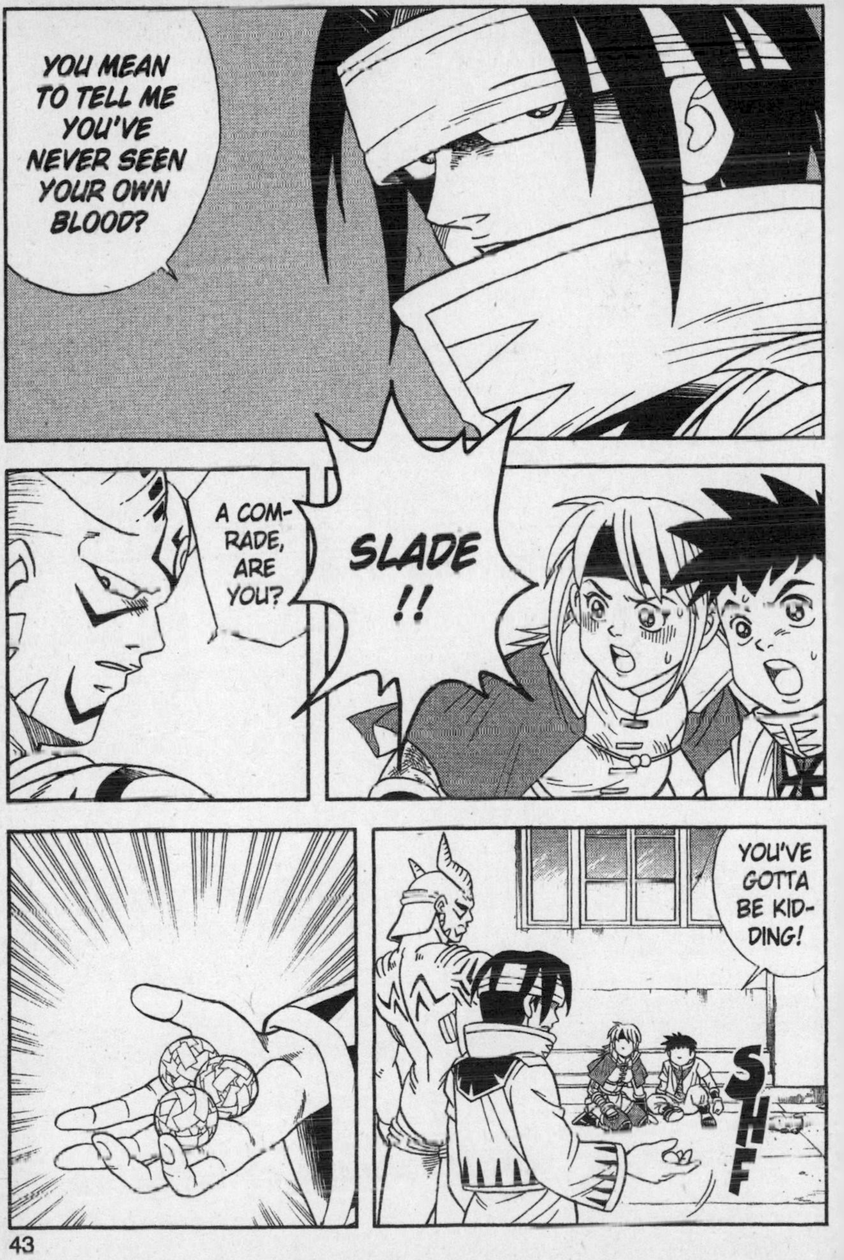
YOU MEAN TO TELL ME YOU'VE NEVER SEEN YOUR OWN BLOOD?
SLADE !!
A COM-RADE, ARE YOU?
YOU'VE GOTTA BE KID-DING!
SHF

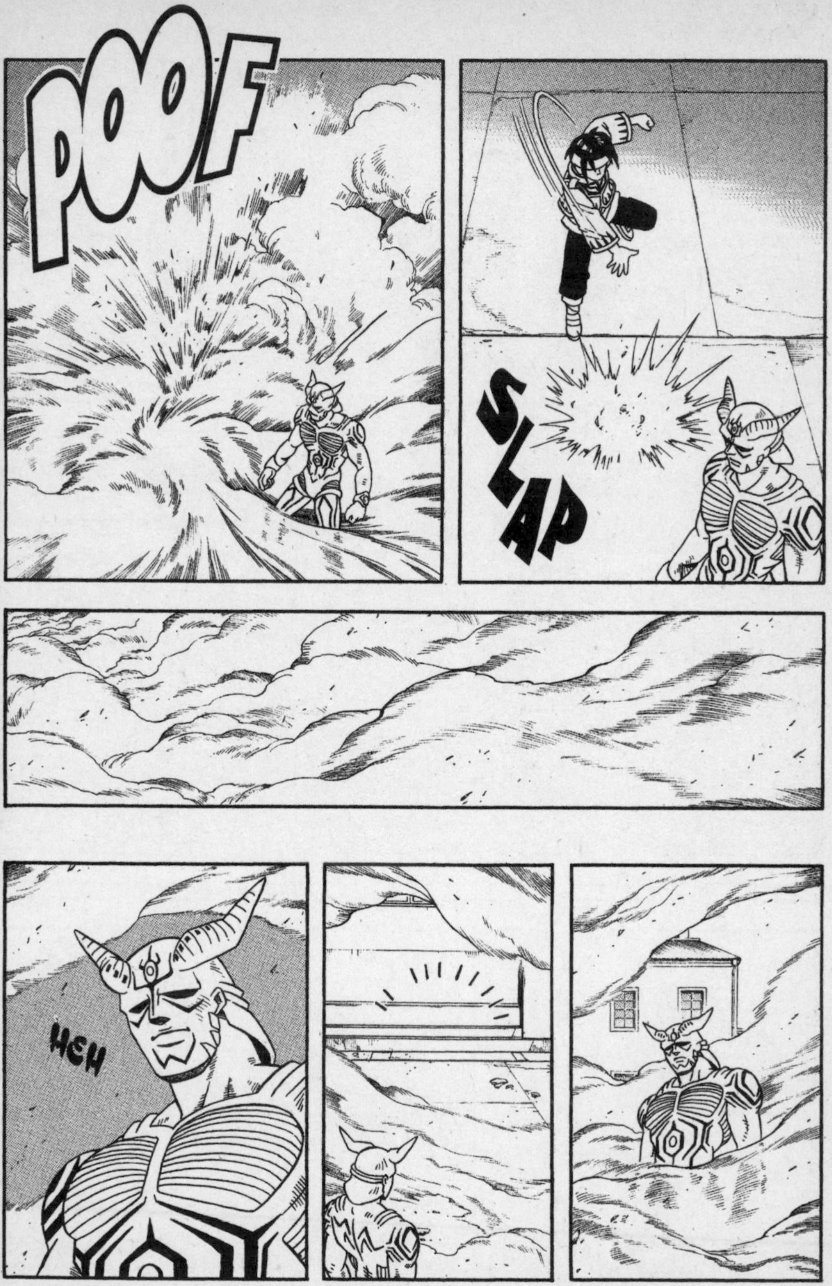
SLAP
POOF
HEH

READ THIS WAY

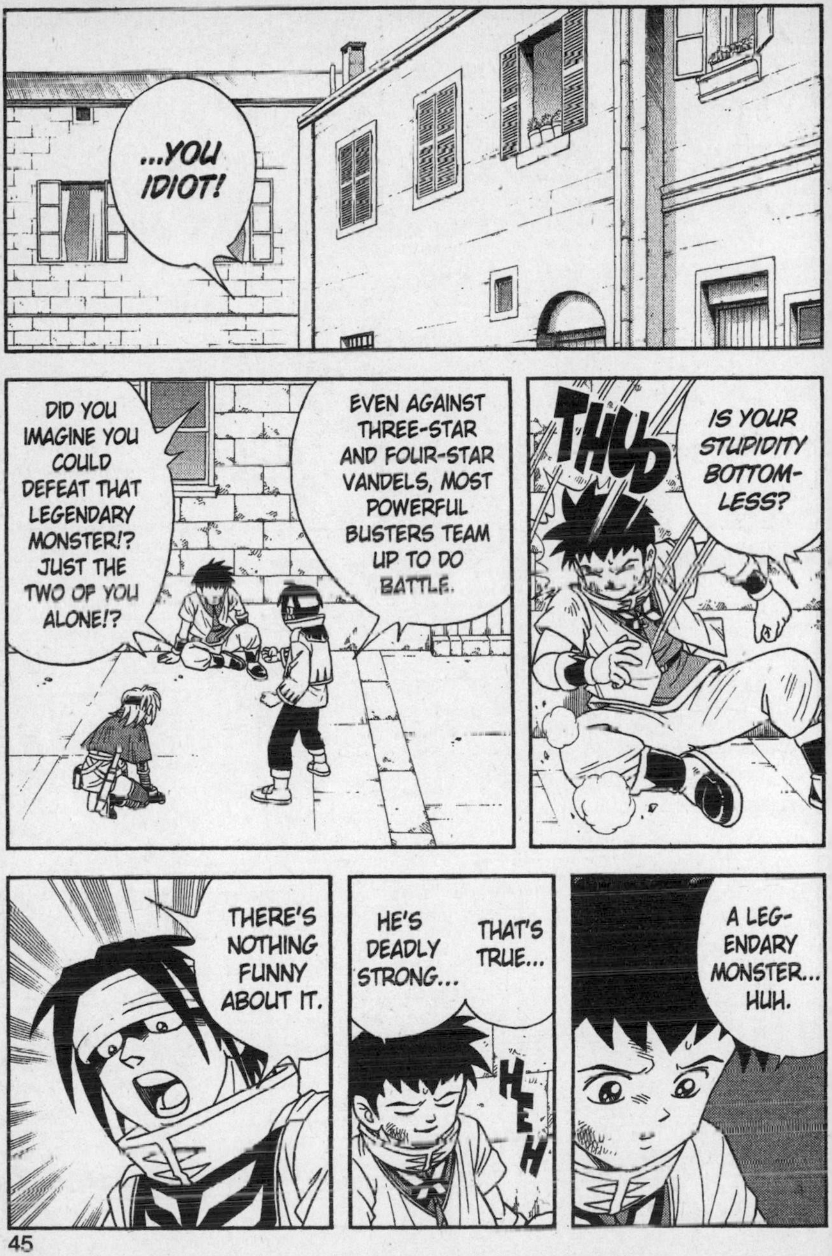
...YOU IDIOT!
THUD
IS YOUR STUPIDITY BOTTOM-LESS?
EVEN AGAINST THREE-STAR AND FOUR-STAR VANDELS, MOST POWERFUL BUSTERS TEAM UP TO DO BATTLE.
DID YOU IMAGINE YOU COULD DEFEAT THAT LEGENDARY MONSTER!? JUST THE TWO OF YOU ALONE!?
A LEG-ENDARY MONSTER... HUH.
THAT'S TRUE...
HE'S DEADLY STRONG...
HEH
THERE'S NOTHING FUNNY ABOUT IT.

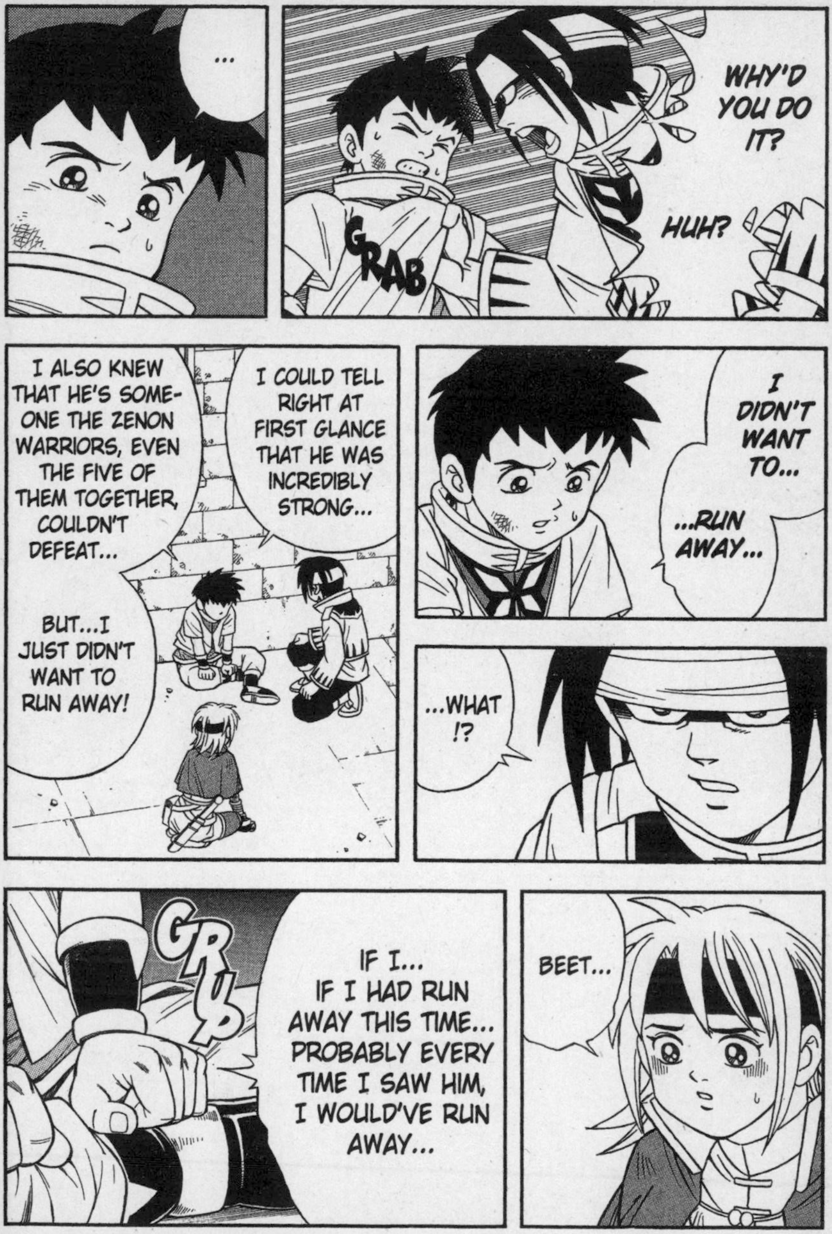
WHY'D YOU DO IT?
HUH?
GRAB
...
I DIDN'T WANT TO...
...RUN AWAY...
...WHAT!?
I COULD TELL RIGHT AT FIRST GLANCE THAT HE WAS INCREDIBLY STRONG...
I ALSO KNEW THAT HE'S SOME-ONE THE ZENON WARRIORS, EVEN THE FIVE OF THEM TOGETHER, COULDN'T DEFEAT...
BUT...I JUST DIDN'T WANT TO RUN AWAY!
BEET...
IF I... IF I HAD RUN AWAY THIS TIME... PROBABLY EVERY TIME I SAW HIM, I WOULD'VE RUN AWAY...
GRUP

READ THIS WAY

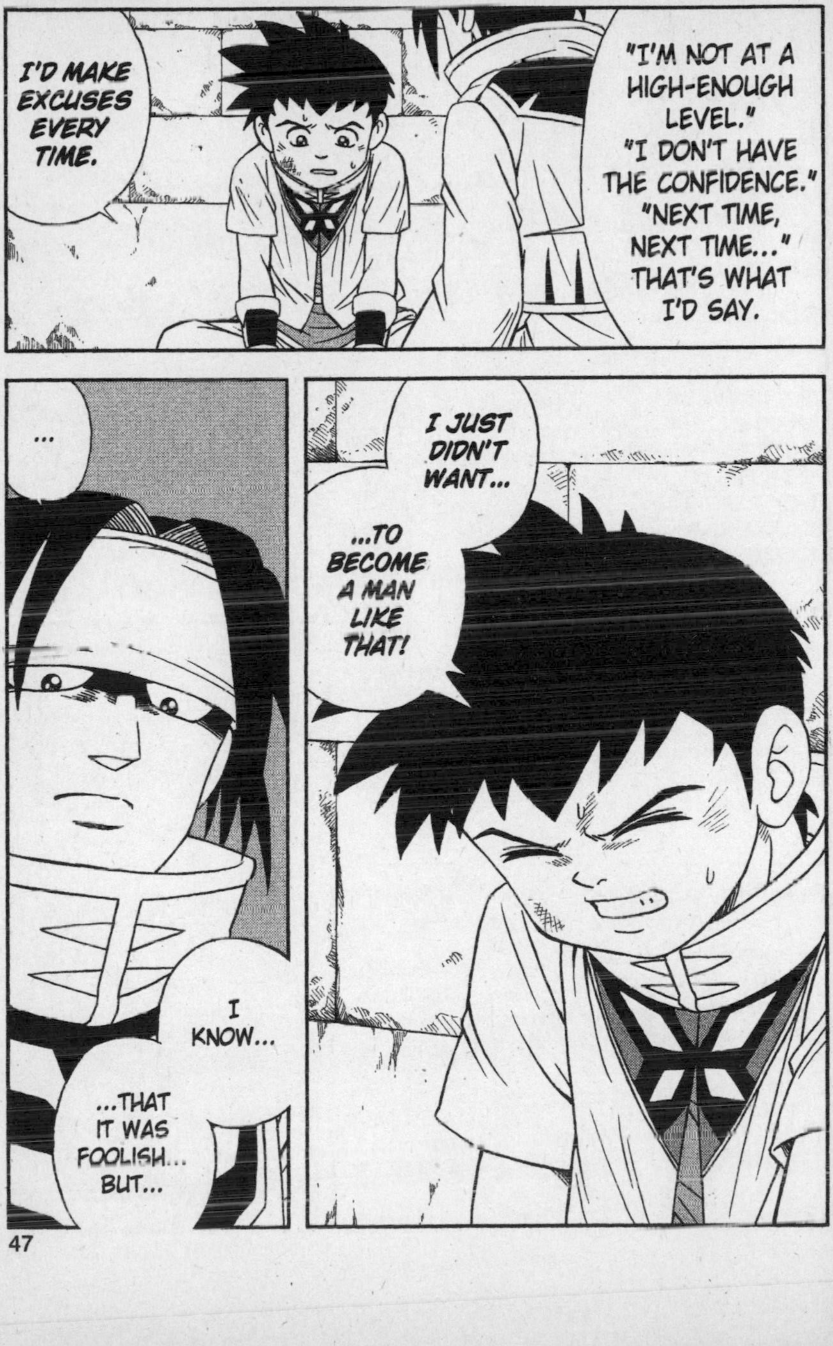
"I'M NOT AT A HIGH-ENOUGH LEVEL." "I DON'T HAVE THE CONFIDENCE." "NEXT TIME, NEXT TIME..." THAT'S WHAT I'D SAY.
I'D MAKE EXCUSES EVERY TIME.
I JUST DIDN'T WANT...
...TO BECOME A MAN LIKE THAT!
...
I KNOW...
...THAT IT WAS FOOLISH... BUT...

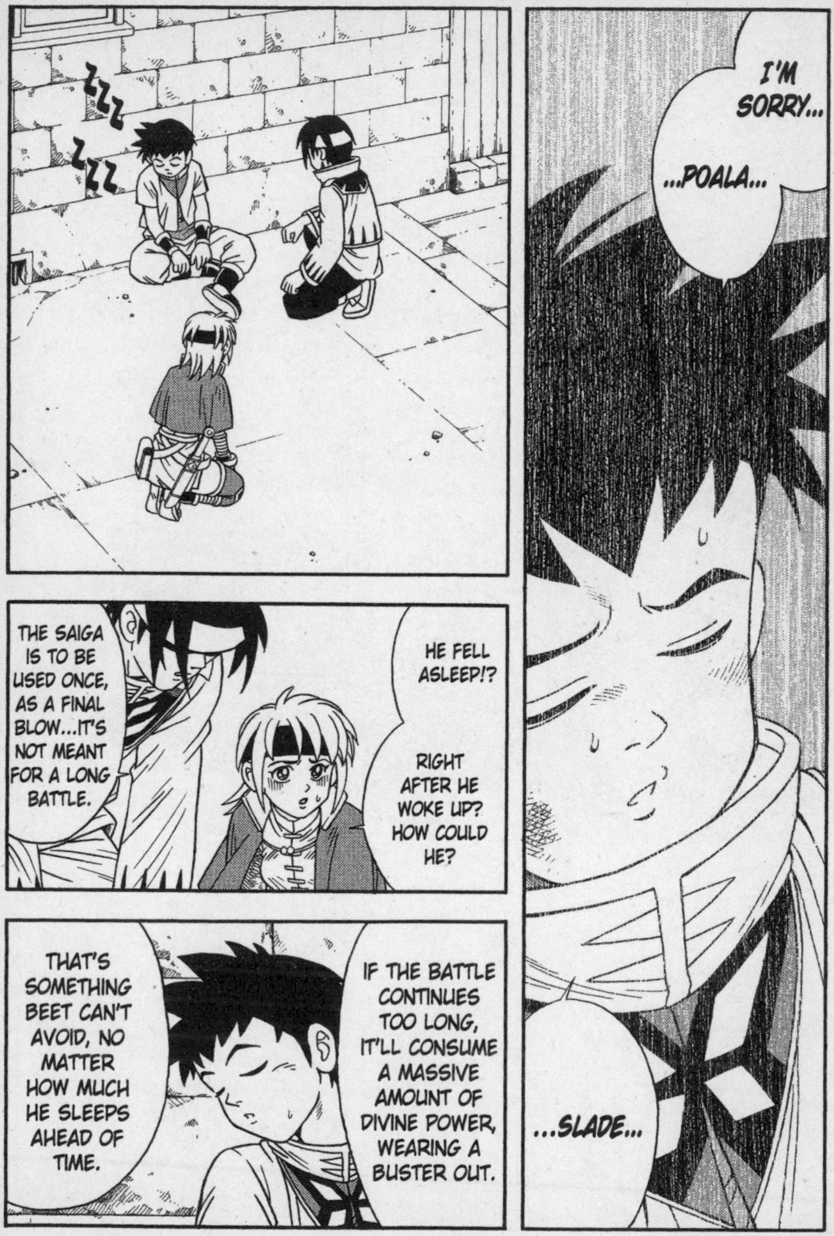
I'M SORRY...
...POALA...
...SLADE...
ZZZ
ZZZ
HE FELL ASLEEP!?
RIGHT AFTER HE WOKE UP? HOW COULD HE?
THE SAIGA IS TO BE USED ONCE, AS A FINAL BLOW...IT'S NOT MEANT FOR A LONG BATTLE.
IF THE BATTLE CONTINUES TOO LONG, IT'LL CONSUME A MASSIVE AMOUNT OF DIVINE POWER, WEARING A BUSTER OUT.
THAT'S SOMETHING BEET CAN'T AVOID, NO MATTER HOW MUCH HE SLEEPS AHEAD OF TIME.

READ THIS WAY

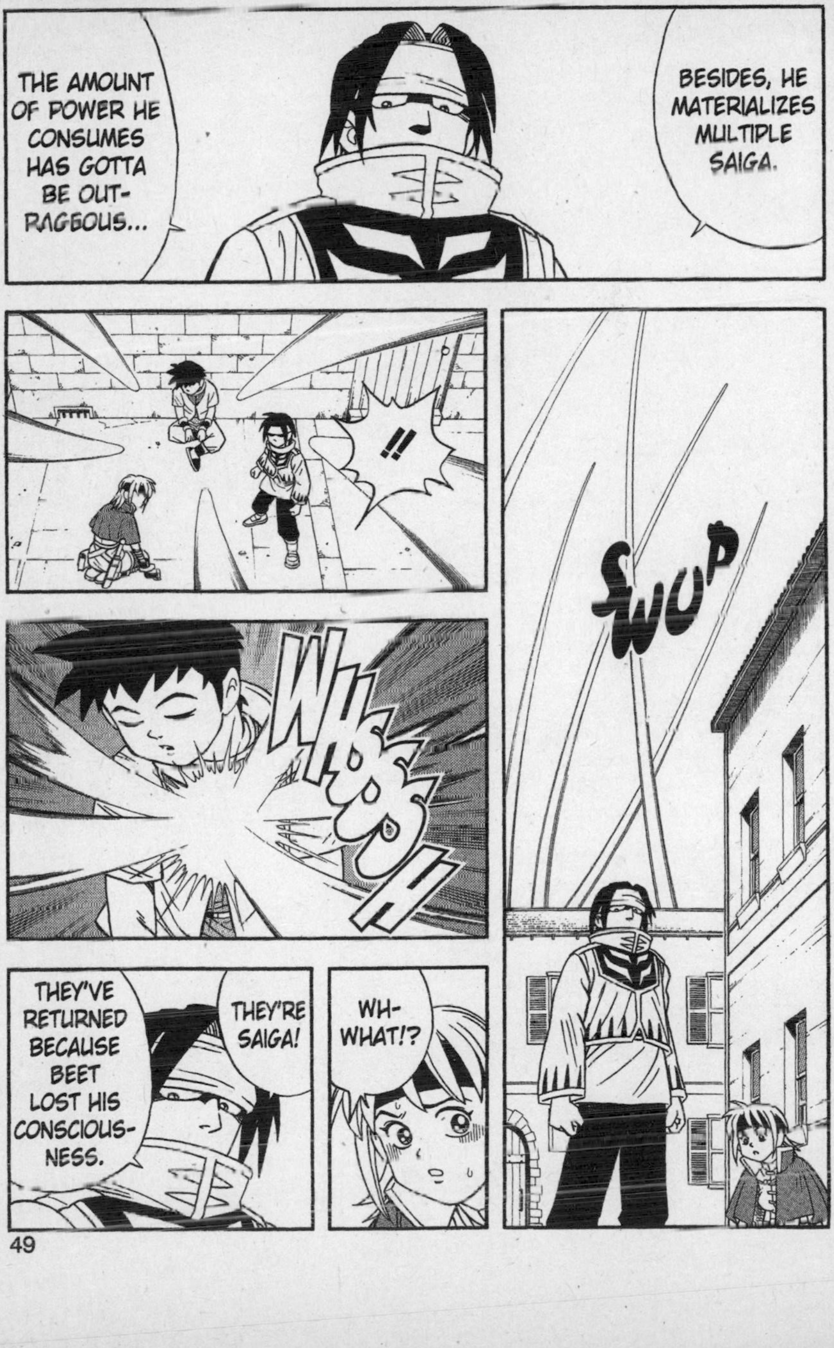
THE AMOUNT OF POWER HE CONSUMES HAS GOTTA BE OUT-RAGEOUS...
BESIDES, HE MATERIALIZES MULTIPLE SAIGA.
SWUP
!!
WHOOSH
WH-WHAT!?
THEY'RE SAIGA!
THEY'VE RETURNED BECAUSE BEET LOST HIS CONSCIOUS-NESS.

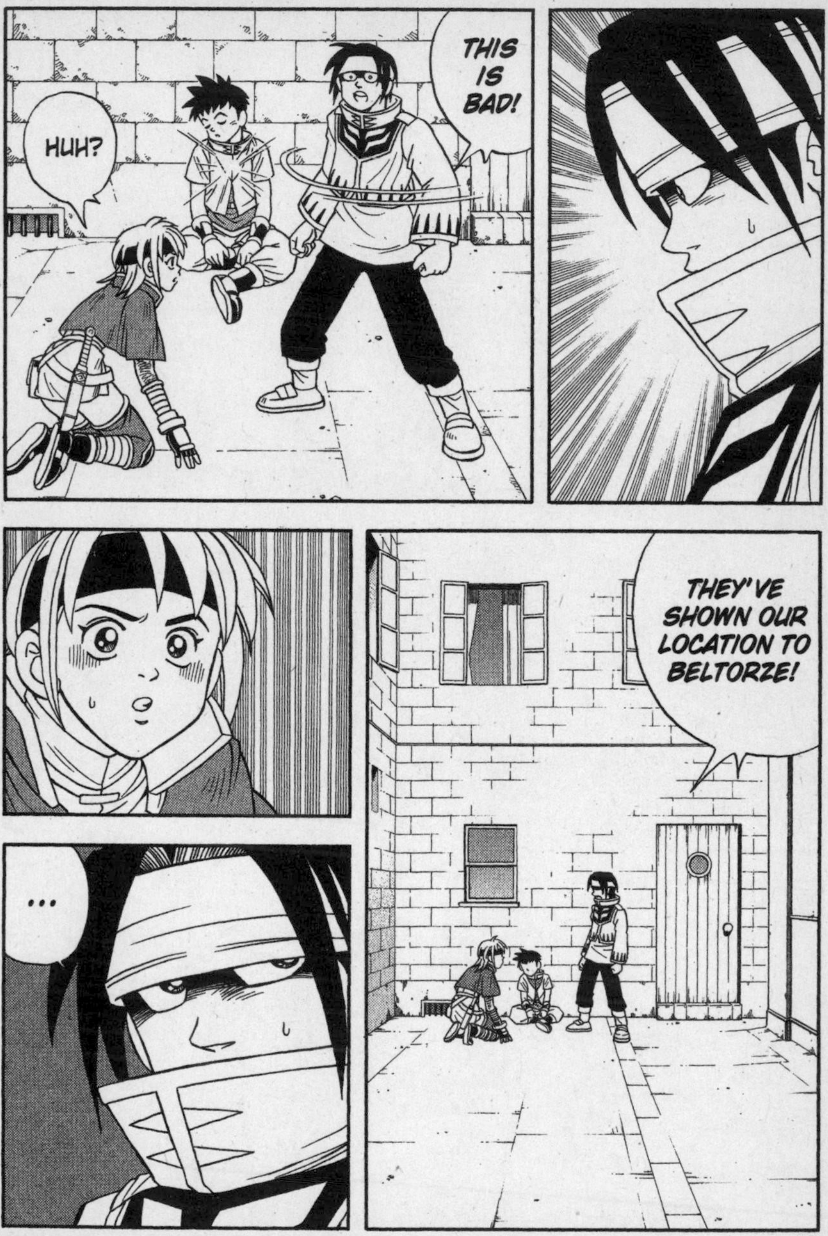
THIS IS BAD!
HUH?
THEY'VE SHOWN OUR LOCATION TO BELTORZE!
...

READ THIS WAY

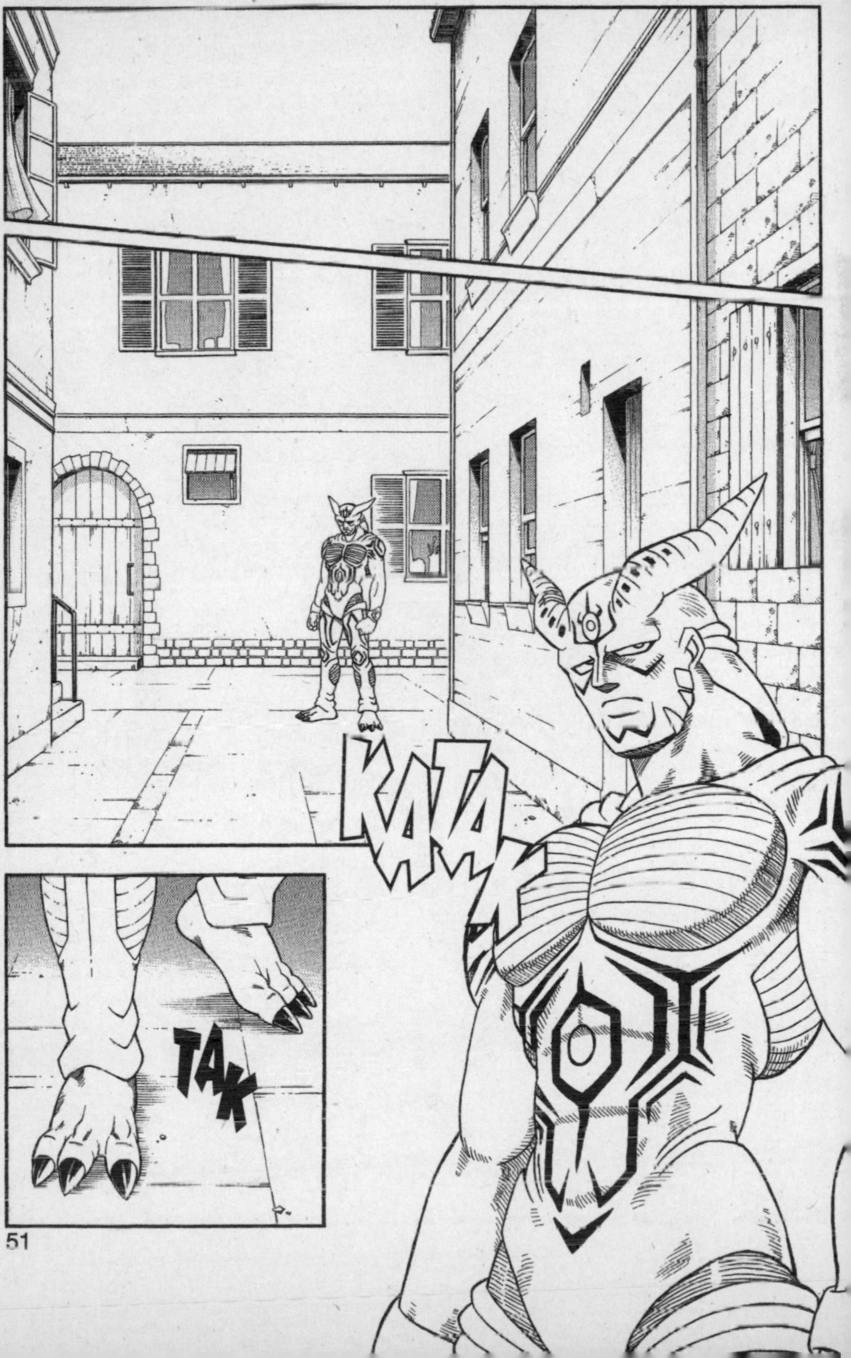
KATAK
TAK

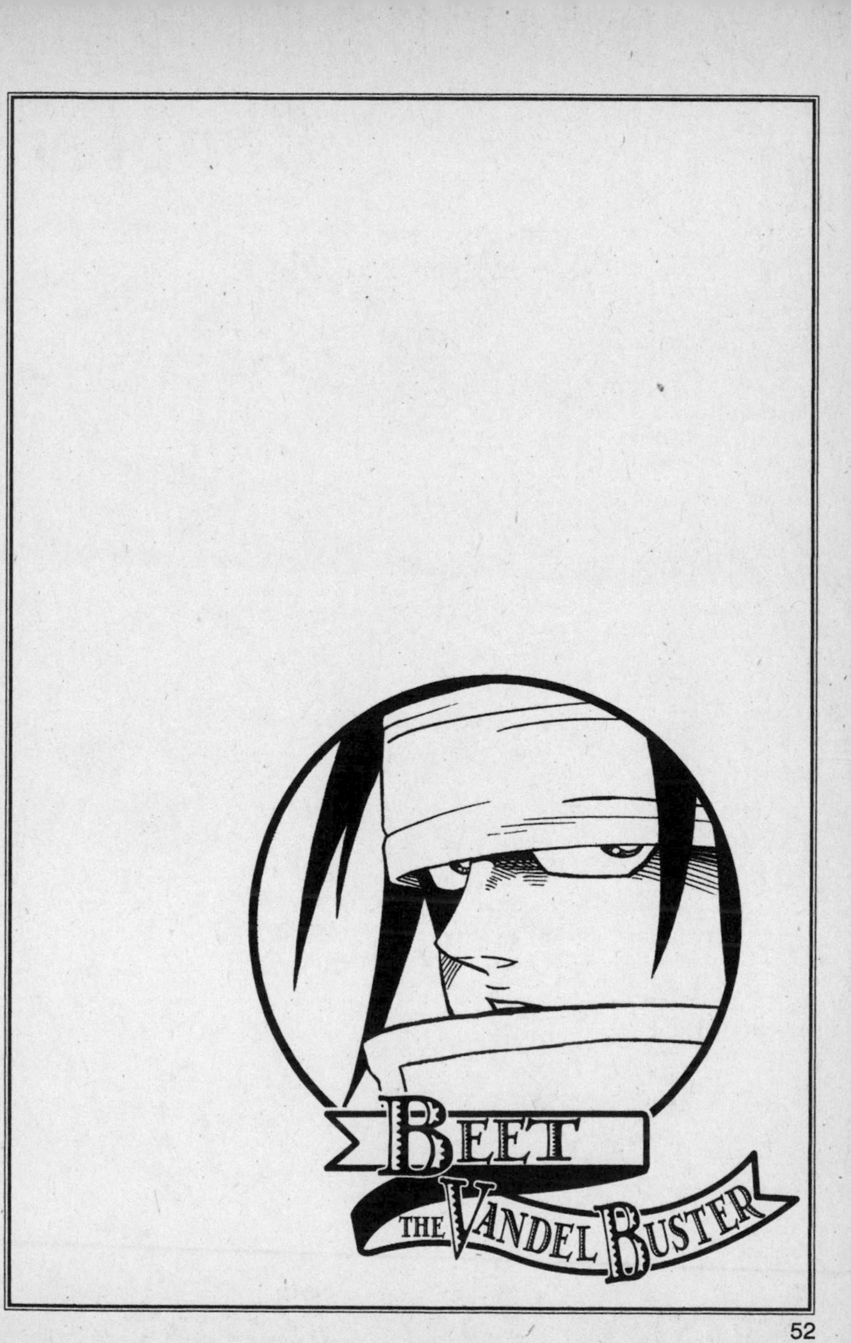
BEET
THE VANDEL BUSTER

Chapter 8

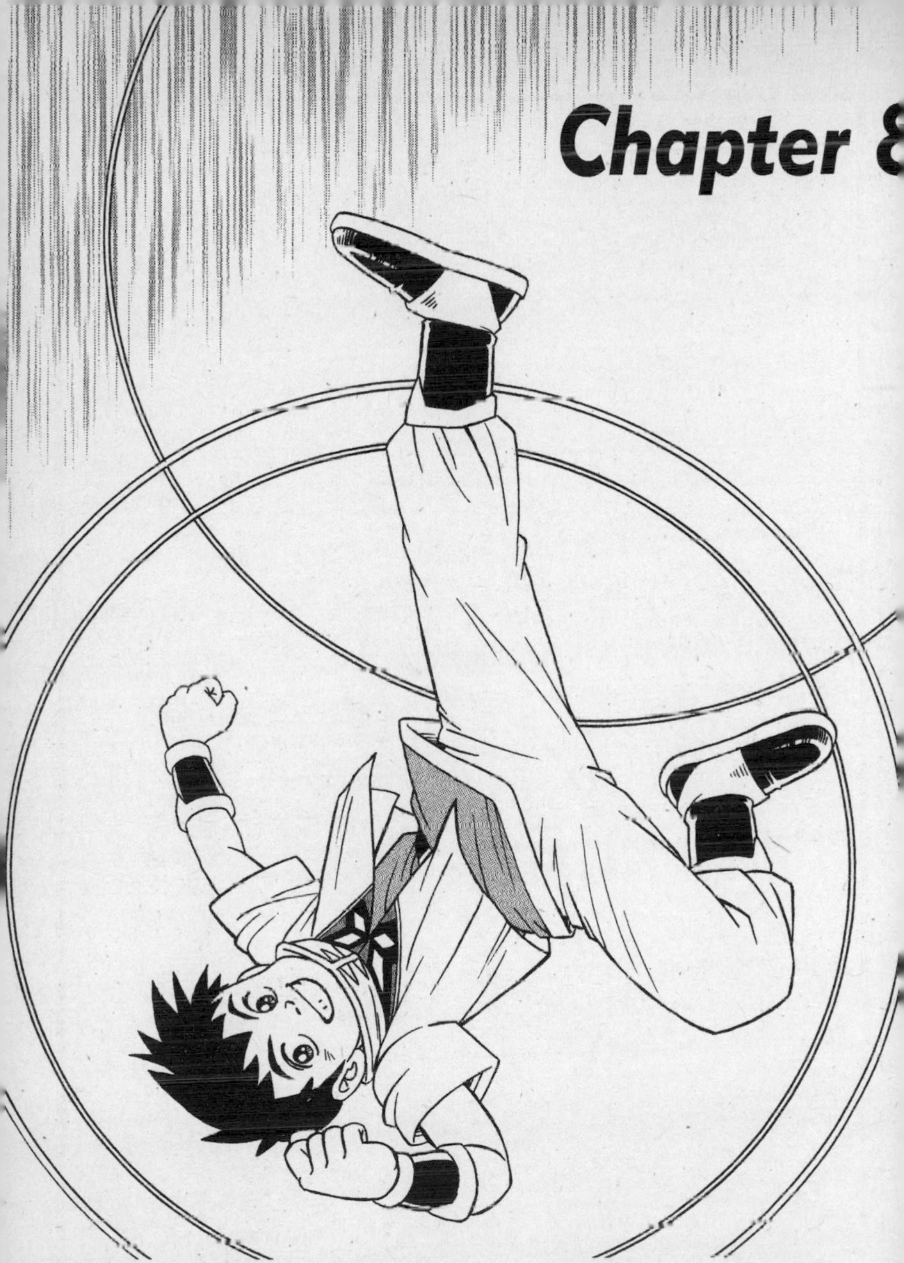

Wake Up, Beet!!

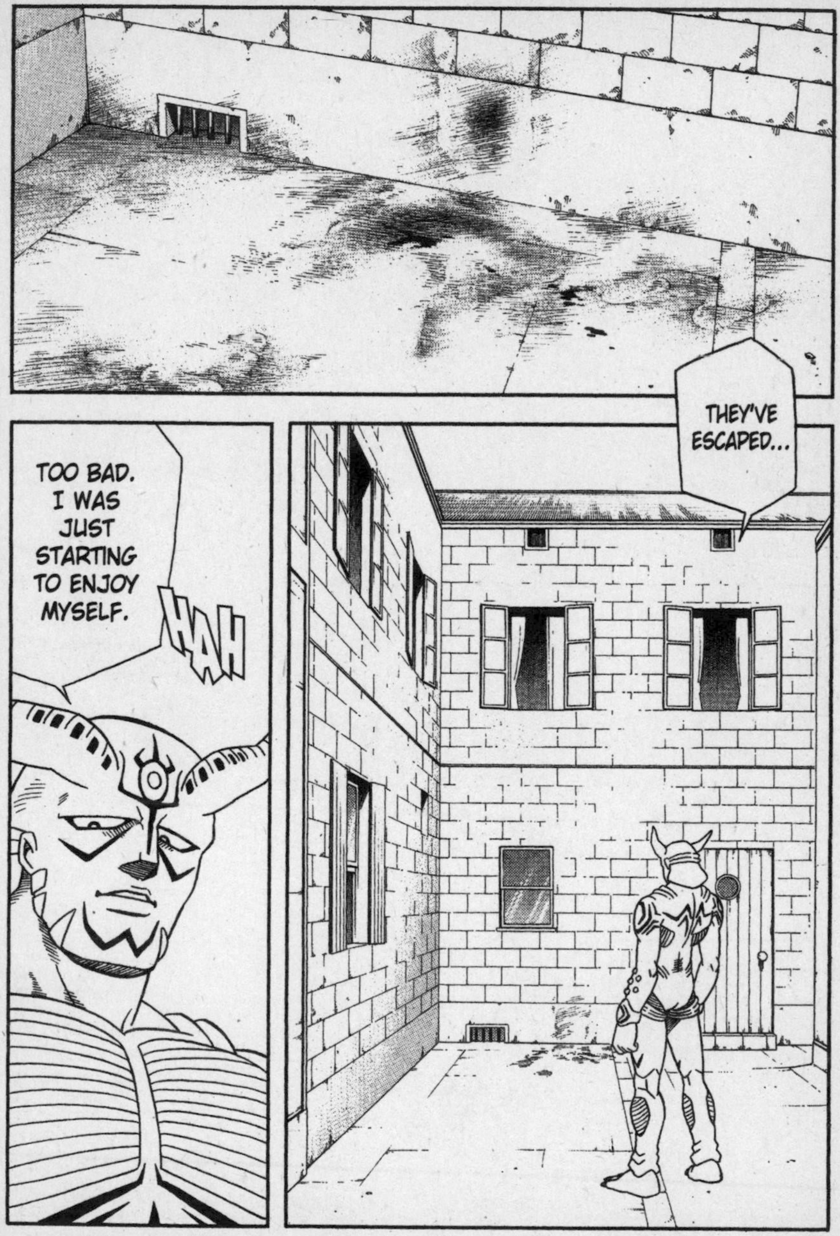
THEY'VE ESCAPED...
TOO BAD. I WAS JUST STARTING TO ENJOY MYSELF.
HAH

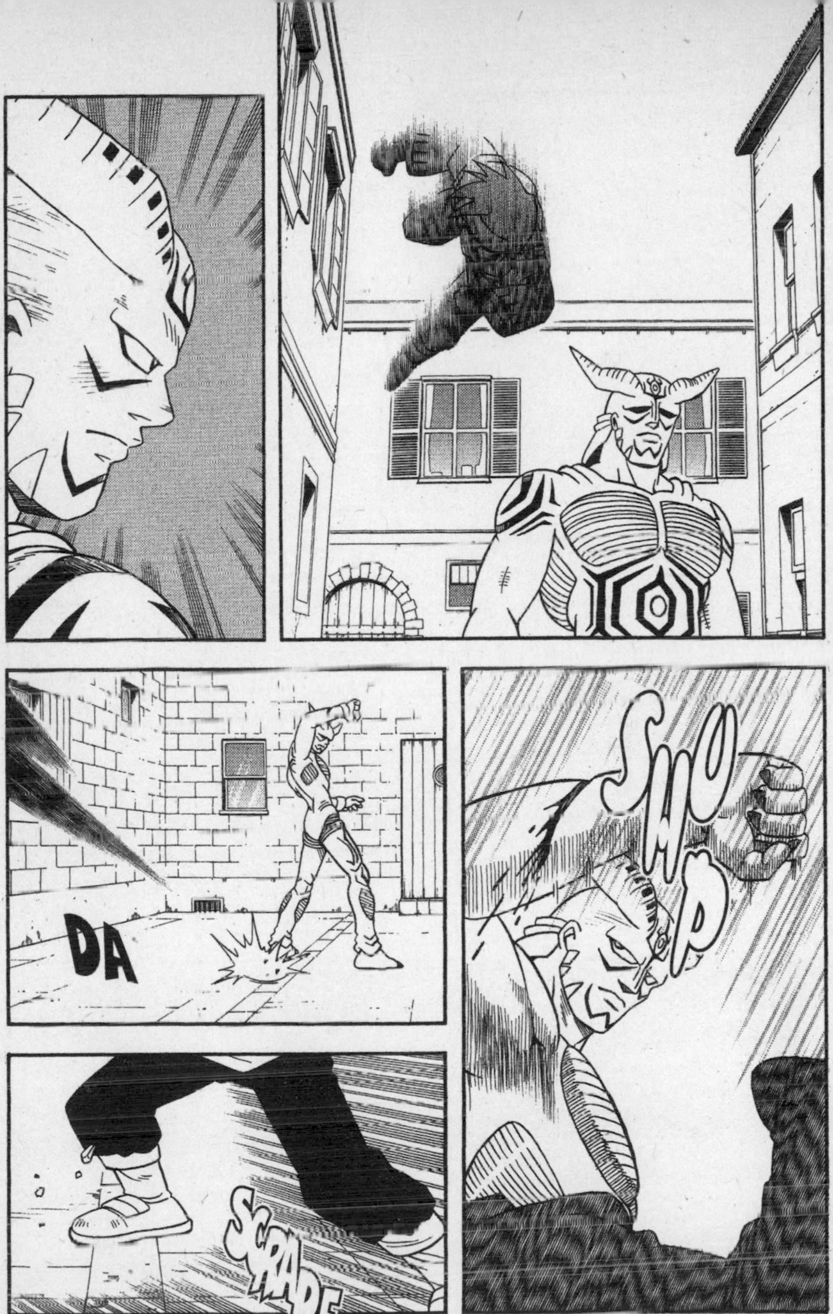
DA
SWOOP
SCRAPE

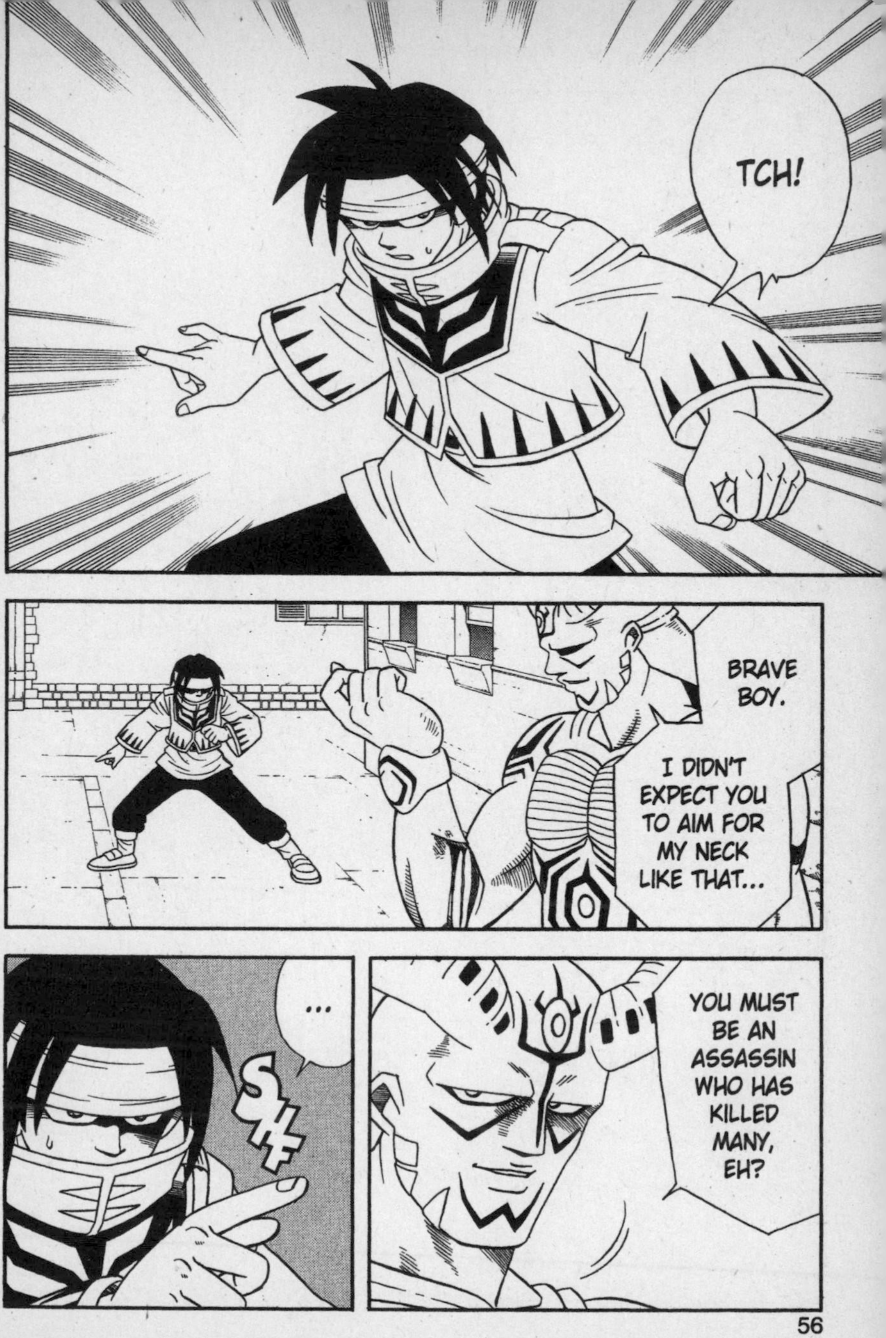
TCH!
BRAVE BOY.
I DIDN'T EXPECT YOU TO AIM FOR MY NECK LIKE THAT...
YOU MUST BE AN ASSASSIN WHO HAS KILLED MANY, EH?
...

READ THIS WAY

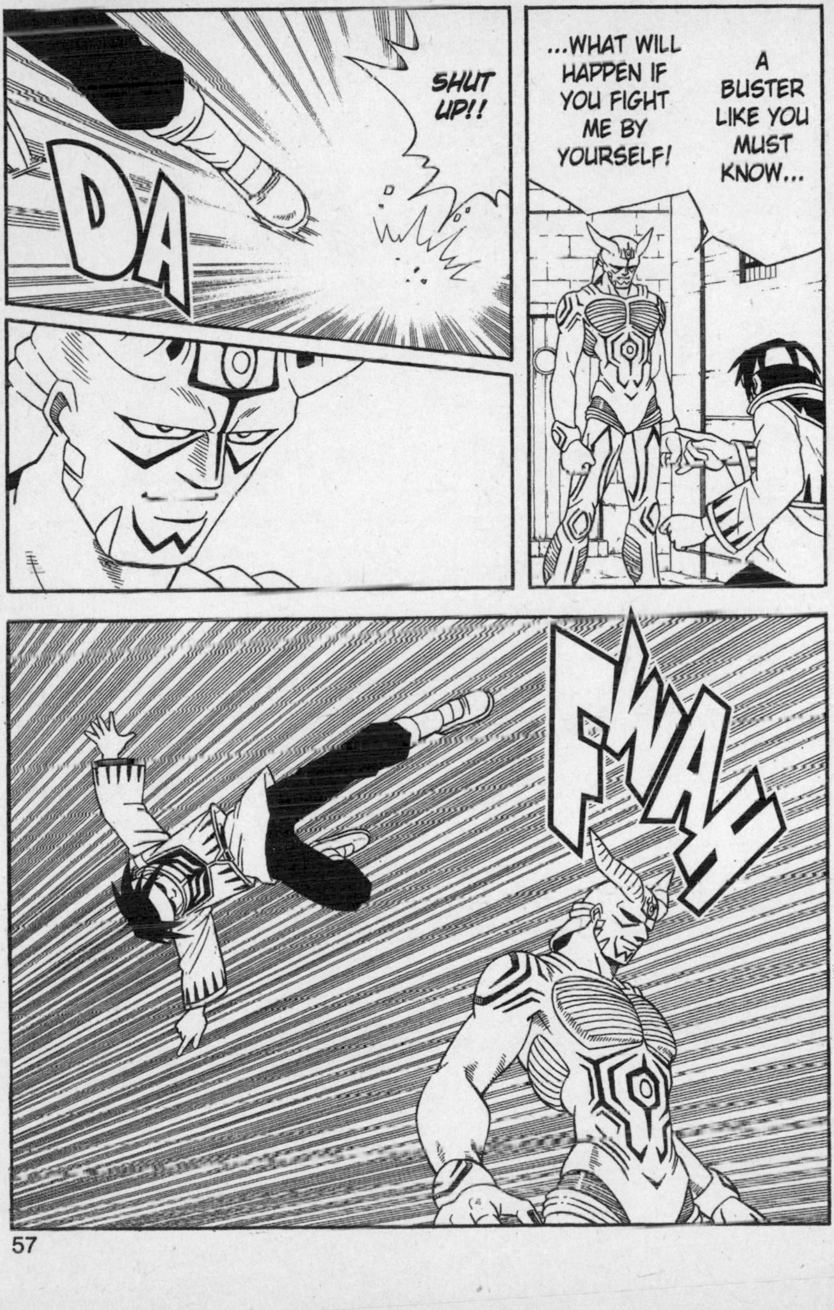
A BUSTER LIKE YOU MUST KNOW...
...WHAT WILL HAPPEN IF YOU FIGHT ME BY YOURSELF!
SHUT UP!!
DA
FWAS

READ THIS WAY

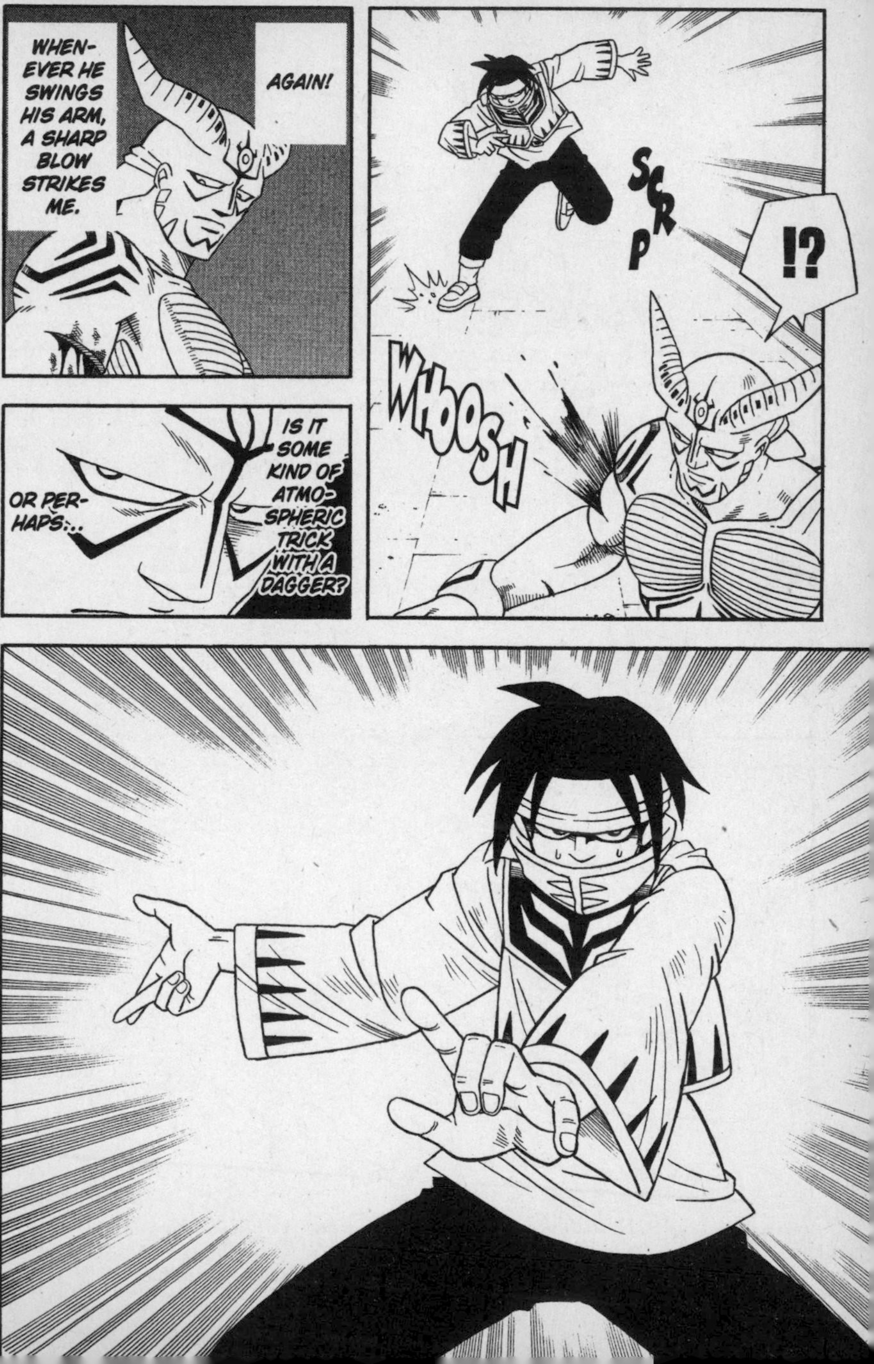
SCRP
!?
WHOOSH
AGAIN!
WHEN-EVER HE SWINGS HIS ARM, A SHARP BLOW STRIKES ME.
IS IT SOME KIND OF ATMO-SPHERIC TRICK WITH A DAGGER?
OR PER-HAPS...

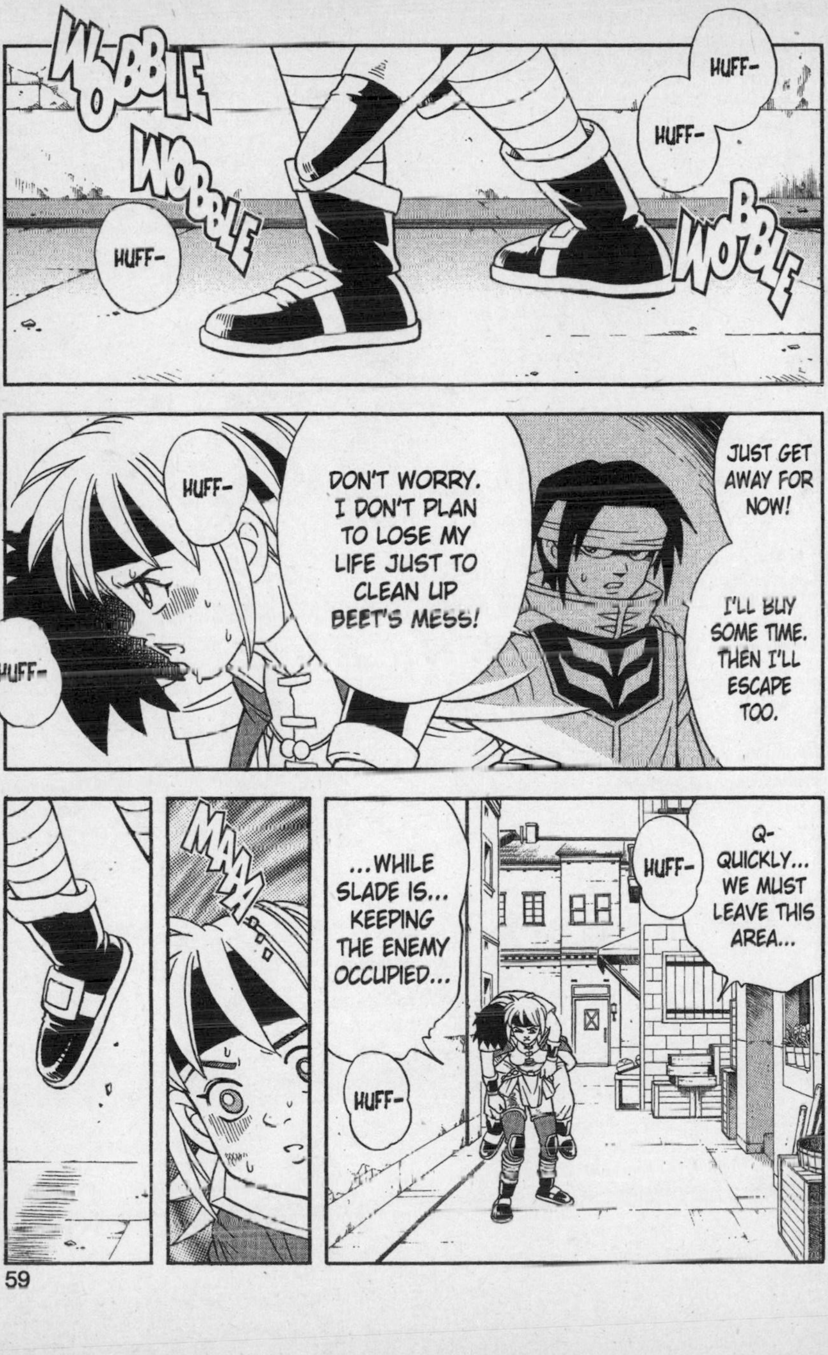
HUFF-
HUFF-
WOBBLE
WOBBLE
WOBBLE
HUFF-
JUST GET AWAY FOR NOW!
I'LL BUY SOME TIME. THEN I'LL ESCAPE TOO.
DON'T WORRY. I DON'T PLAN TO LOSE MY LIFE JUST TO CLEAN UP BEET'S MESS!
HUFF-
HUFF-
Q-QUICKLY... WE MUST LEAVE THIS AREA...
HUFF-
...WHILE SLADE IS... KEEPING THE ENEMY OCCUPIED...
HUFF-
MAAA

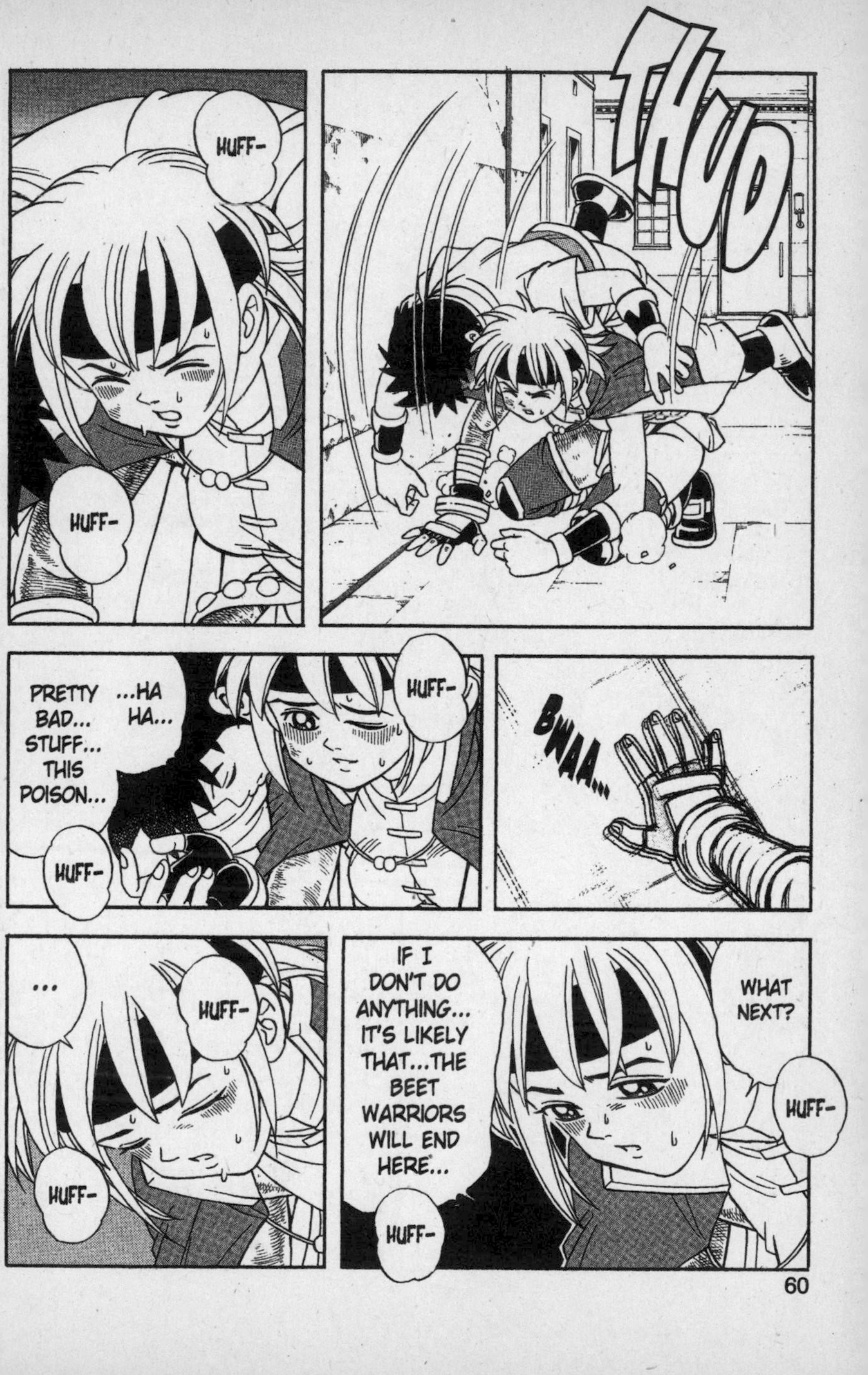
THUD
HUFF-
HUFF-
BWAA...
HUFF-
...HA HA...
PRETTY BAD... STUFF... THIS POISON...
HUFF-
WHAT NEXT?
HUFF-
IF I DON'T DO ANYTHING... IT'S LIKELY THAT...THE BEET WARRIORS WILL END HERE...
HUFF-
HUFF-
...
HUFF-

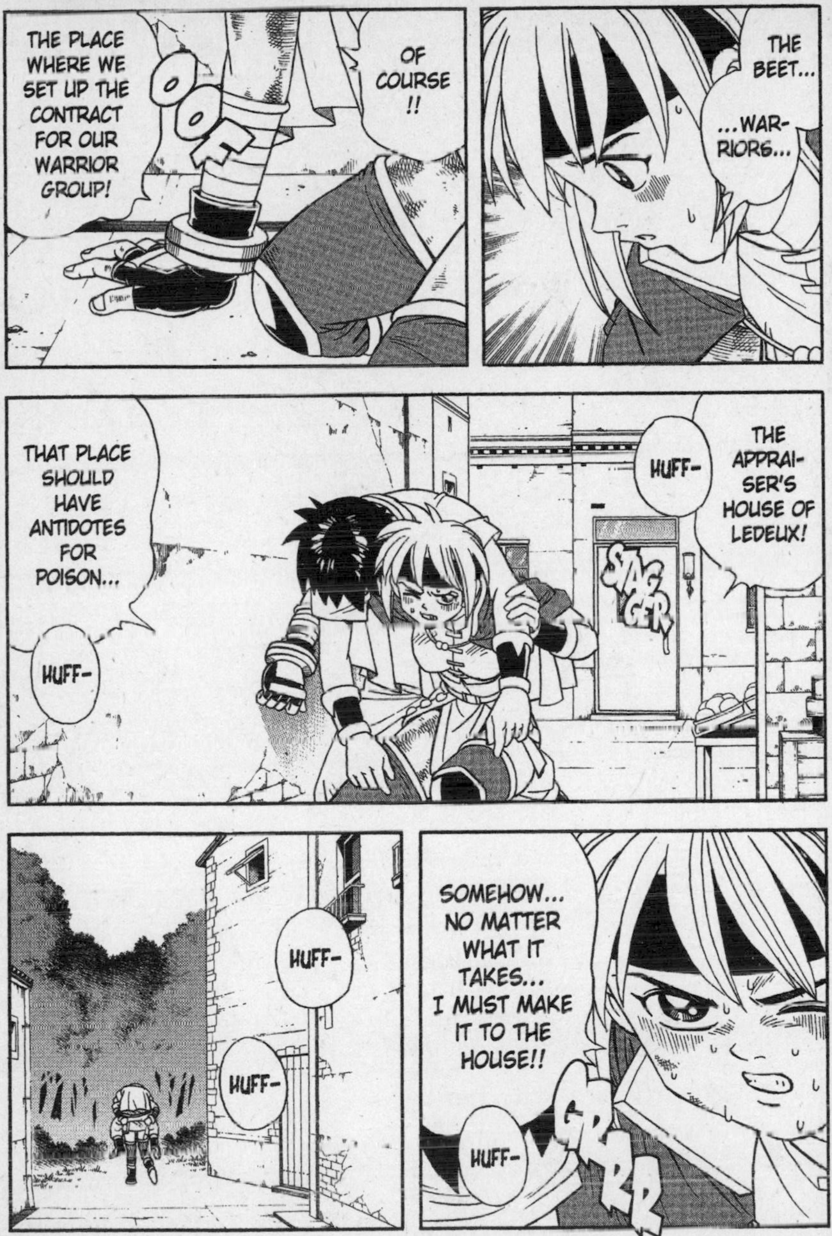
THE BEET...
...WARRIORS...
OF COURSE !!
THE PLACE WHERE WE SET UP THE CONTRACT FOR OUR WARRIOR GROUP!
OOF
THE APPRAISER'S HOUSE OF LEDEUX!
HUFF-
STAGGER
THAT PLACE SHOULD HAVE ANTIDOTES FOR POISON...
HUFF-
SOMEHOW... NO MATTER WHAT IT TAKES... I MUST MAKE IT TO THE HOUSE!!
GRRR
HUFF-
HUFF-
HUFF-

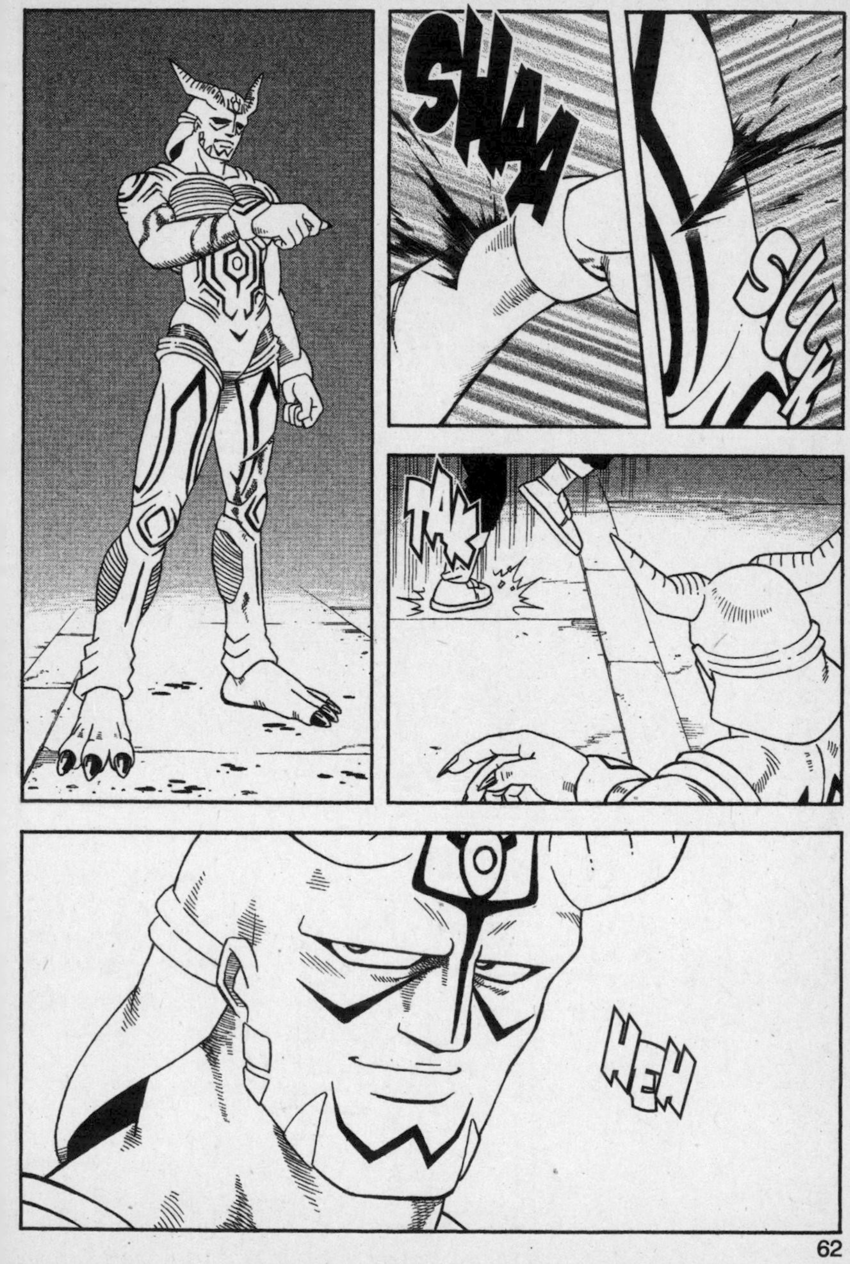
SLICK
SHAA
TAK
HEH

READ THIS WAY

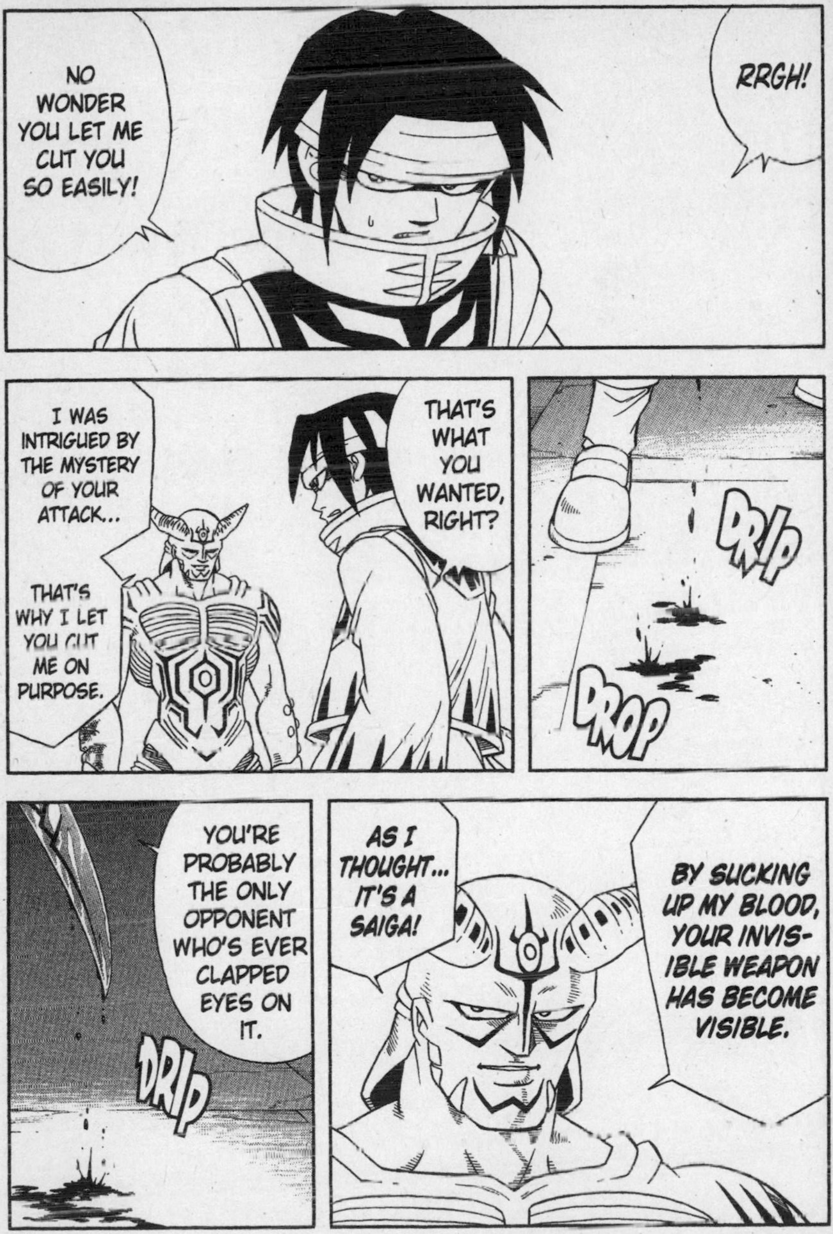
RRGH!
NO WONDER YOU LET ME CUT YOU SO EASILY!
DRIP
DROP
THAT'S WHAT YOU WANTED, RIGHT?
I WAS INTRIGUED BY THE MYSTERY OF YOUR ATTACK...
THAT'S WHY I LET YOU CUT ME ON PURPOSE.
BY SUCKING UP MY BLOOD, YOUR INVISIBLE WEAPON HAS BECOME VISIBLE.
AS I THOUGHT... IT'S A SAIGA!
YOU'RE PROBABLY THE ONLY OPPONENT WHO'S EVER CLAPPED EYES ON IT.
DRIP

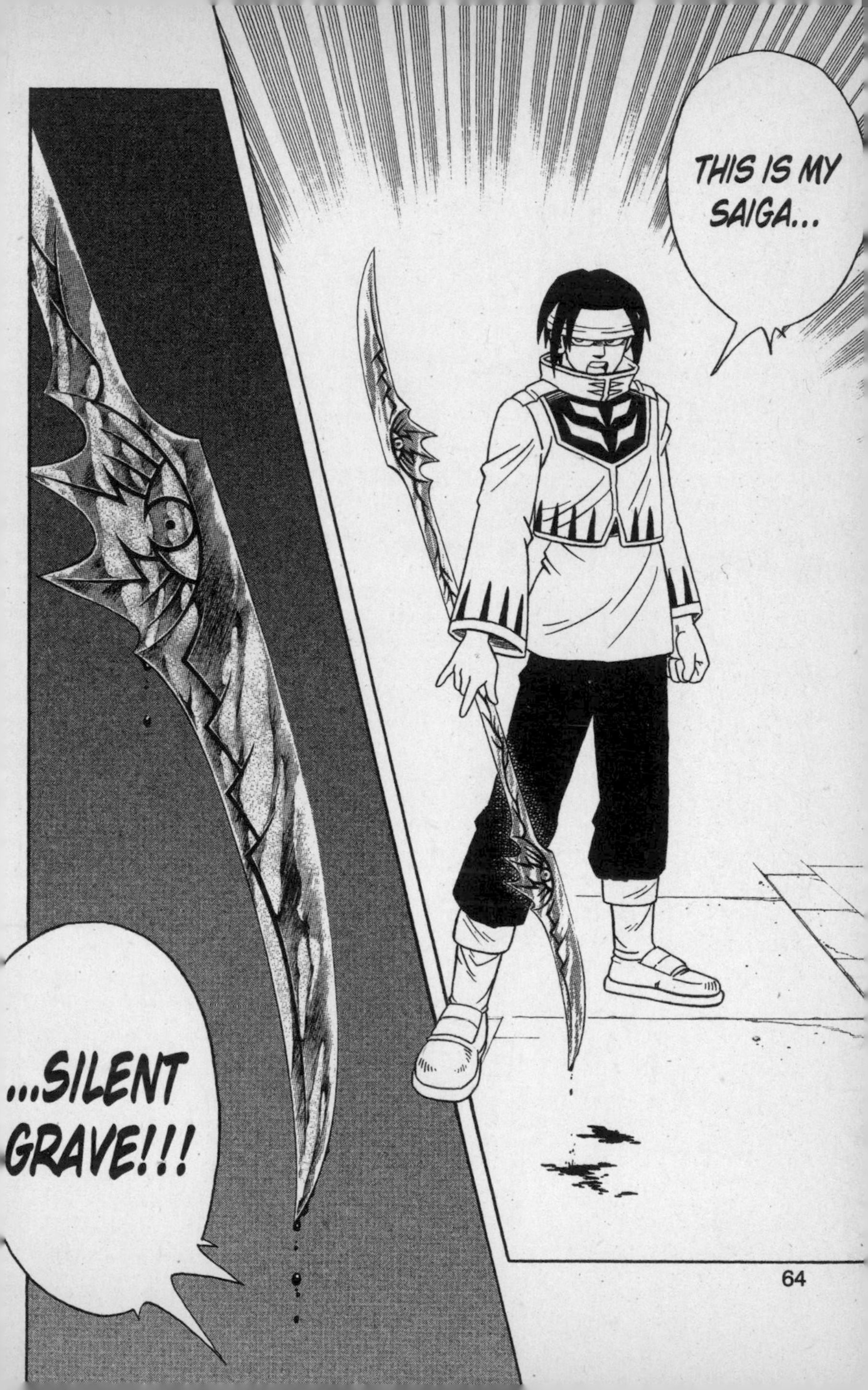
THIS IS MY SAIGA...
...SILENT GRAVE!!!

READ THIS WAY

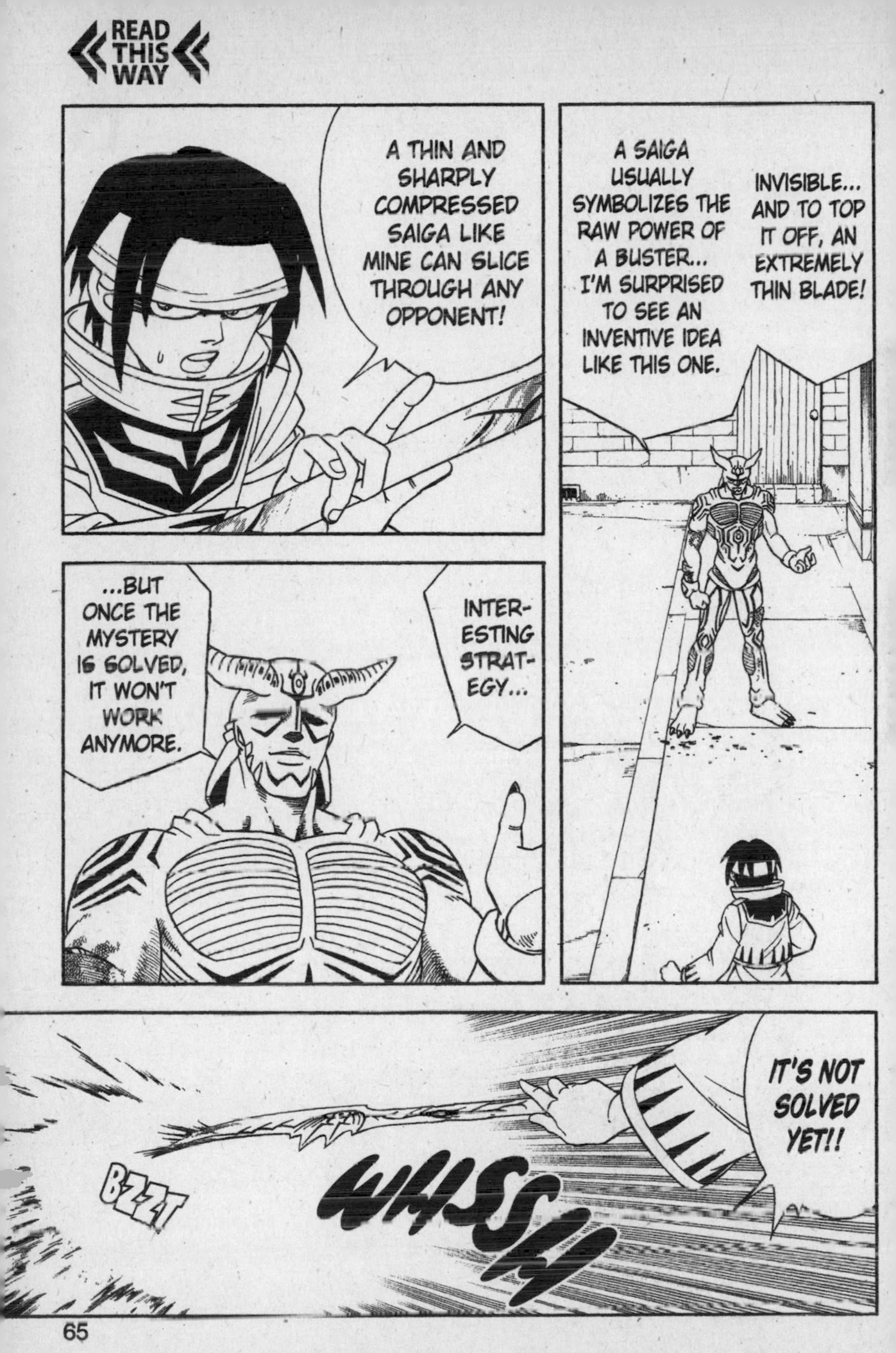

INVISIBLE... AND TO TOP IT OFF, AN EXTREMELY THIN BLADE!
A SAIGA USUALLY SYMBOLIZES THE RAW POWER OF A BUSTER... I'M SURPRISED TO SEE AN INVENTIVE IDEA LIKE THIS ONE.
A THIN AND SHARPLY COMPRESSED SAIGA LIKE MINE CAN SLICE THROUGH ANY OPPONENT!
INTER-ESTING STRAT-EGY...
...BUT ONCE THE MYSTERY IS SOLVED, IT WON'T WORK ANYMORE.
IT'S NOT SOLVED YET!!
WHSSH
BZZT

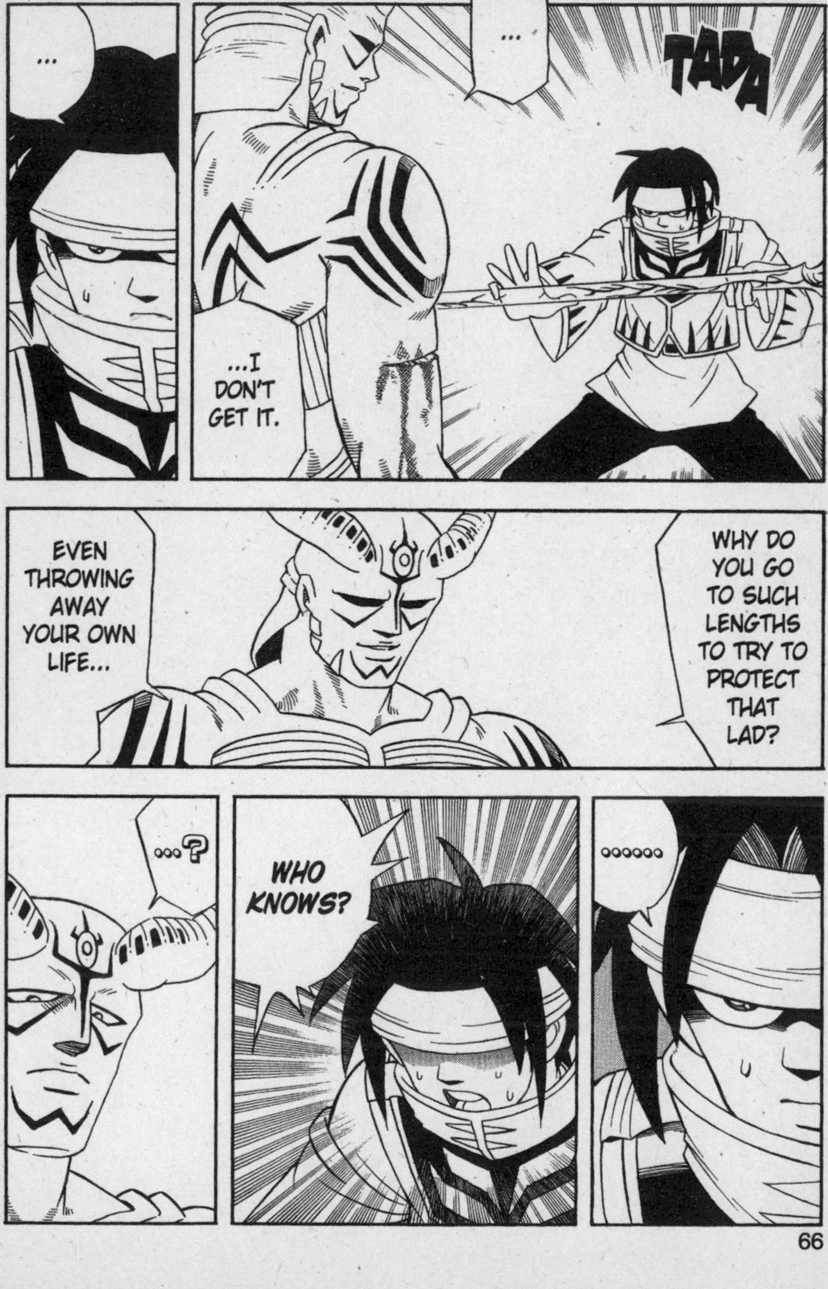
TADA
...
...I DON'T GET IT.
...
WHY DO YOU GO TO SUCH LENGTHS TO TRY TO PROTECT THAT LAD?
EVEN THROWING AWAY YOUR OWN LIFE...
......
WHO KNOWS?
...?

READ THIS WAY

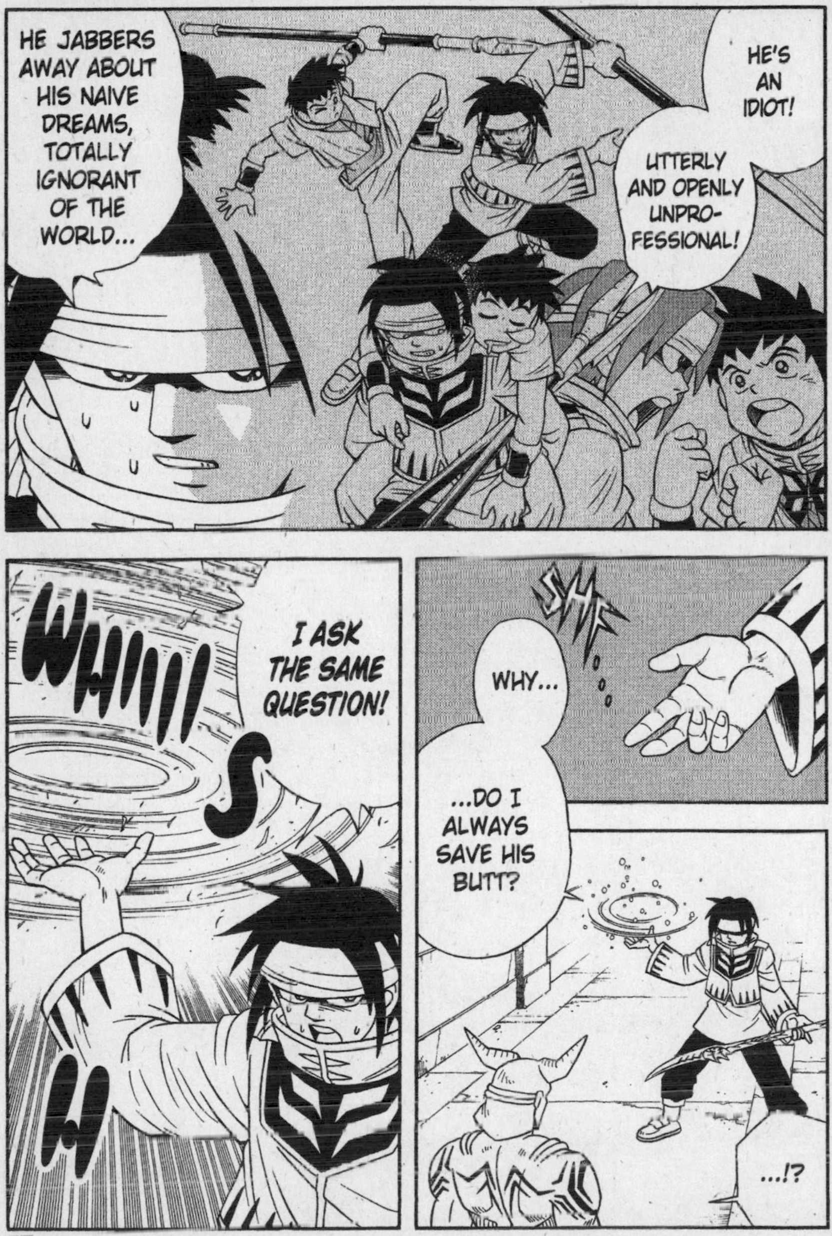
HE'S AN IDIOT!
UTTERLY AND OPENLY UNPRO-FESSIONAL!
HE JABBERS AWAY ABOUT HIS NAIVE DREAMS, TOTALLY IGNORANT OF THE WORLD...
WHY...
...DO I ALWAYS SAVE HIS BUTT?
...!?
I ASK THE SAME QUESTION!

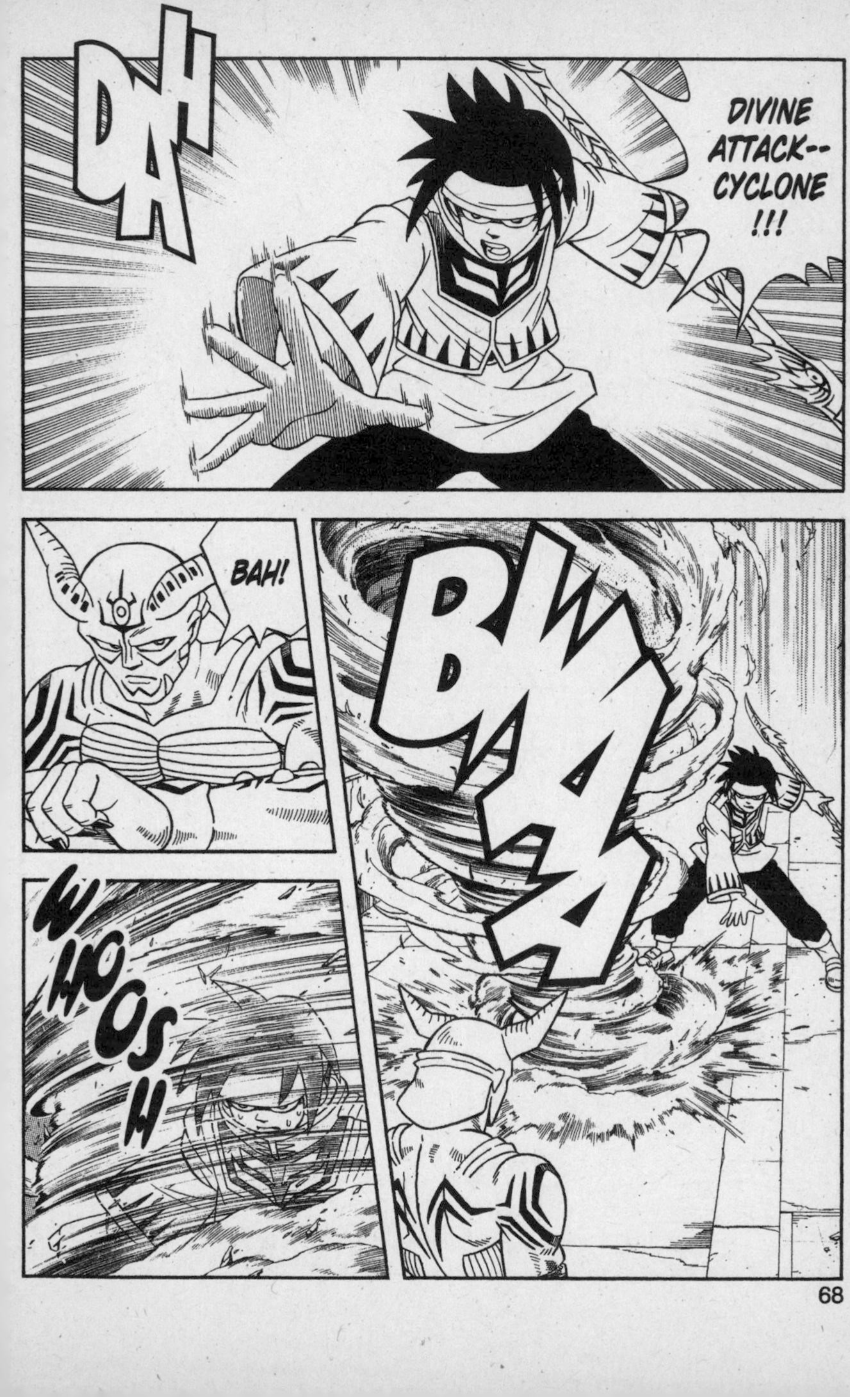
DIVINE ATTACK-- CYCLONE !!!
DAH
BWA
BAH!
WHOOSH

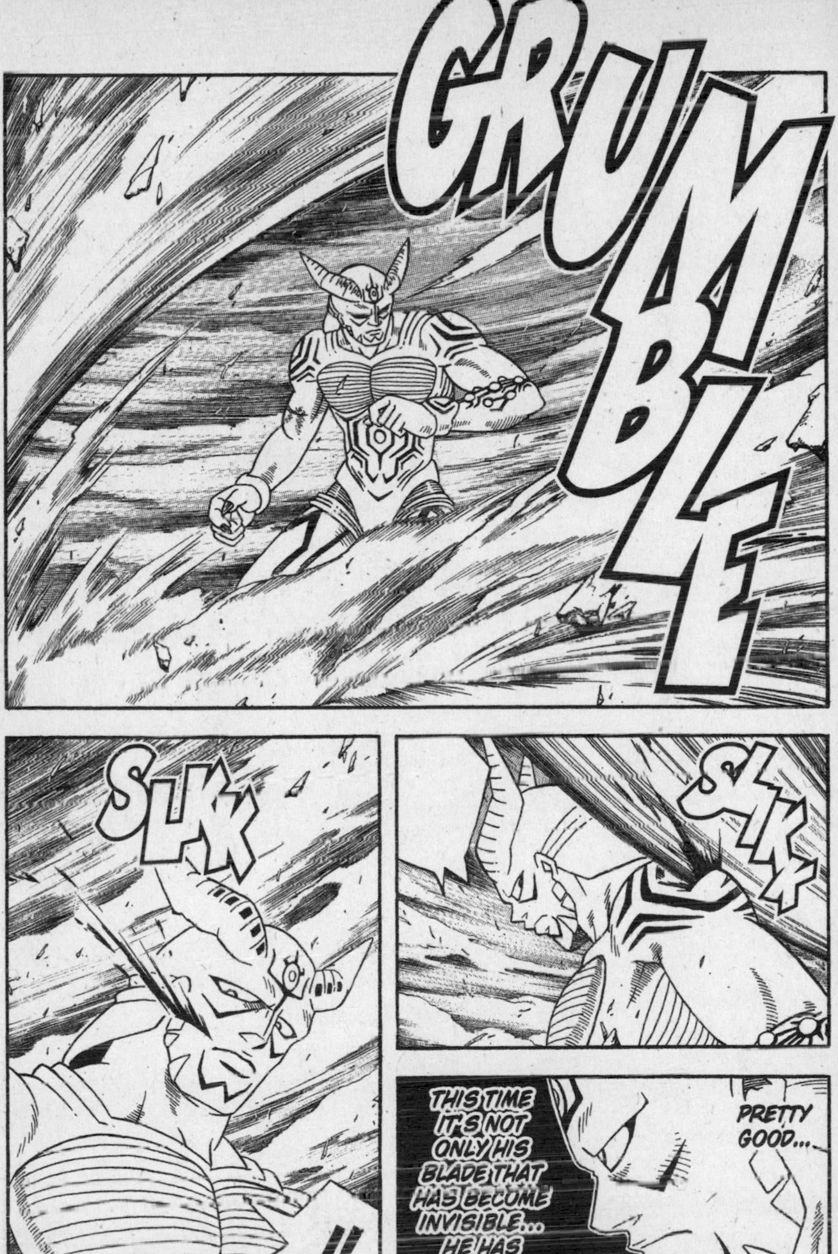
GRUMBLE
SLKK
PRETTY GOOD...
THIS TIME IT'S NOT ONLY HIS BLADE THAT HAS BECOME INVISIBLE... HE HAS AS WELL.
SLKK
!!

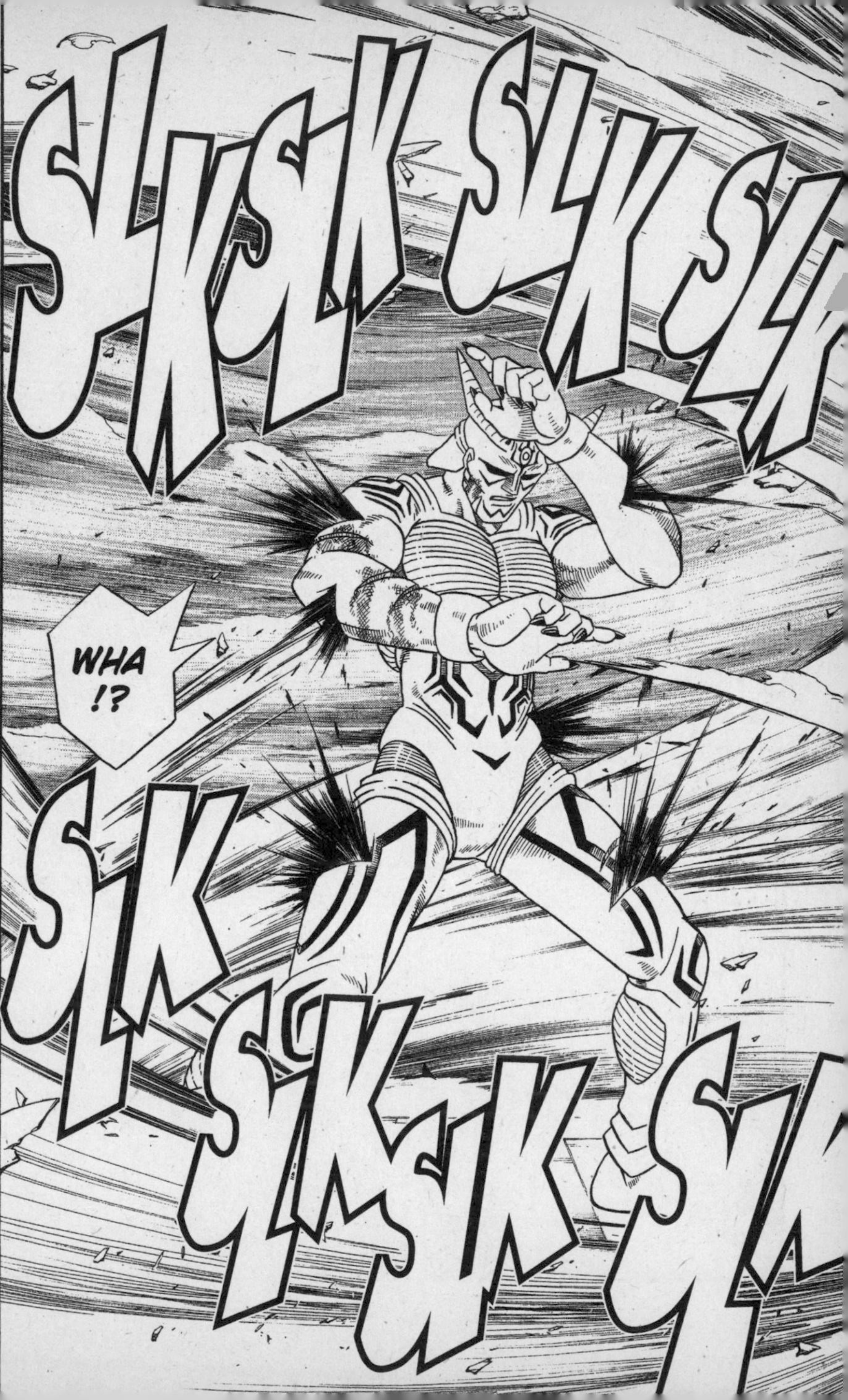
WHA !?

READ THIS WAY

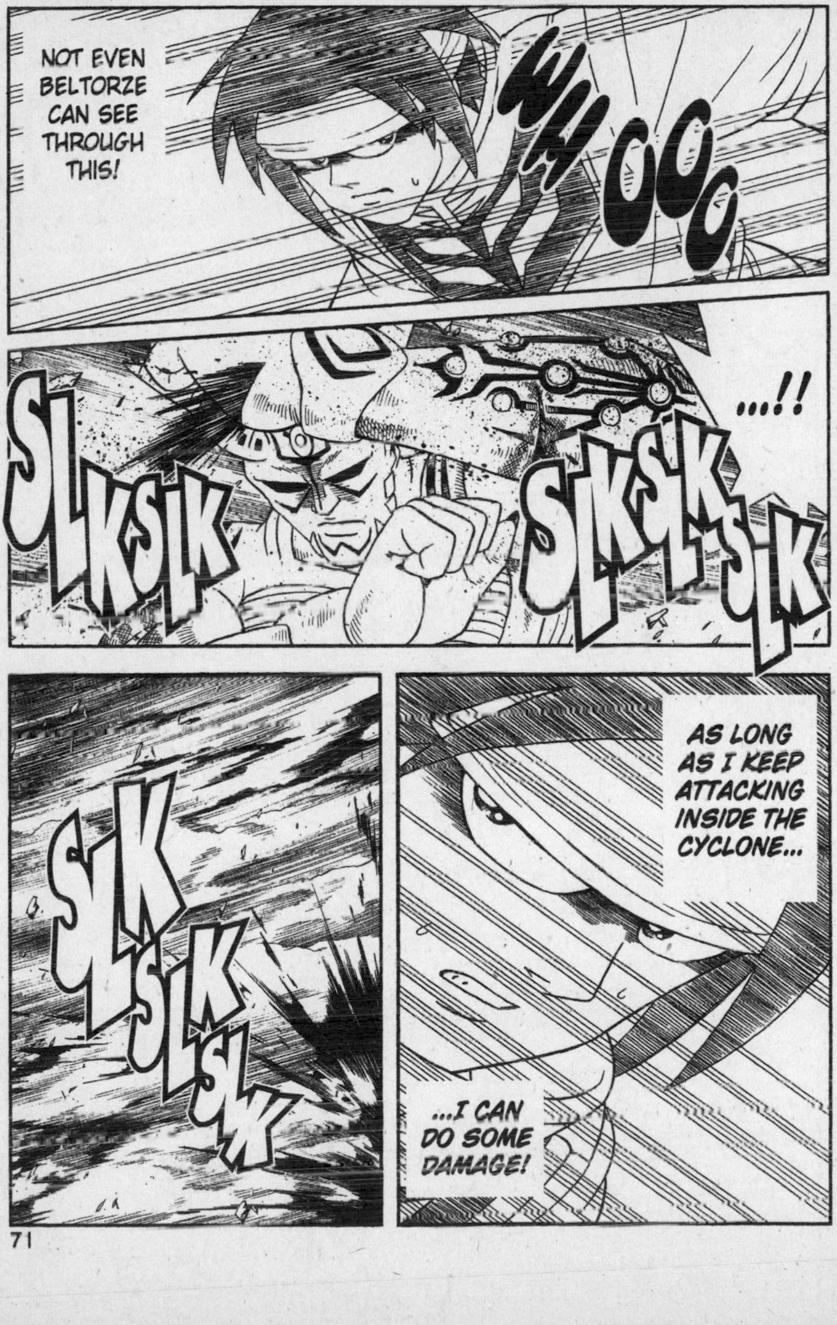
NOT EVEN BELTORZE CAN SEE THROUGH THIS!
WHOOOO
...!!
SLKSLKSLK
SLKSLK
AS LONG AS I KEEP ATTACKING INSIDE THE CYCLONE...
...I CAN DO SOME DAMAGE!
SLKSLKSLK

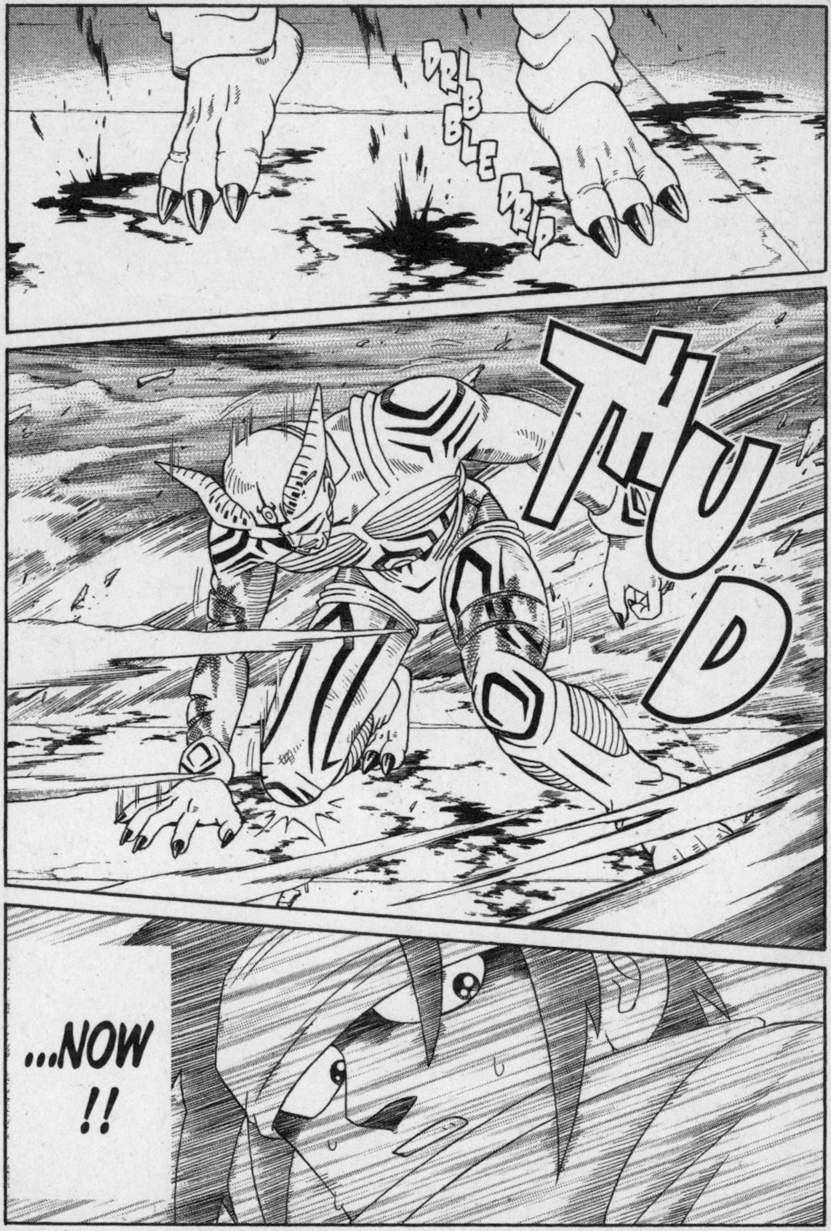
DRIBBLE DRIP
THUD
...NOW !!

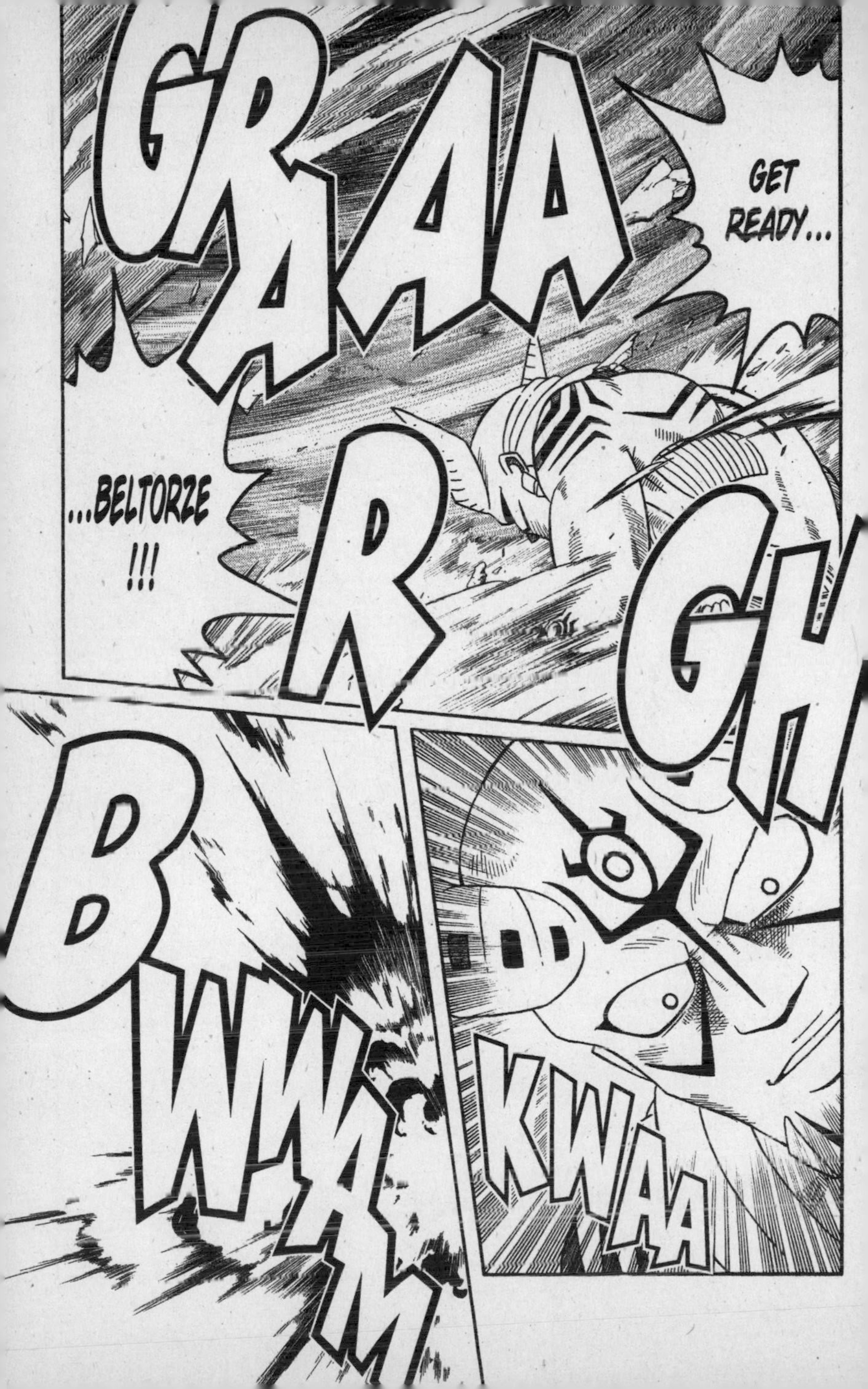
GET READY...
...BELTORZE !!!
GRAARGH
KWAA
BWWAM

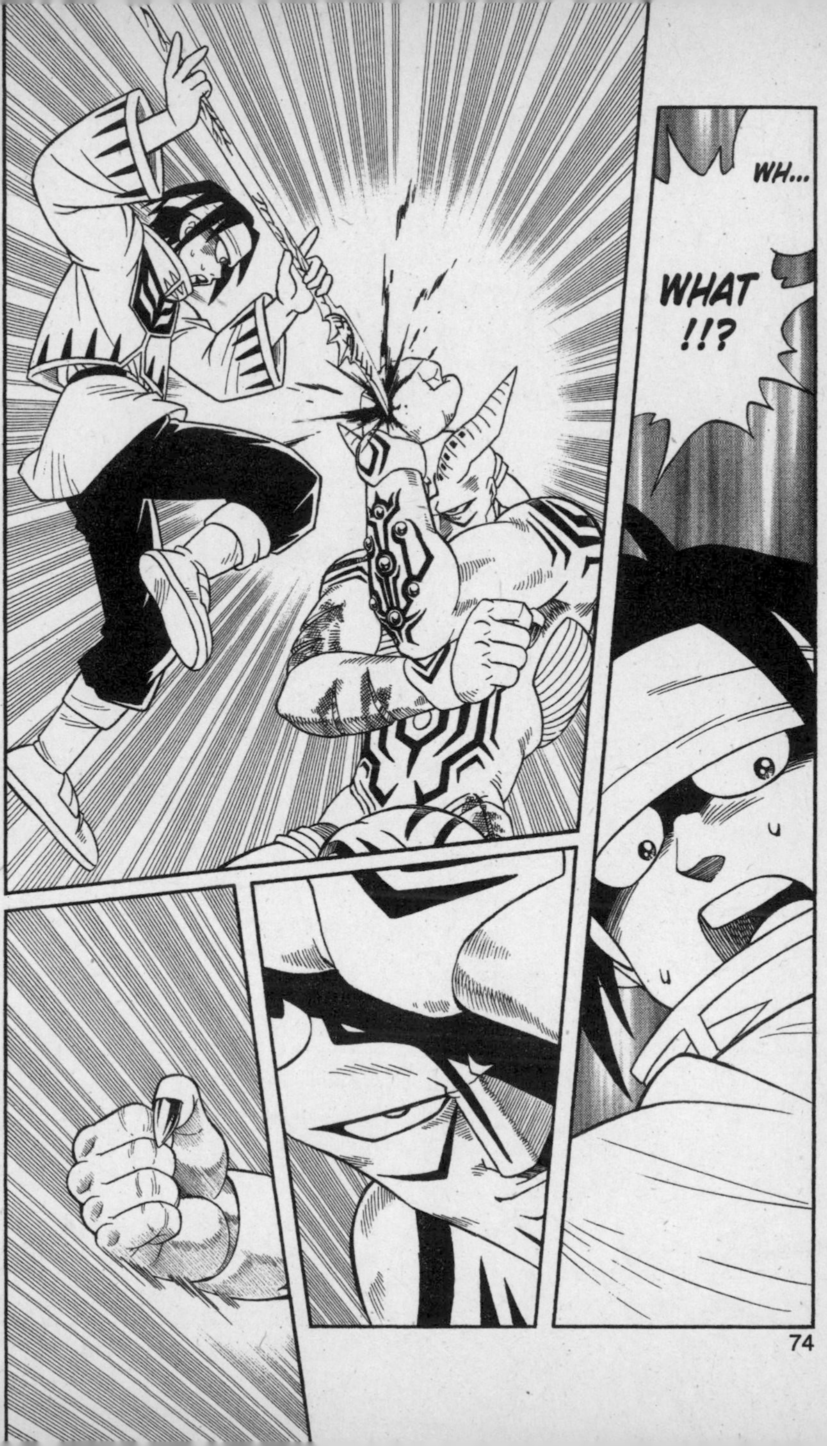
WH...
WHAT !!?

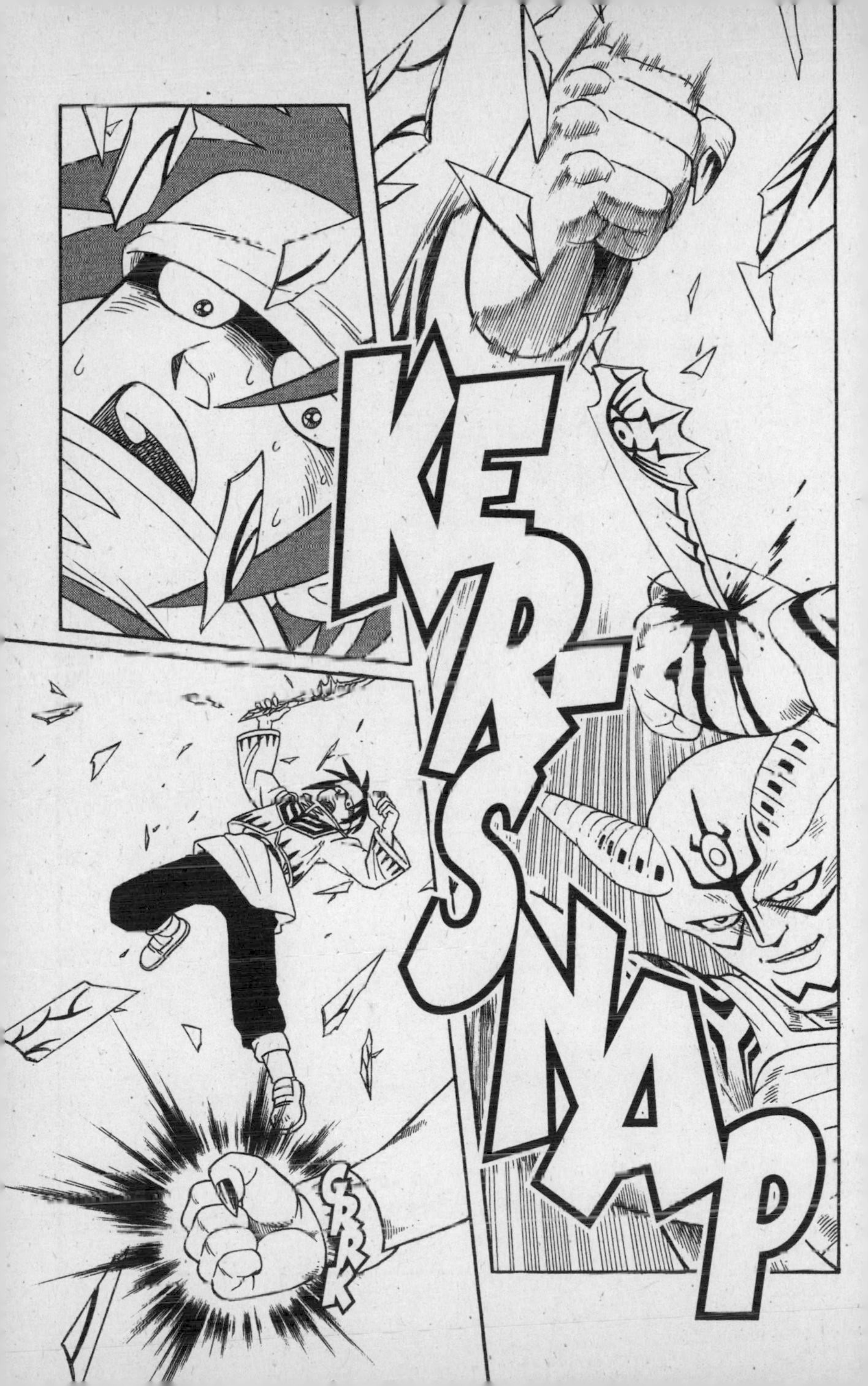
KRA-SNAP
GRRK

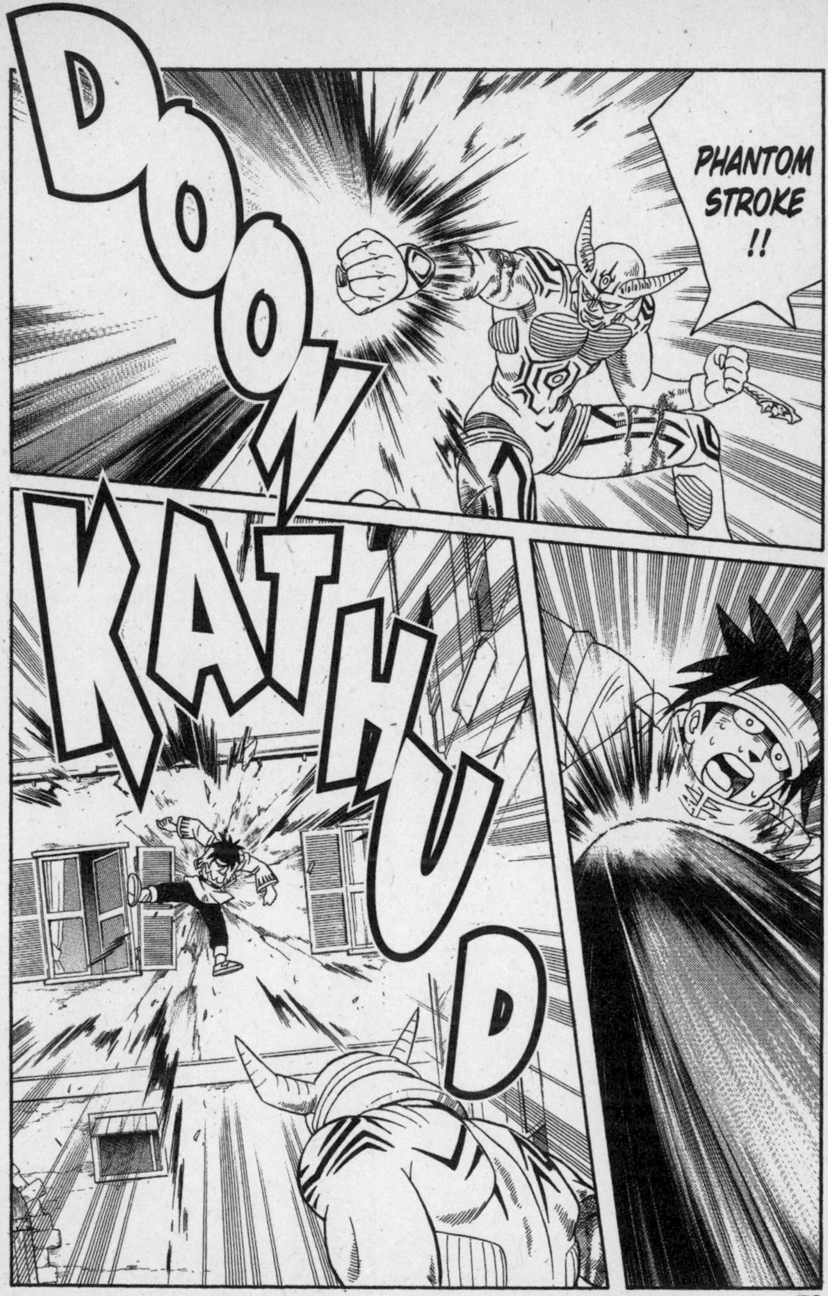
PHANTOM STROKE !!
DOOON
KATHUD

READ THIS WAY

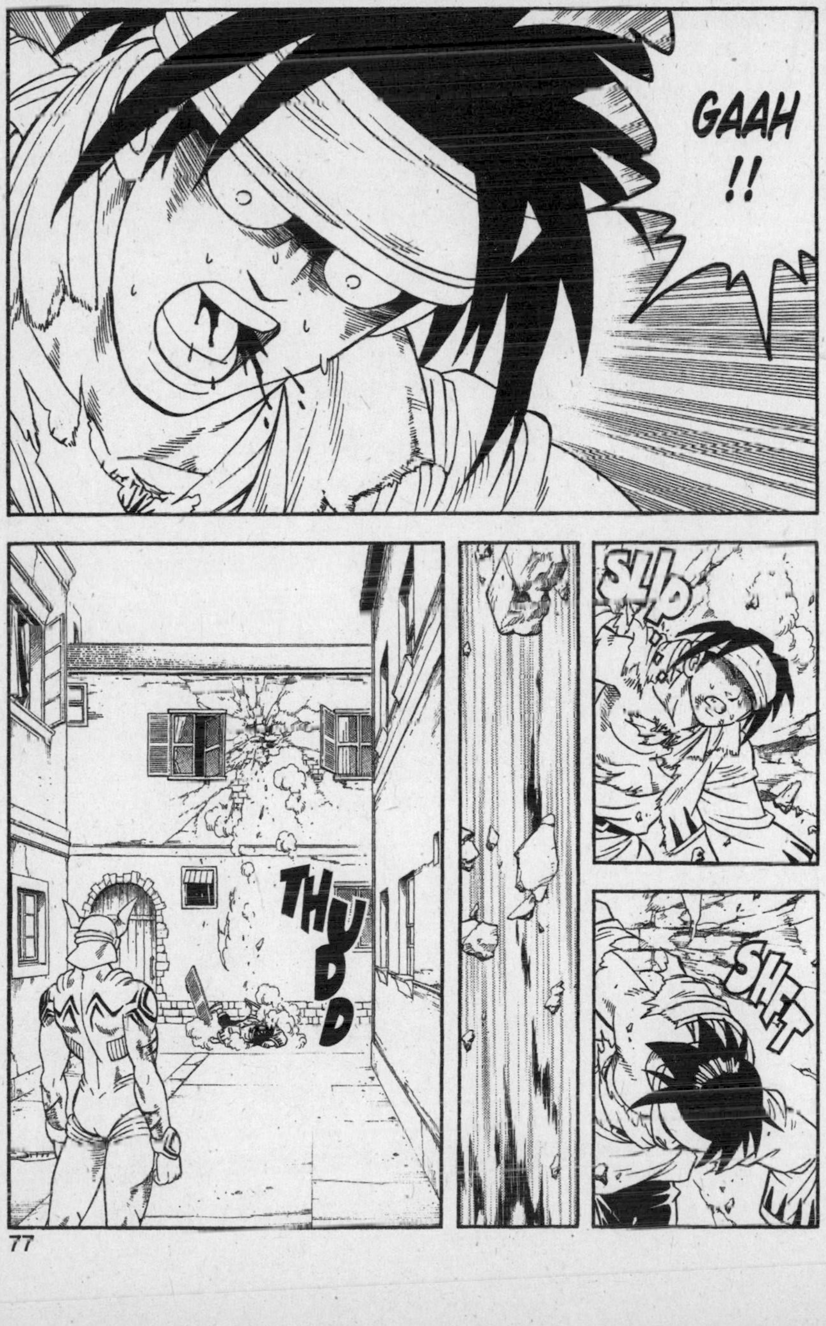
GAAH !!
SLIP
SHFT
THUDD

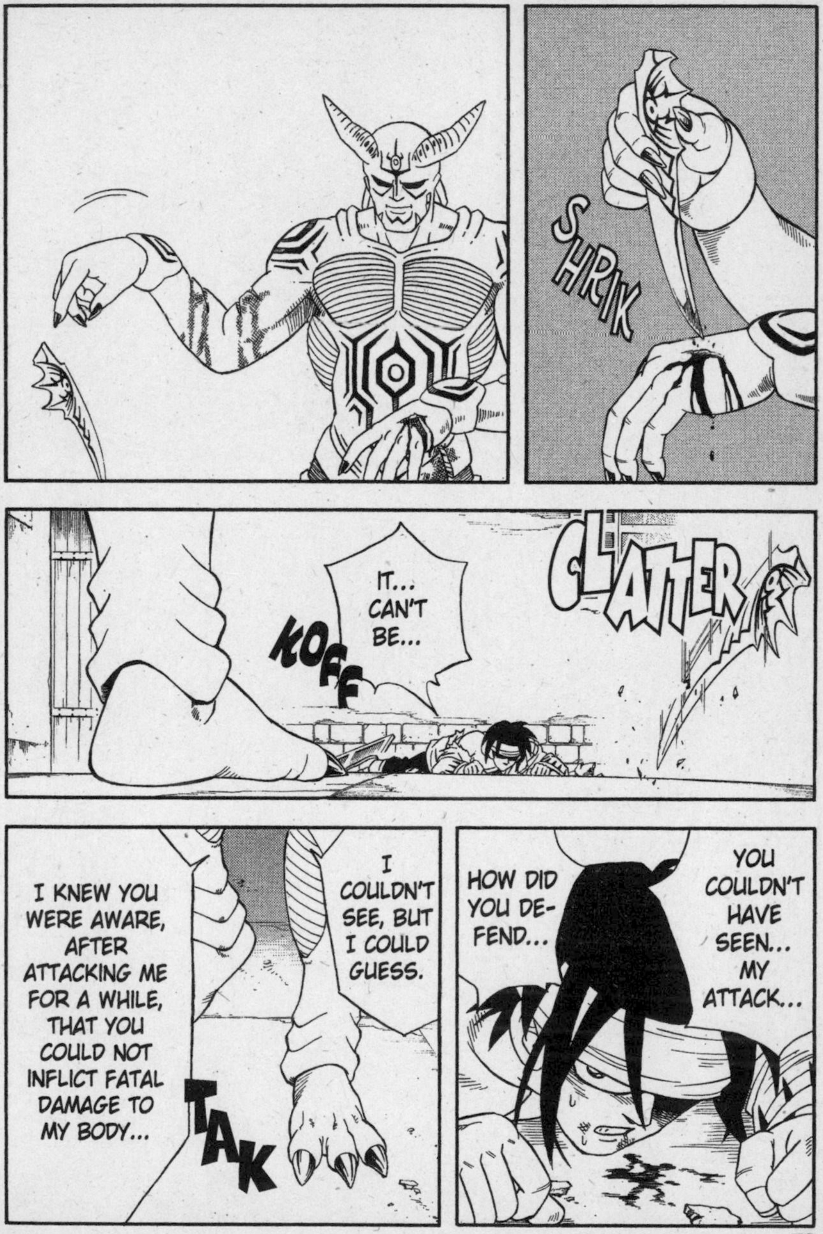
SHRIK
CLATTER
IT... CAN'T BE...
KOFF
YOU COULDN'T HAVE SEEN... MY ATTACK...
HOW DID YOU DE- FEND...
I COULDN'T SEE, BUT I COULD GUESS.
I KNEW YOU WERE AWARE, AFTER ATTACKING ME FOR A WHILE, THAT YOU COULD NOT INFLICT FATAL DAMAGE TO MY BODY...
TAK

READ THIS WAY

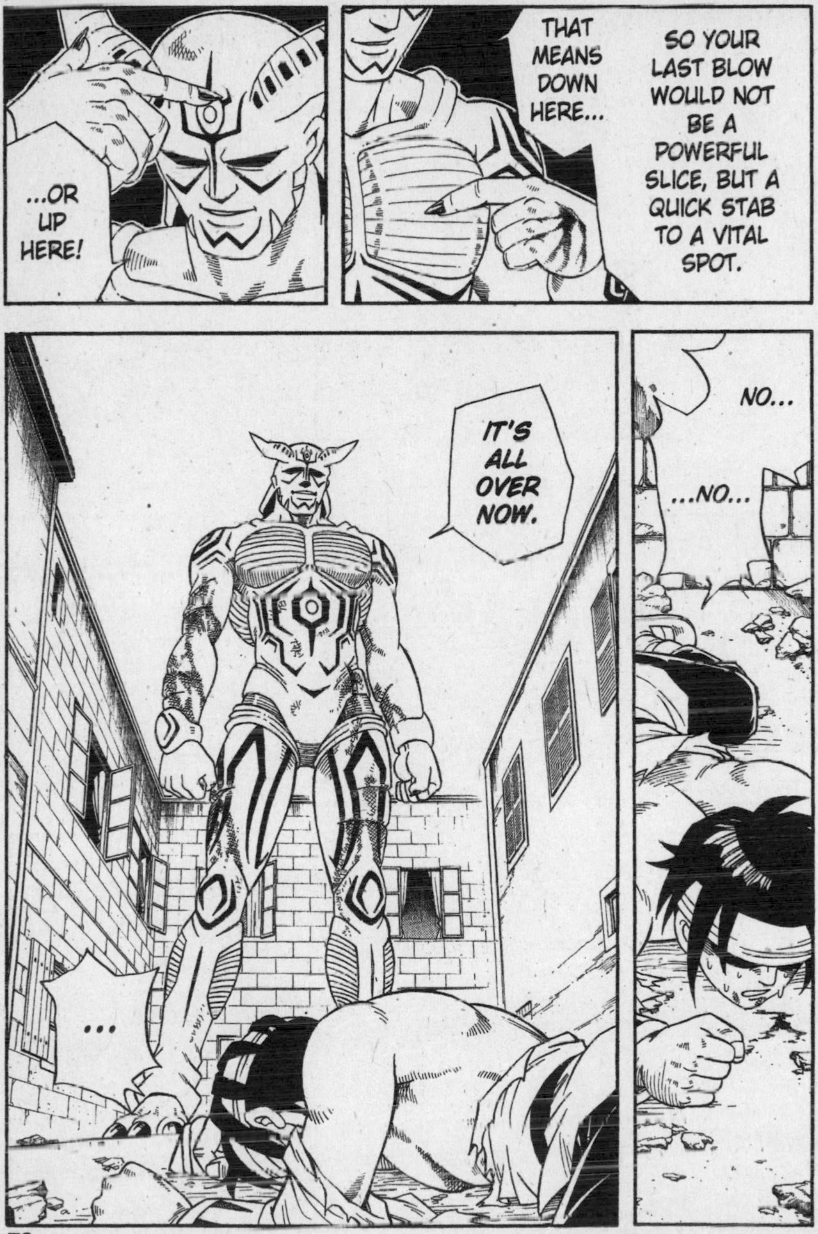
SO YOUR LAST BLOW WOULD NOT BE A POWERFUL SLICE, BUT A QUICK STAB TO A VITAL SPOT.
THAT MEANS DOWN HERE...
...OR UP HERE!
NO...
...NO...
IT'S ALL OVER NOW.
...

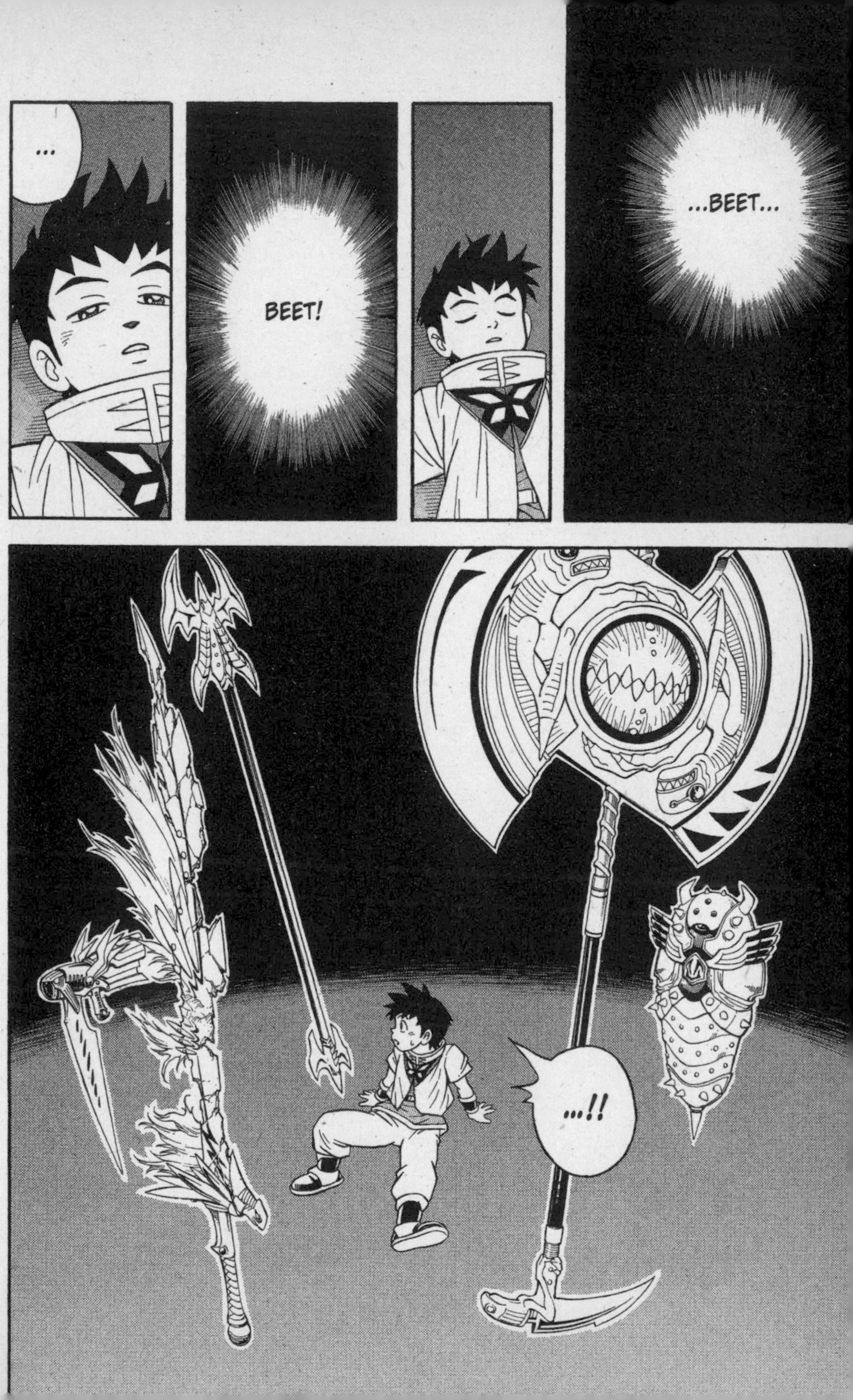
...BEET...
BEET!
...
...!!

READ THIS WAY

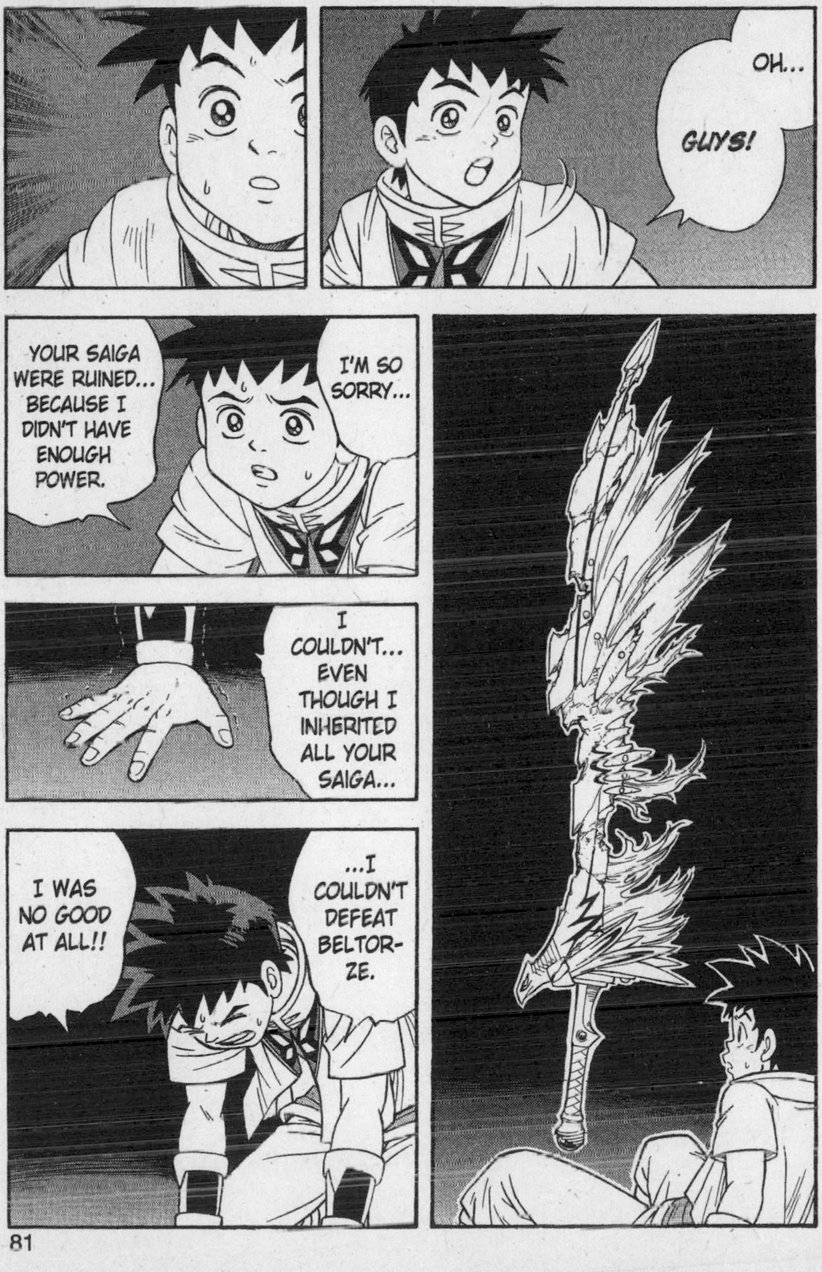
OH...
GUYS!
I'M SO SORRY...
YOUR SAIGA WERE RUINED... BECAUSE I DIDN'T HAVE ENOUGH POWER.
I COULDN'T... EVEN THOUGH I INHERITED ALL YOUR SAIGA...
...I COULDN'T DEFEAT BELTOR-ZE.
I WAS NO GOOD AT ALL!!

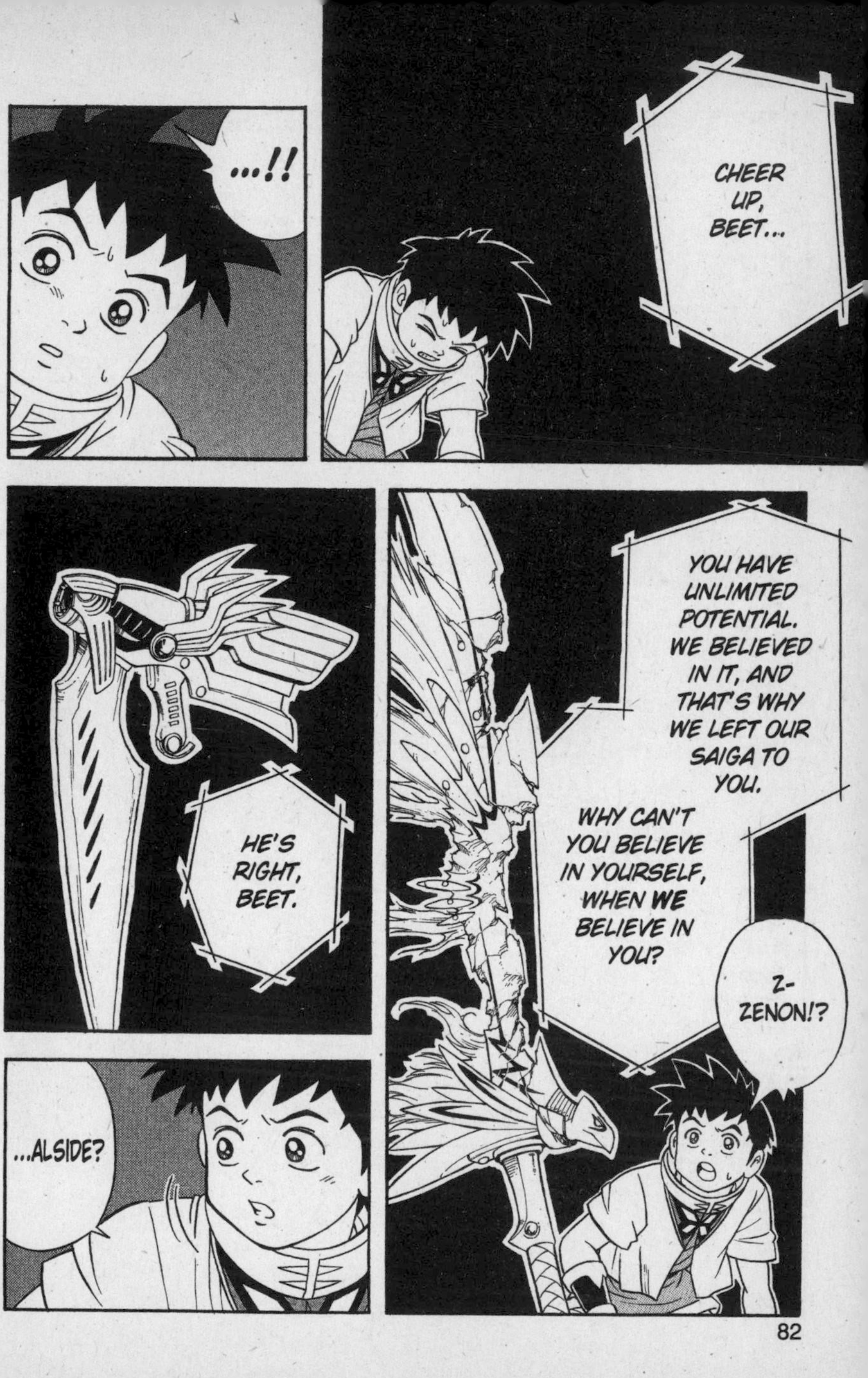
CHEER UP, BEET...
...!!
YOU HAVE UNLIMITED POTENTIAL. WE BELIEVED IN IT, AND THAT'S WHY WE LEFT OUR SAIGA TO YOU.
WHY CAN'T YOU BELIEVE IN YOURSELF, WHEN WE BELIEVE IN YOU?
Z-ZENON!?
HE'S RIGHT, BEET.
...ALSIDE?

READ THIS WAY

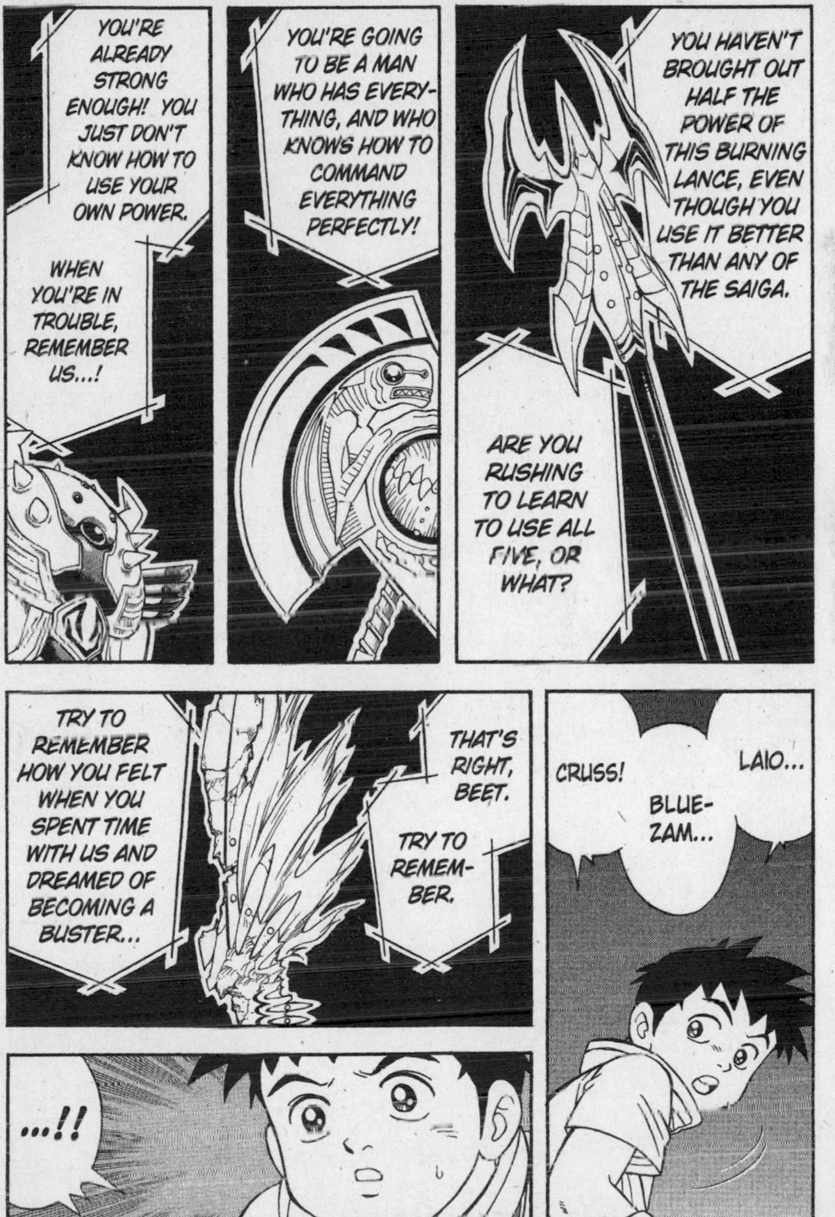
YOU HAVEN'T BROUGHT OUT HALF THE POWER OF THIS BURNING LANCE, EVEN THOUGH YOU USE IT BETTER THAN ANY OF THE SAIGA.
ARE YOU RUSHING TO LEARN TO USE ALL FIVE, OR WHAT?
YOU'RE GOING TO BE A MAN WHO HAS EVERY-THING, AND WHO KNOWS HOW TO COMMAND EVERYTHING PERFECTLY!
YOU'RE ALREADY STRONG ENOUGH! YOU JUST DON'T KNOW HOW TO USE YOUR OWN POWER.
WHEN YOU'RE IN TROUBLE, REMEMBER US...!
LAIO...
BLUE-ZAM...
CRUSS!
THAT'S RIGHT, BEET.
TRY TO REMEM-BER.
TRY TO REMEMBER HOW YOU FELT WHEN YOU SPENT TIME WITH US AND DREAMED OF BECOMING A BUSTER...
...!!

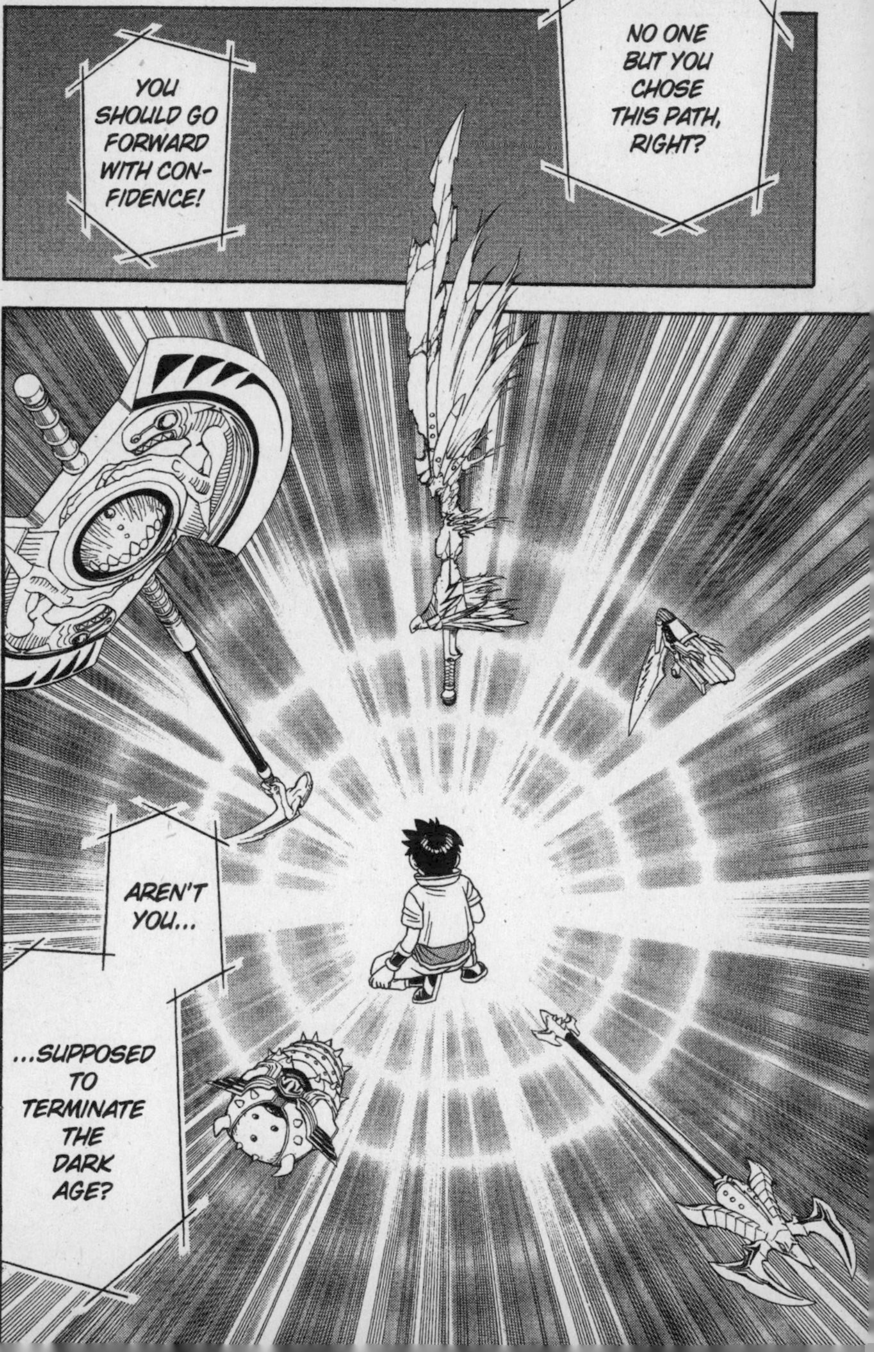
NO ONE BUT YOU CHOSE THIS PATH, RIGHT?
YOU SHOULD GO FORWARD WITH CON-FIDENCE!
AREN'T YOU...
...SUPPOSED TO TERMINATE THE DARK AGE?

READ THIS WAY

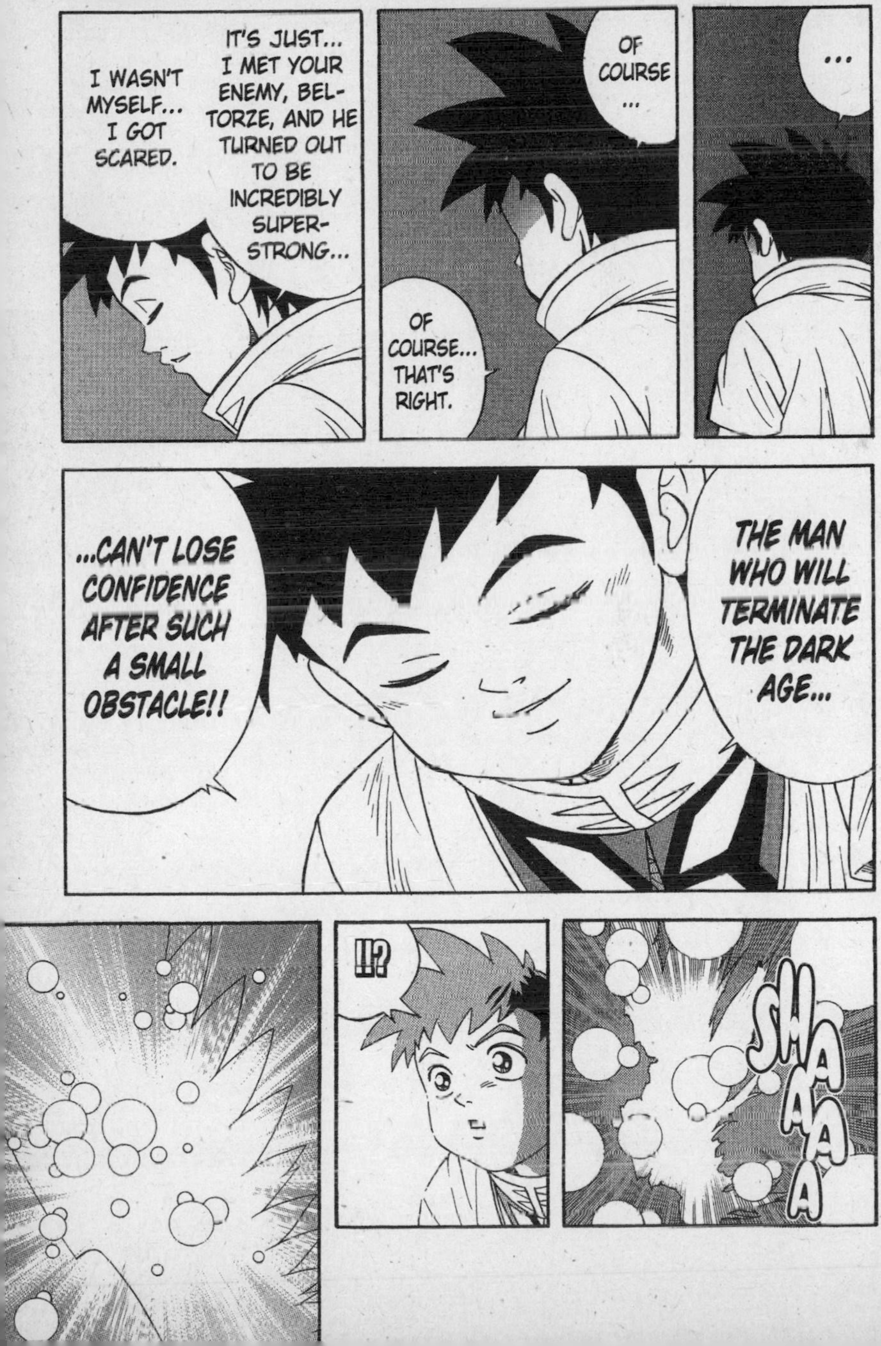

...
OF COURSE...
OF COURSE... THAT'S RIGHT.
IT'S JUST... I MET YOUR ENEMY, BEL-TORZE, AND HE TURNED OUT TO BE INCREDIBLY SUPER-STRONG...
I WASN'T MYSELF... I GOT SCARED.
THE MAN WHO WILL TERMINATE THE DARK AGE...
...CAN'T LOSE CONFIDENCE AFTER SUCH A SMALL OBSTACLE!!
SHAAAAA
!!?

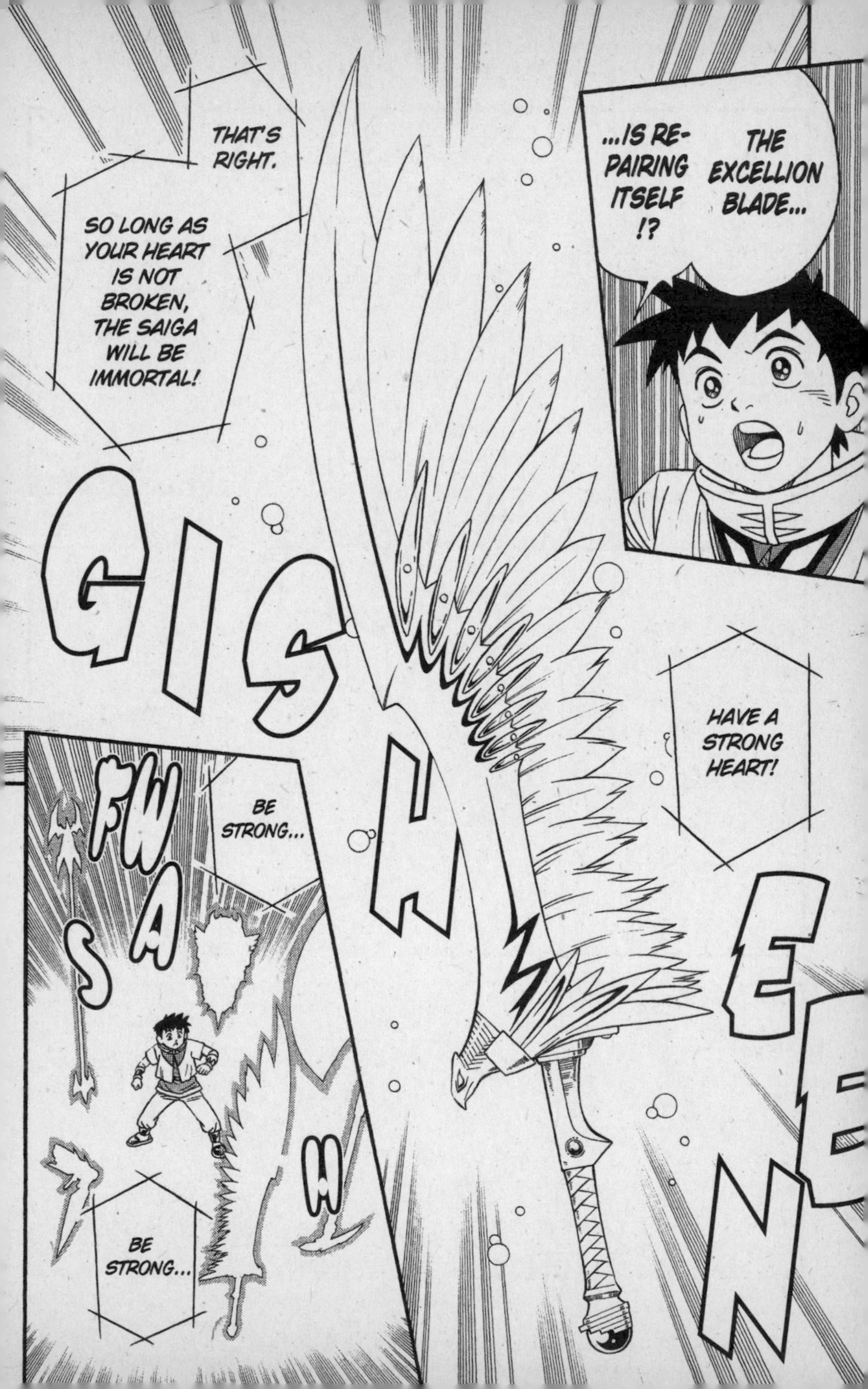
THE EXCELLION BLADE...
...IS RE-PAIRING ITSELF!?
THAT'S RIGHT.
SO LONG AS YOUR HEART IS NOT BROKEN, THE SAIGA WILL BE IMMORTAL!
HAVE A STRONG HEART!
GISHEEN
FWASH
BE STRONG...
BE STRONG...

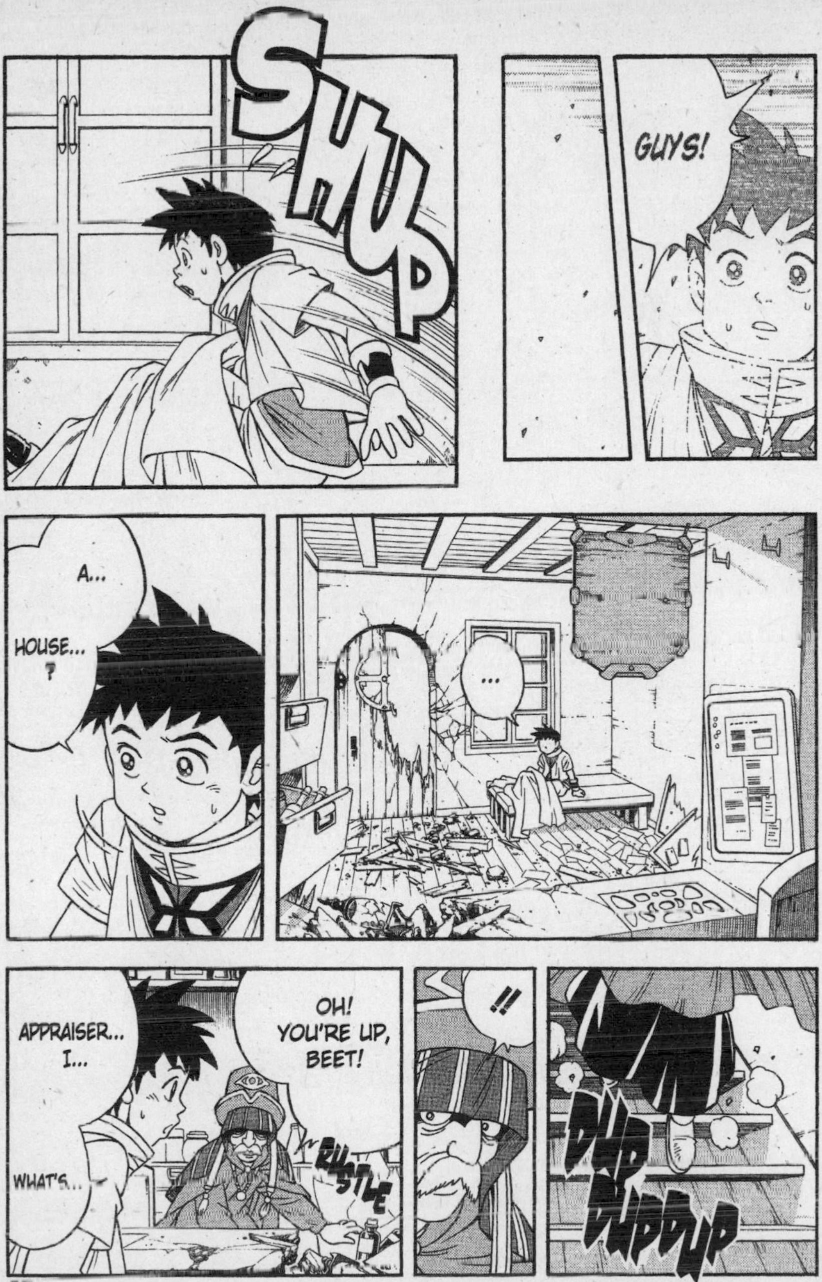
GUYS!
SHUP
...
A...
HOUSE... ?
DUP DUDDUP
!!
OH! YOU'RE UP, BEET!
APPRAISER... I...
RUSTLE
WHAT'S...

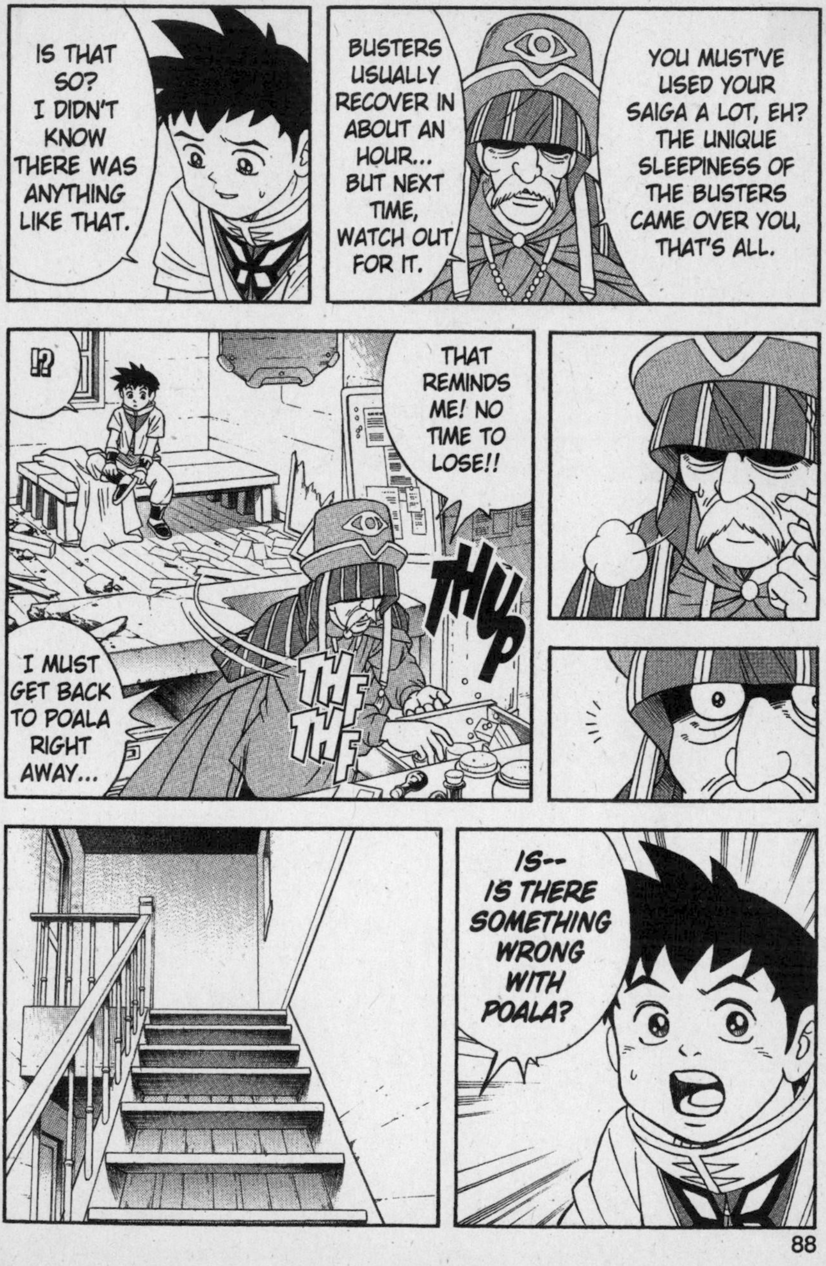
YOU MUST'VE USED YOUR SAIGA A LOT, EH? THE UNIQUE SLEEPINESS OF THE BUSTERS CAME OVER YOU, THAT'S ALL.
BUSTERS USUALLY RECOVER IN ABOUT AN HOUR... BUT NEXT TIME, WATCH OUT FOR IT.
IS THAT SO? I DIDN'T KNOW THERE WAS ANYTHING LIKE THAT.
THAT REMINDS ME! NO TIME TO LOSE!!
!?
THUP
THF THF
I MUST GET BACK TO POALA RIGHT AWAY...
IS-- IS THERE SOMETHING WRONG WITH POALA?

READ THIS WAY

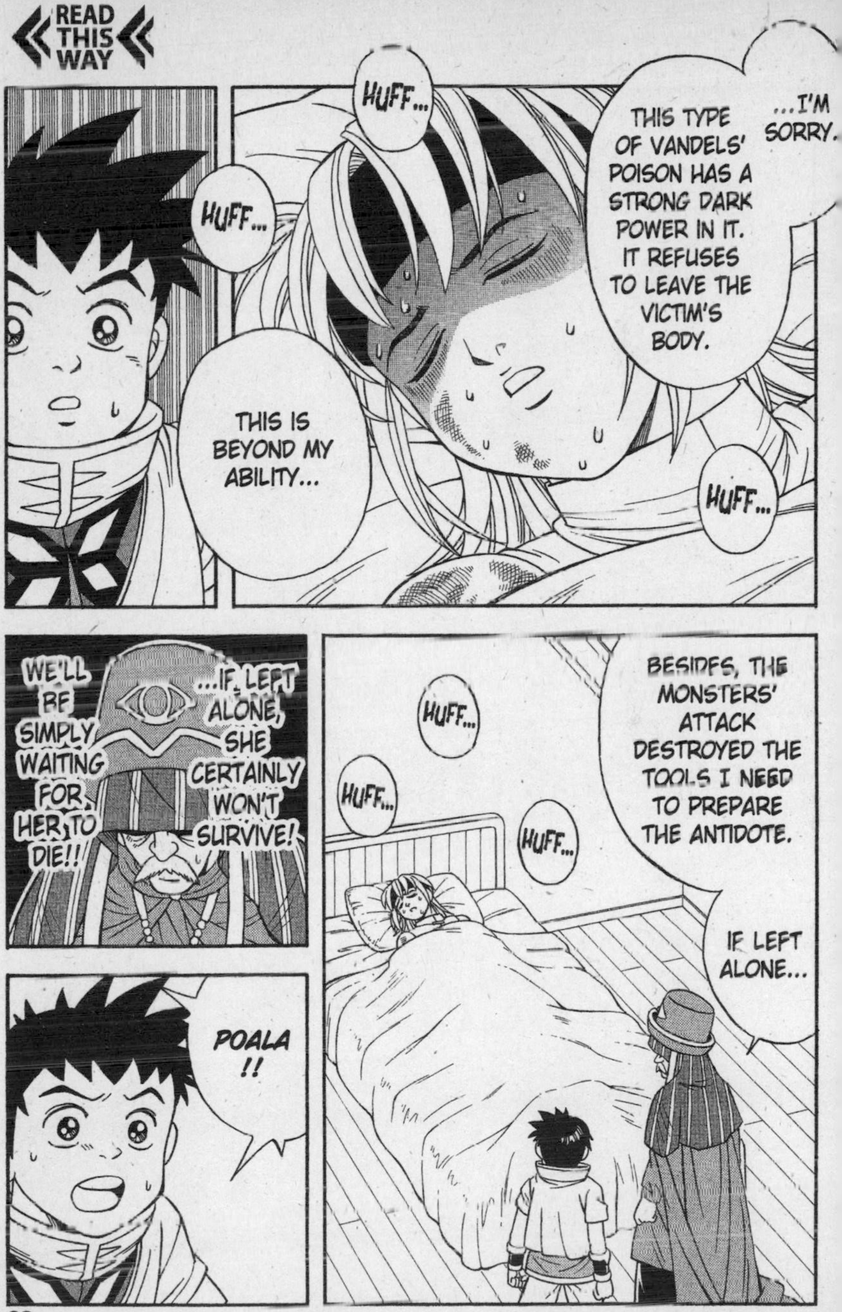
...I'M SORRY.
THIS TYPE OF VANDELS' POISON HAS A STRONG DARK POWER IN IT. IT REFUSES TO LEAVE THE VICTIM'S BODY.
HUFF...
HUFF...
THIS IS BEYOND MY ABILITY...
HUFF...
BESIDES, THE MONSTERS' ATTACK DESTROYED THE TOOLS I NEED TO PREPARE THE ANTIDOTE.
HUFF...
HUFF...
HUFF...
IF LEFT ALONE...
...IF, LEFT ALONE, SHE CERTAINLY WON'T SURVIVE!
WE'LL BE SIMPLY WAITING FOR HER TO DIE!!
POALA !!

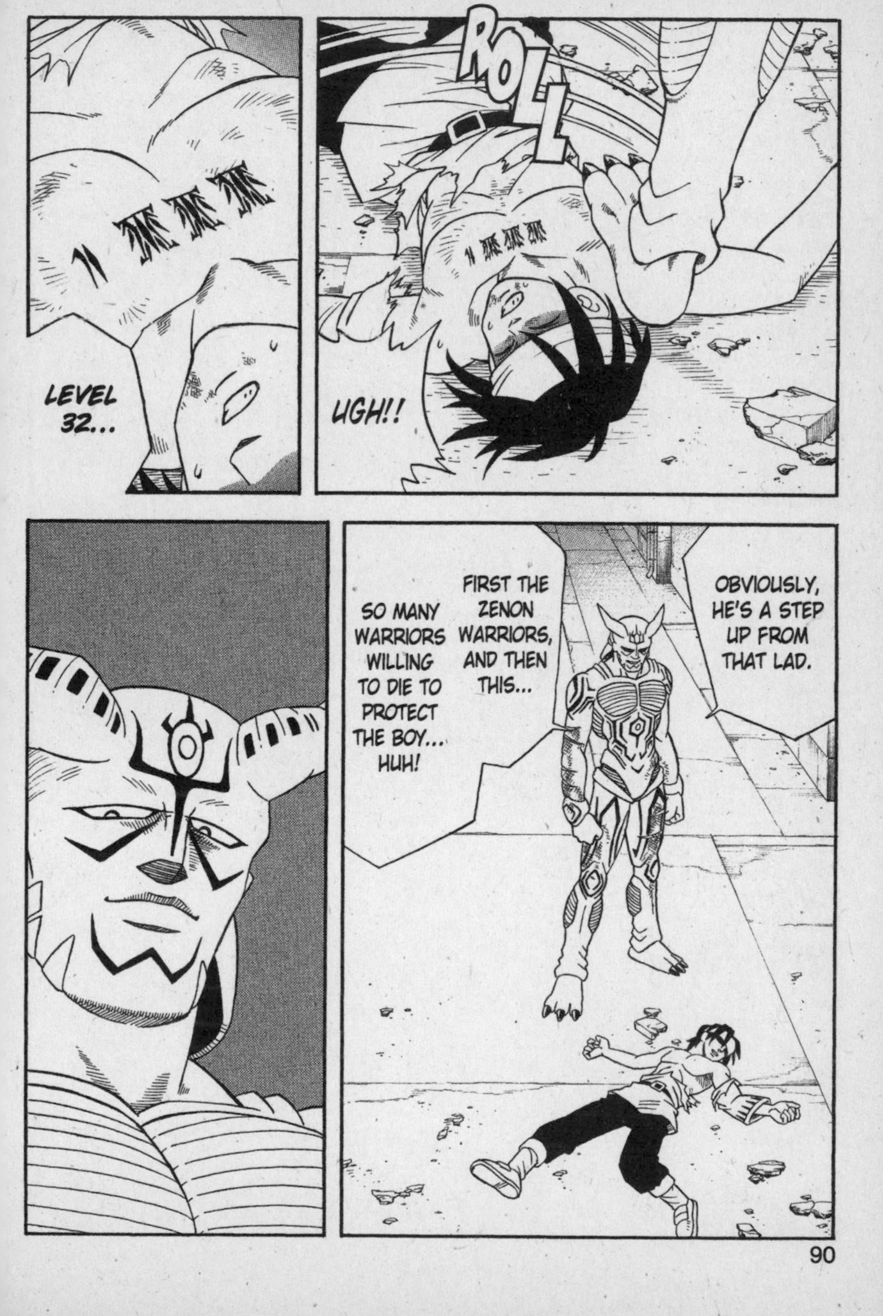
ROLL
UGH!!
LEVEL 32...
OBVIOUSLY, HE'S A STEP UP FROM THAT LAD.
FIRST THE ZENON WARRIORS, AND THEN THIS...
SO MANY WARRIORS WILLING TO DIE TO PROTECT THE BOY... HUH!

READ THIS WAY

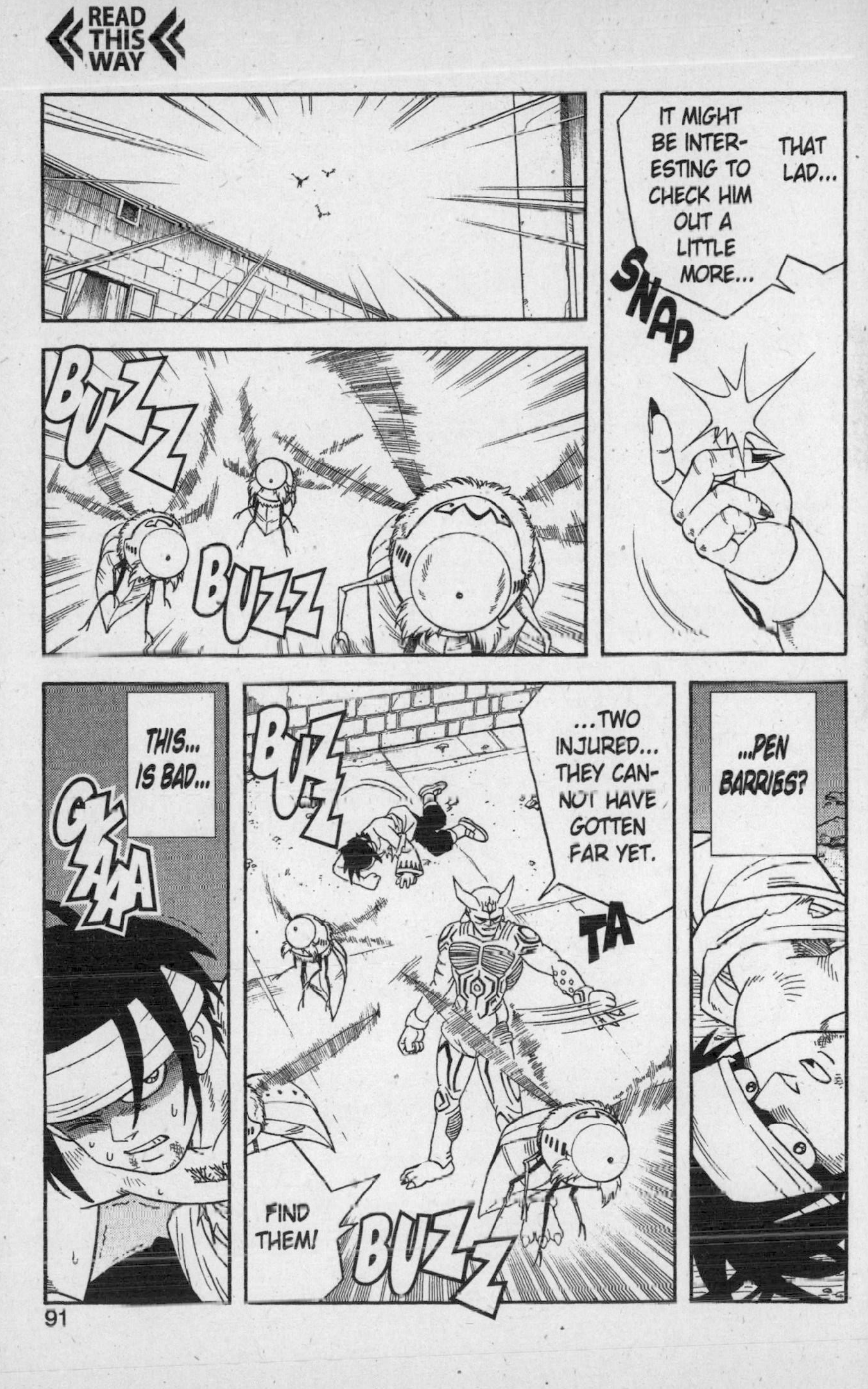

THAT LAD...
IT MIGHT BE INTER-ESTING TO CHECK HIM OUT A LITTLE MORE...
SNAP
BUZZ
BUZZ
...PEN BARRIES?
BUZZ
...TWO INJURED... THEY CAN-NOT HAVE GOTTEN FAR YET.
TA
FIND THEM!
BUZZ
THIS... IS BAD...
GYAAA

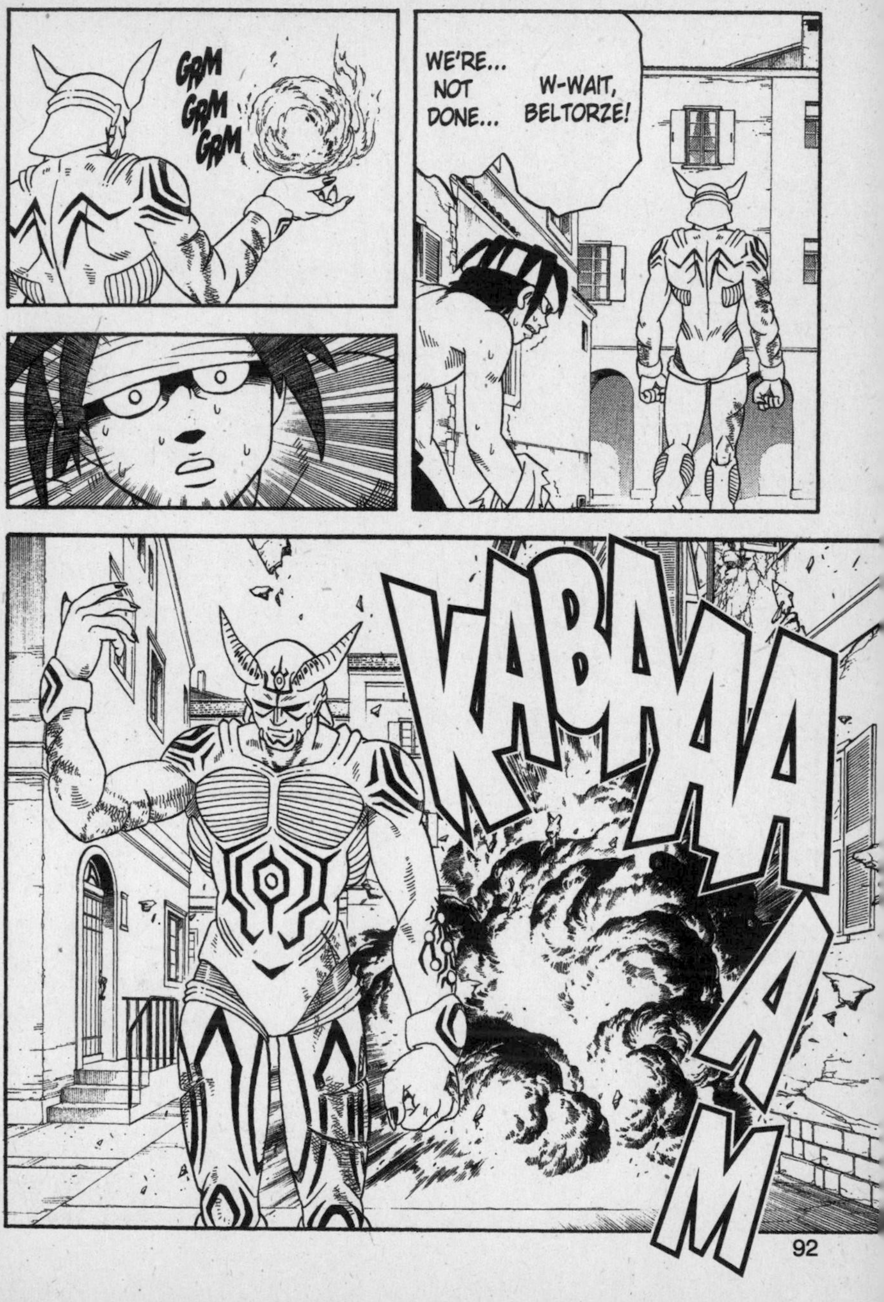
W-WAIT, BELTORZE!
WE'RE... NOT DONE...
GRM GRM GRM
KABAAAAAM

READ THIS WAY

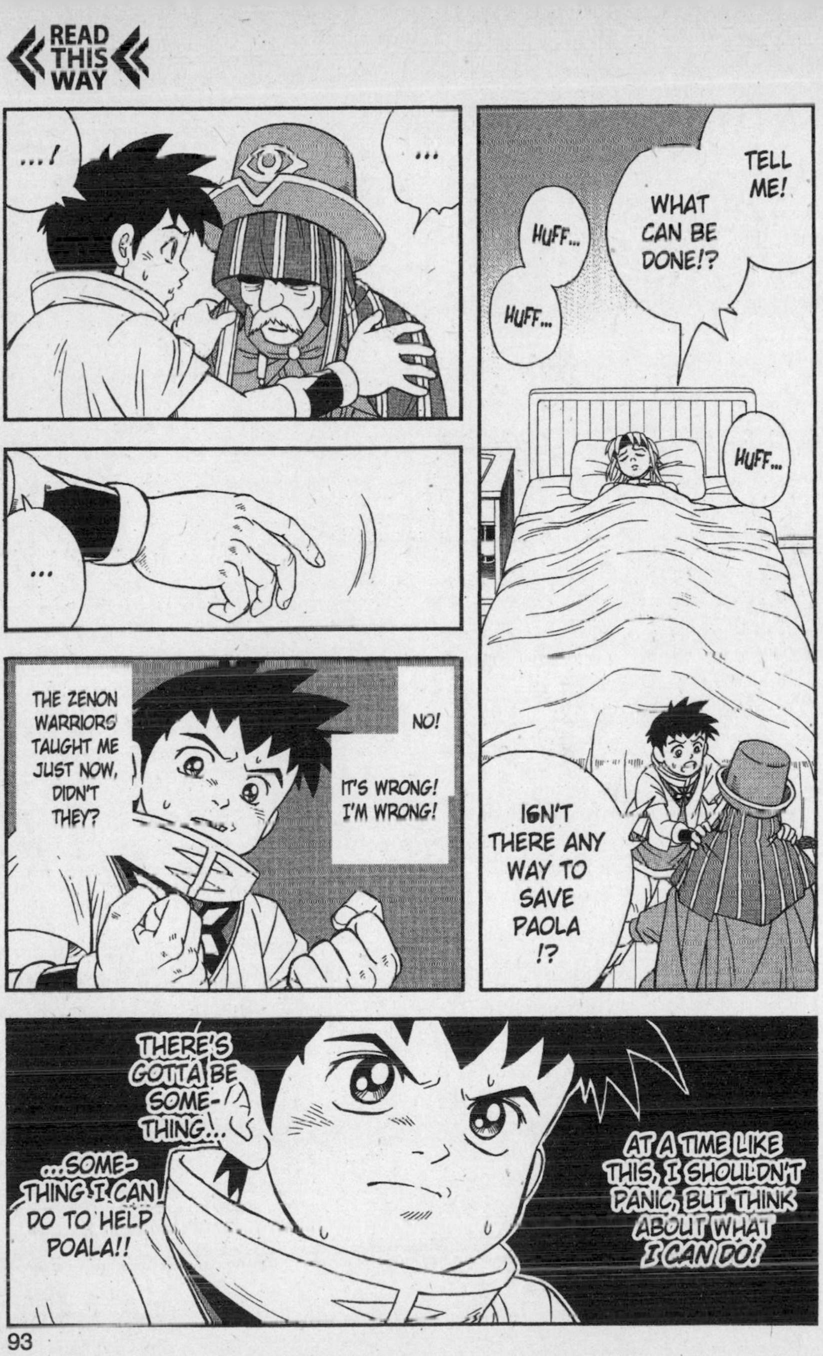
TELL ME!
WHAT CAN BE DONE!?
HUFF...
HUFF...
HUFF...
ISN'T THERE ANY WAY TO SAVE PAOLA !?
...
...!
...
NO!
IT'S WRONG! I'M WRONG!
THE ZENON WARRIORS TAUGHT ME JUST NOW, DIDN'T THEY?
AT A TIME LIKE THIS, I SHOULDN'T PANIC, BUT THINK ABOUT WHAT I CAN DO!
THERE'S GOTTA BE SOME-THING...
...SOME-THING I CAN DO TO HELP POALA!!

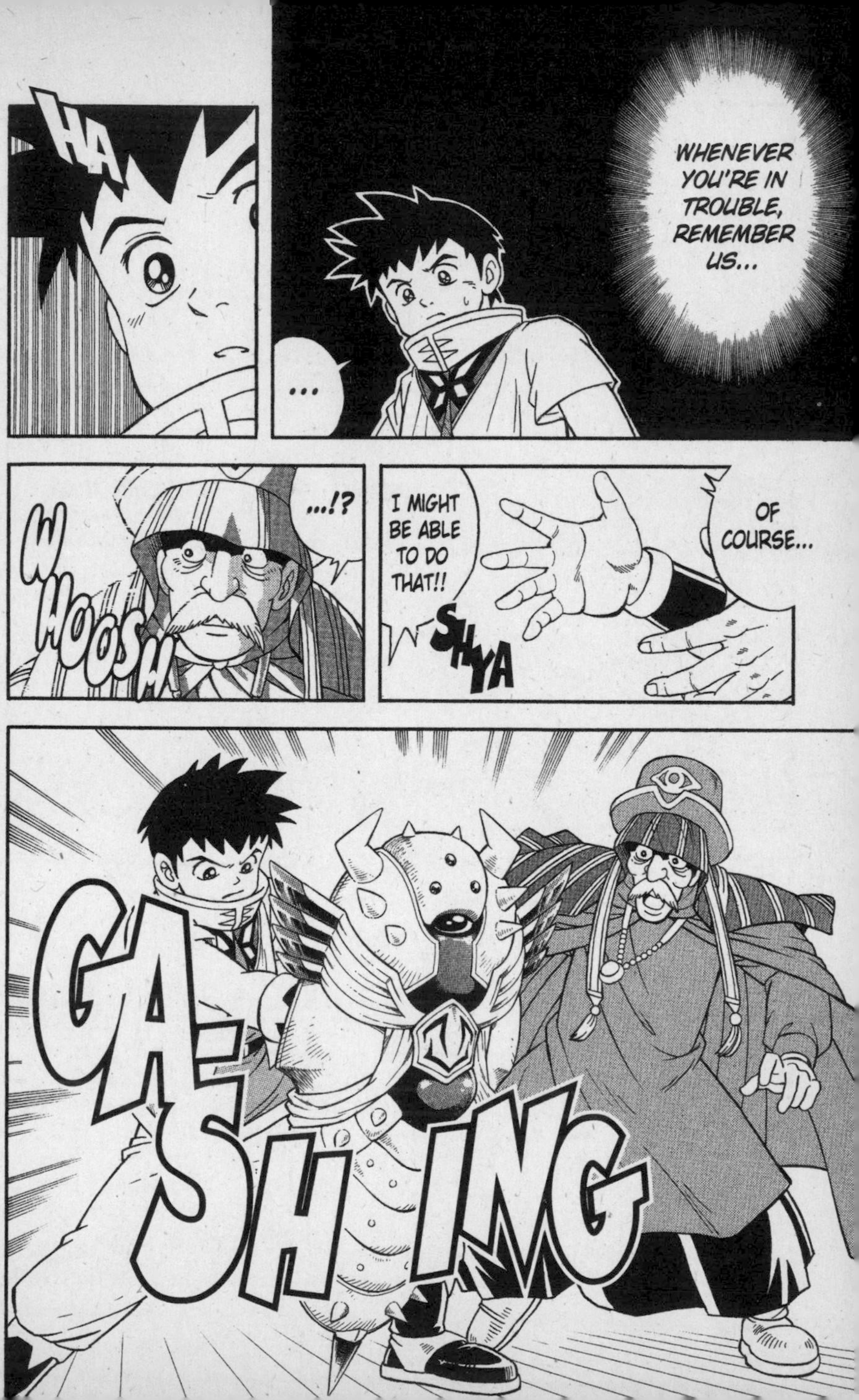
WHENEVER YOU'RE IN TROUBLE, REMEMBER US...
...
HA
OF COURSE...
I MIGHT BE ABLE TO DO THAT!!
SHYA
...!?
WHOOSH
GA-SHING

READ THIS WAY

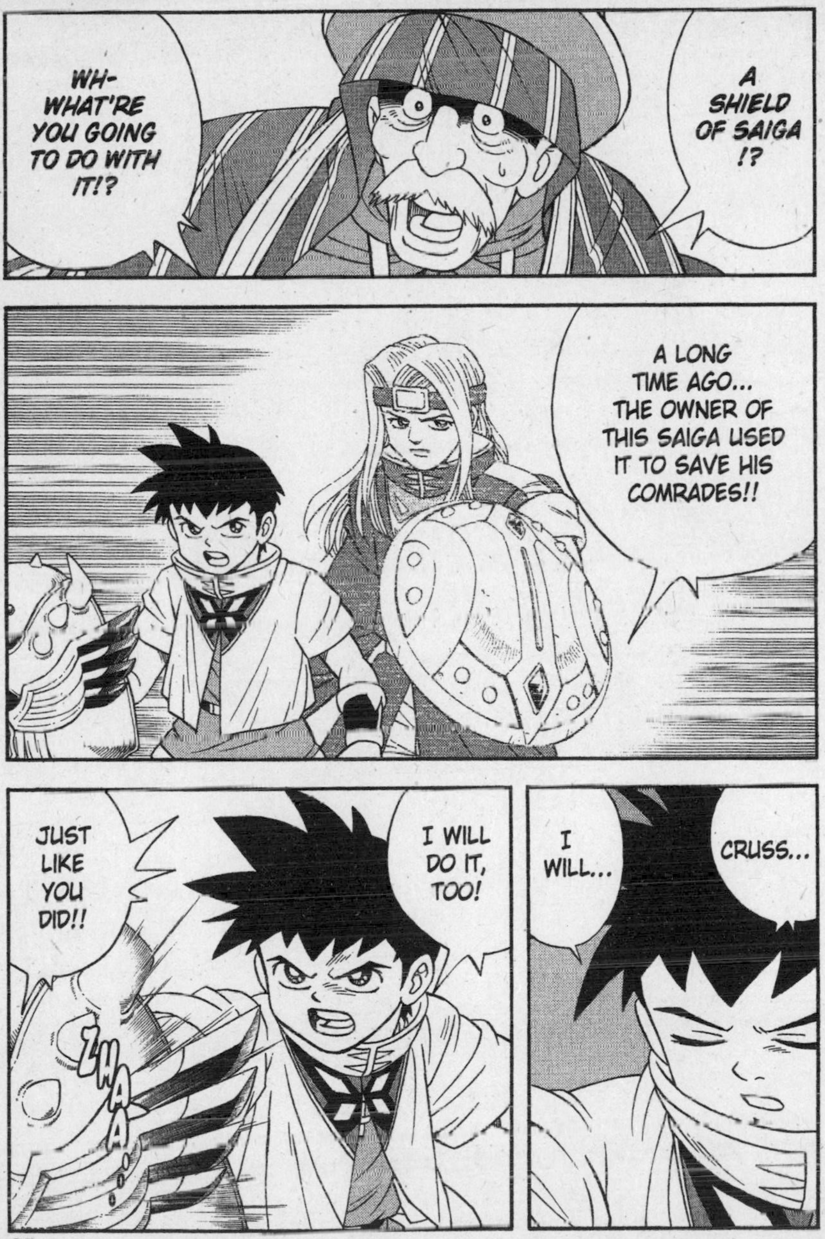
A SHIELD OF SAIGA !?
WH- WHAT'RE YOU GOING TO DO WITH IT!?
A LONG TIME AGO... THE OWNER OF THIS SAIGA USED IT TO SAVE HIS COMRADES!!
CRUSS...
I WILL...
I WILL DO IT, TOO!
JUST LIKE YOU DID!!
ZHAA

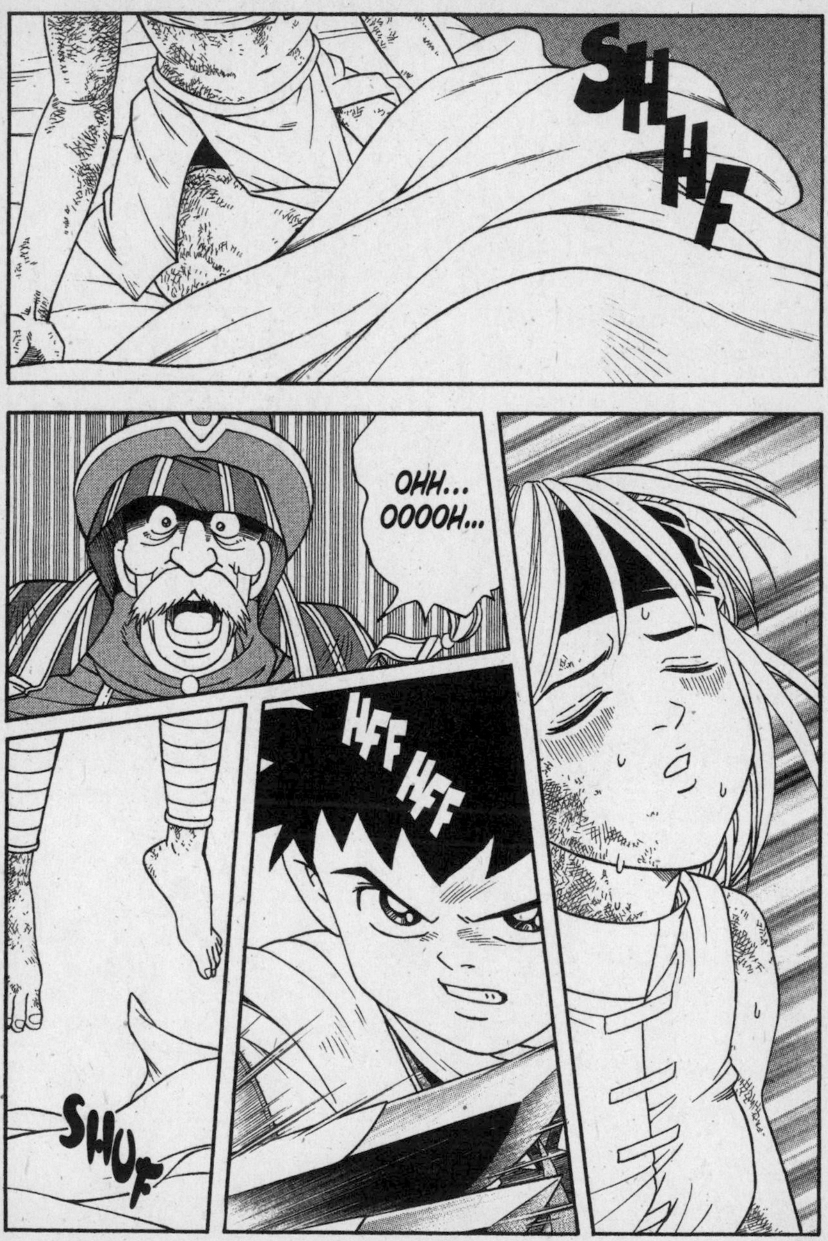
SHHF
OHH... OOOOH...
HFF HFF
SHUF

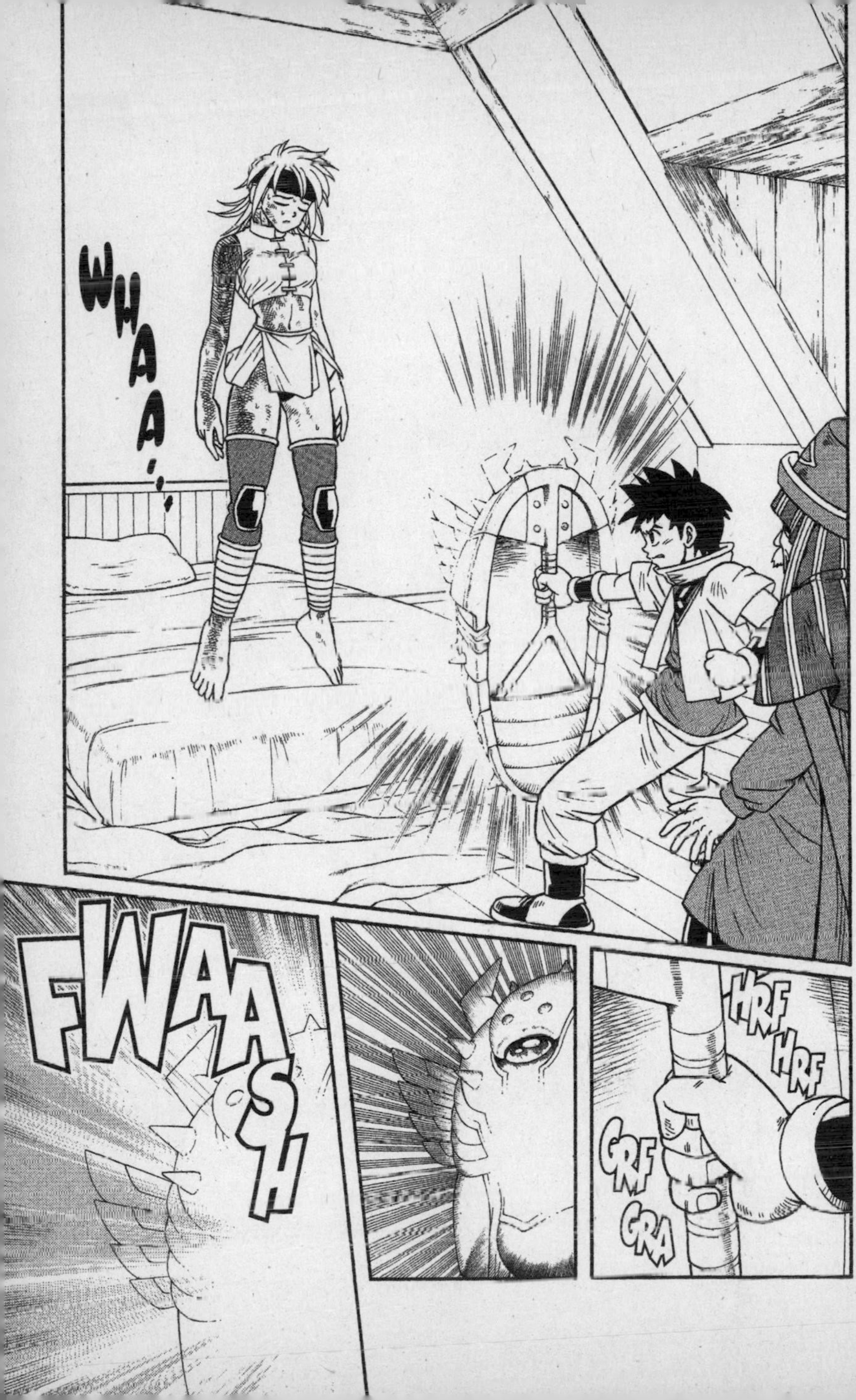
WHAA...
HRF HRF
GRF GRA
FWAASH

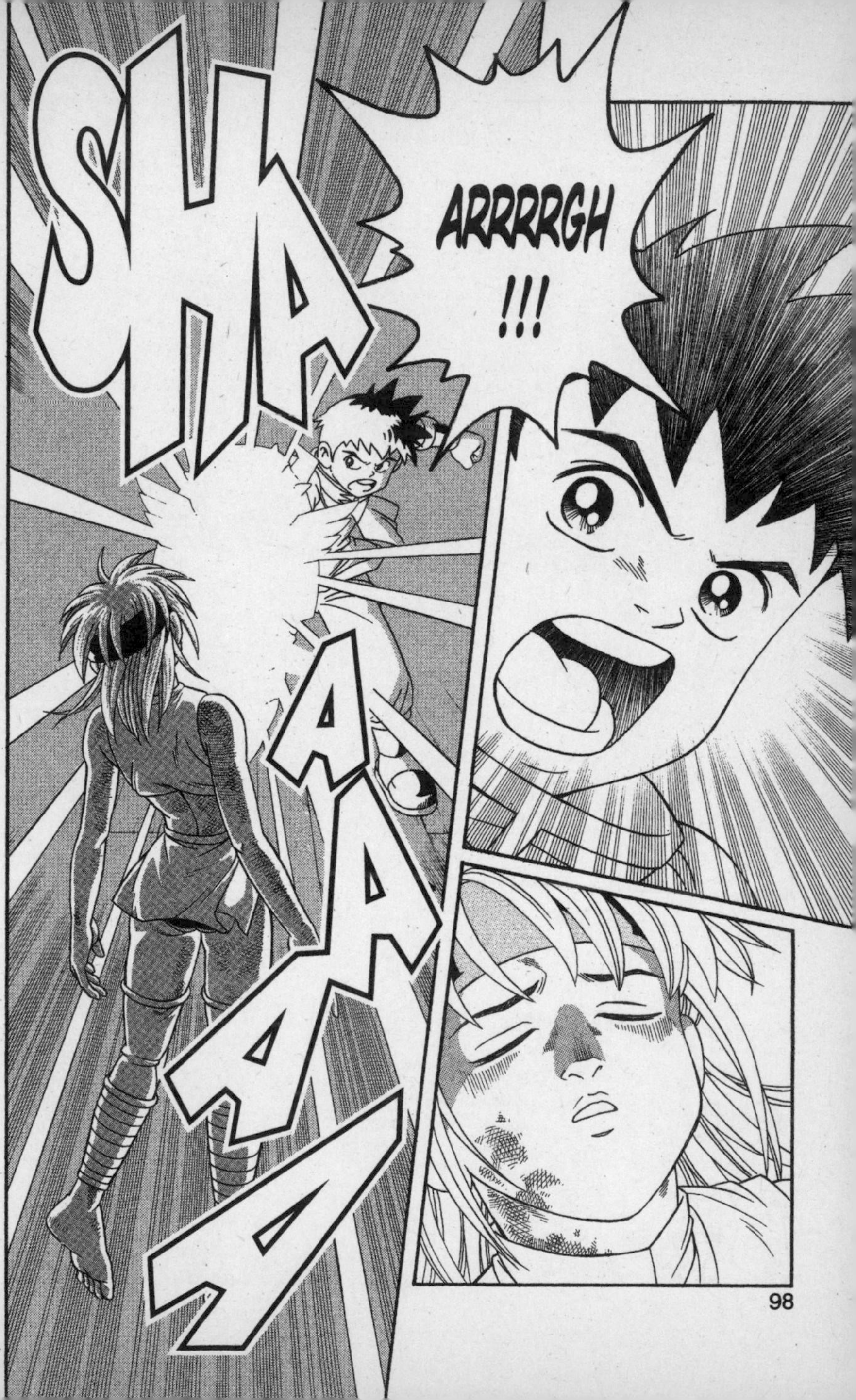
ARRRRGH !!!
SHAAAAA

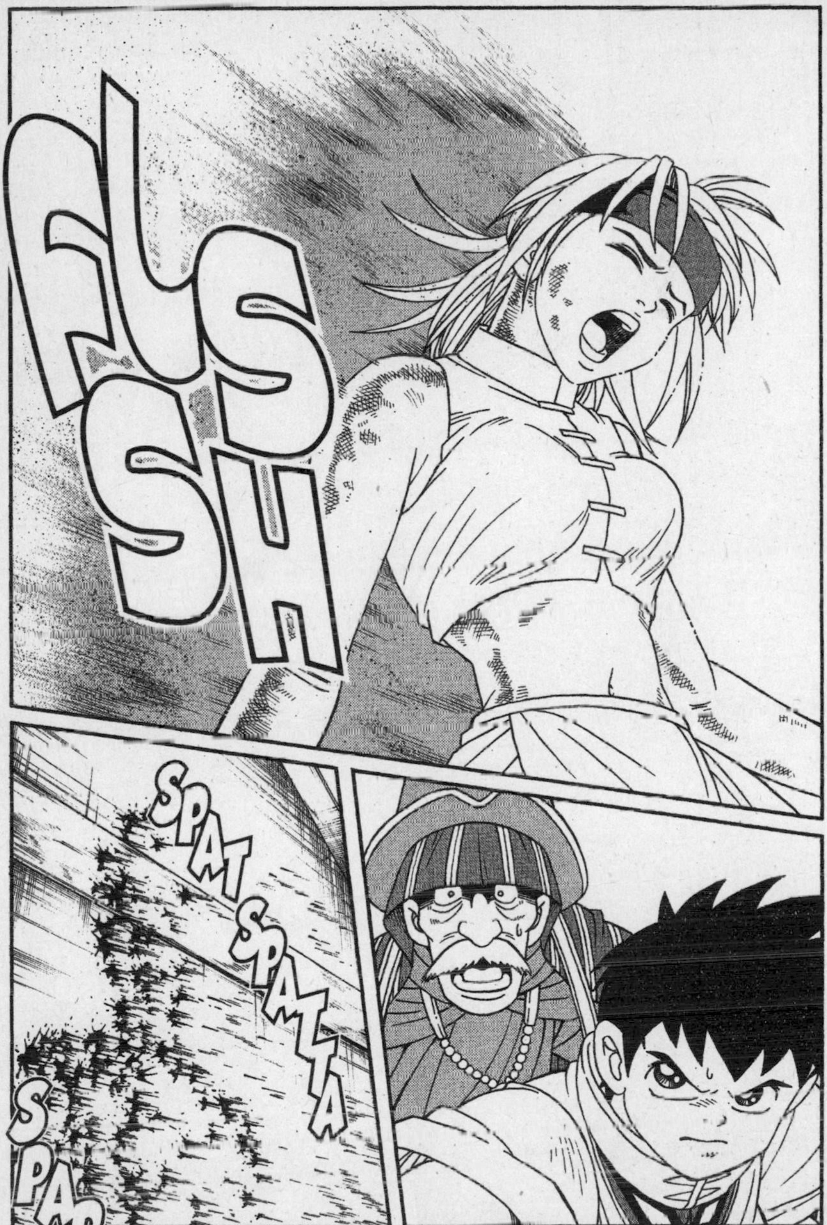
FUSSH
SPAT
SPATTA
SPAP

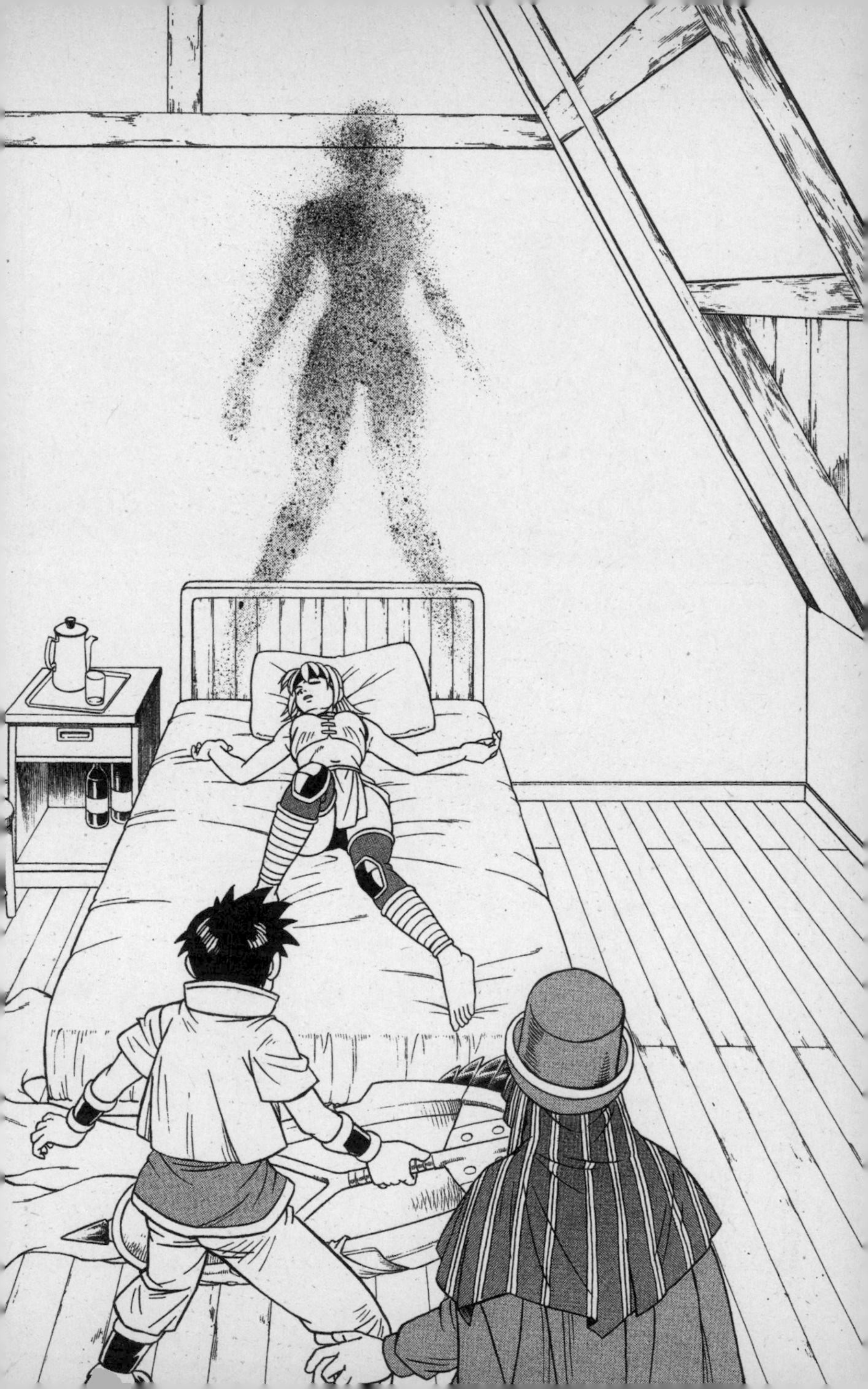

READ THIS WAY

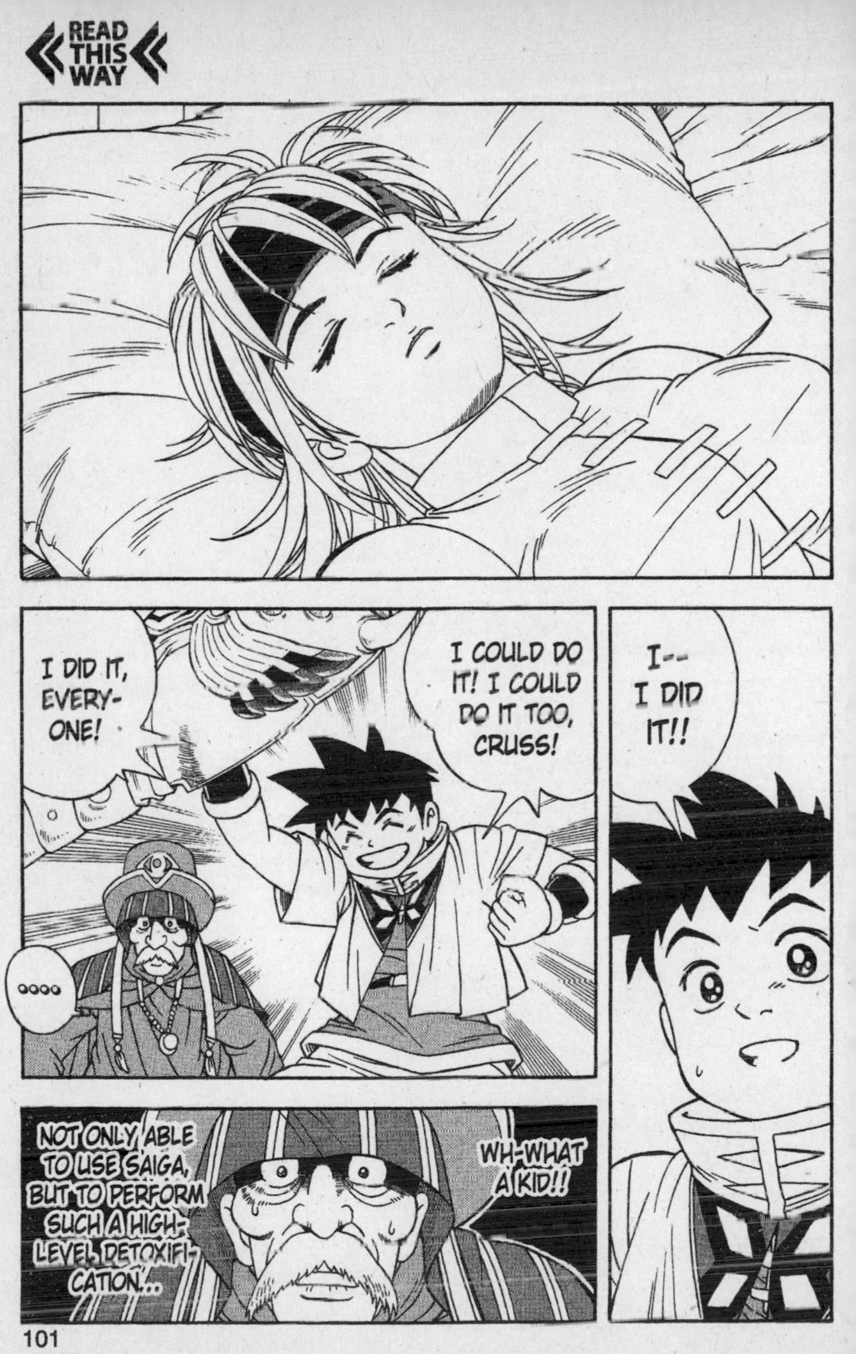
I-- I DID IT!!
I COULD DO IT! I COULD DO IT TOO, CRUSS!
I DID IT, EVERY-ONE!
....
WH-WHAT A KID!!
NOT ONLY ABLE TO USE SAIGA, BUT TO PERFORM SUCH A HIGH-LEVEL DETOXIFI-CATION...

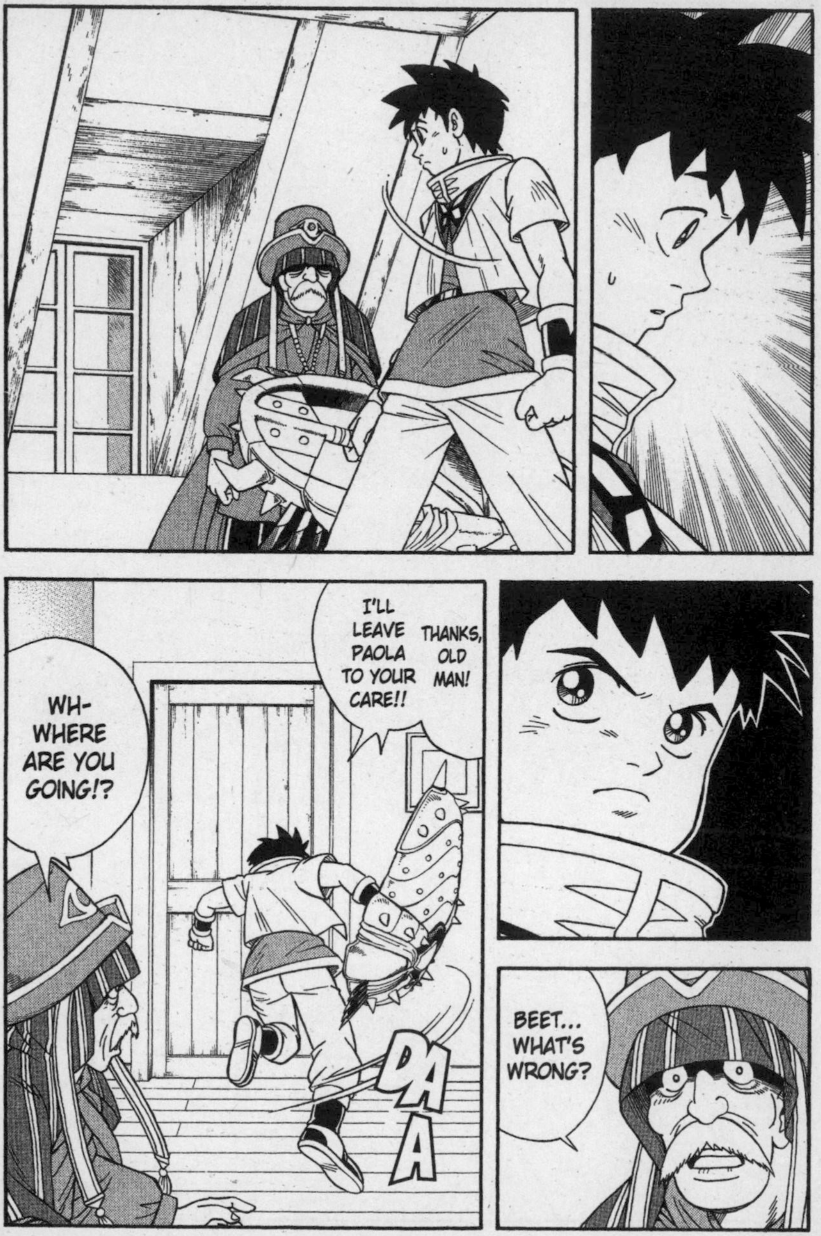
BEET... WHAT'S WRONG?
I'LL LEAVE PAOLA TO YOUR CARE!!
THANKS, OLD MAN!
WH- WHERE ARE YOU GOING!?
DA A

READ THIS WAY

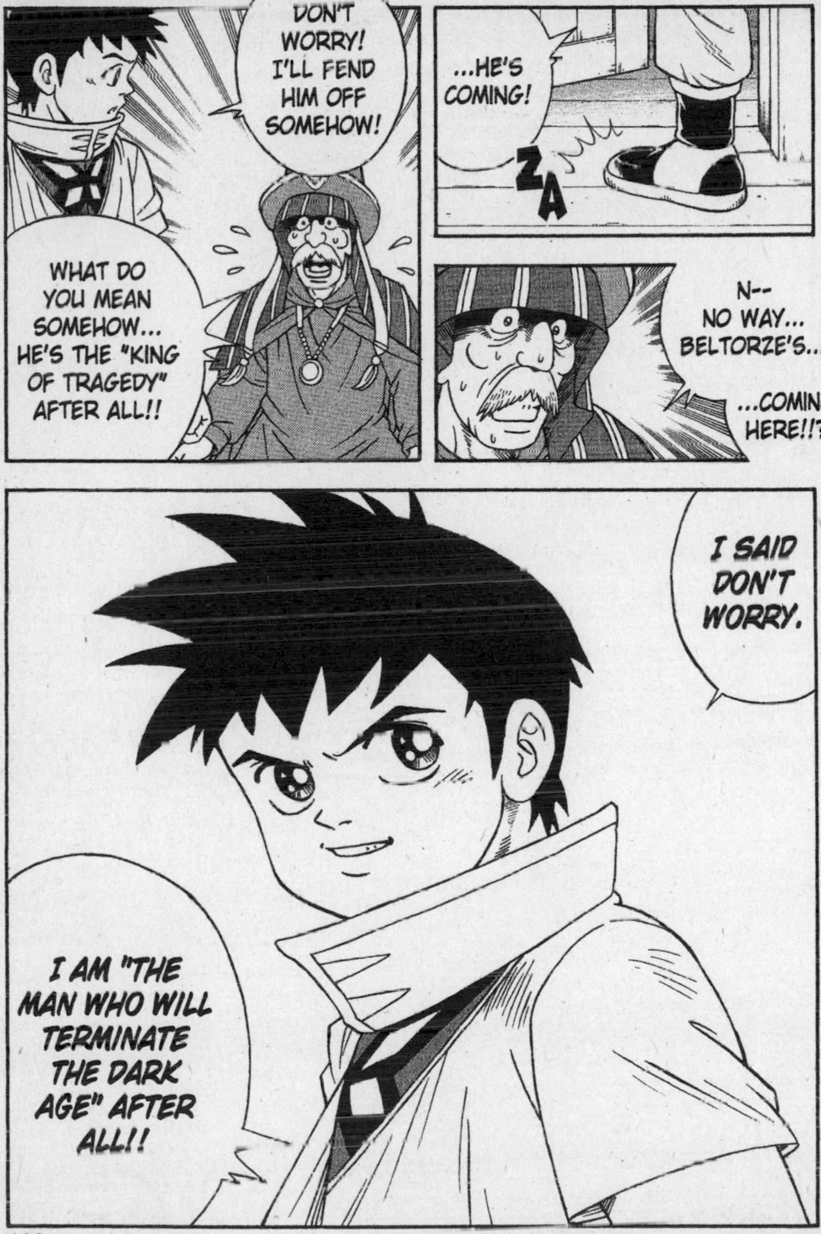
...HE'S COMING!
ZA
N-- NO WAY... BELTORZE'S...
...COMING HERE!!?
DON'T WORRY! I'LL FEND HIM OFF SOMEHOW!
WHAT DO YOU MEAN SOMEHOW... HE'S THE "KING OF TRAGEDY" AFTER ALL!!
I SAID DON'T WORRY.
I AM "THE MAN WHO WILL TERMINATE THE DARK AGE" AFTER ALL!!

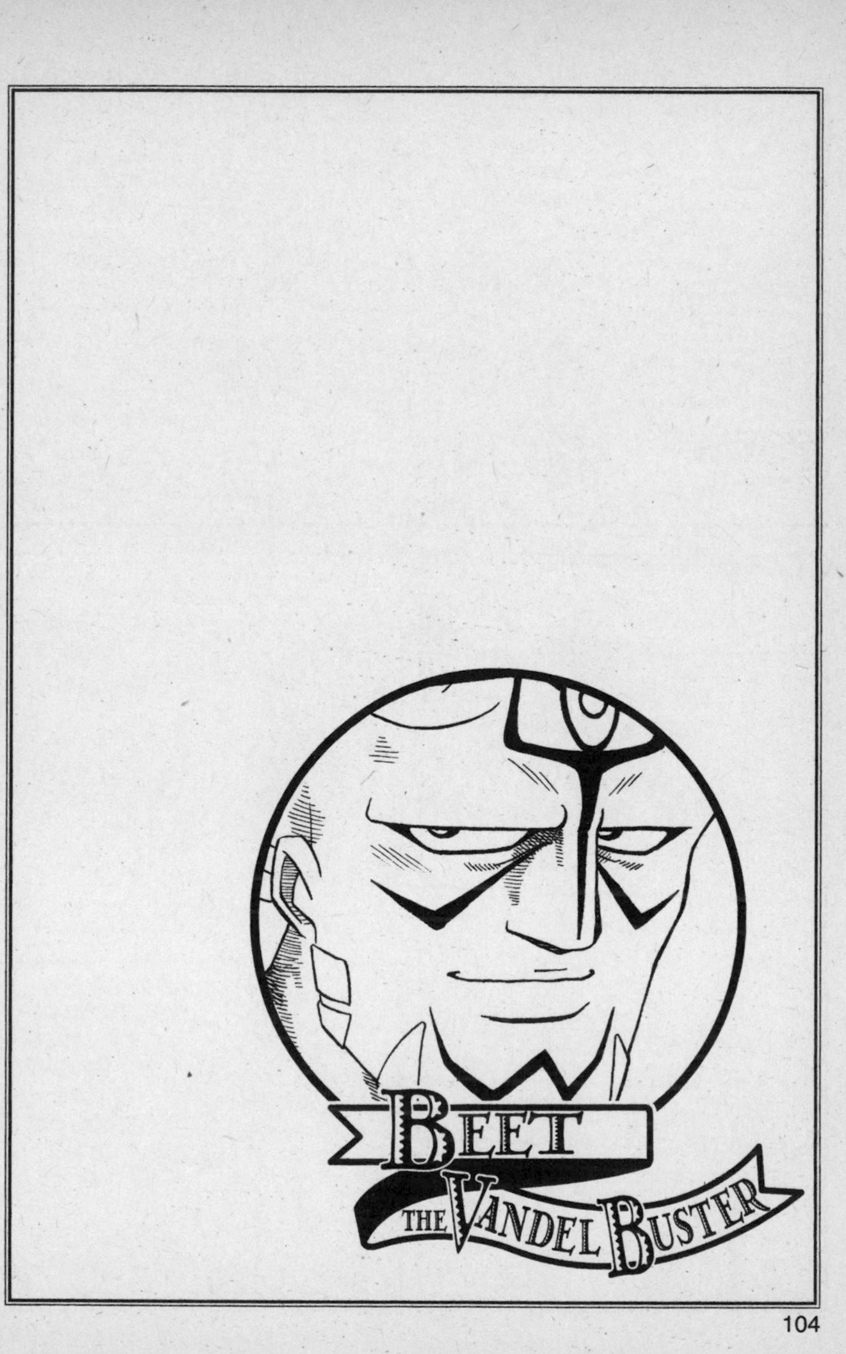
BEET
THE VANDEL BUSTER

Chapter 9: The Death Match!!

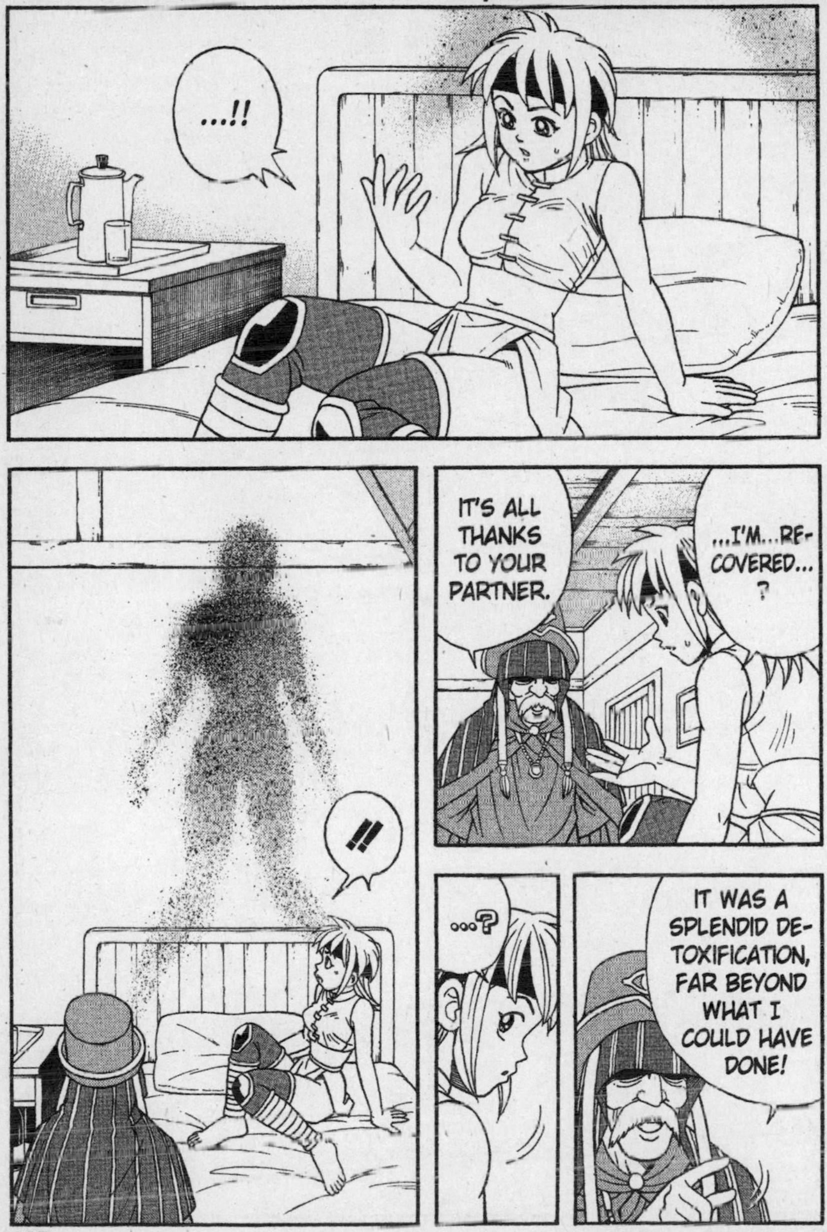
...!!
...I'M...RE-COVERED...?
IT'S ALL THANKS TO YOUR PARTNER.
IT WAS A SPLENDID DE-TOXIFICATION, FAR BEYOND WHAT I COULD HAVE DONE!
...?
!!

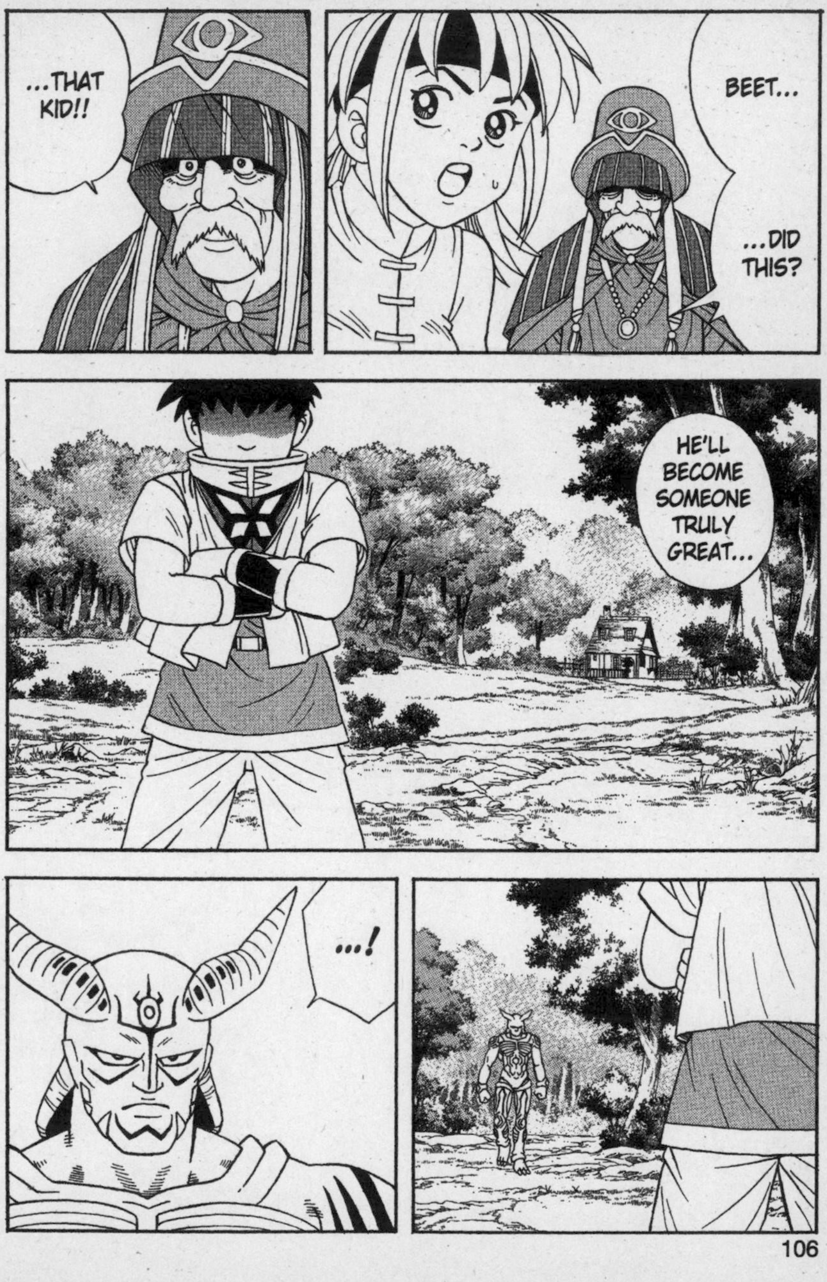
BEET...
...DID THIS?
...THAT KID!!
HE'LL BECOME SOMEONE TRULY GREAT...
...!

Chapter 9: The Death Match!!

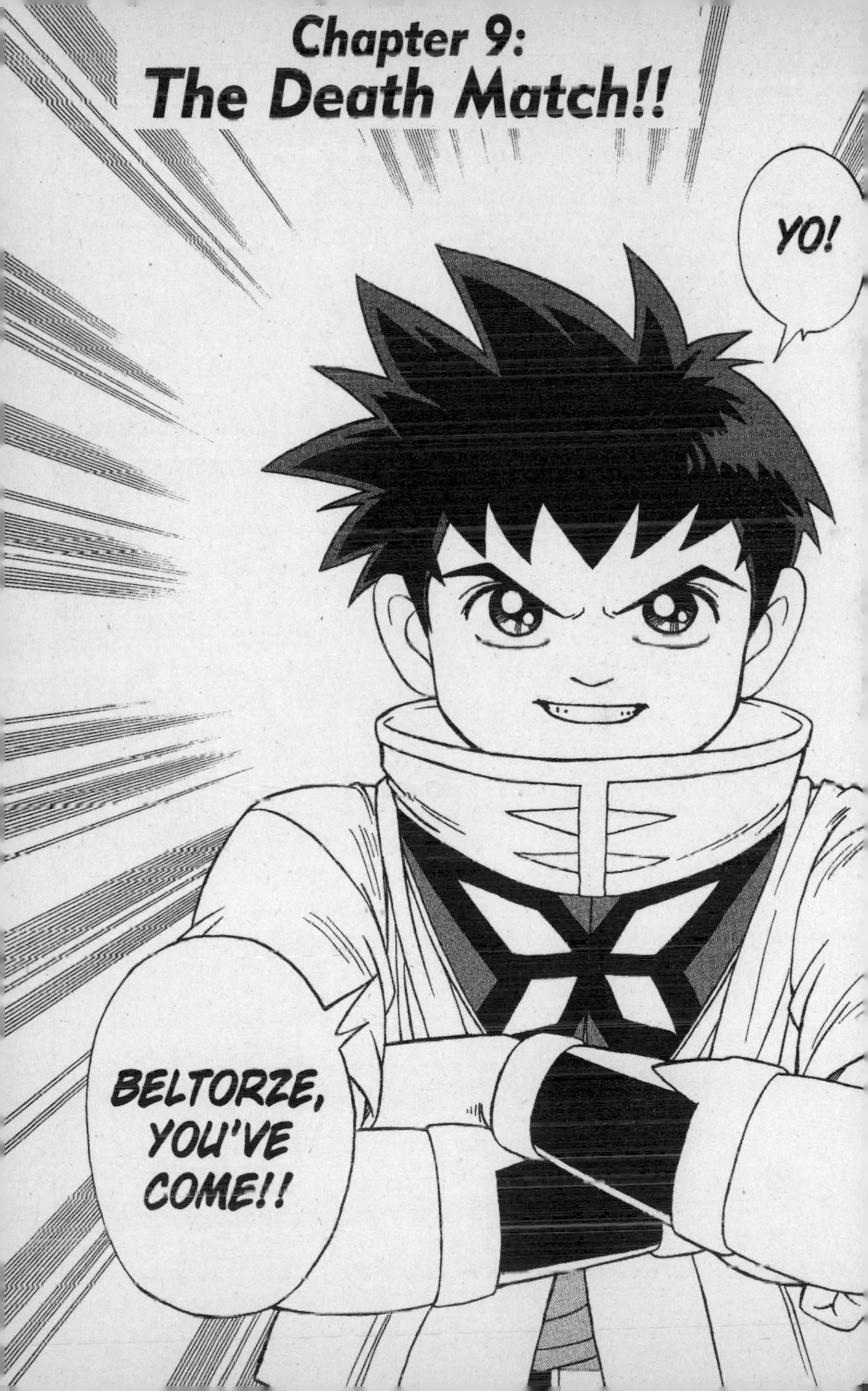
YO!
BELTORZE, YOU'VE COME!!

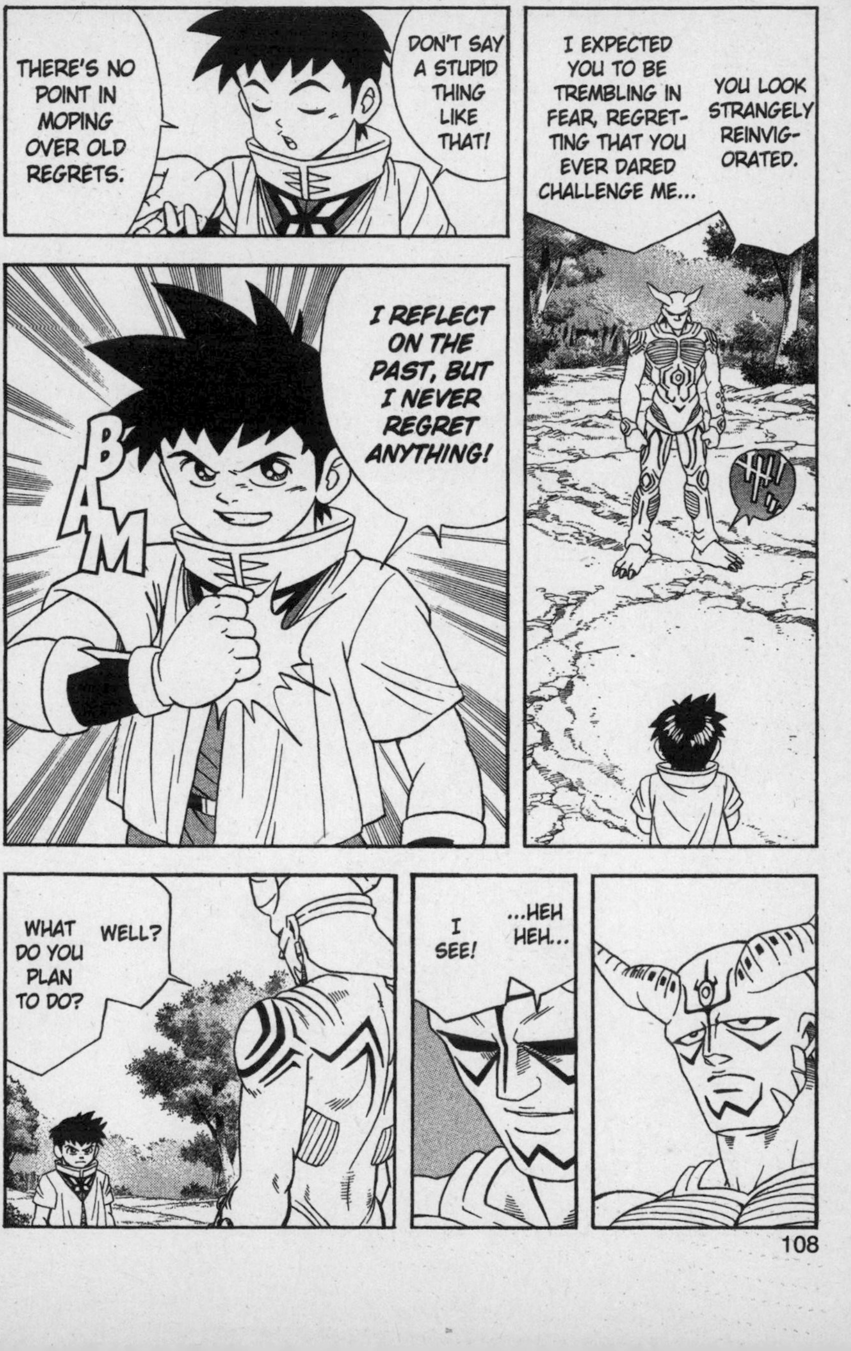
YOU LOOK STRANGELY REINVIG-ORATED.
I EXPECTED YOU TO BE TREMBLING IN FEAR, REGRET-TING THAT YOU EVER DARED CHALLENGE ME...
DON'T SAY A STUPID THING LIKE THAT!
THERE'S NO POINT IN MOPING OVER OLD REGRETS.
I REFLECT ON THE PAST, BUT I NEVER REGRET ANYTHING!
BAM
...HEH HEH...
I SEE!
WELL?
WHAT DO YOU PLAN TO DO?

READ THIS WAY

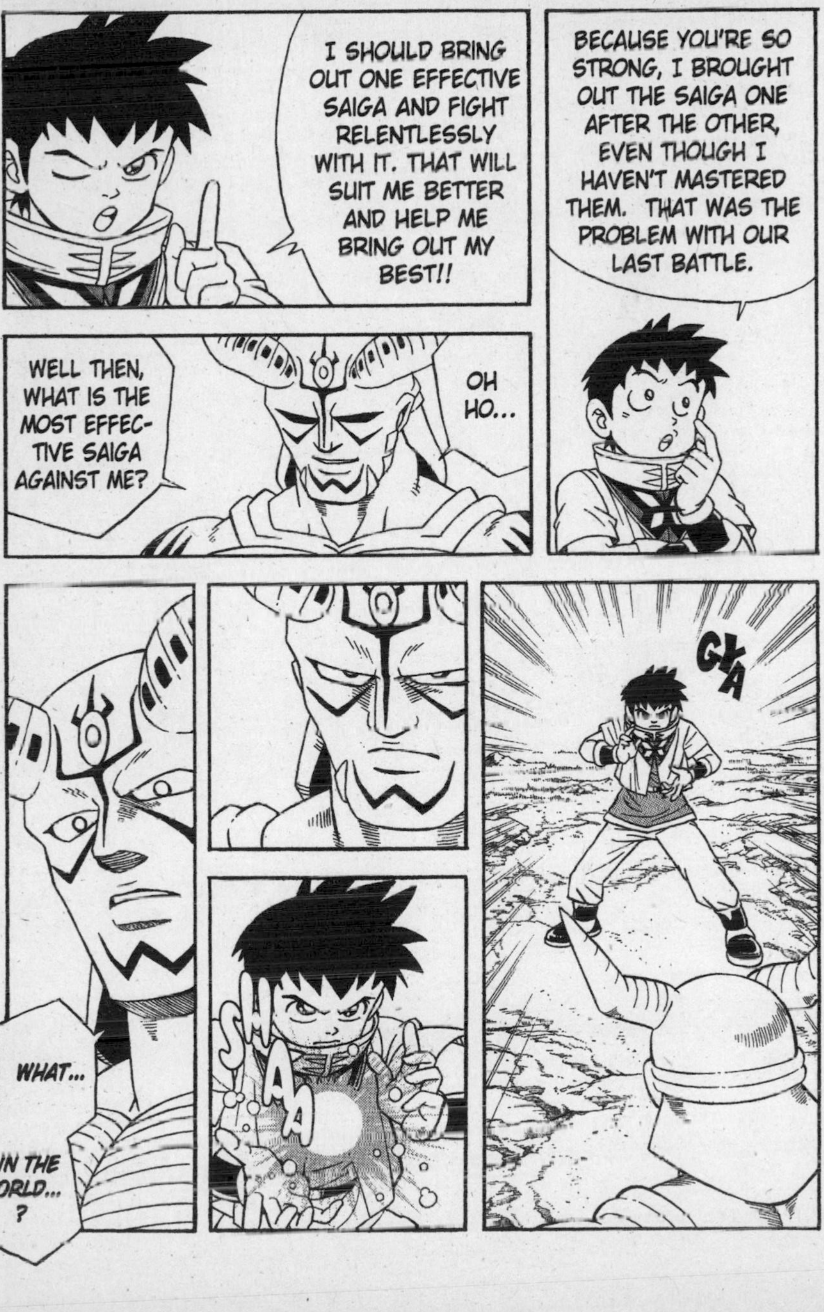
BECAUSE YOU'RE SO STRONG, I BROUGHT OUT THE SAIGA ONE AFTER THE OTHER, EVEN THOUGH I HAVEN'T MASTERED THEM. THAT WAS THE PROBLEM WITH OUR LAST BATTLE.
I SHOULD BRING OUT ONE EFFECTIVE SAIGA AND FIGHT RELENTLESSLY WITH IT. THAT WILL SUIT ME BETTER AND HELP ME BRING OUT MY BEST!!
OH HO...
WELL THEN, WHAT IS THE MOST EFFEC-TIVE SAIGA AGAINST ME?
GYA
SHAAA
WHAT...
...IN THE WORLD...?

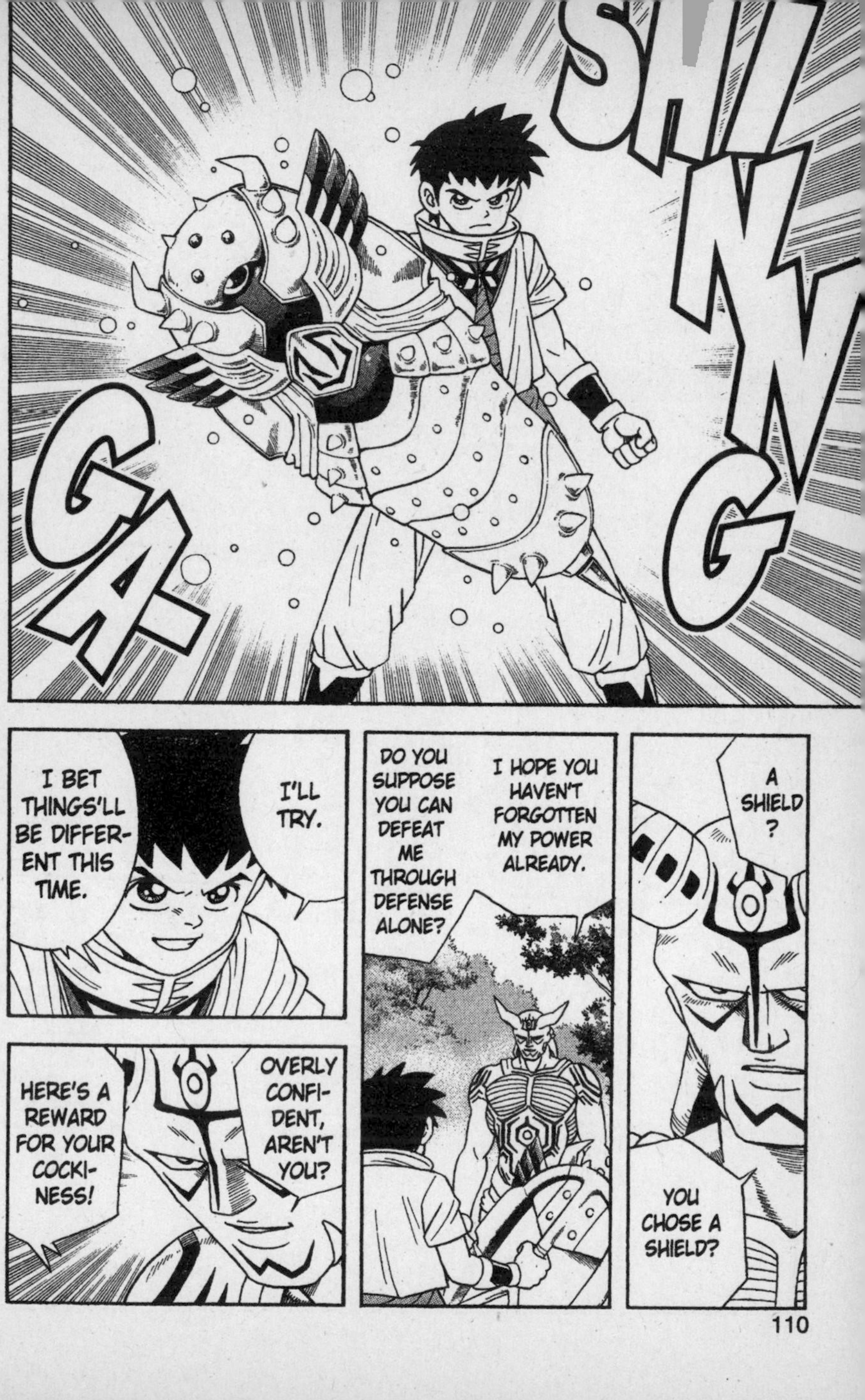
SHINNG
GA-
A SHIELD?
YOU CHOSE A SHIELD?
I HOPE YOU HAVEN'T FORGOTTEN MY POWER ALREADY.
DO YOU SUPPOSE YOU CAN DEFEAT ME THROUGH DEFENSE ALONE?
I'LL TRY.
I BET THINGS'LL BE DIFFERENT THIS TIME.
OVERLY CONFIDENT, AREN'T YOU?
HERE'S A REWARD FOR YOUR COCKINESS!

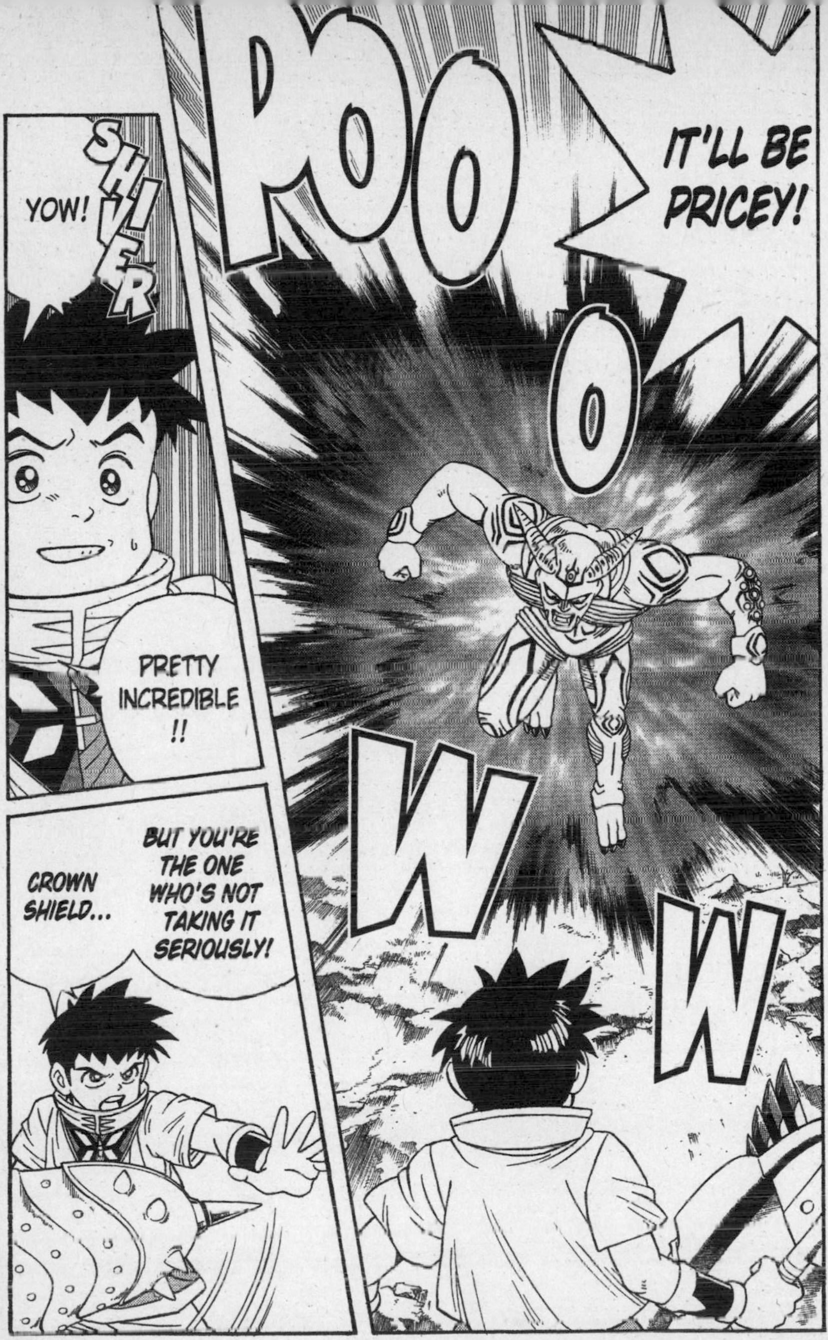
POOOOWWW
IT'LL BE PRICEY!
SHIVER
YOW!
PRETTY INCREDIBLE !!
BUT YOU'RE THE ONE WHO'S NOT TAKING IT SERIOUSLY!
CROWN SHIELD...

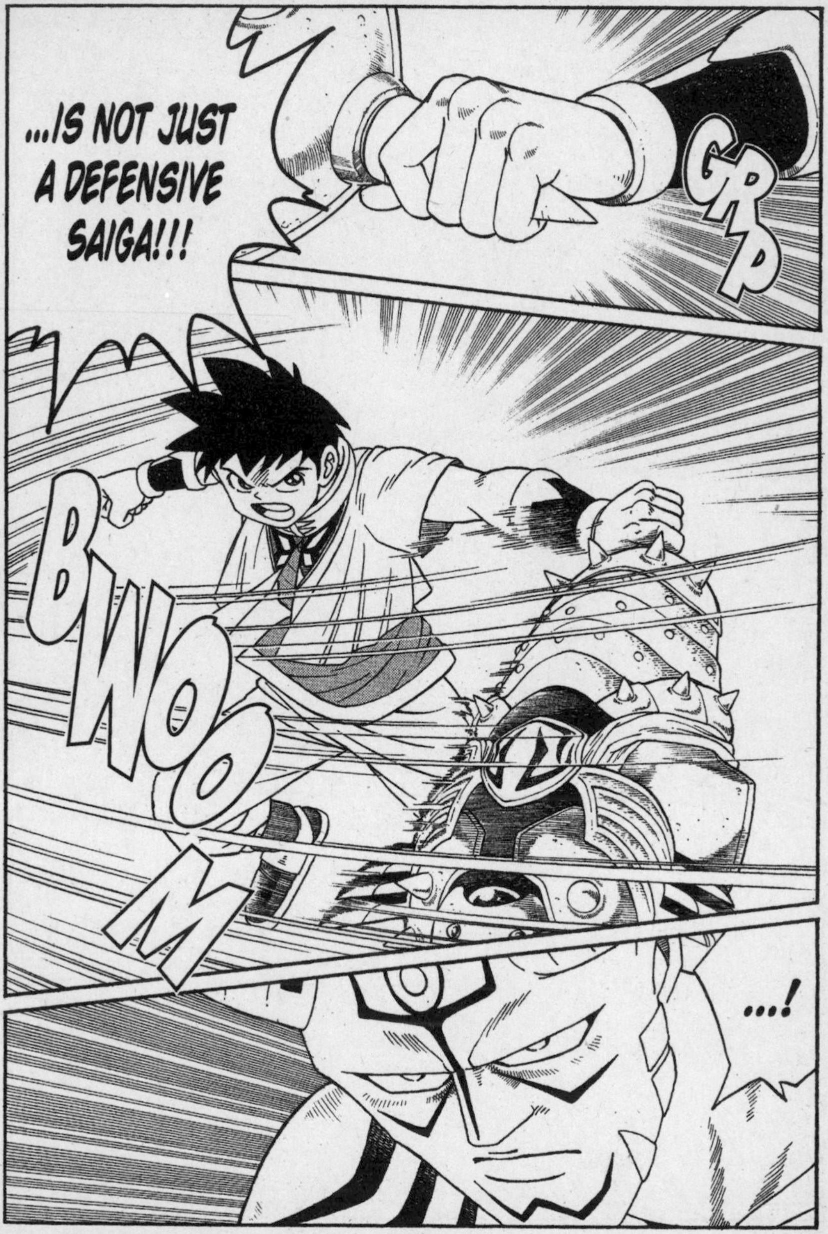

GRP
...IS NOT JUST A DEFENSIVE SAIGA!!!
BWOOM
...!

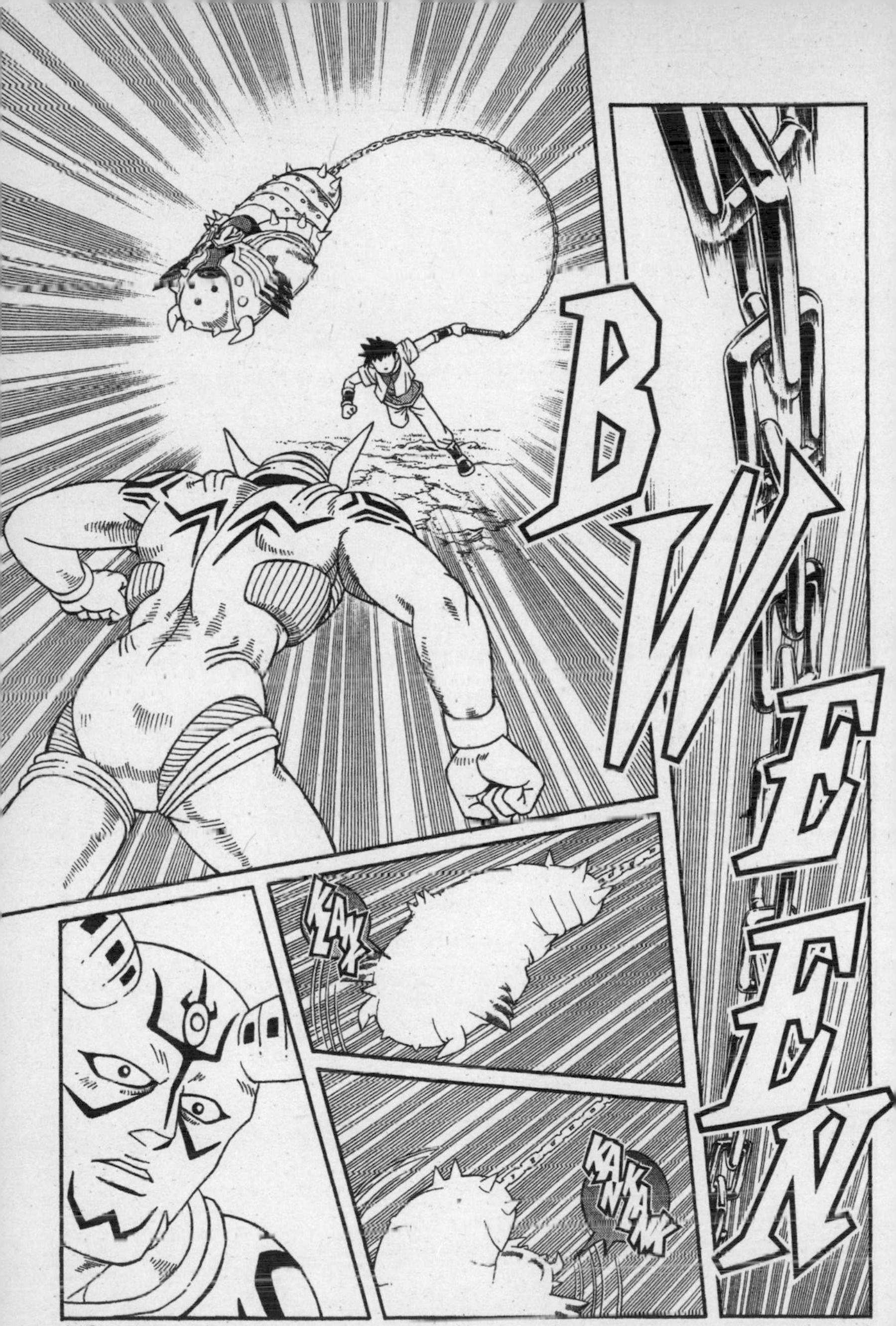
BWEEEN
KLANK
KANKANK

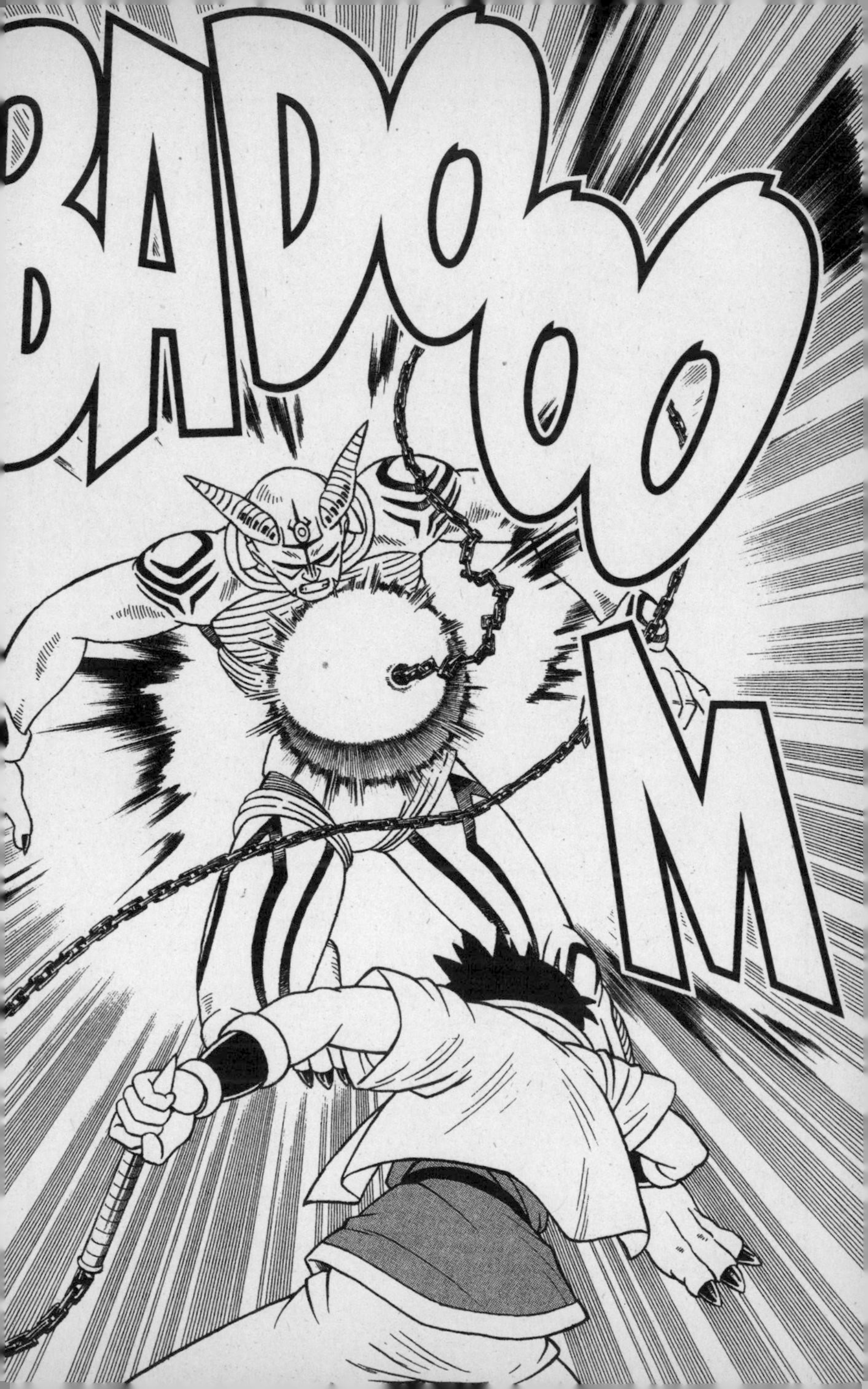
BADOOOM

READ THIS WAY

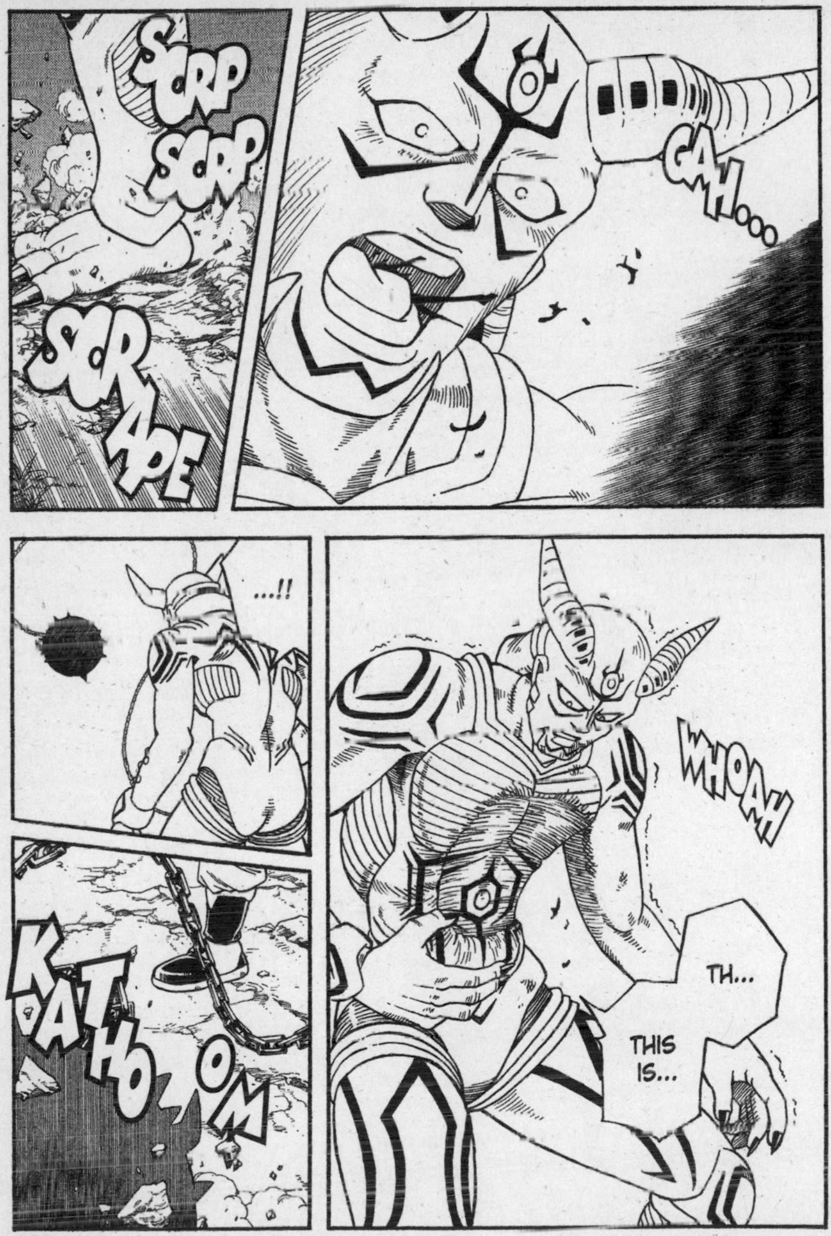

...
GAH...
SCRP
SCRP
SCRAPE
WHOAH
TH...
THIS IS...
...!!
KATHOOM

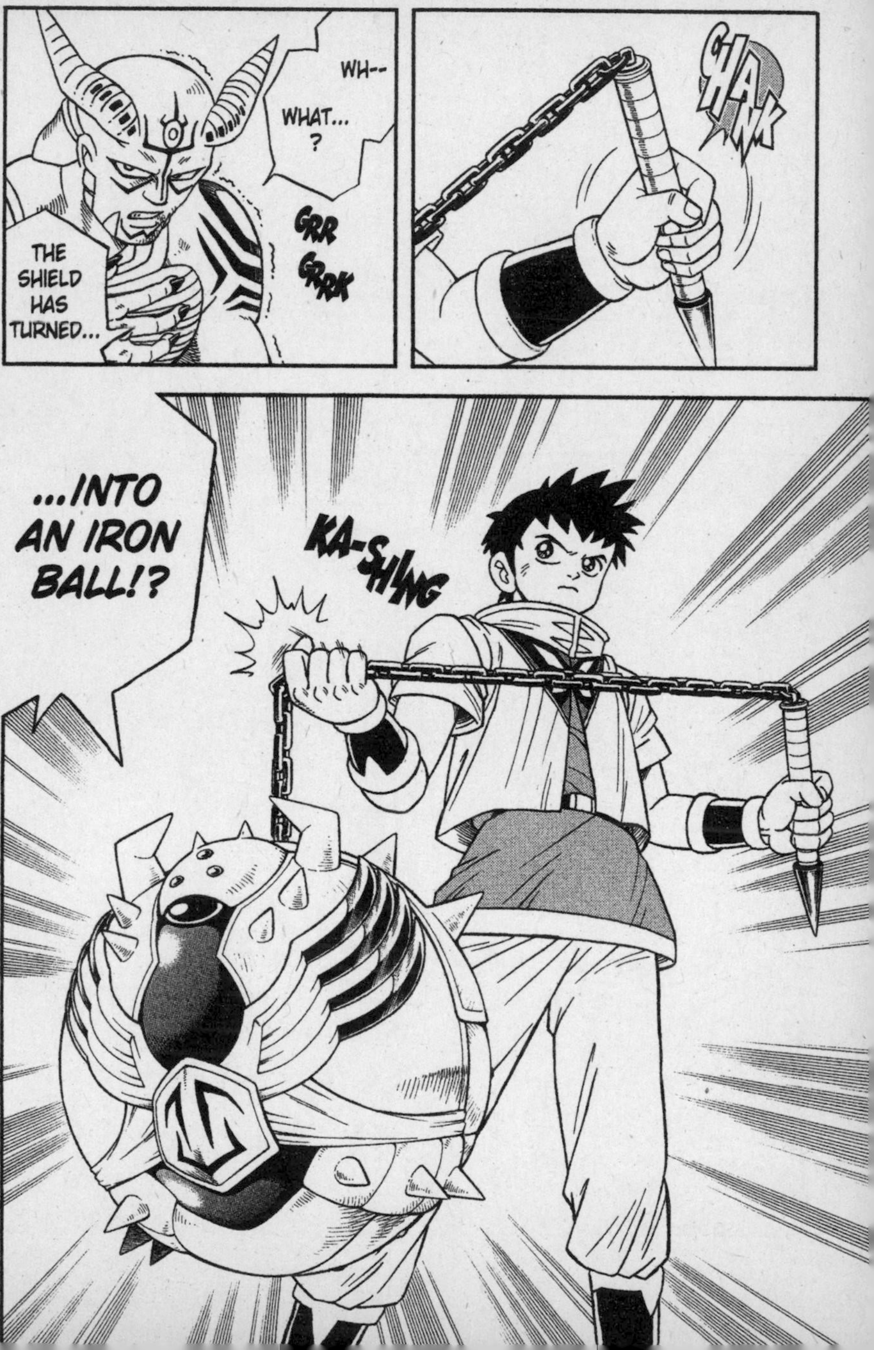
CHANK
WH--
WHAT...?
GRR GRRK
THE SHIELD HAS TURNED...
KA-SHING
...INTO AN IRON BALL!?

READ THIS WAY

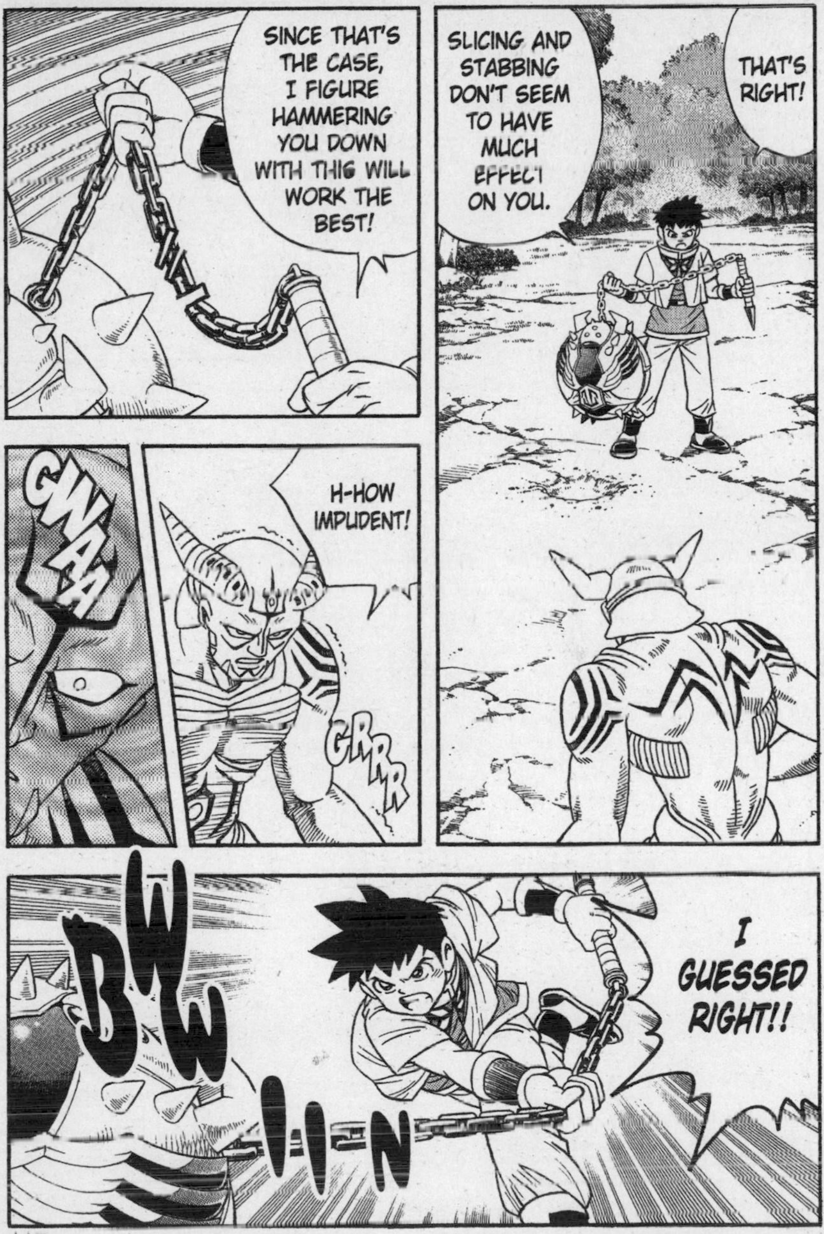
THAT'S RIGHT!
SLICING AND STABBING DON'T SEEM TO HAVE MUCH EFFECT ON YOU.
SINCE THAT'S THE CASE, I FIGURE HAMMERING YOU DOWN WITH THIS WILL WORK THE BEST!
H-HOW IMPUDENT!
GRRR
GWAAA
I GUESSED RIGHT!!
BWWI-I-N

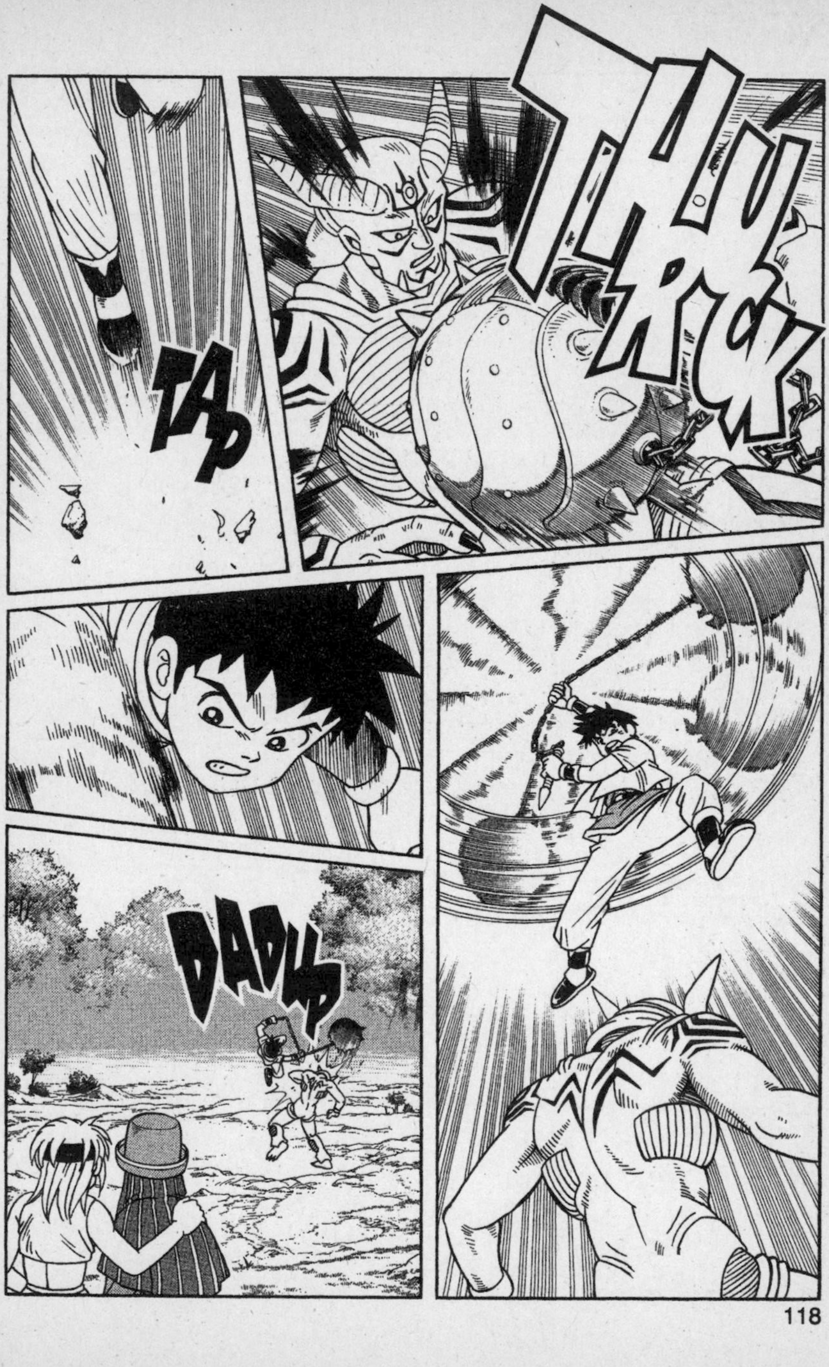
THURACK
TAP
DADUP

READ THIS WAY

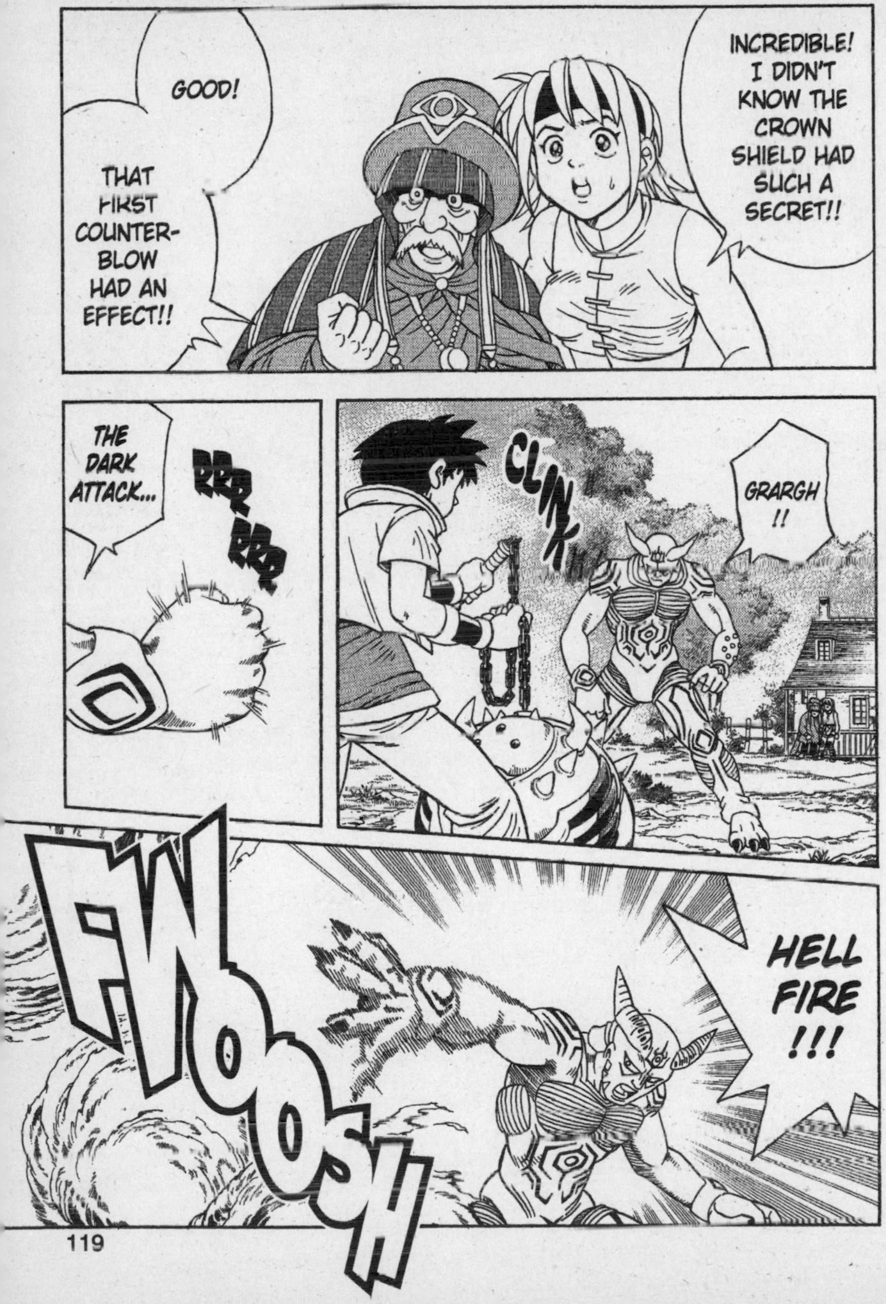

INCREDIBLE! I DIDN'T KNOW THE CROWN SHIELD HAD SUCH A SECRET!!
GOOD!
THAT FIRST COUNTER-BLOW HAD AN EFFECT!!
GRARGH !!
CLINK
THE DARK ATTACK...
RRR RRR
HELL FIRE !!!
FWOOSH

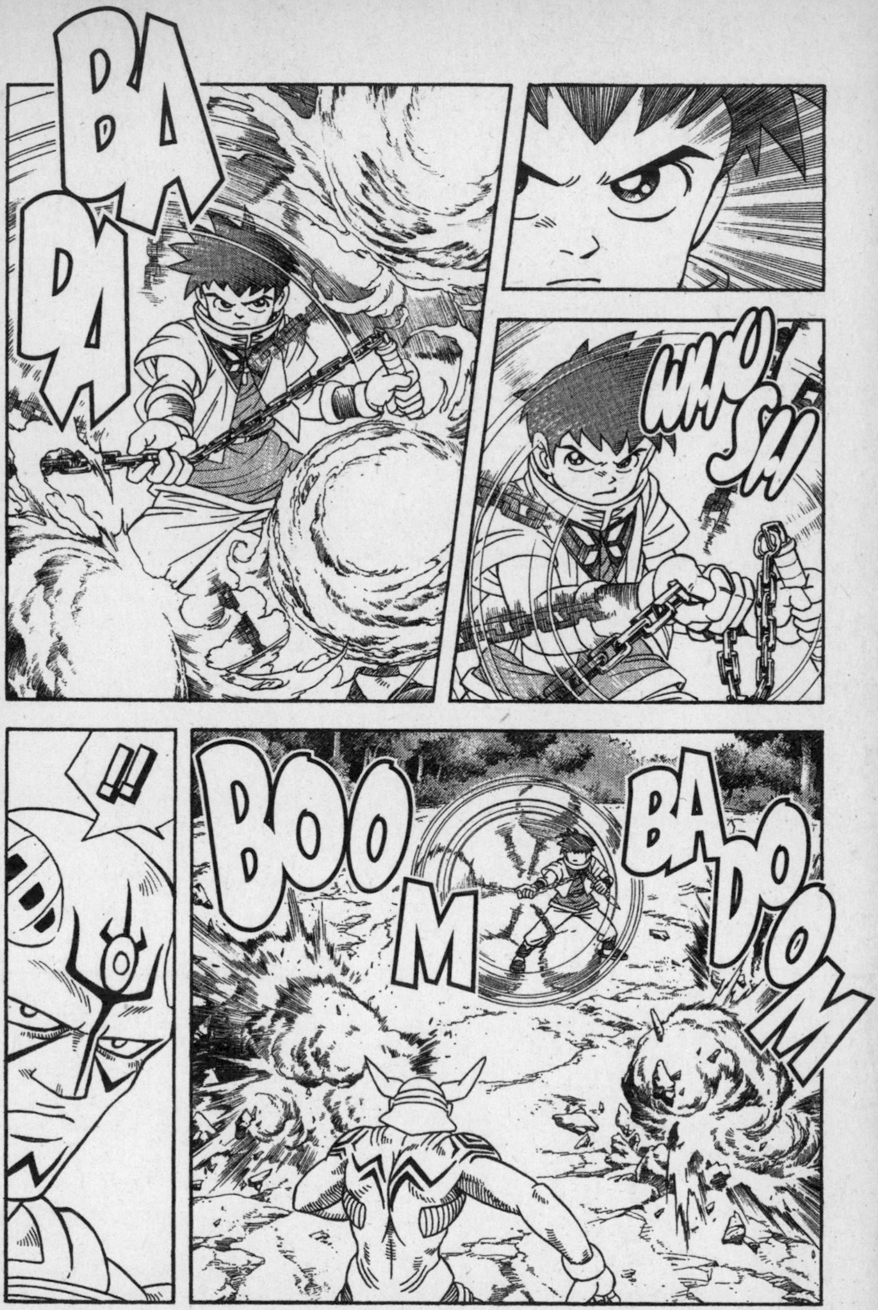
WHOOSH
BADA
BOOM
BADOOM
!!

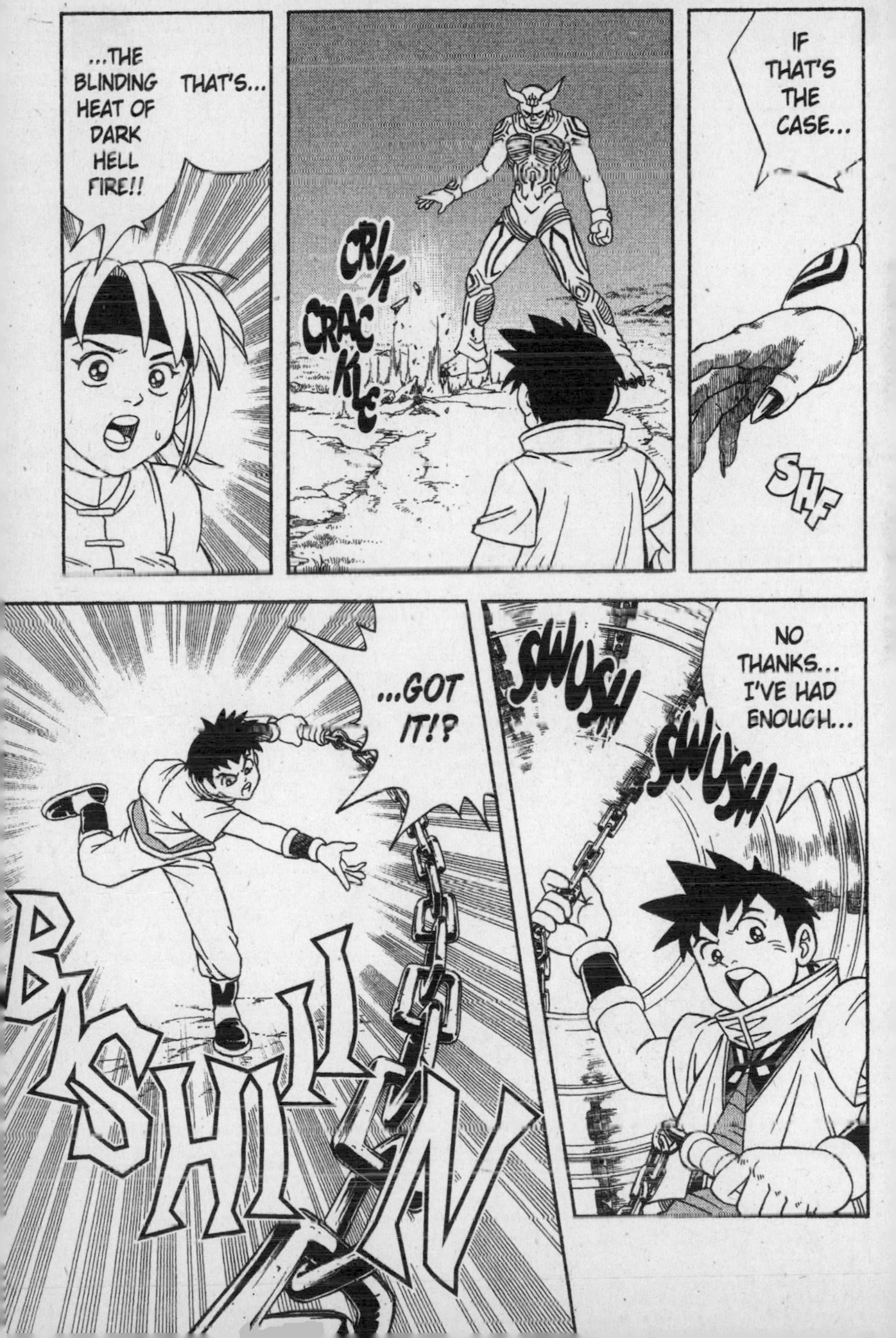
IF THAT'S THE CASE...
SHF
CRIK CRACKLE
THAT'S...
...THE BLINDING HEAT OF DARK HELL FIRE!!
NO THANKS... I'VE HAD ENOUGH...
SWOSH
SWOSH
...GOT IT!?
BSHIIIN

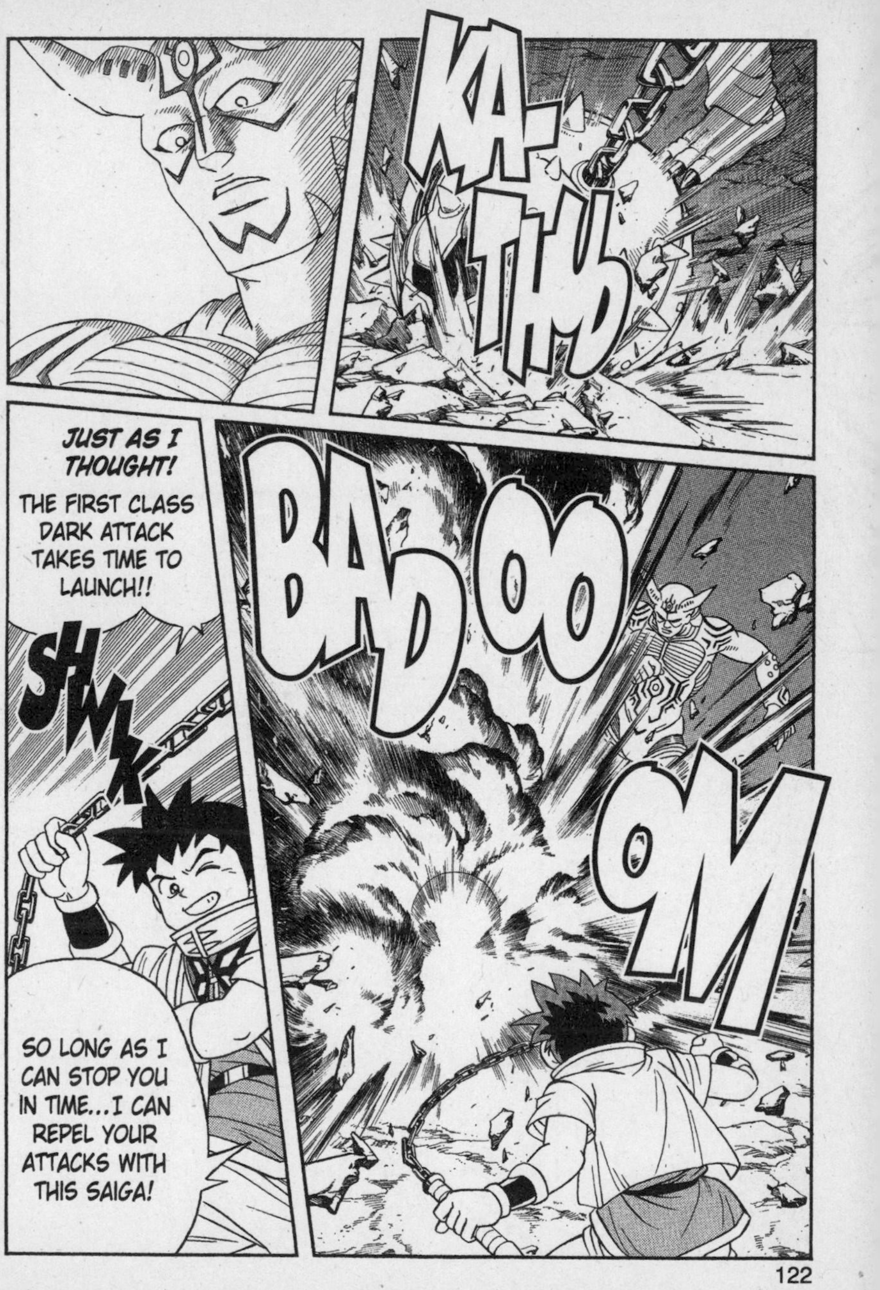
KA-THUD
BADOOOM
JUST AS I THOUGHT!
THE FIRST CLASS DARK ATTACK TAKES TIME TO LAUNCH!!
SHWK
SO LONG AS I CAN STOP YOU IN TIME...I CAN REPEL YOUR ATTACKS WITH THIS SAIGA!

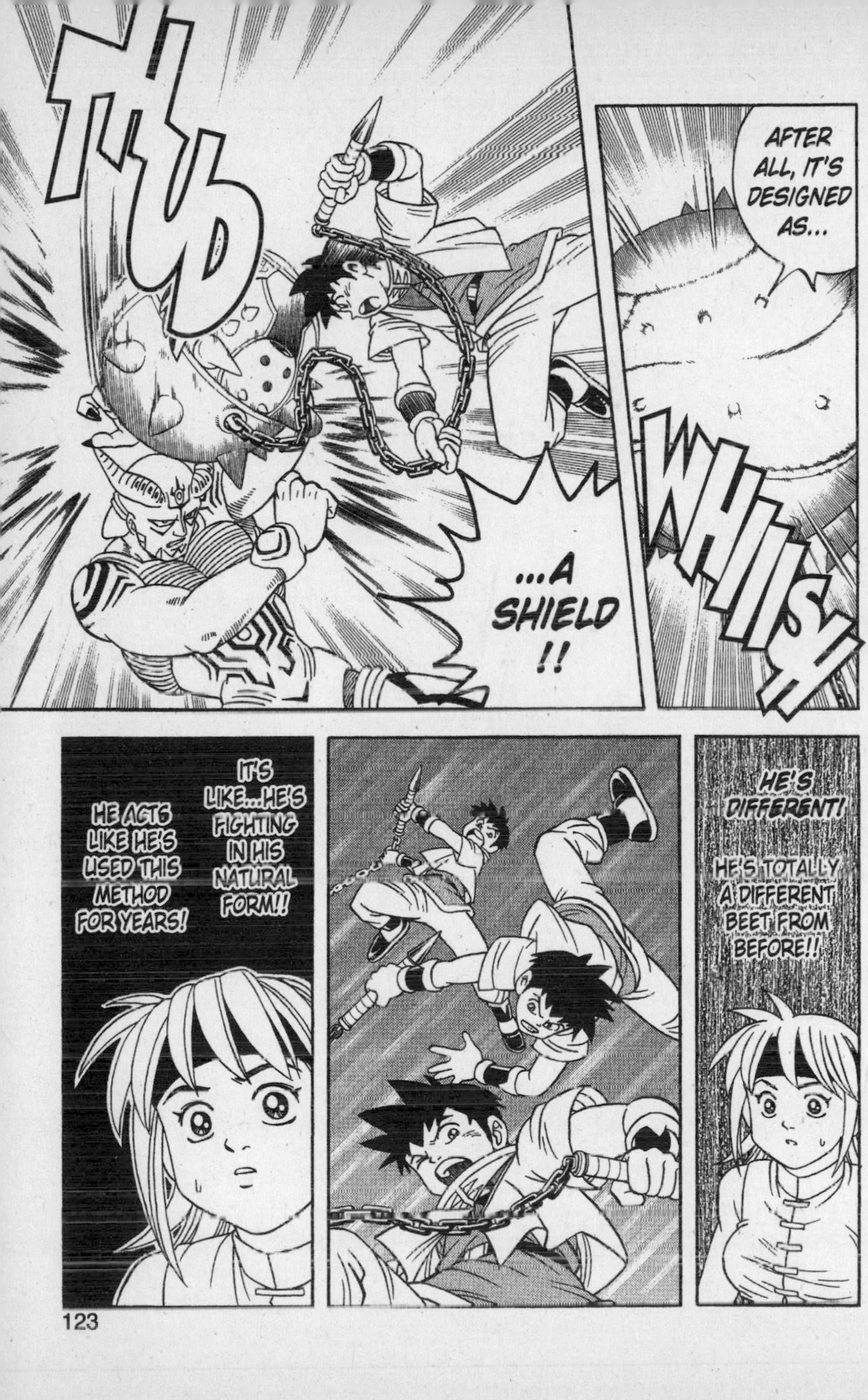
AFTER ALL, IT'S DESIGNED AS...
WHIISH
THUD
...A SHIELD!!
HE'S DIFFERENT!
HE'S TOTALLY A DIFFERENT BEET FROM BEFORE!!
IT'S LIKE...HE'S FIGHTING IN HIS NATURAL FORM!!
HE ACTS LIKE HE'S USED THIS METHOD FOR YEARS!

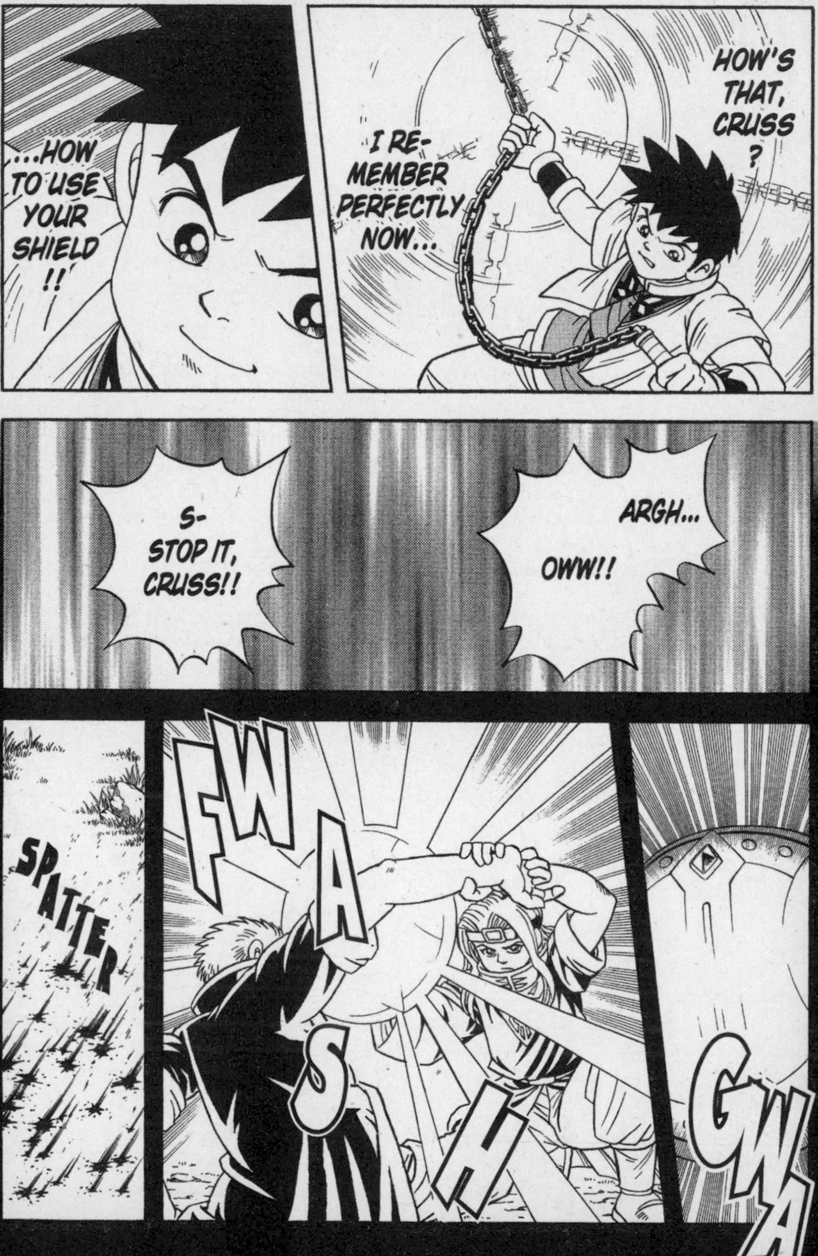
HOW'S THAT, CRUSS?
I RE-MEMBER PERFECTLY NOW...
...HOW TO USE YOUR SHIELD!!
ARGH...
OWW!!
S- STOP IT, CRUSS!!
GWA
FWASH
SPATTER

READ THIS WAY

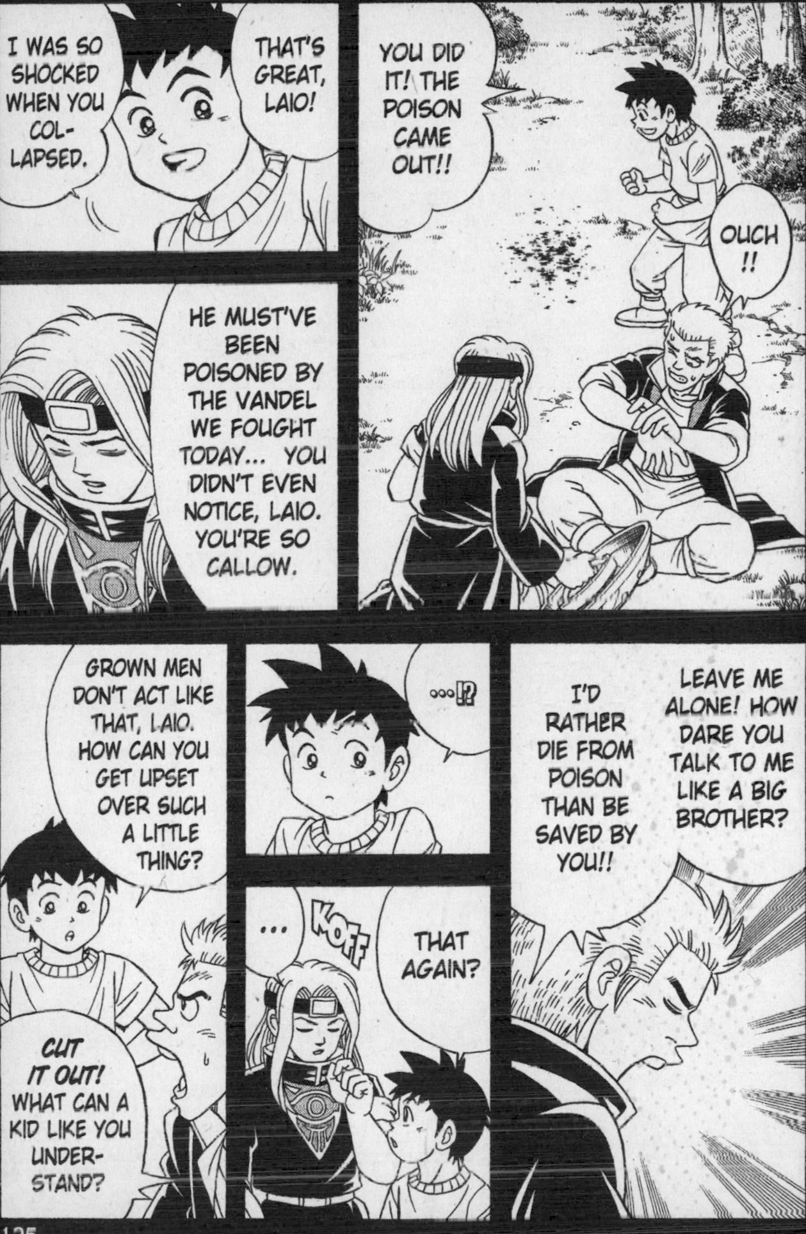

YOU DID IT! THE POISON CAME OUT!!
OUCH!!
THAT'S GREAT, LAIO!
I WAS SO SHOCKED WHEN YOU COL-LAPSED.
HE MUST'VE BEEN POISONED BY THE VANDEL WE FOUGHT TODAY... YOU DIDN'T EVEN NOTICE, LAIO. YOU'RE SO CALLOW.
LEAVE ME ALONE! HOW DARE YOU TALK TO ME LIKE A BIG BROTHER?
I'D RATHER DIE FROM POISON THAN BE SAVED BY YOU!!
...!?
THAT AGAIN?
KOFF
...
GROWN MEN DON'T ACT LIKE THAT, LAIO. HOW CAN YOU GET UPSET OVER SUCH A LITTLE THING?
CUT IT OUT! WHAT CAN A KID LIKE YOU UNDER-STAND?

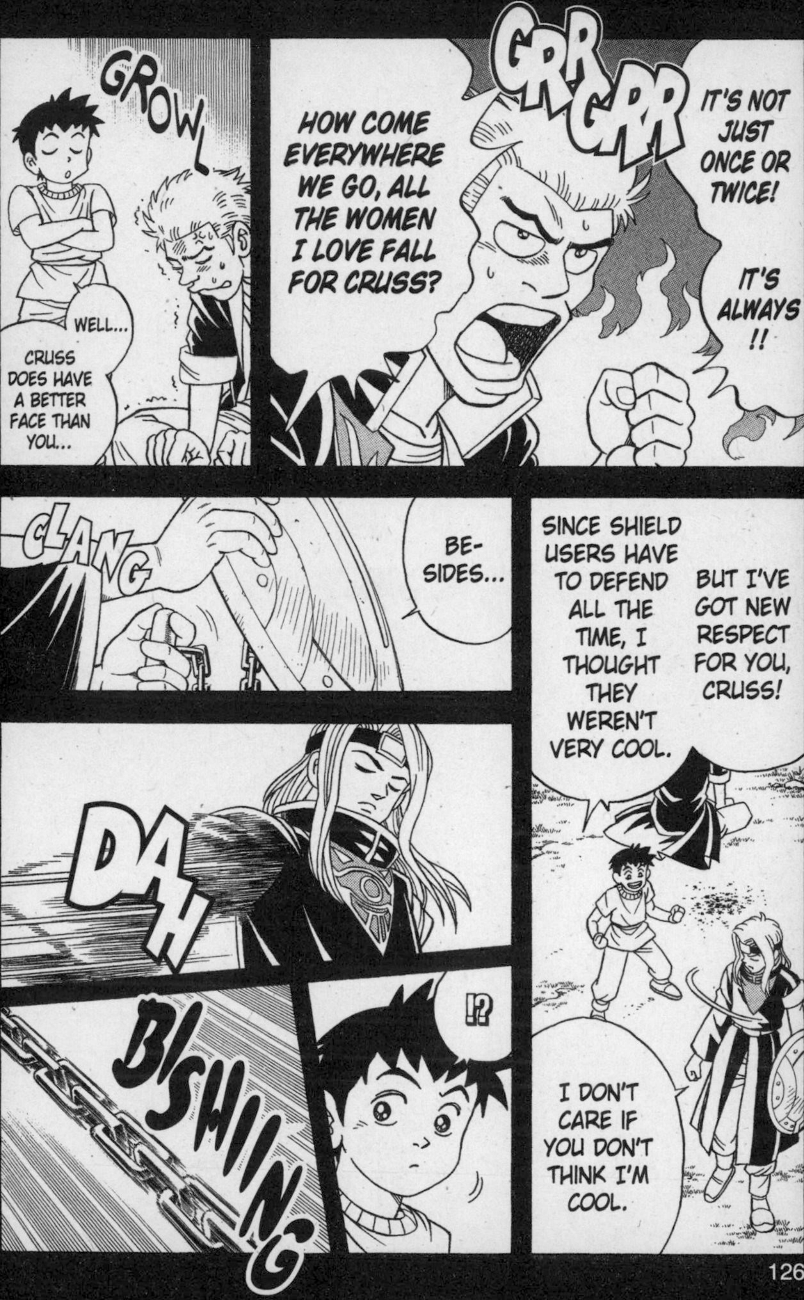
IT'S NOT JUST ONCE OR TWICE!
GRGRR
HOW COME EVERYWHERE WE GO, ALL THE WOMEN I LOVE FALL FOR CRUSS?
IT'S ALWAYS!!
GROWL
WELL...
CRUSS DOES HAVE A BETTER FACE THAN YOU...
SINCE SHIELD USERS HAVE TO DEFEND ALL THE TIME, I THOUGHT THEY WEREN'T VERY COOL.
BUT I'VE GOT NEW RESPECT FOR YOU, CRUSS!
I DON'T CARE IF YOU DON'T THINK I'M COOL.
BE-SIDES...
CLANG
DAH
!?
BISHING

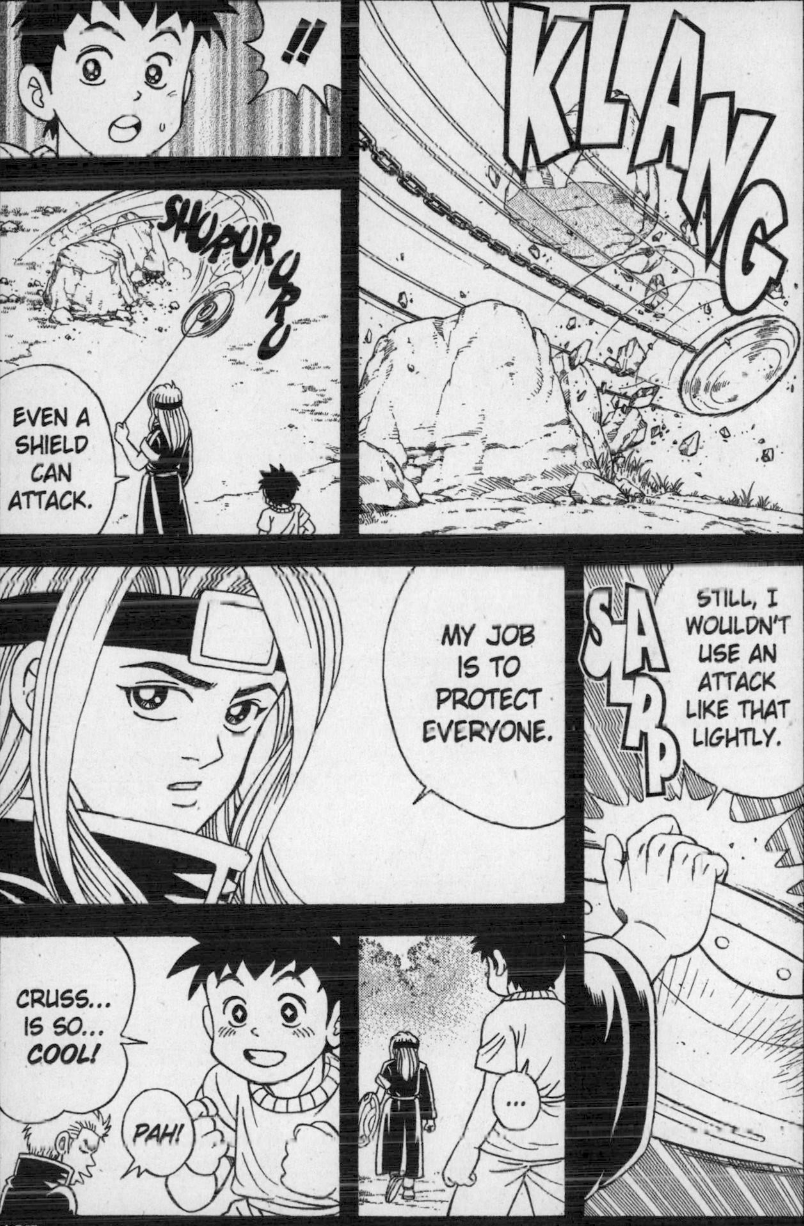
KLANG
!!
SHUPURURU
EVEN A SHIELD CAN ATTACK.
SLAP
STILL, I WOULDN'T USE AN ATTACK LIKE THAT LIGHTLY.
MY JOB IS TO PROTECT EVERYONE.
...
CRUSS... IS SO... COOL!
PAH!

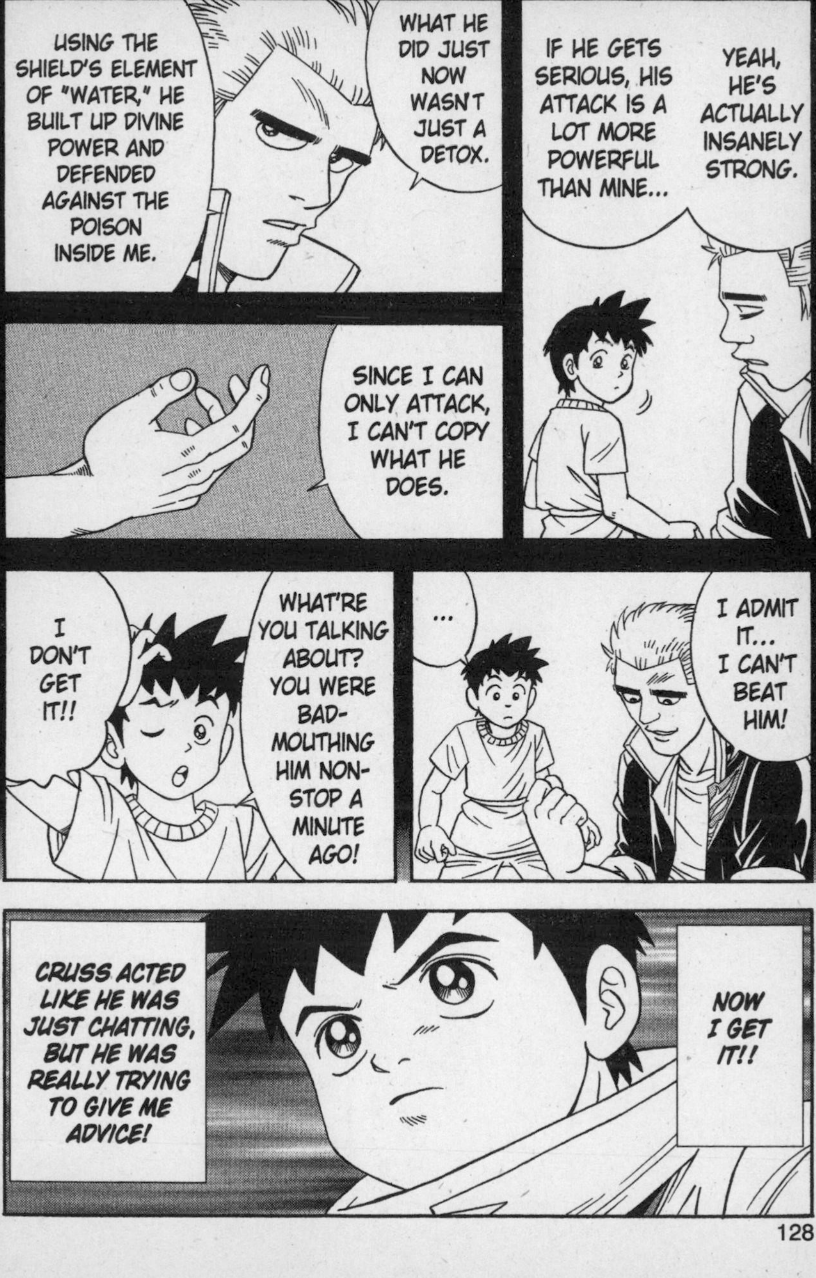
YEAH, HE'S ACTUALLY INSANELY STRONG.
IF HE GETS SERIOUS, HIS ATTACK IS A LOT MORE POWERFUL THAN MINE...
WHAT HE DID JUST NOW WASN'T JUST A DETOX.
USING THE SHIELD'S ELEMENT OF "WATER," HE BUILT UP DIVINE POWER AND DEFENDED AGAINST THE POISON INSIDE ME.
SINCE I CAN ONLY ATTACK, I CAN'T COPY WHAT HE DOES.
I ADMIT IT... I CAN'T BEAT HIM!
...
WHAT'RE YOU TALKING ABOUT? YOU WERE BAD-MOUTHING HIM NON-STOP A MINUTE AGO!
I DON'T GET IT!!
NOW I GET IT!!
CRUSS ACTED LIKE HE WAS JUST CHATTING, BUT HE WAS REALLY TRYING TO GIVE ME ADVICE!

READ THIS WAY

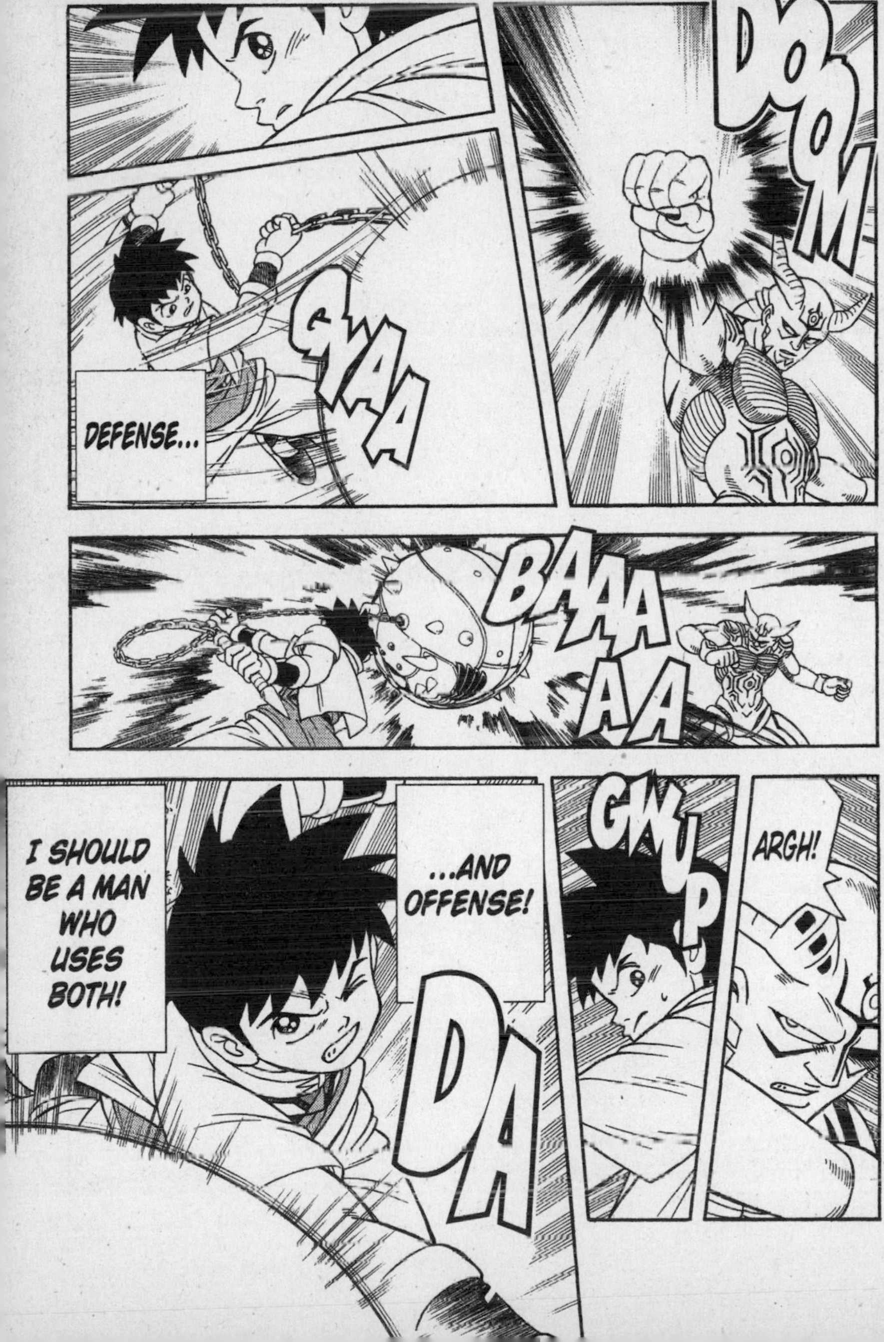
DOOOM
GYAA
DEFENSE...
BAAAAAA
ARGH!
GWUP
...AND OFFENSE!
I SHOULD BE A MAN WHO USES BOTH!
DA

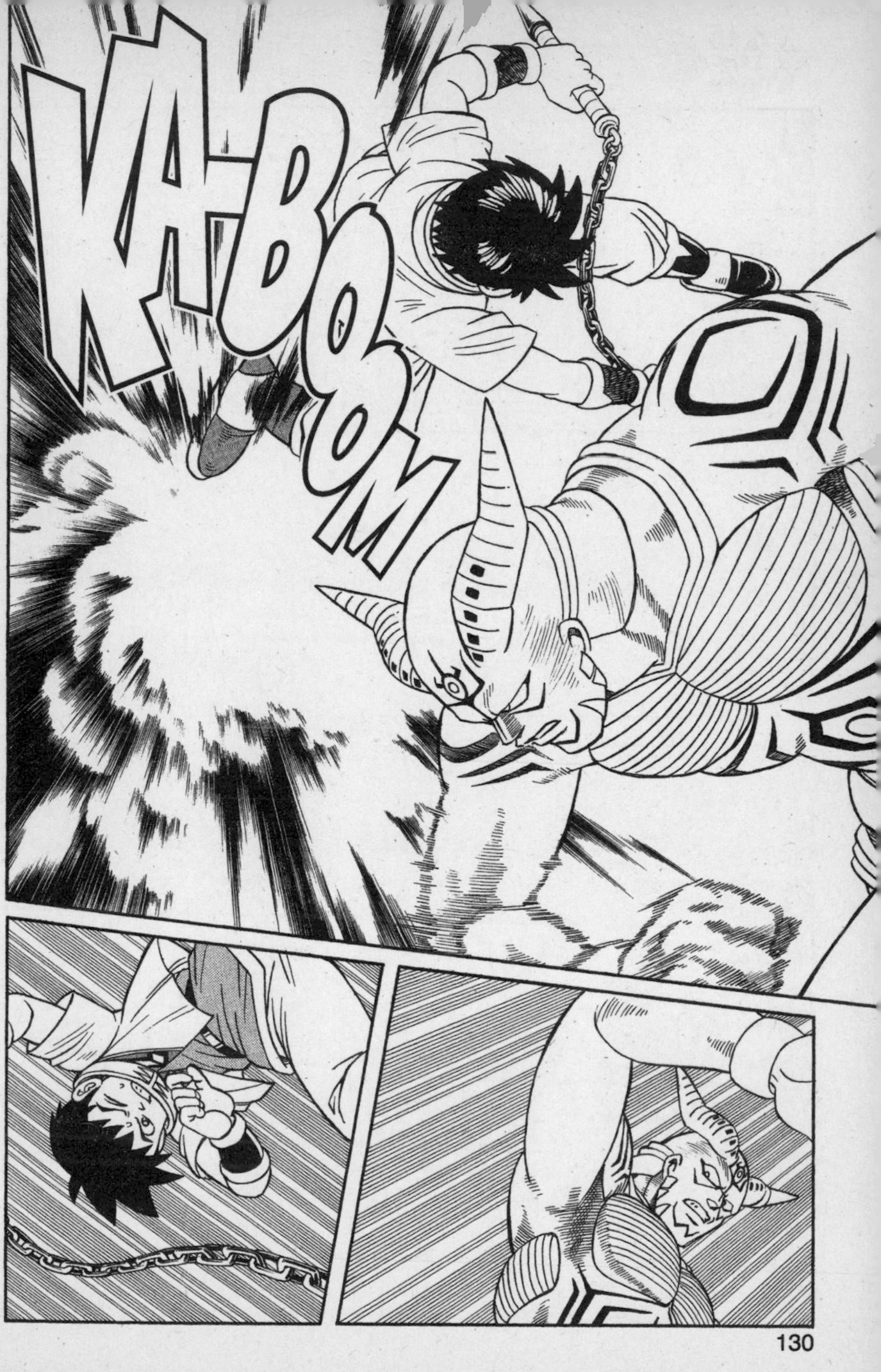
KA-BOOM

READ THIS WAY

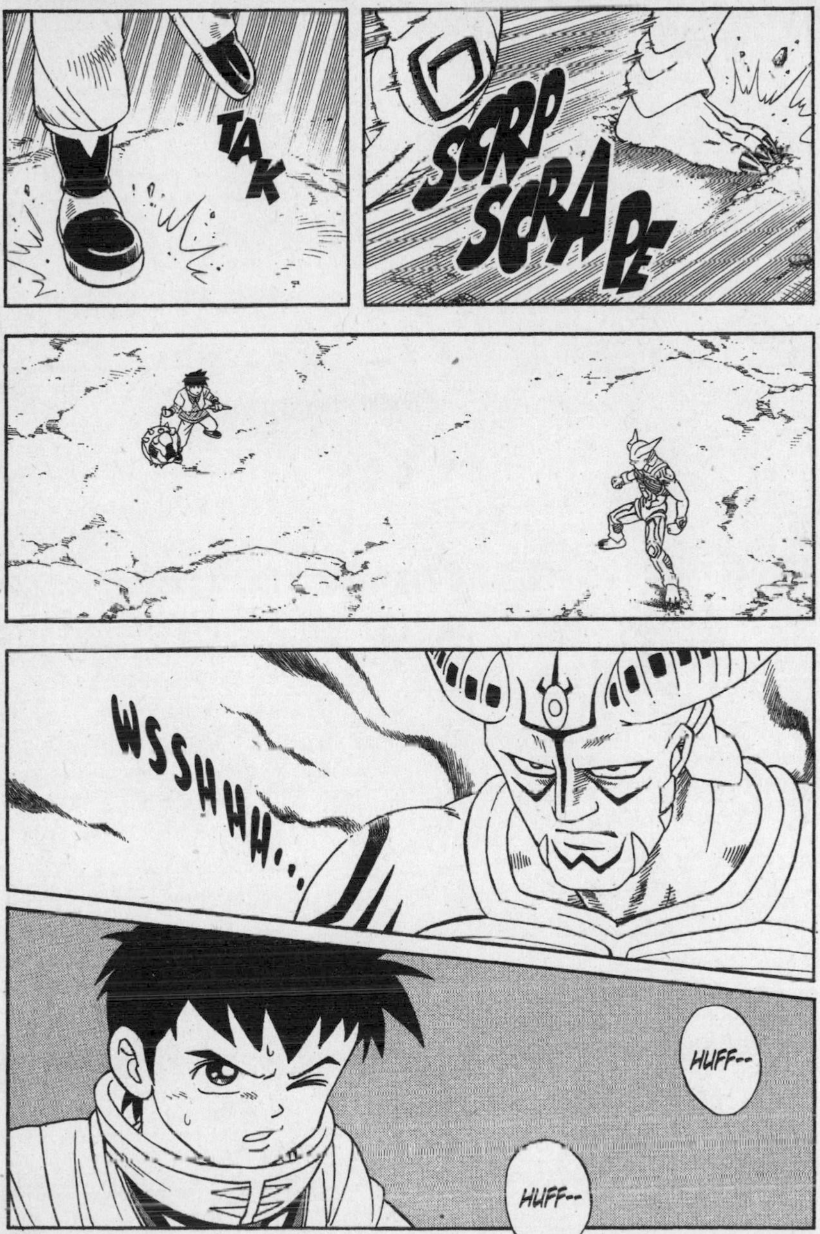
SCRP
SCRAPE
TAK
WSSHHH...
HUFF--
HUFF--

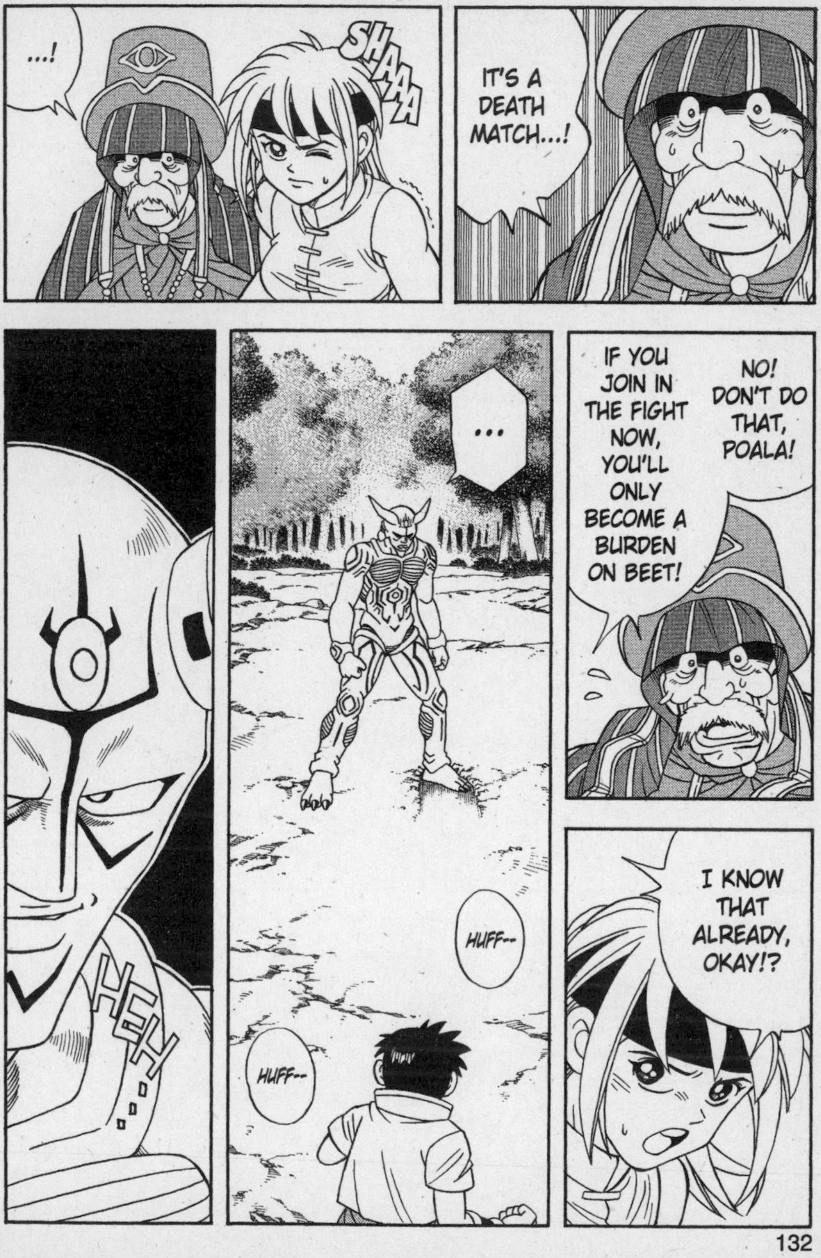
IT'S A DEATH MATCH...!
SHAAAA
...!
NO! DON'T DO THAT, POALA!
IF YOU JOIN IN THE FIGHT NOW, YOU'LL ONLY BECOME A BURDEN ON BEET!
I KNOW THAT ALREADY, OKAY!?
...
HUFF--
HUFF--
HEH

READ THIS WAY

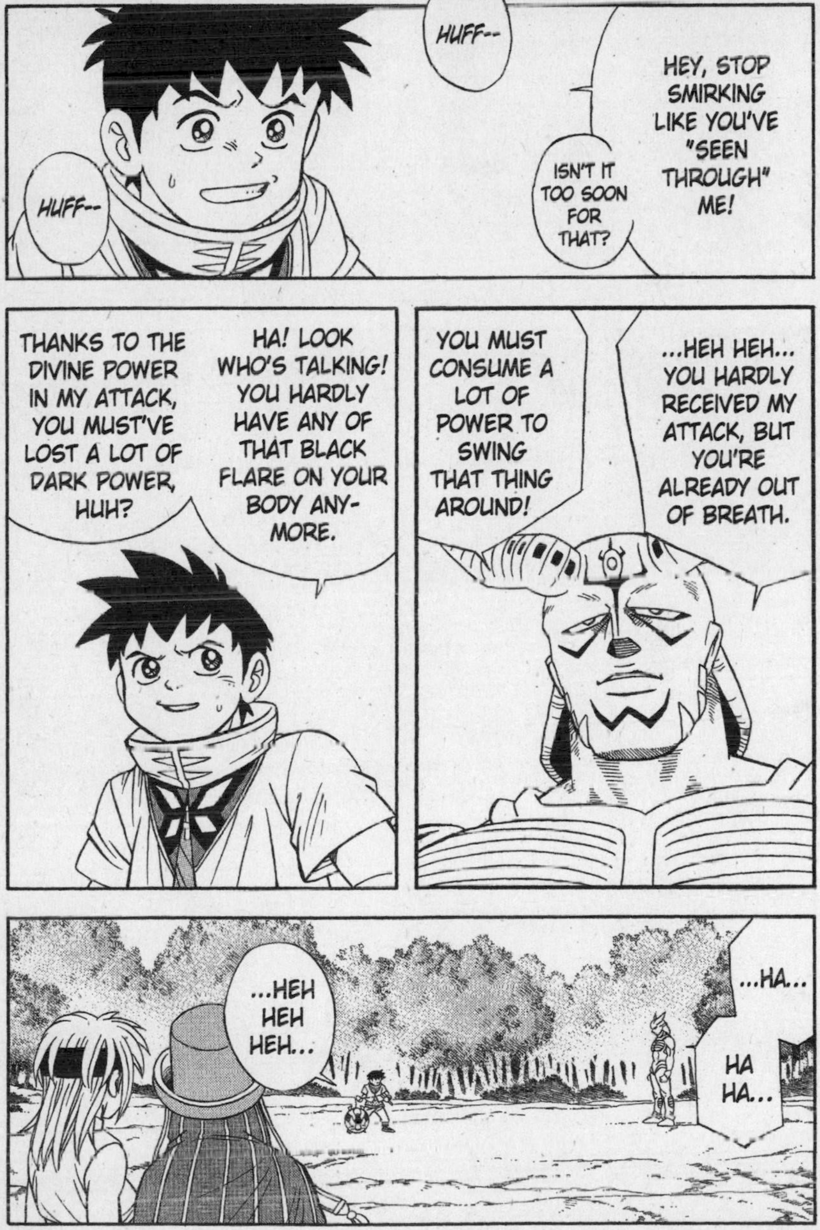

HEY, STOP SMIRKING LIKE YOU'VE "SEEN THROUGH" ME!
HUFF--
ISN'T IT TOO SOON FOR THAT?
HUFF--
...HEH HEH... YOU HARDLY RECEIVED MY ATTACK, BUT YOU'RE ALREADY OUT OF BREATH.
YOU MUST CONSUME A LOT OF POWER TO SWING THAT THING AROUND!
HA! LOOK WHO'S TALKING! YOU HARDLY HAVE ANY OF THAT BLACK FLARE ON YOUR BODY ANY-MORE.
THANKS TO THE DIVINE POWER IN MY ATTACK, YOU MUST'VE LOST A LOT OF DARK POWER, HUH?
...HA...
HA HA...
...HEH HEH HEH...

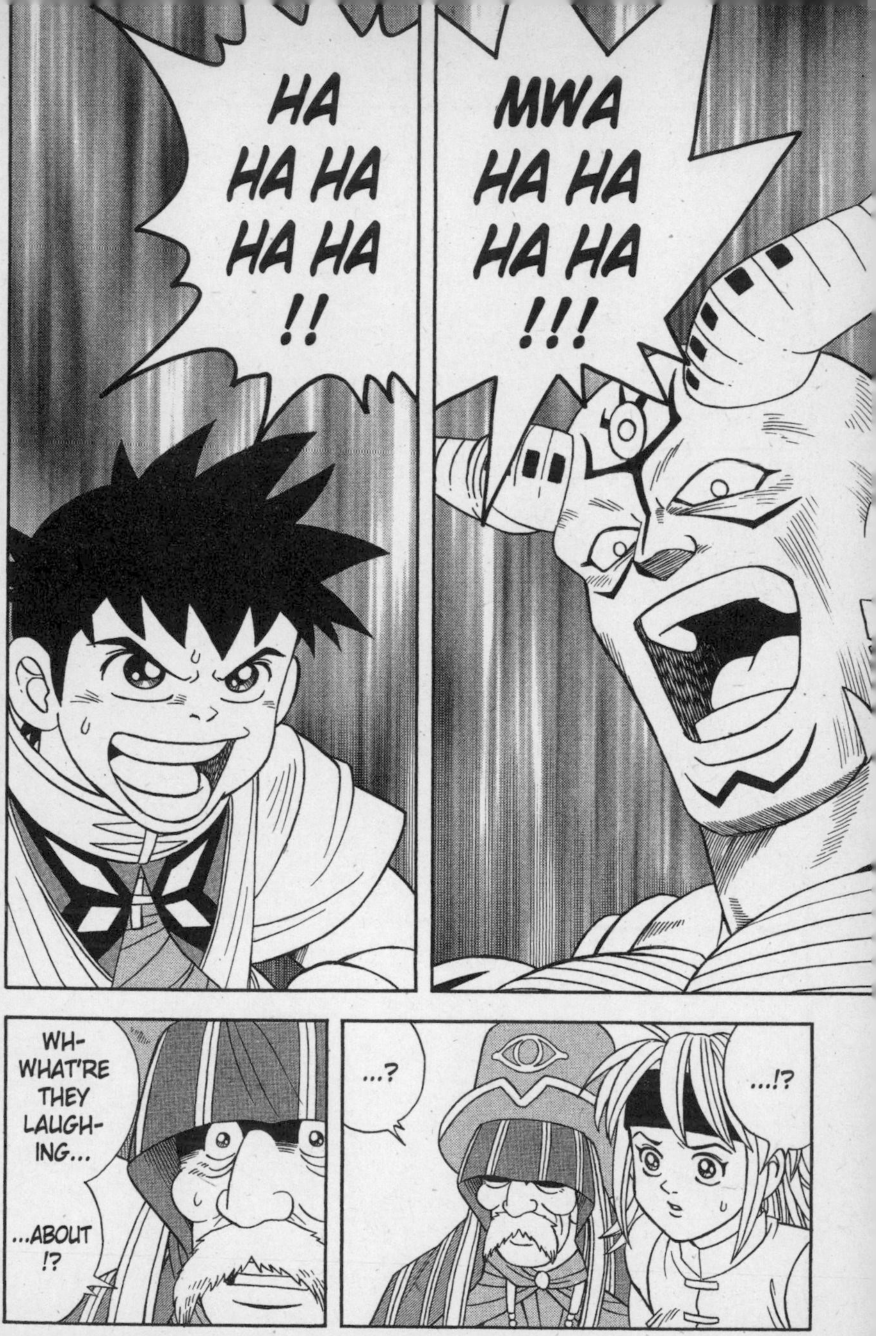
MWA HA HA HA HA!!!
HA HA HA HA HA!!
...!?
...?
WH-WHAT'RE THEY LAUGH-ING...
...ABOUT !?

READ THIS WAY

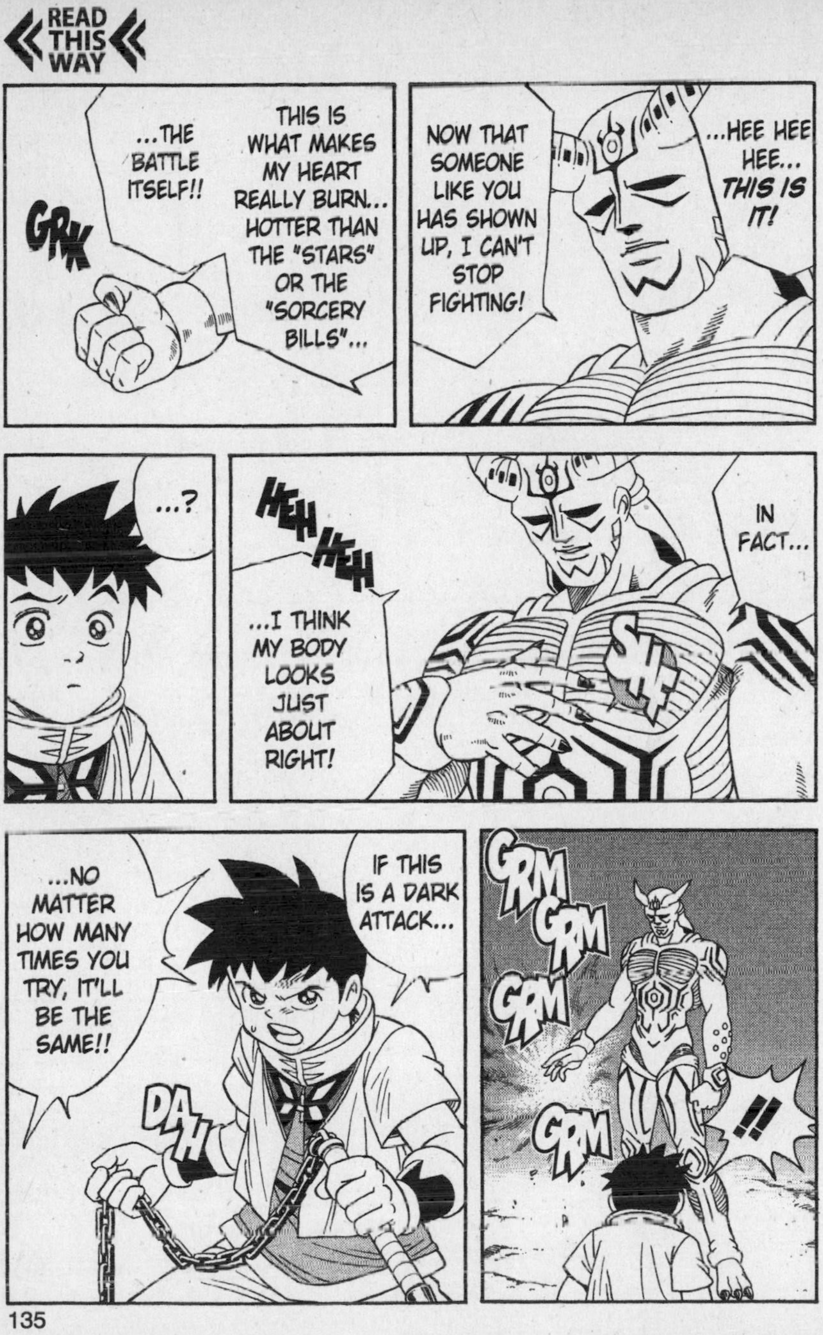
...HEE HEE HEE... THIS IS IT!
NOW THAT SOMEONE LIKE YOU HAS SHOWN UP, I CAN'T STOP FIGHTING!
THIS IS WHAT MAKES MY HEART REALLY BURN... HOTTER THAN THE "STARS" OR THE "SORCERY BILLS"...
...THE BATTLE ITSELF!!
IN FACT...
HEH HEH
...I THINK MY BODY LOOKS JUST ABOUT RIGHT!
...?
GRM GRM
GRM
GRM
!!
IF THIS IS A DARK ATTACK...
...NO MATTER HOW MANY TIMES YOU TRY, IT'LL BE THE SAME!!
DAH

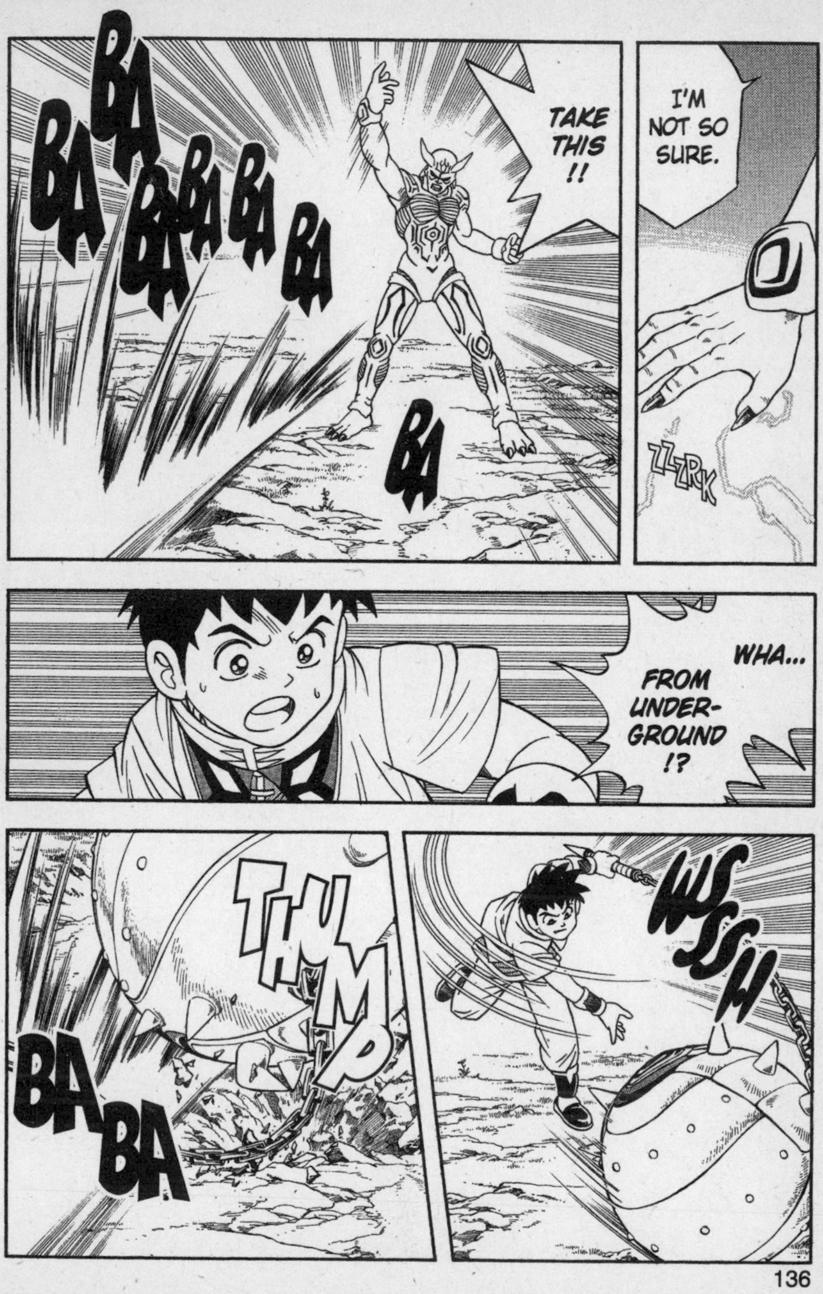
I'M NOT SO SURE.
ZZZRK
TAKE THIS !!
BA BA BA BA BA BA BA BA
BA
WHA...
FROM UNDER-GROUND !?
WSSH
THUMP
BA BA

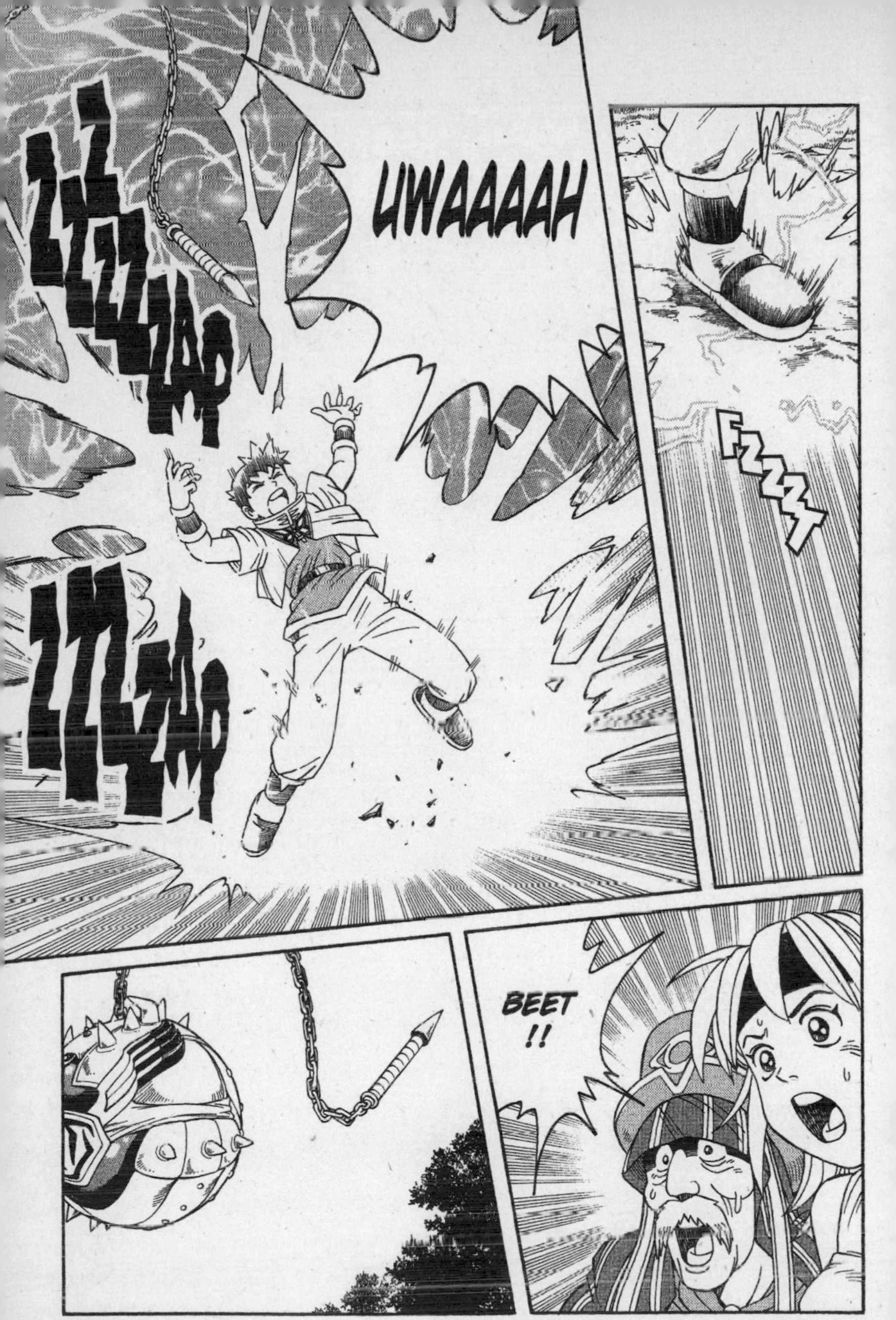
FZZZT
UWAAAAH
ZZZZZAP
ZZZZAP
BEET !!

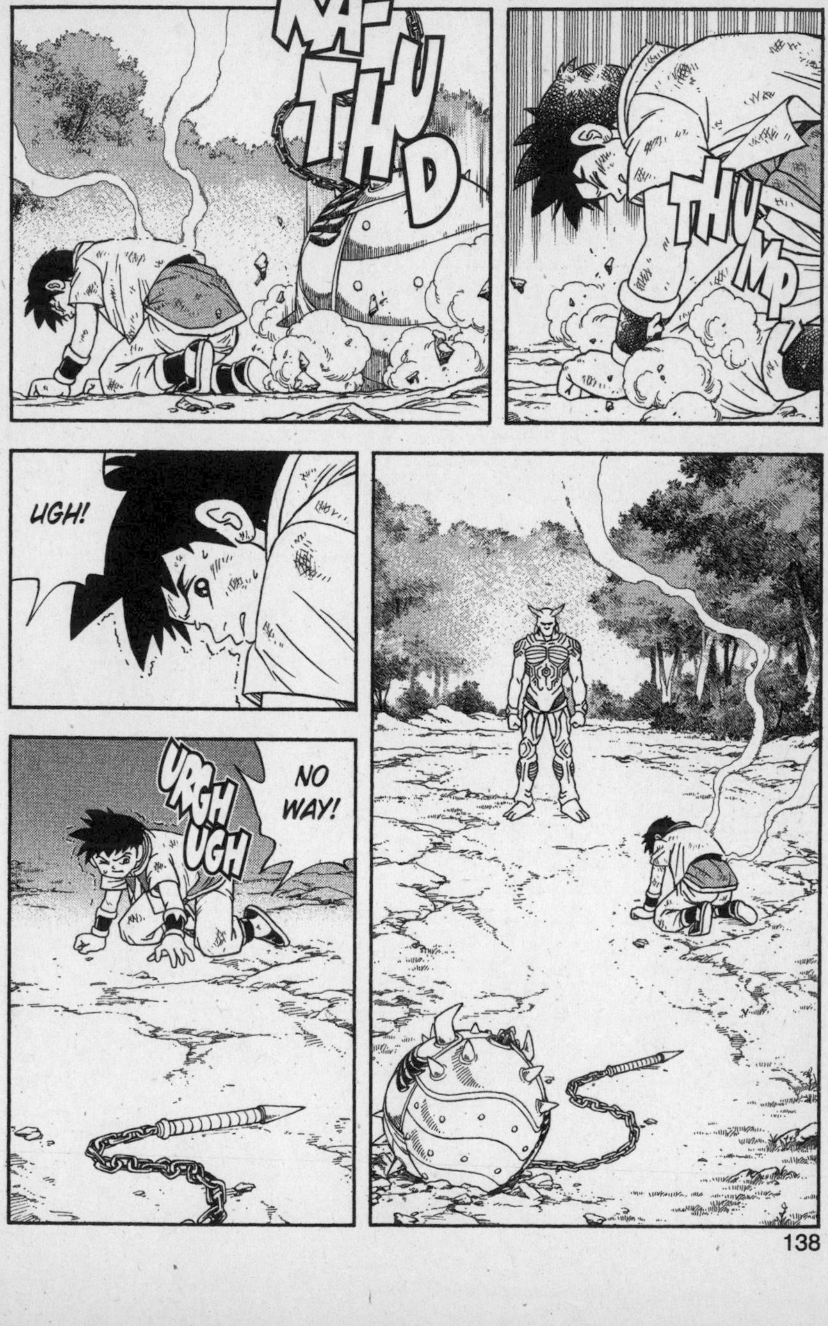
THUMP
KA-THUD
UGH!
NO WAY!
URGH UGH

READ THIS WAY

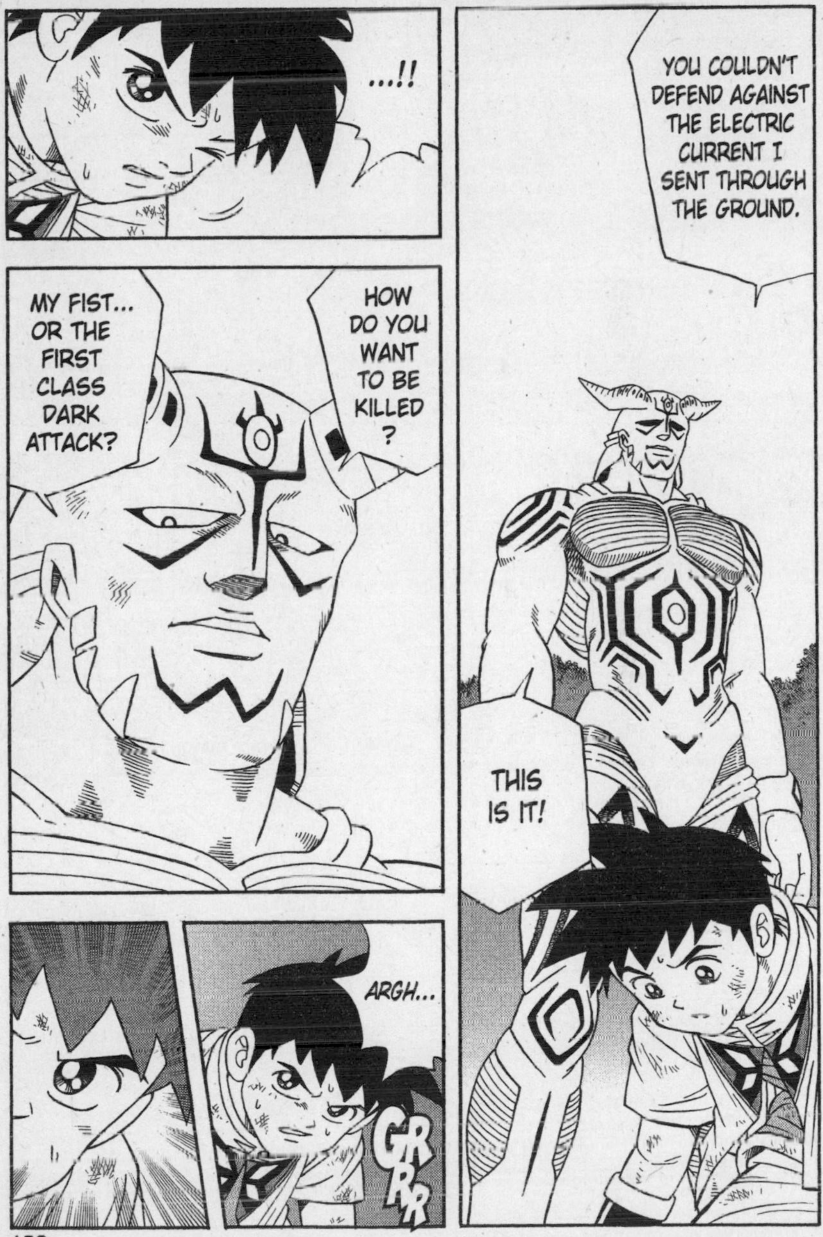
YOU COULDN'T DEFEND AGAINST THE ELECTRIC CURRENT I SENT THROUGH THE GROUND.
THIS IS IT!
...!!
HOW DO YOU WANT TO BE KILLED?
MY FIST... OR THE FIRST CLASS DARK ATTACK?
ARGH...
GRRR

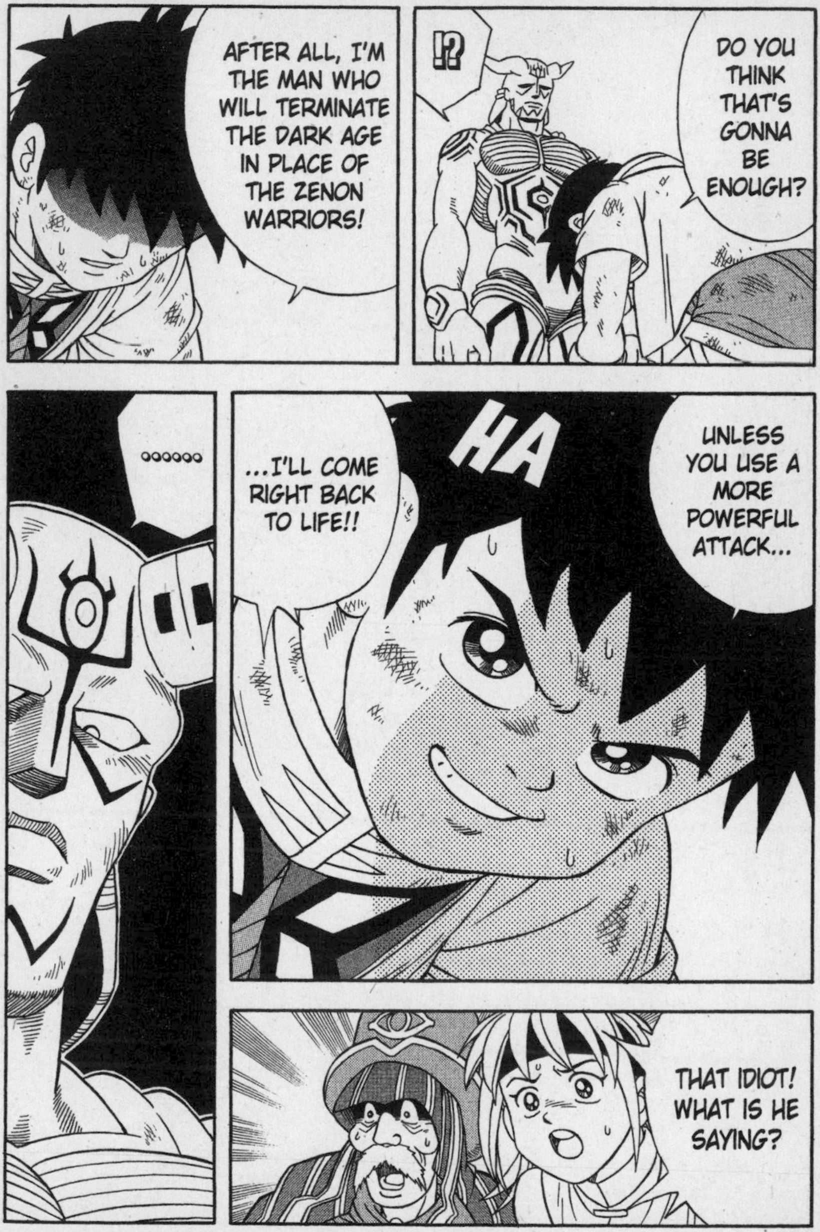
DO YOU THINK THAT'S GONNA BE ENOUGH?
!?
AFTER ALL, I'M THE MAN WHO WILL TERMINATE THE DARK AGE IN PLACE OF THE ZENON WARRIORS!
UNLESS YOU USE A MORE POWERFUL ATTACK...
HA
...I'LL COME RIGHT BACK TO LIFE!!
THAT IDIOT! WHAT IS HE SAYING?
oooooo

READ THIS WAY

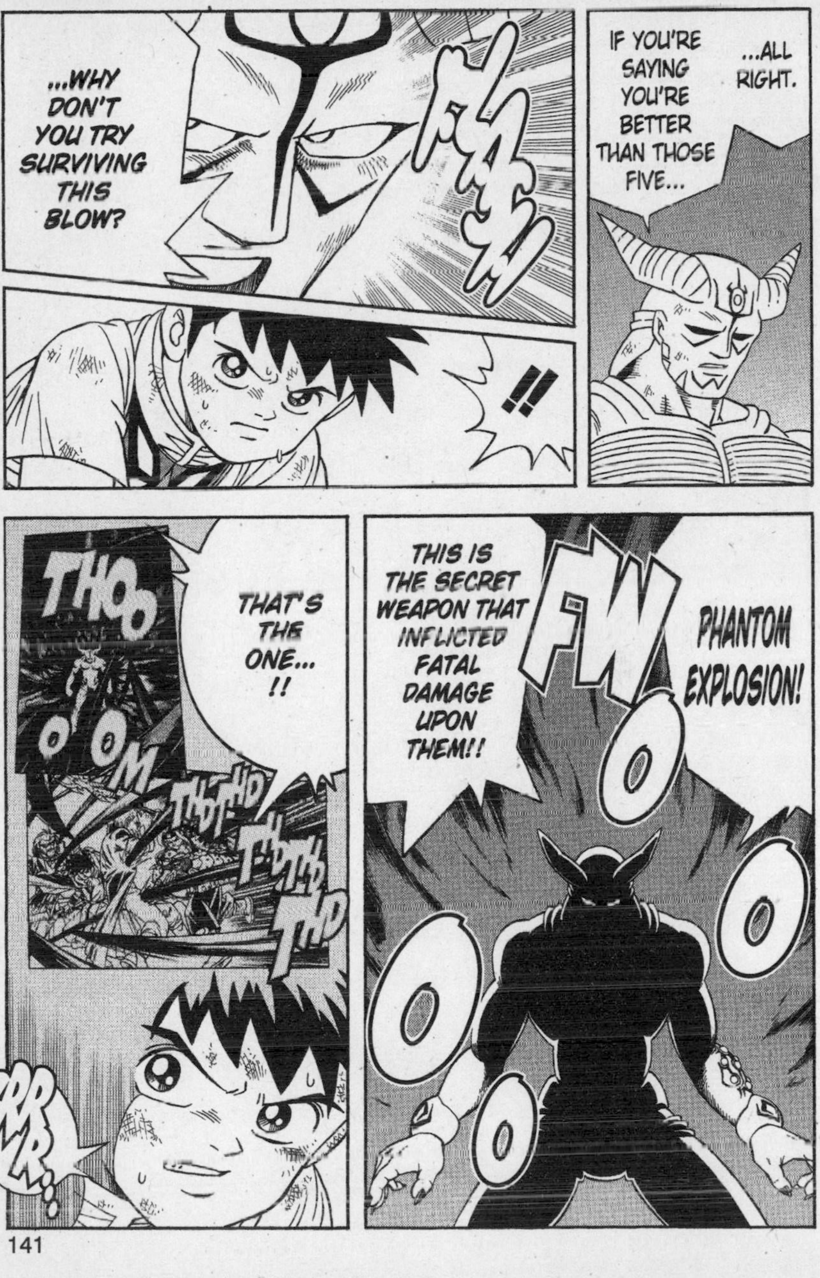
IF YOU'RE SAYING YOU'RE BETTER THAN THOSE FIVE...
...ALL RIGHT.
...WHY DON'T YOU TRY SURVIVING THIS BLOW?
!!
THIS IS THE SECRET WEAPON THAT INFLICTED FATAL DAMAGE UPON THEM!!
PHANTOM EXPLOSION!
THOOOOM
THD THD THD THD THD
THAT'S THE ONE... !!
GRRR...

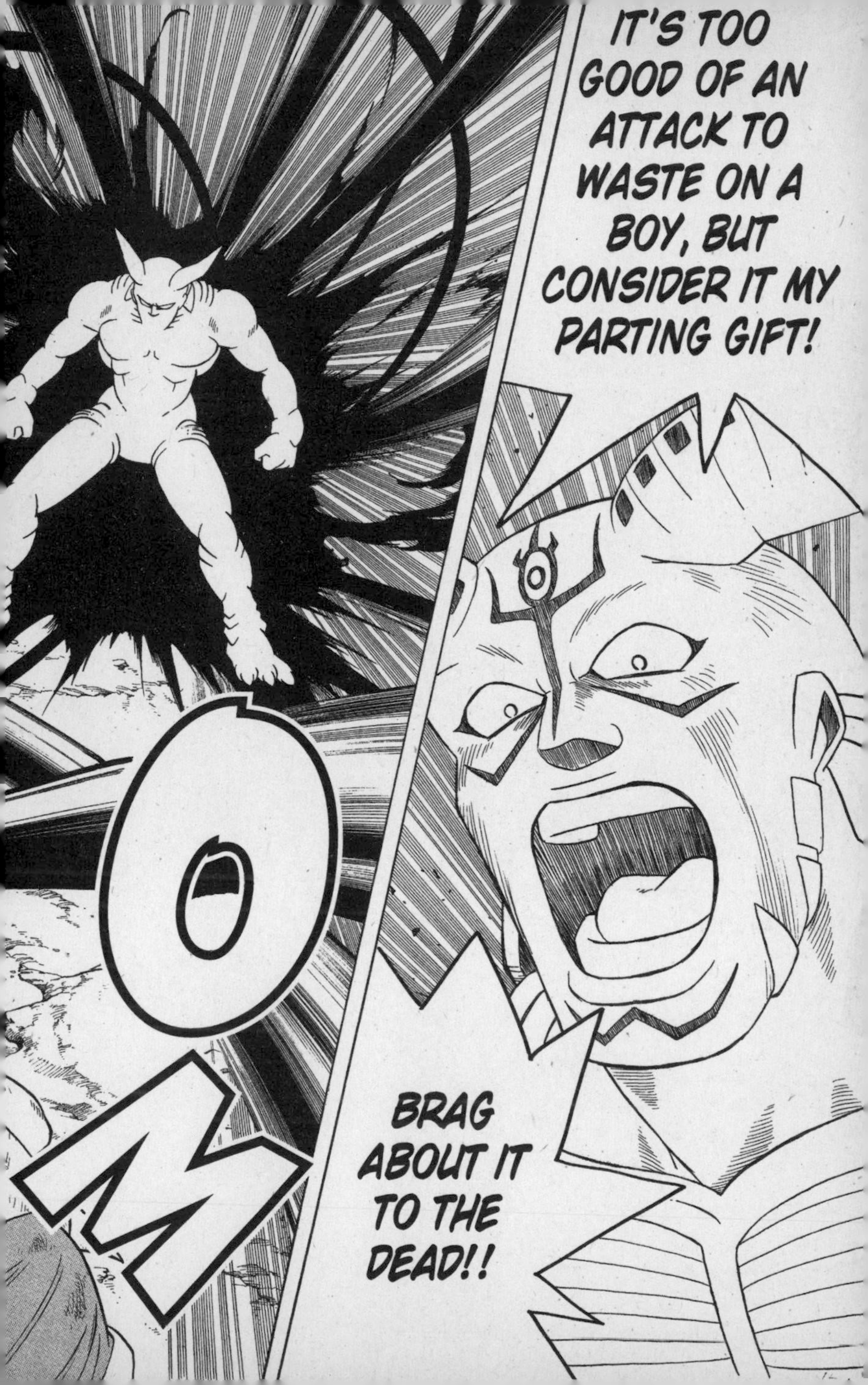
IT'S TOO GOOD OF AN ATTACK TO WASTE ON A BOY, BUT CONSIDER IT MY PARTING GIFT!
BRAG ABOUT IT TO THE DEAD!!
OOM

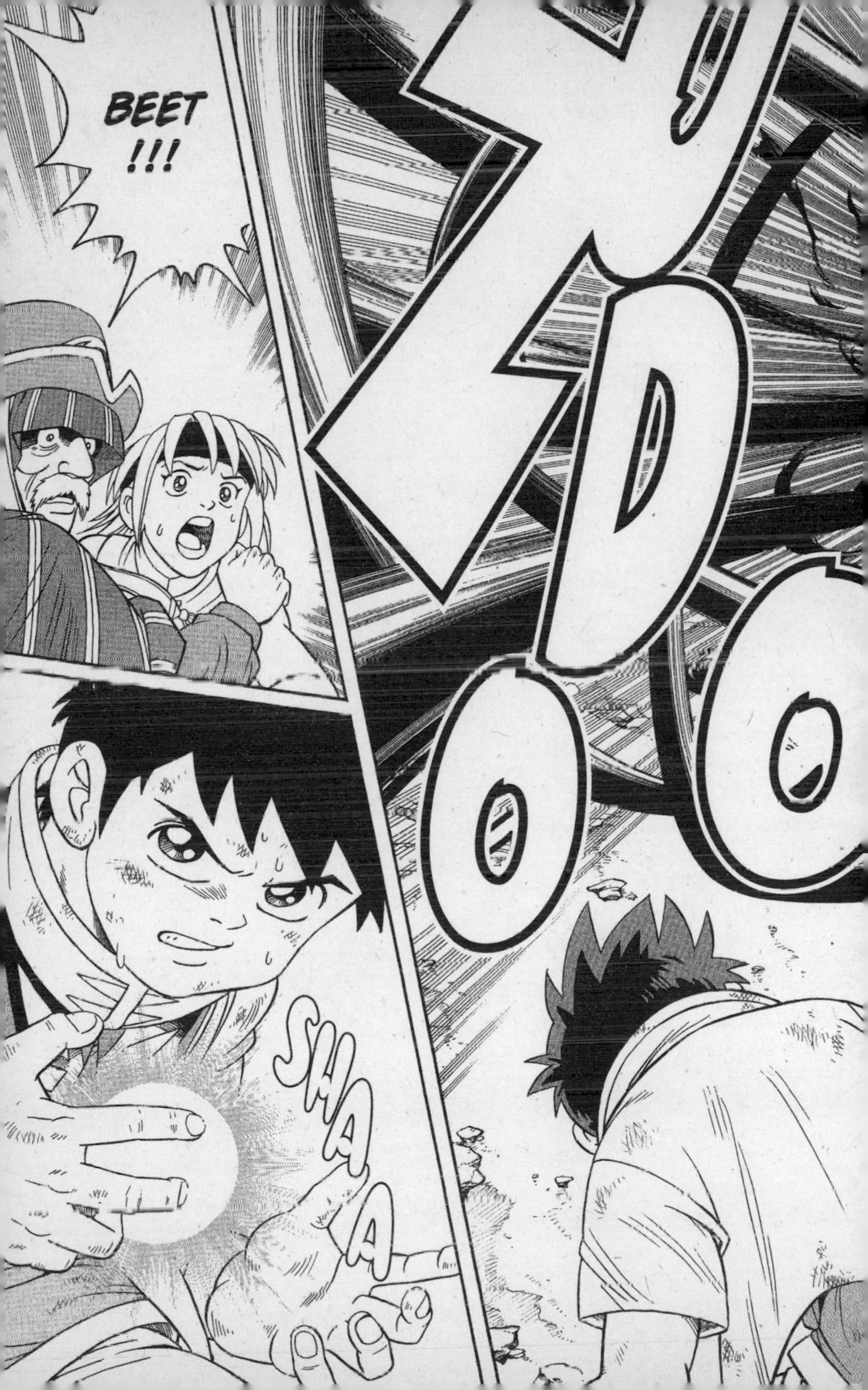
DOO
BEET !!!
SHAA

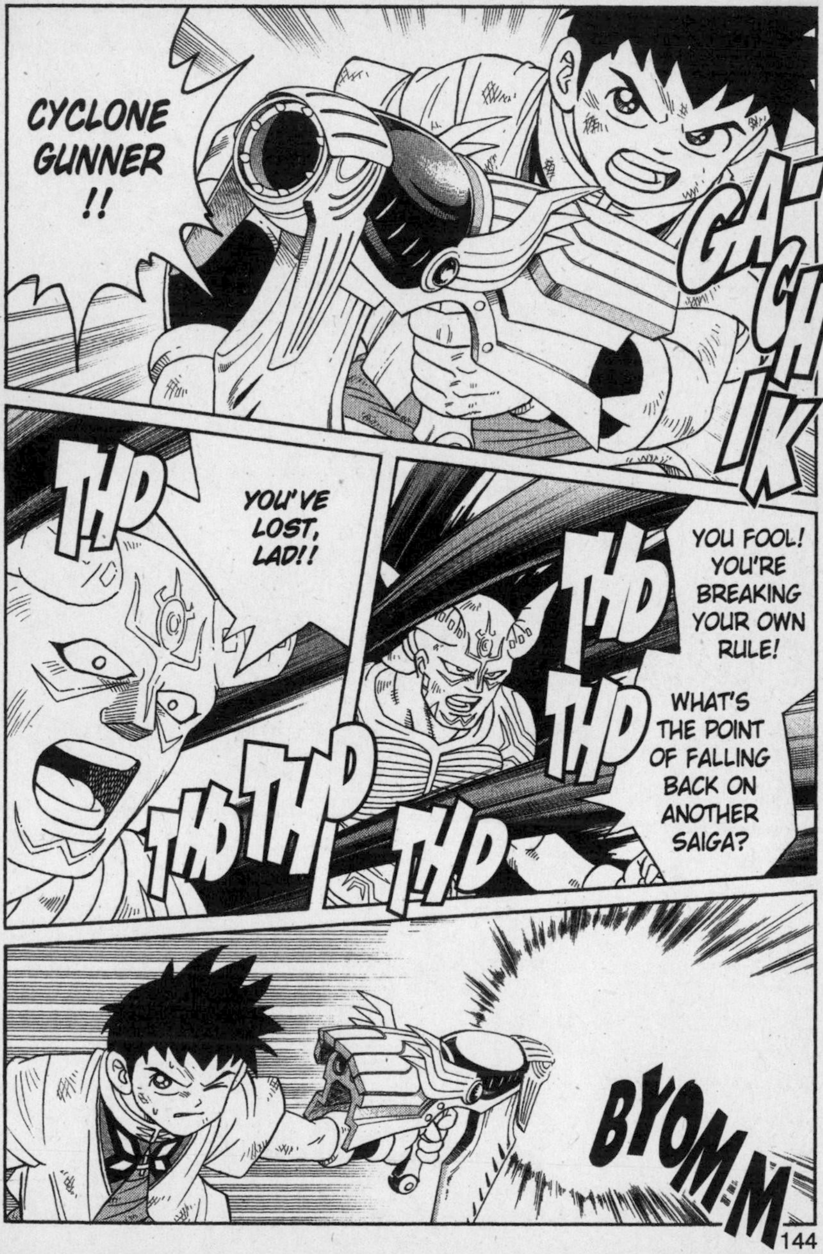
CYCLONE GUNNER!!
GACHIK
YOU FOOL! YOU'RE BREAKING YOUR OWN RULE!
WHAT'S THE POINT OF FALLING BACK ON ANOTHER SAIGA?
THD
THD
THD
THD
YOU'VE LOST, LAD!!
THD
THD
BYOMMM

READ THIS WAY

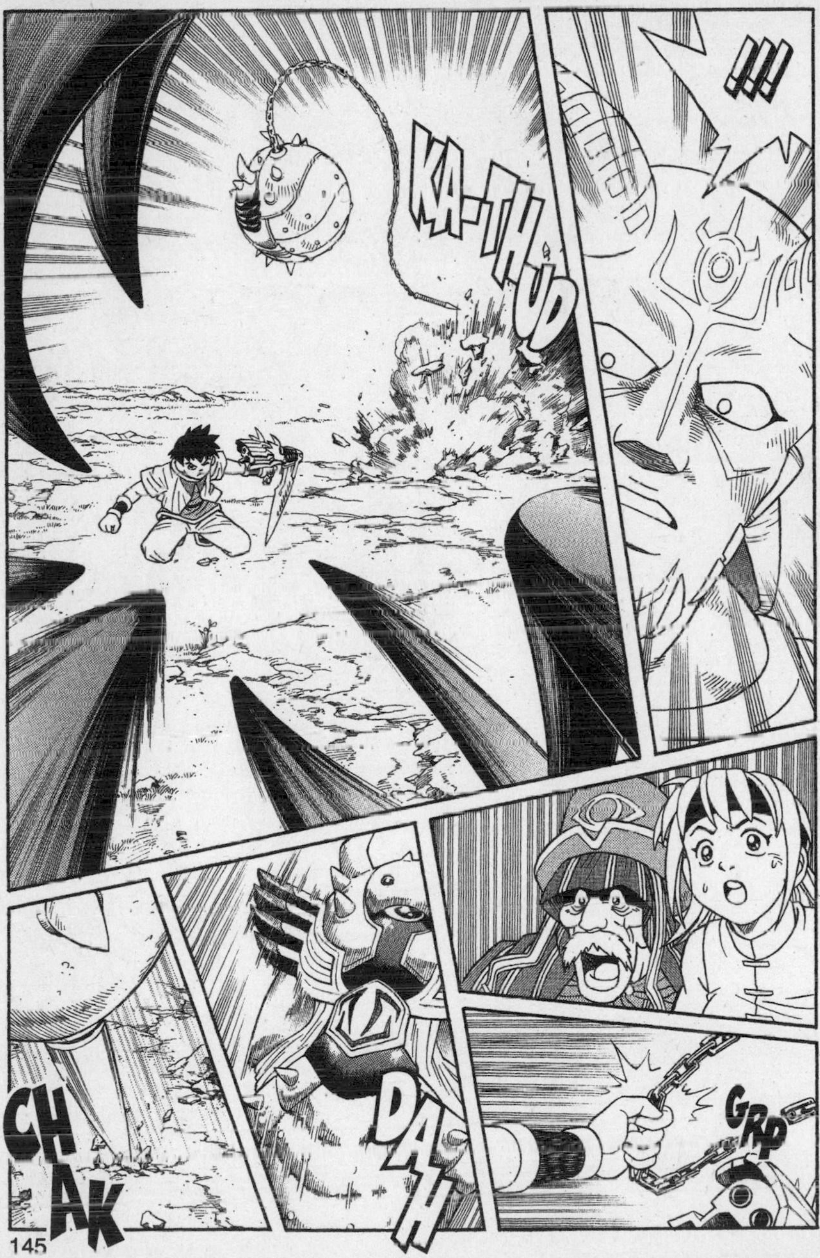
!!!
KA-THUD
GRP
DASH
CHAK

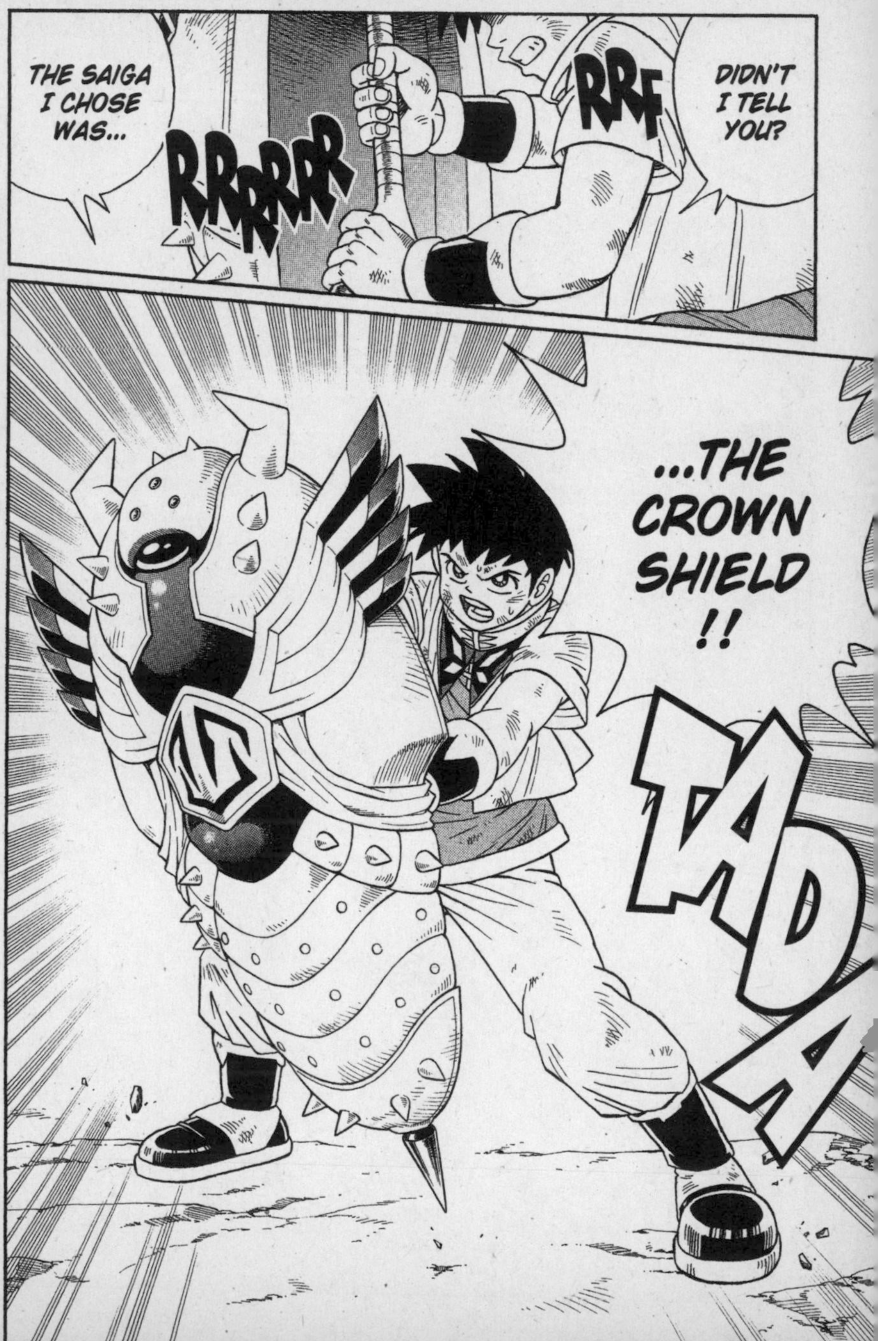
DIDN'T I TELL YOU?
RRF
RRRRRR
THE SAIGA I CHOSE WAS...
...THE CROWN SHIELD !!
TADA

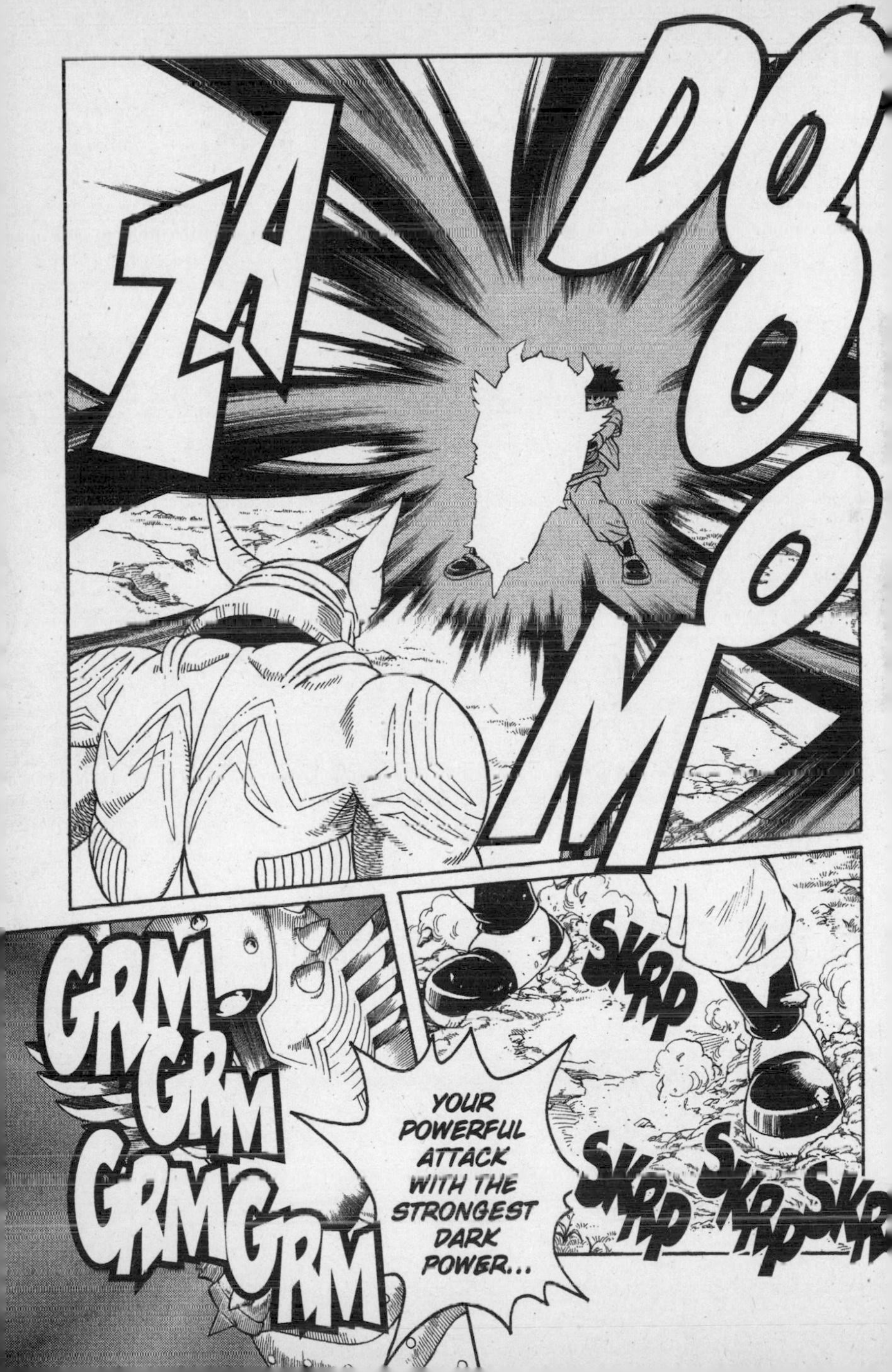
ZA
DOOOM
SKRP
SKRP SKRP SKRP SKR
GRM GRM GRM GRM GRM
YOUR POWERFUL ATTACK WITH THE STRONGEST DARK POWER...

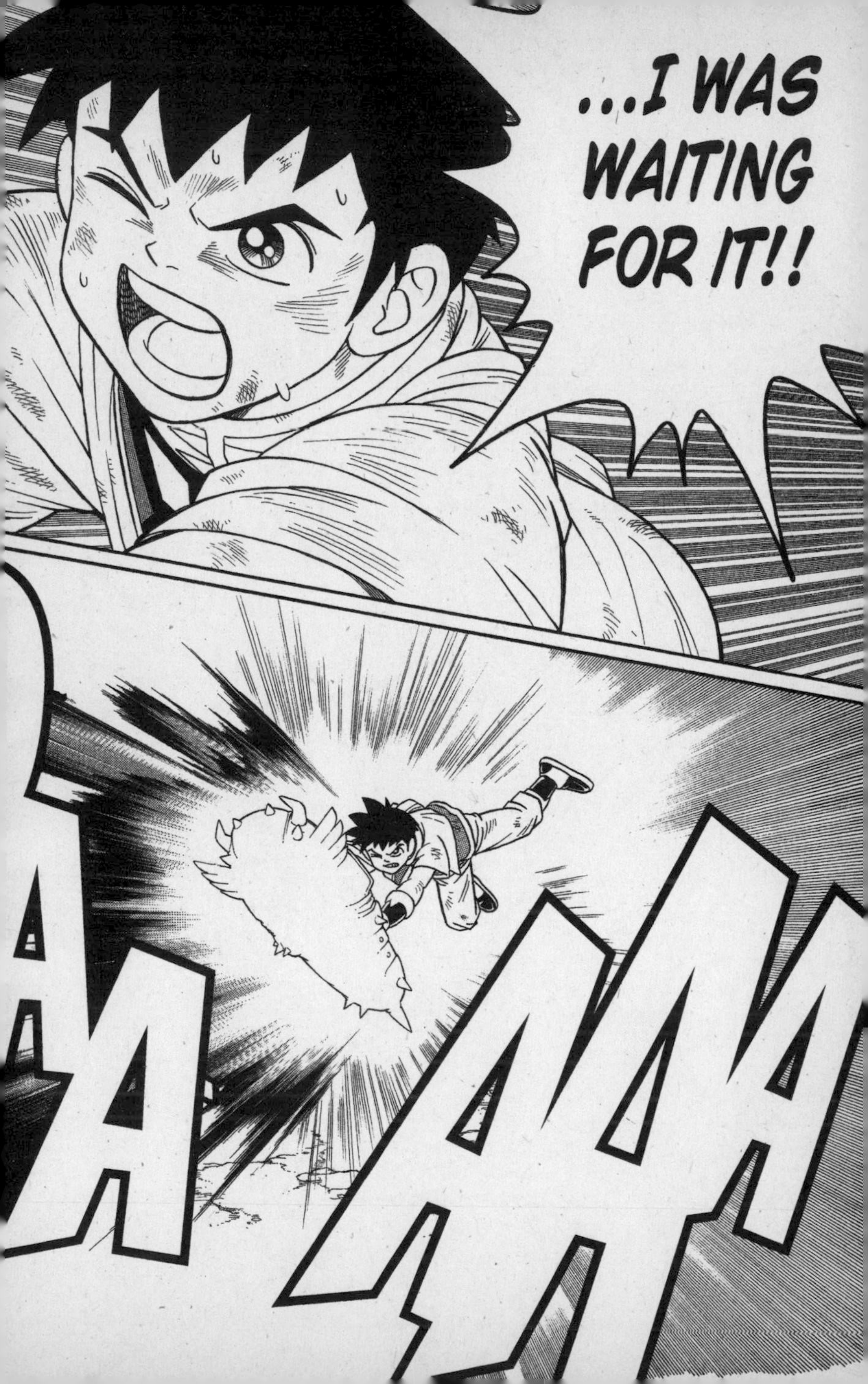
...I WAS WAITING FOR IT!!
AAAA

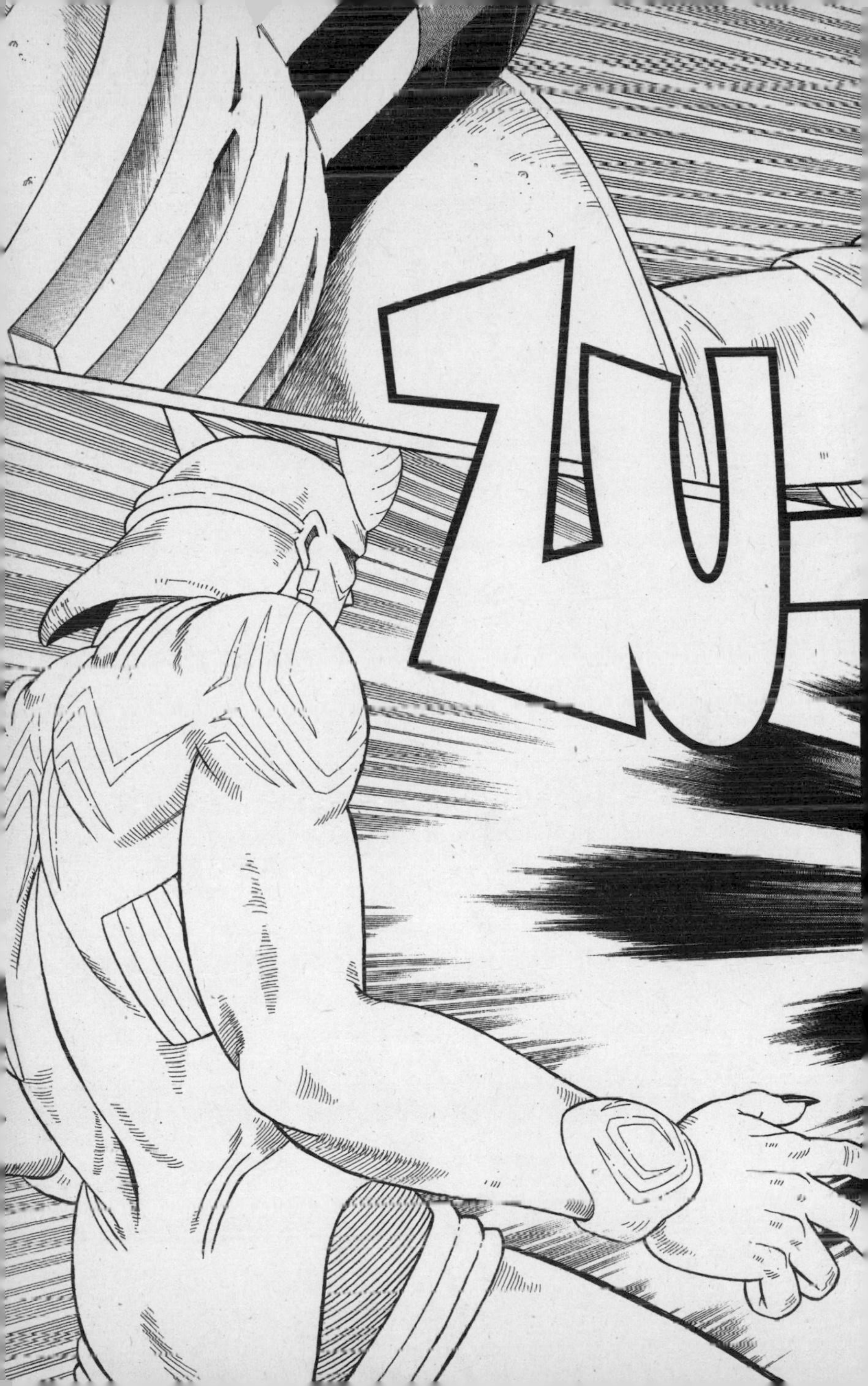
ZU

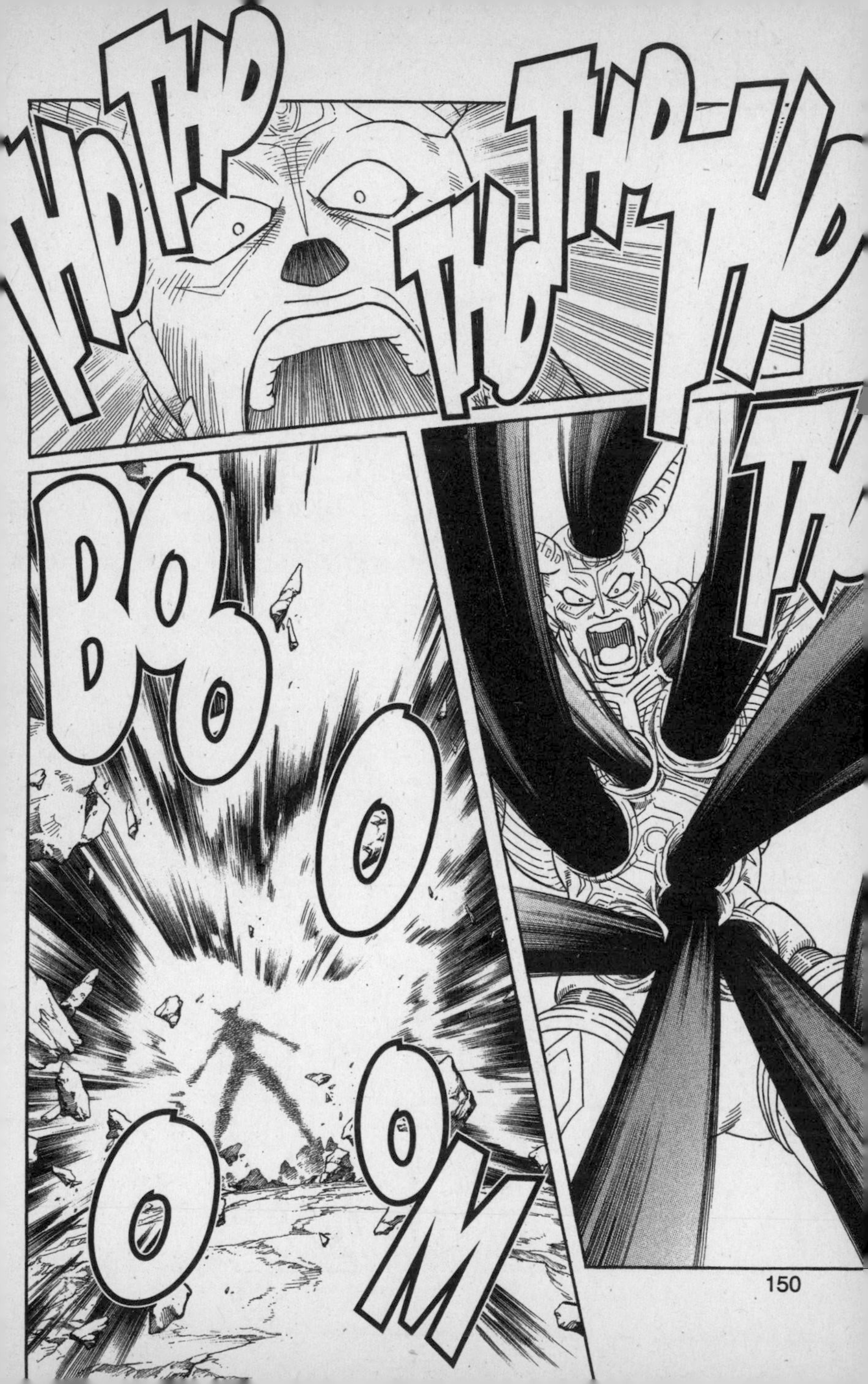
THD THD-THD-THD
THD THD
BOOOOM

READ THIS WAY

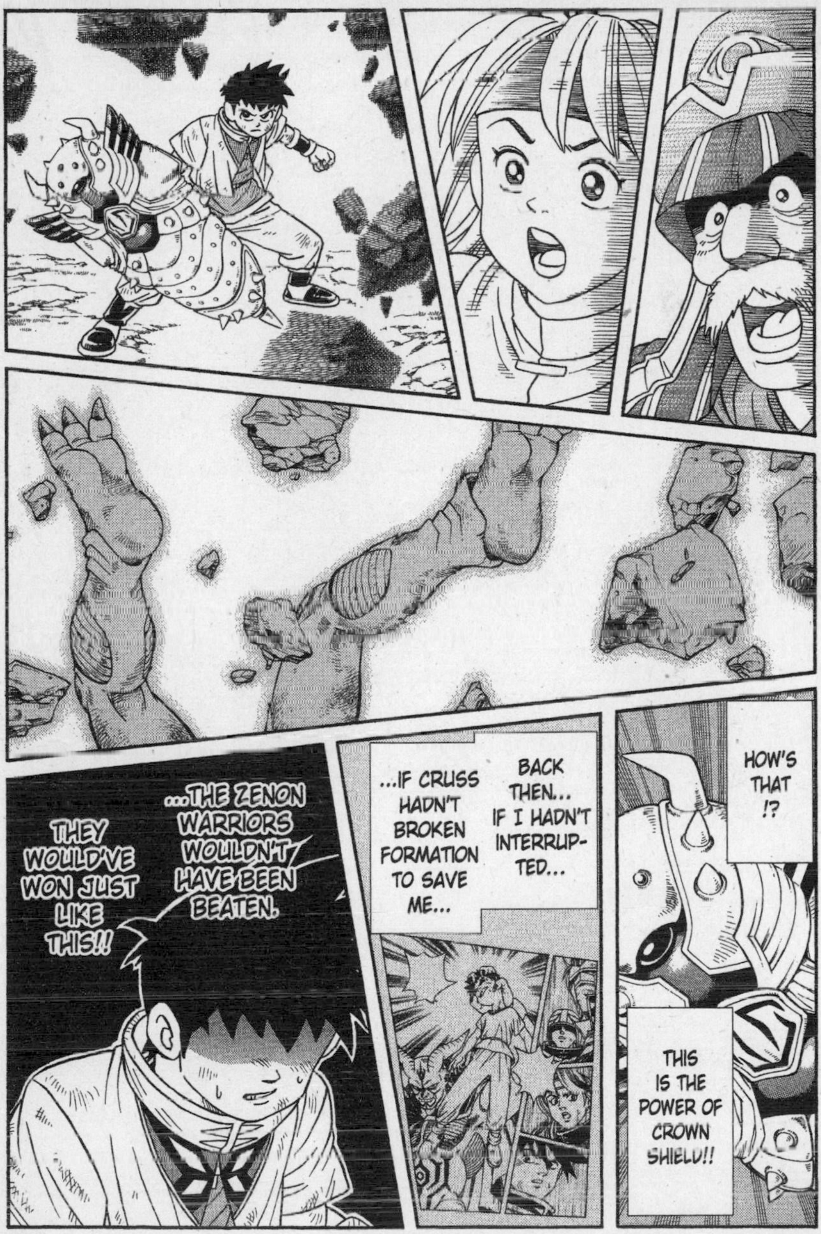
HOW'S THAT !?
THIS IS THE POWER OF CROWN SHIELD!!
BACK THEN... IF I HADN'T INTERRUP- TED...
...IF CRUSS HADN'T BROKEN FORMATION TO SAVE ME...
...THE ZENON WARRIORS WOULDN'T HAVE BEEN BEATEN.
THEY WOULD'VE WON JUST LIKE THIS!!

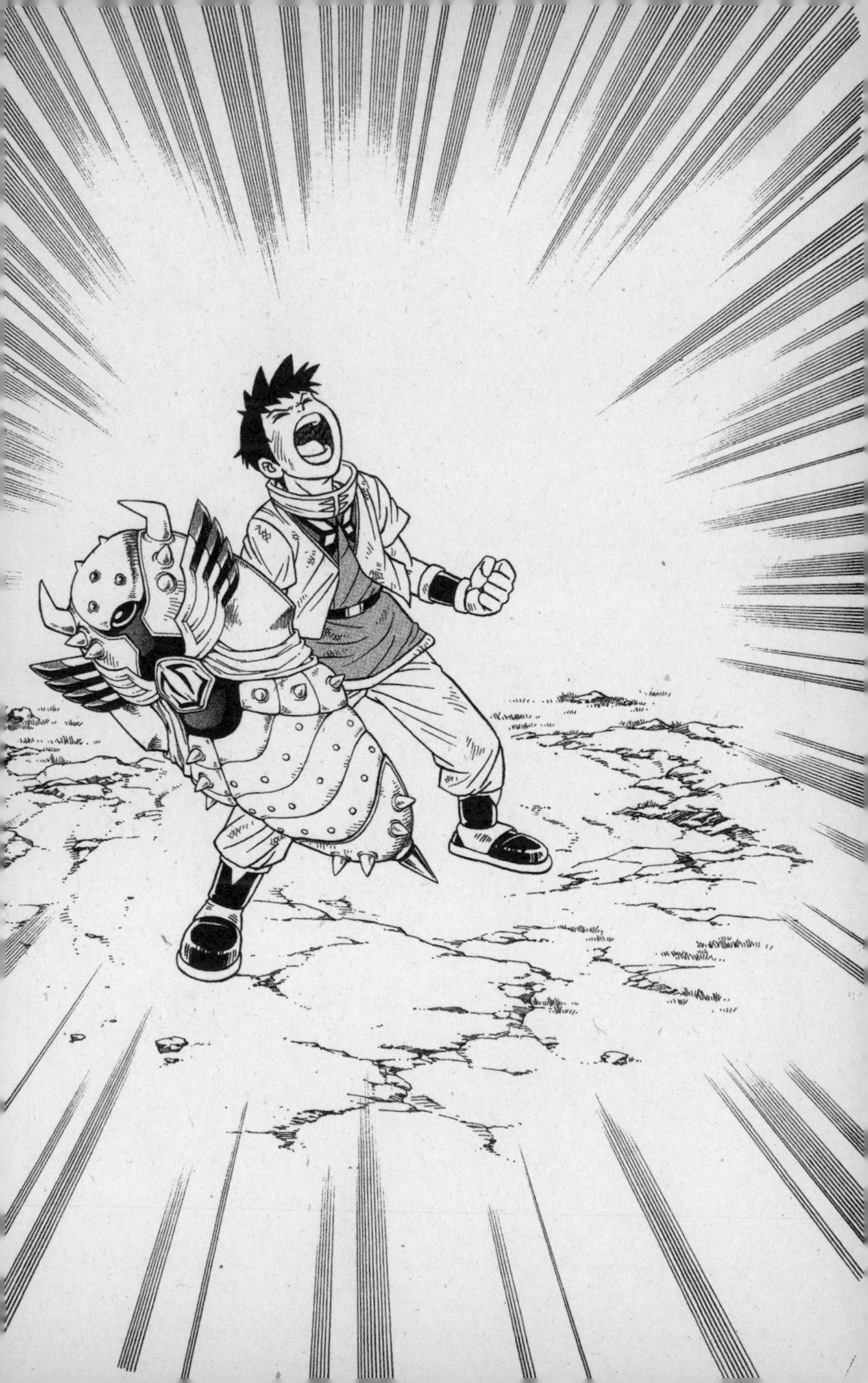

READ THIS WAY

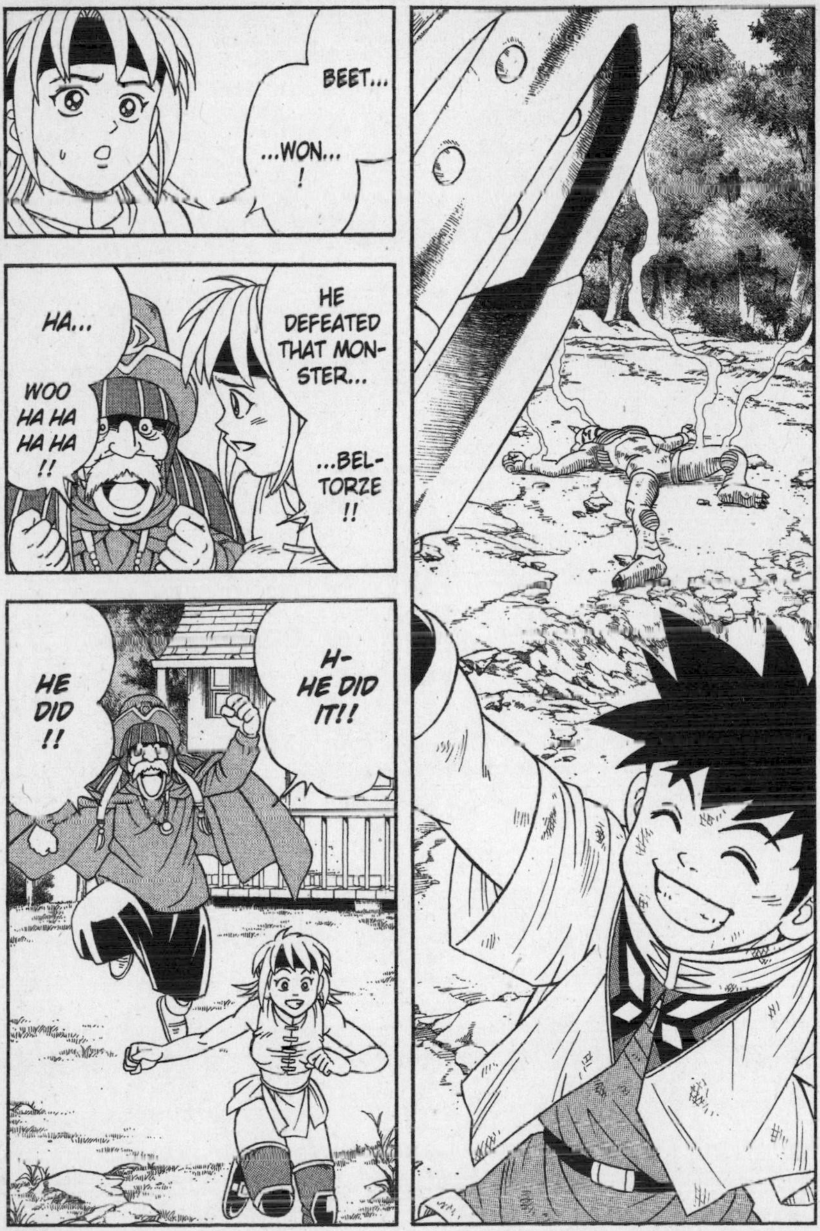
BEET...
...WON...!
HE DEFEATED THAT MON-STER...
...BEL-TORZE!!
HA...
WOO HA HA HA HA!!
H-HE DID IT!!
HE DID!!

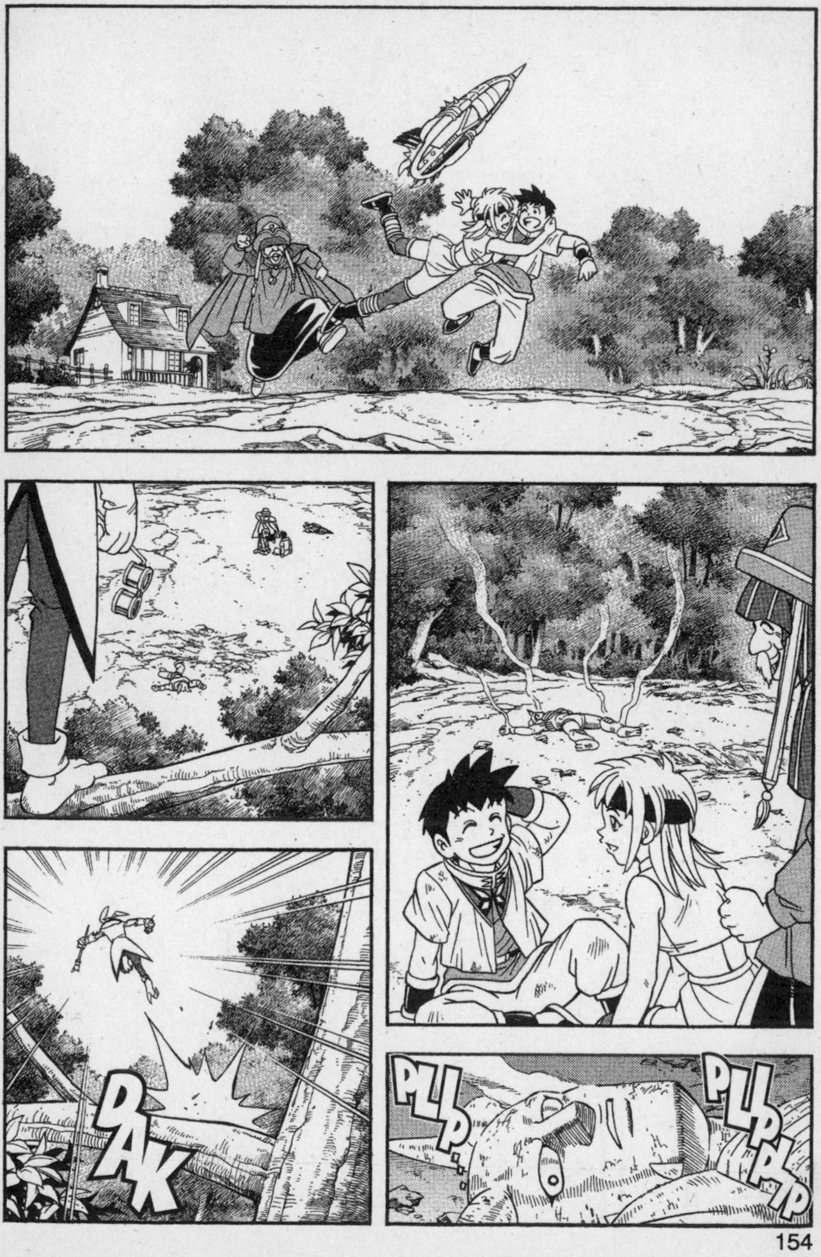
PLIPIPIP
PLIP...
DAK

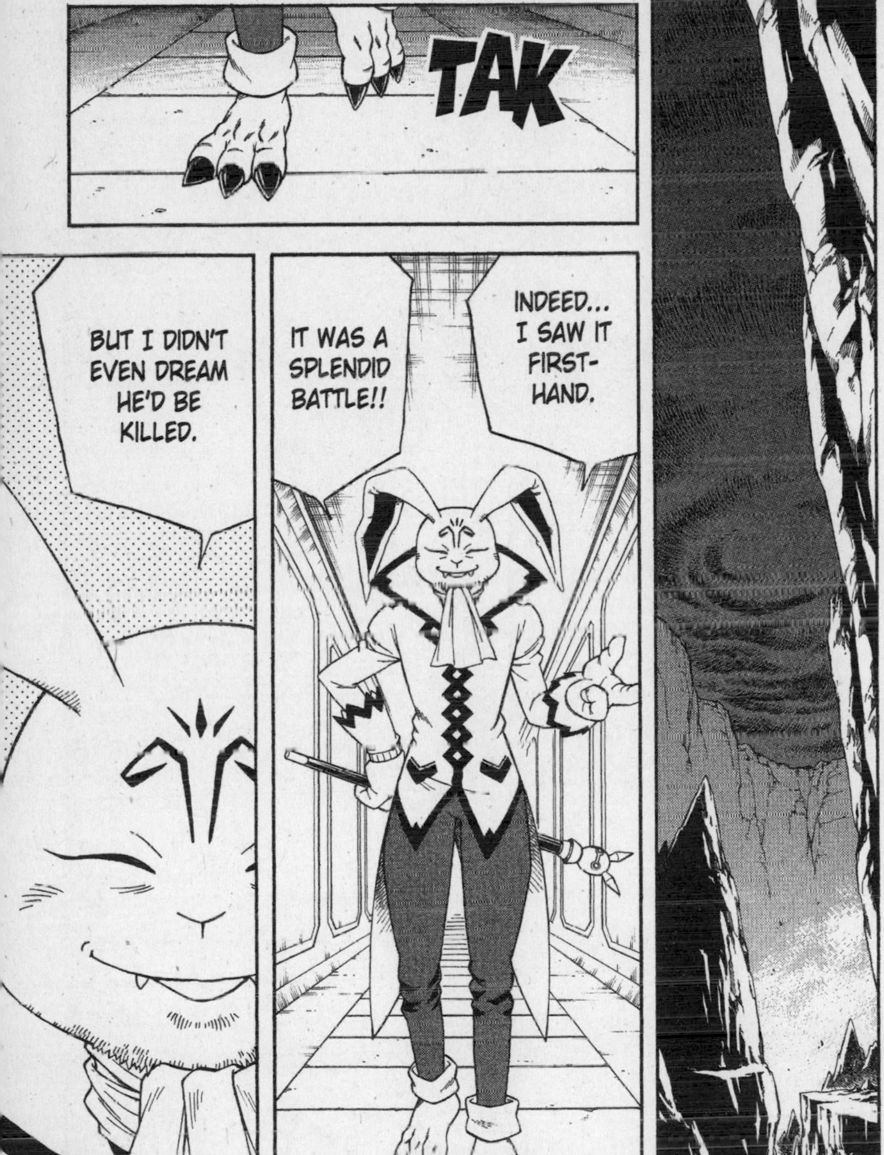
TAK
INDEED... I SAW IT FIRST-HAND.
IT WAS A SPLENDID BATTLE!!
BUT I DIDN'T EVEN DREAM HE'D BE KILLED.

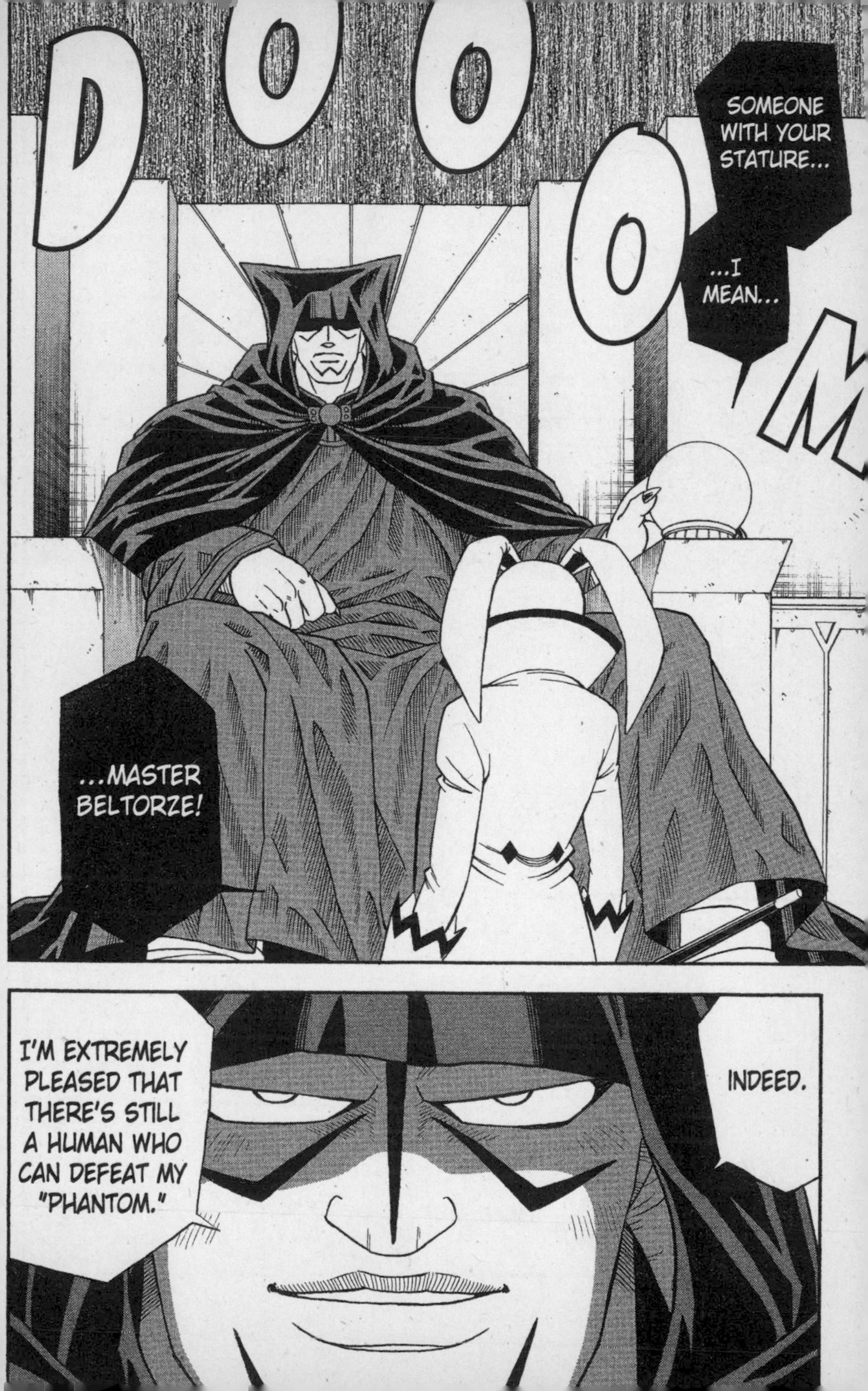
SOMEONE WITH YOUR STATURE...
...I MEAN...
DOOOOM
...MASTER BELTORZE!
INDEED.
I'M EXTREMELY PLEASED THAT THERE'S STILL A HUMAN WHO CAN DEFEAT MY "PHANTOM."

READ THIS WAY

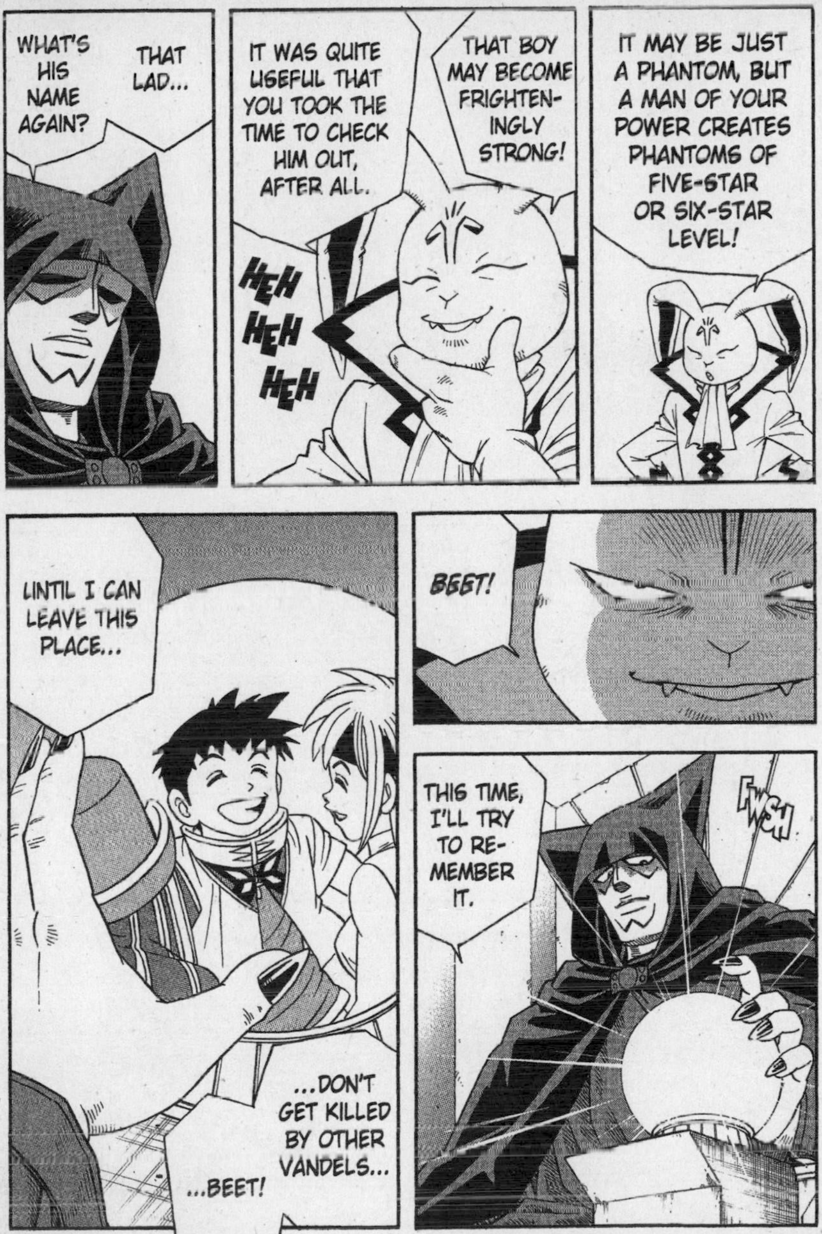
IT MAY BE JUST A PHANTOM, BUT A MAN OF YOUR POWER CREATES PHANTOMS OF FIVE-STAR OR SIX-STAR LEVEL!
THAT BOY MAY BECOME FRIGHTEN-INGLY STRONG!
IT WAS QUITE USEFUL THAT YOU TOOK THE TIME TO CHECK HIM OUT, AFTER ALL.
HEH HEH HEH
THAT LAD...
WHAT'S HIS NAME AGAIN?
BEET!
THIS TIME, I'LL TRY TO RE-MEMBER IT.
FWSH
UNTIL I CAN LEAVE THIS PLACE...
...DON'T GET KILLED BY OTHER VANDELS...
...BEET!

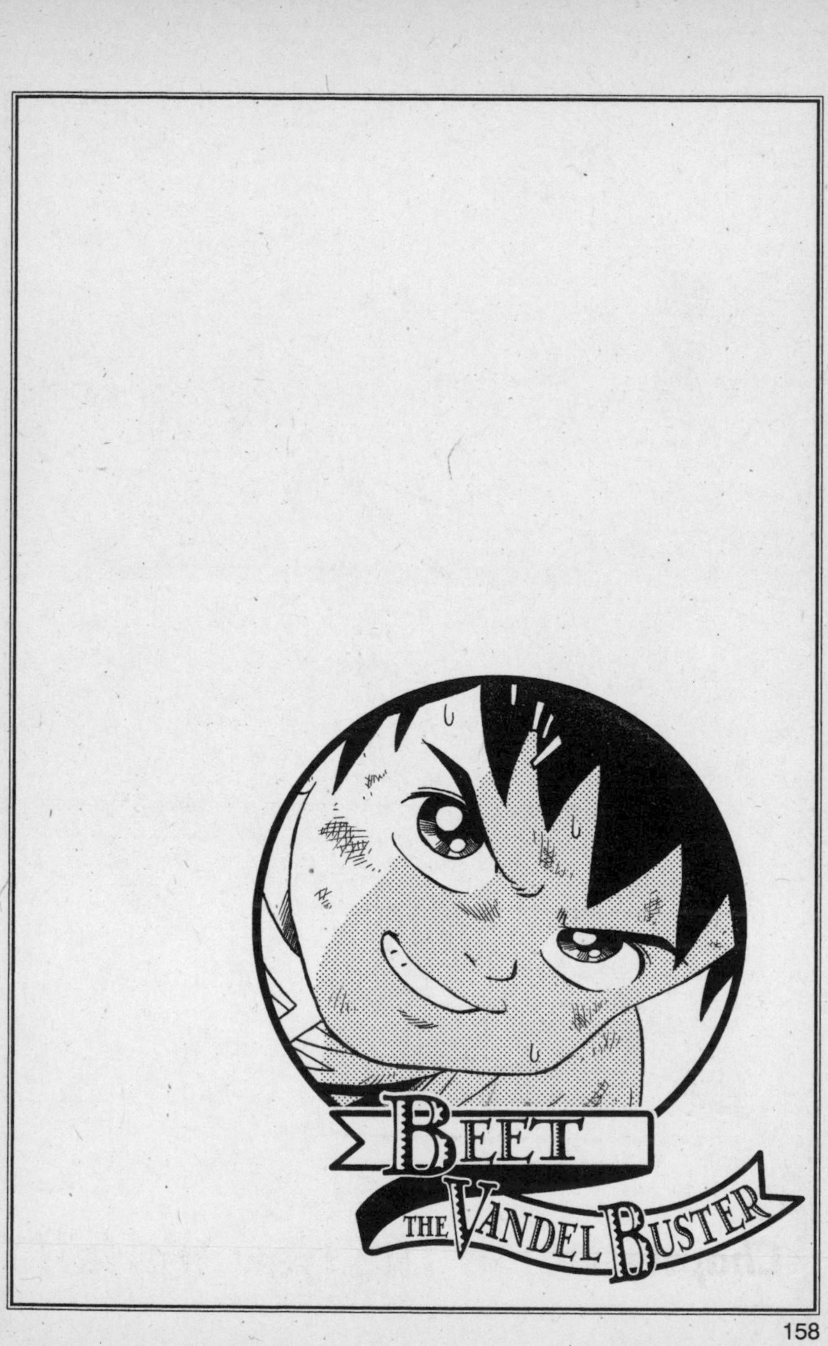
BEET
THE VANDEL BUSTER

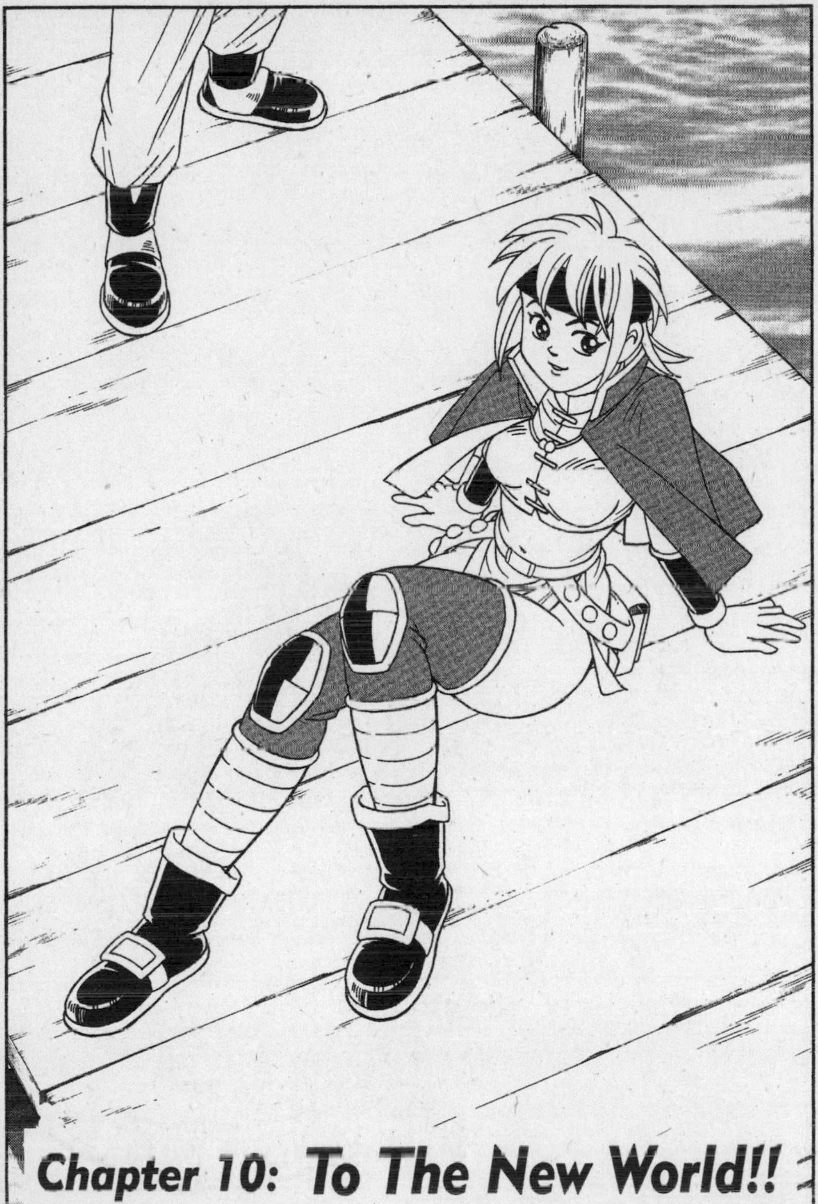
Chapter 10: To The New World!!

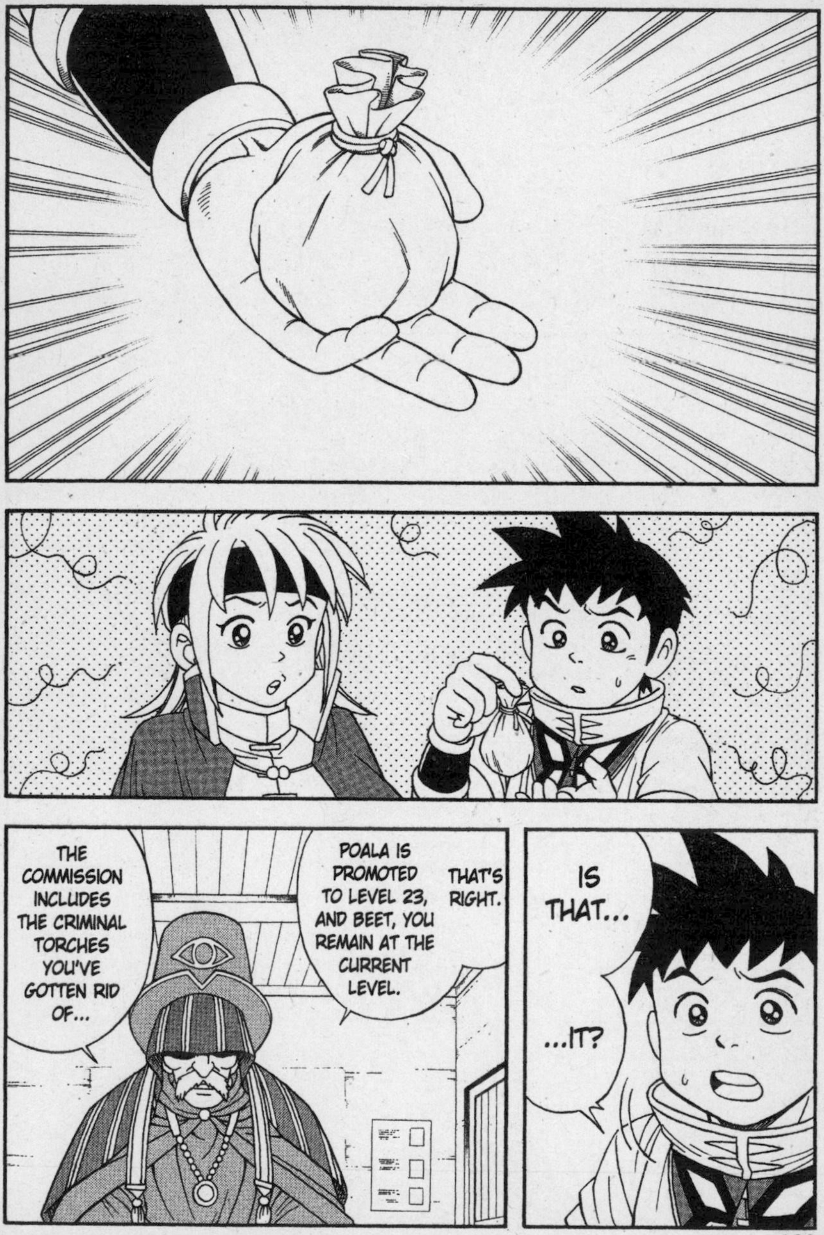
IS THAT...
...IT?
THAT'S RIGHT.
POALA IS PROMOTED TO LEVEL 23, AND BEET, YOU REMAIN AT THE CURRENT LEVEL.
THE COMMISSION INCLUDES THE CRIMINAL TORCHES YOU'VE GOTTEN RID OF...

READ THIS WAY

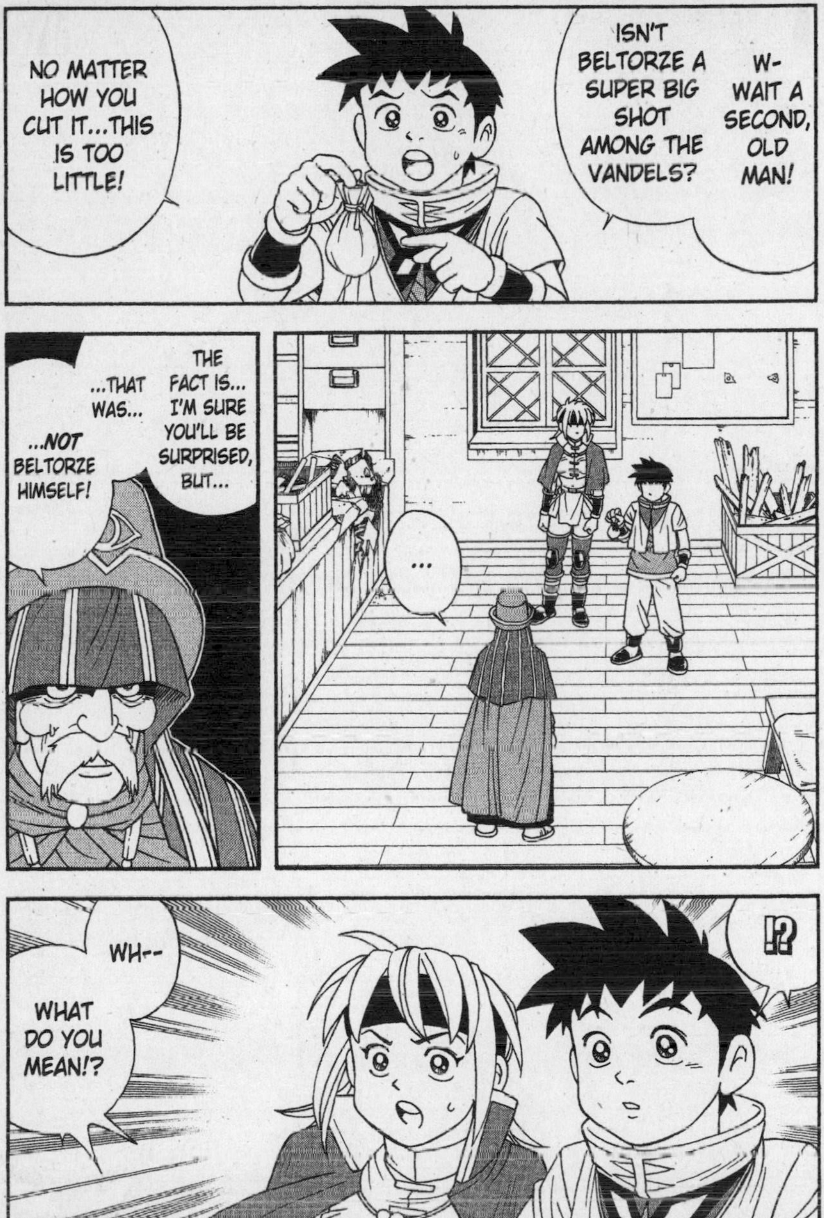
W- WAIT A SECOND, OLD MAN!
ISN'T BELTORZE A SUPER BIG SHOT AMONG THE VANDELS?
NO MATTER HOW YOU CUT IT...THIS IS TOO LITTLE!
...
THE FACT IS... I'M SURE YOU'LL BE SURPRISED, BUT...
...THAT WAS...
...*NOT* BELTORZE HIMSELF!
!?
WH-- WHAT DO YOU MEAN!?

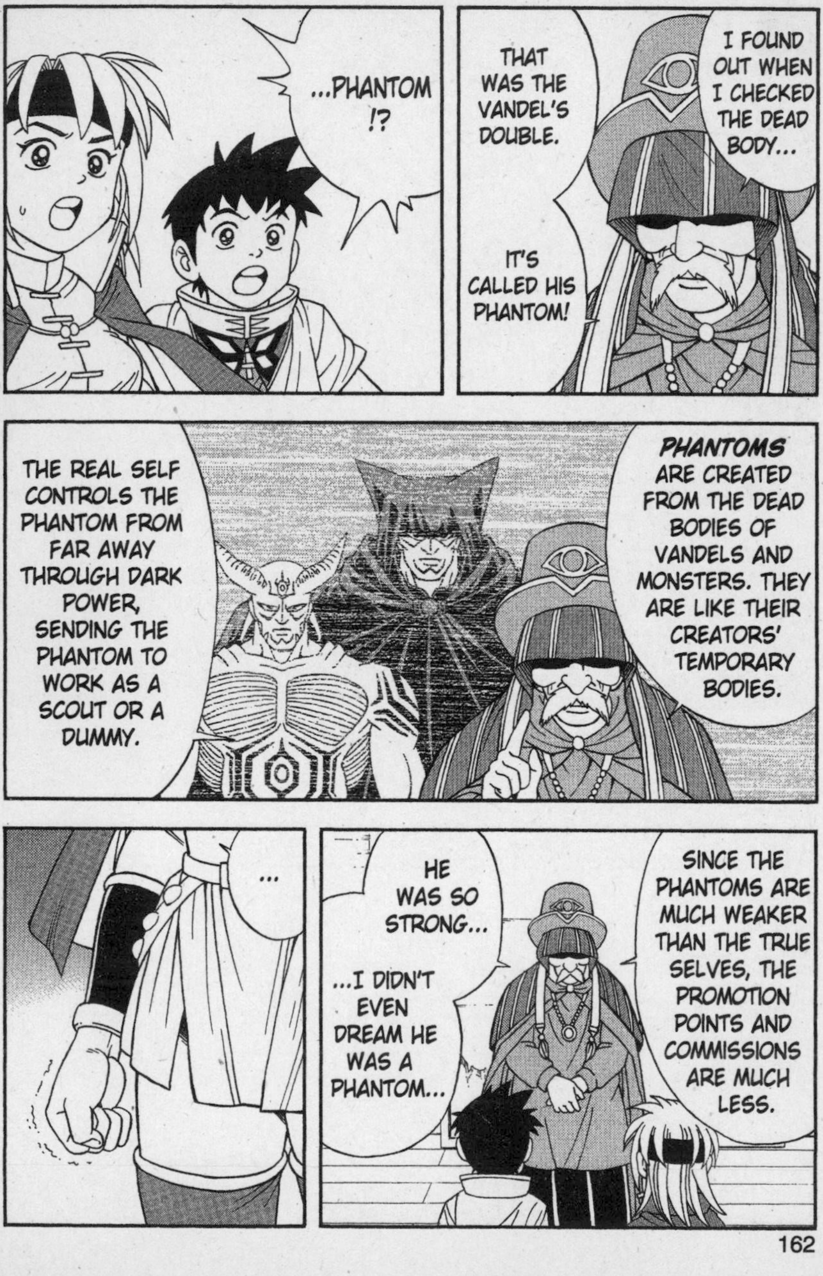
I FOUND OUT WHEN I CHECKED THE DEAD BODY...
THAT WAS THE VANDEL'S DOUBLE.
IT'S CALLED HIS PHANTOM!
...PHANTOM !?
PHANTOMS ARE CREATED FROM THE DEAD BODIES OF VANDELS AND MONSTERS. THEY ARE LIKE THEIR CREATORS' TEMPORARY BODIES.
THE REAL SELF CONTROLS THE PHANTOM FROM FAR AWAY THROUGH DARK POWER, SENDING THE PHANTOM TO WORK AS A SCOUT OR A DUMMY.
SINCE THE PHANTOMS ARE MUCH WEAKER THAN THE TRUE SELVES, THE PROMOTION POINTS AND COMMISSIONS ARE MUCH LESS.
HE WAS SO STRONG...
...I DIDN'T EVEN DREAM HE WAS A PHANTOM...
...

READ THIS WAY

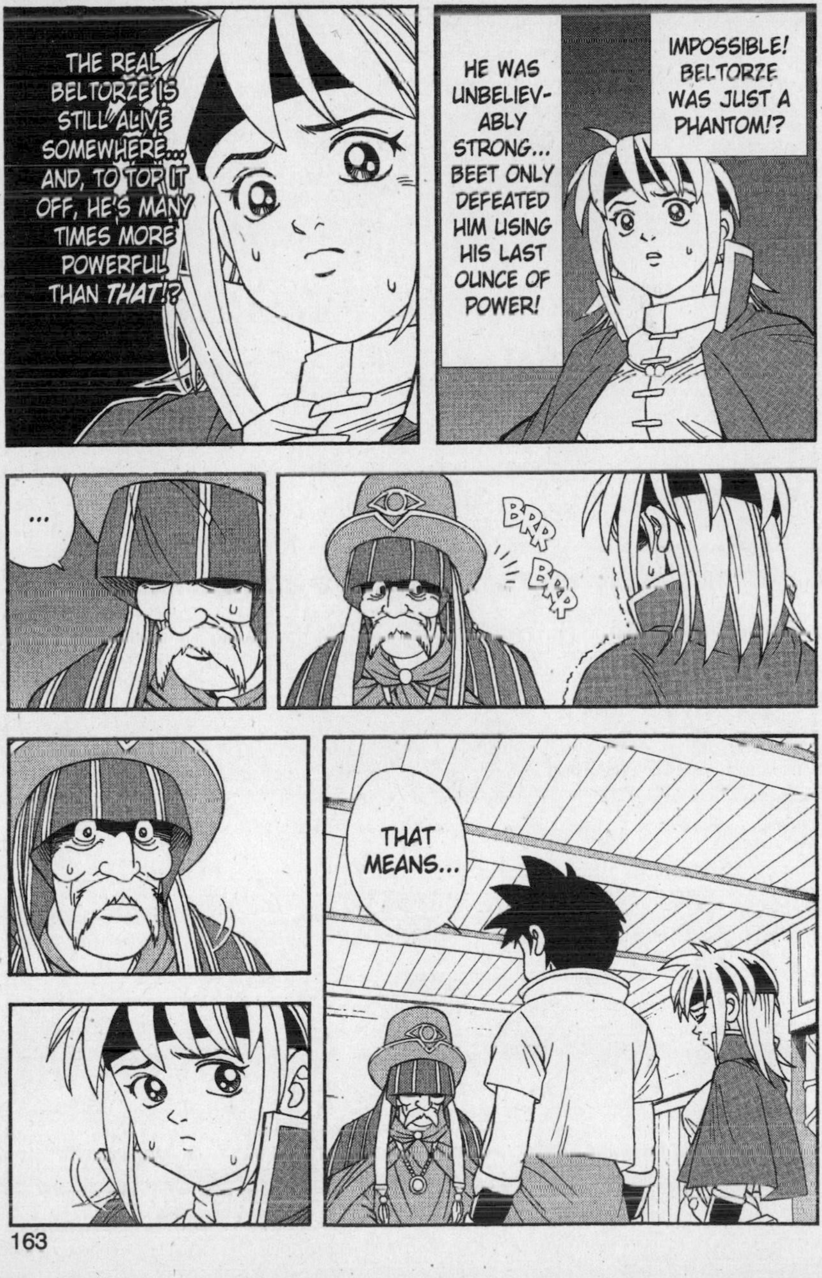
IMPOSSIBLE! BELTORZE WAS JUST A PHANTOM!?
HE WAS UNBELIEV-ABLY STRONG... BEET ONLY DEFEATED HIM USING HIS LAST OUNCE OF POWER!
THE REAL BELTORZE IS STILL ALIVE SOMEWHERE... AND, TO TOP IT OFF, HE'S MANY TIMES MORE POWERFUL THAN *THAT*!?
BRR
BRR
...
THAT MEANS...

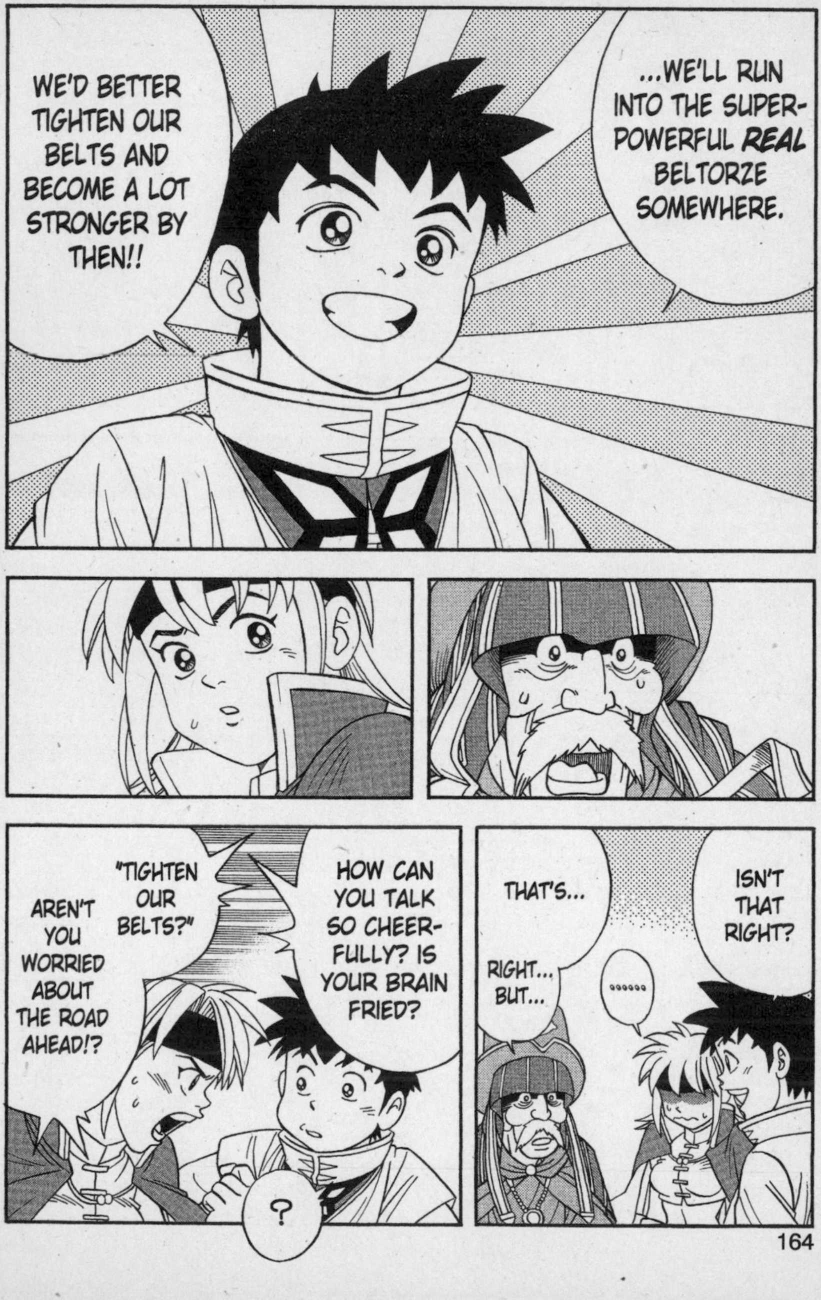
...WE'LL RUN INTO THE SUPER-POWERFUL *REAL* BELTORZE SOMEWHERE.
WE'D BETTER TIGHTEN OUR BELTS AND BECOME A LOT STRONGER BY THEN!!
ISN'T THAT RIGHT?
THAT'S...
......
RIGHT... BUT...
HOW CAN YOU TALK SO CHEER-FULLY? IS YOUR BRAIN FRIED?
"TIGHTEN OUR BELTS?"
AREN'T YOU WORRIED ABOUT THE ROAD AHEAD!?
?

READ THIS WAY

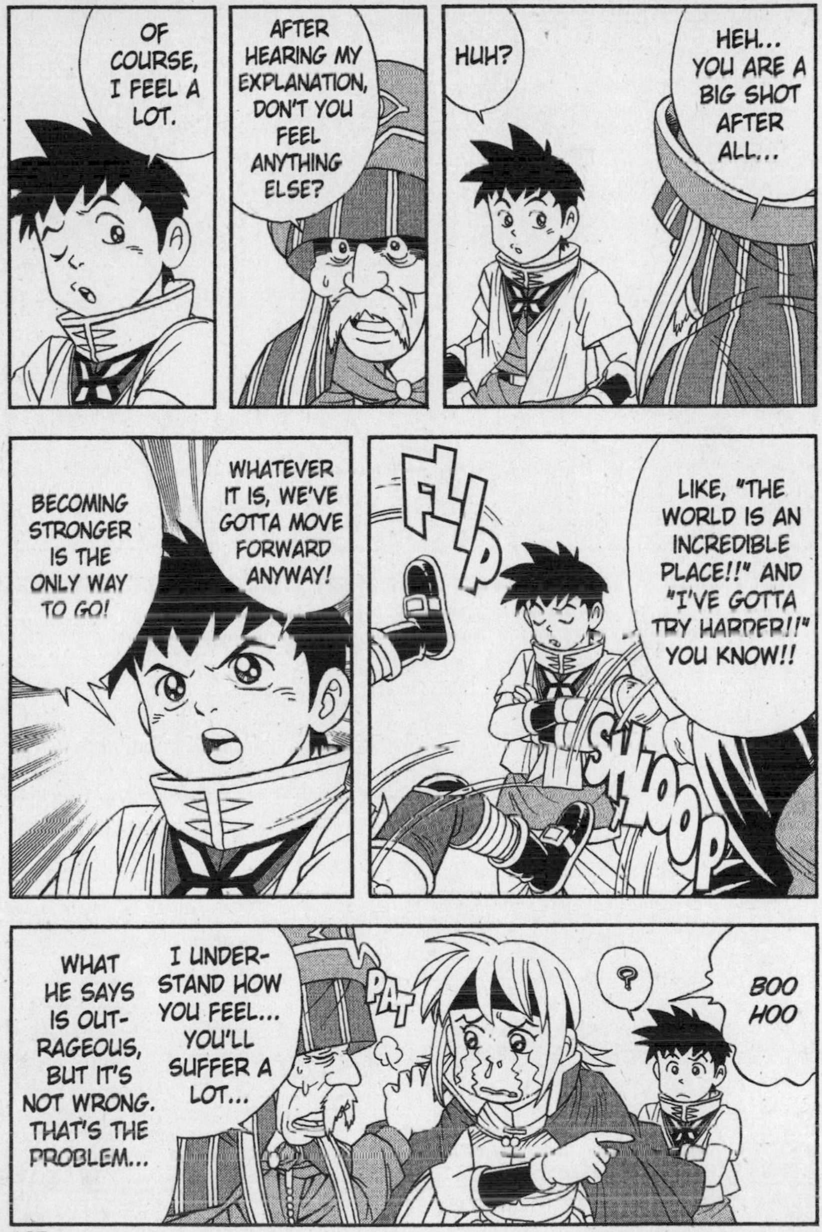
HEH... YOU ARE A BIG SHOT AFTER ALL...
HUH?
AFTER HEARING MY EXPLANATION, DON'T YOU FEEL ANYTHING ELSE?
OF COURSE, I FEEL A LOT.
LIKE, "THE WORLD IS AN INCREDIBLE PLACE!!" AND "I'VE GOTTA TRY HARDER!!" YOU KNOW!!
FLIP
SHOOOP
WHATEVER IT IS, WE'VE GOTTA MOVE FORWARD ANYWAY!
BECOMING STRONGER IS THE ONLY WAY TO GO!
BOO HOO
?
PAT
I UNDER-STAND HOW YOU FEEL... YOU'LL SUFFER A LOT...
WHAT HE SAYS IS OUT-RAGEOUS, BUT IT'S NOT WRONG. THAT'S THE PROBLEM...

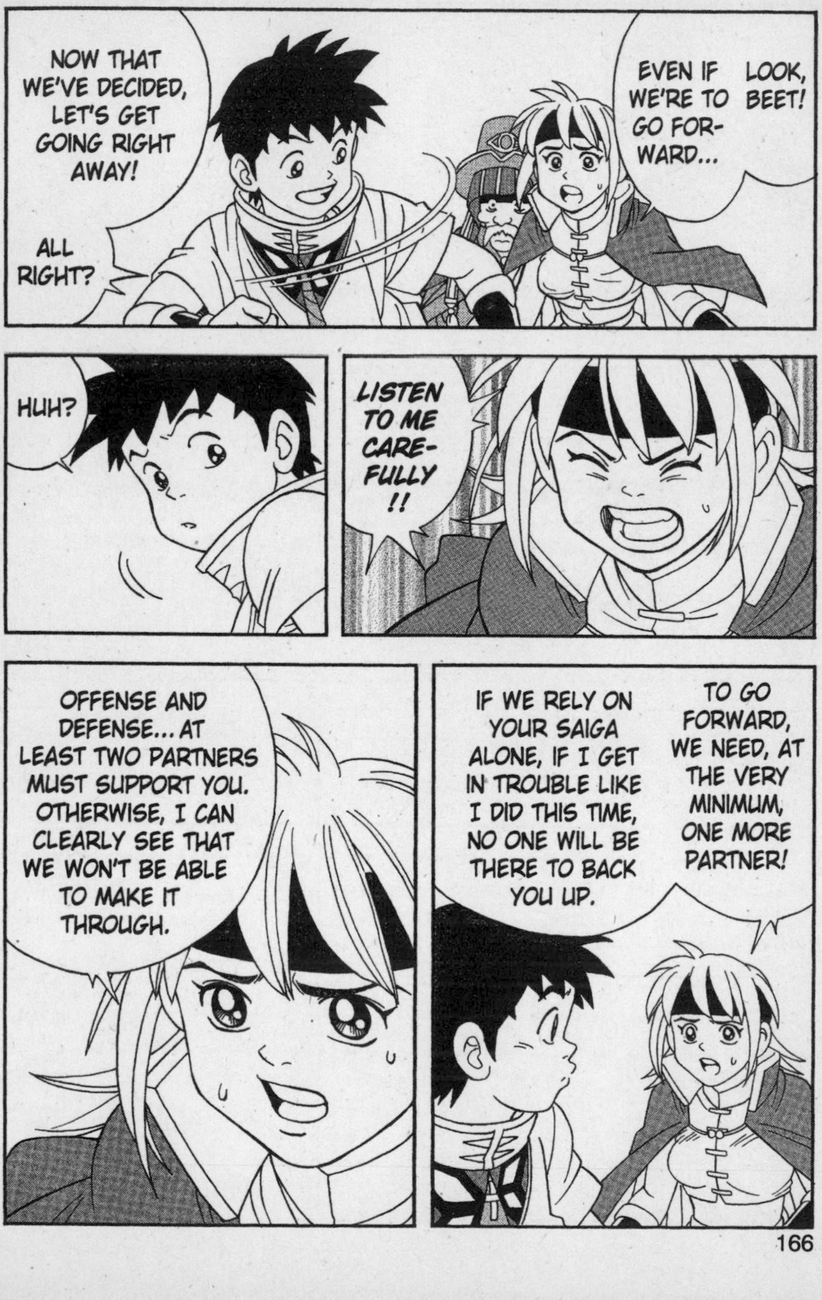
LOOK, BEET!
EVEN IF WE'RE TO GO FORWARD...
NOW THAT WE'VE DECIDED, LET'S GET GOING RIGHT AWAY!
ALL RIGHT?
LISTEN TO ME CAREFULLY!!
HUH?
TO GO FORWARD, WE NEED, AT THE VERY MINIMUM, ONE MORE PARTNER!
IF WE RELY ON YOUR SAIGA ALONE, IF I GET IN TROUBLE LIKE I DID THIS TIME, NO ONE WILL BE THERE TO BACK YOU UP.
OFFENSE AND DEFENSE... AT LEAST TWO PARTNERS MUST SUPPORT YOU. OTHERWISE, I CAN CLEARLY SEE THAT WE WON'T BE ABLE TO MAKE IT THROUGH.

READ THIS WAY

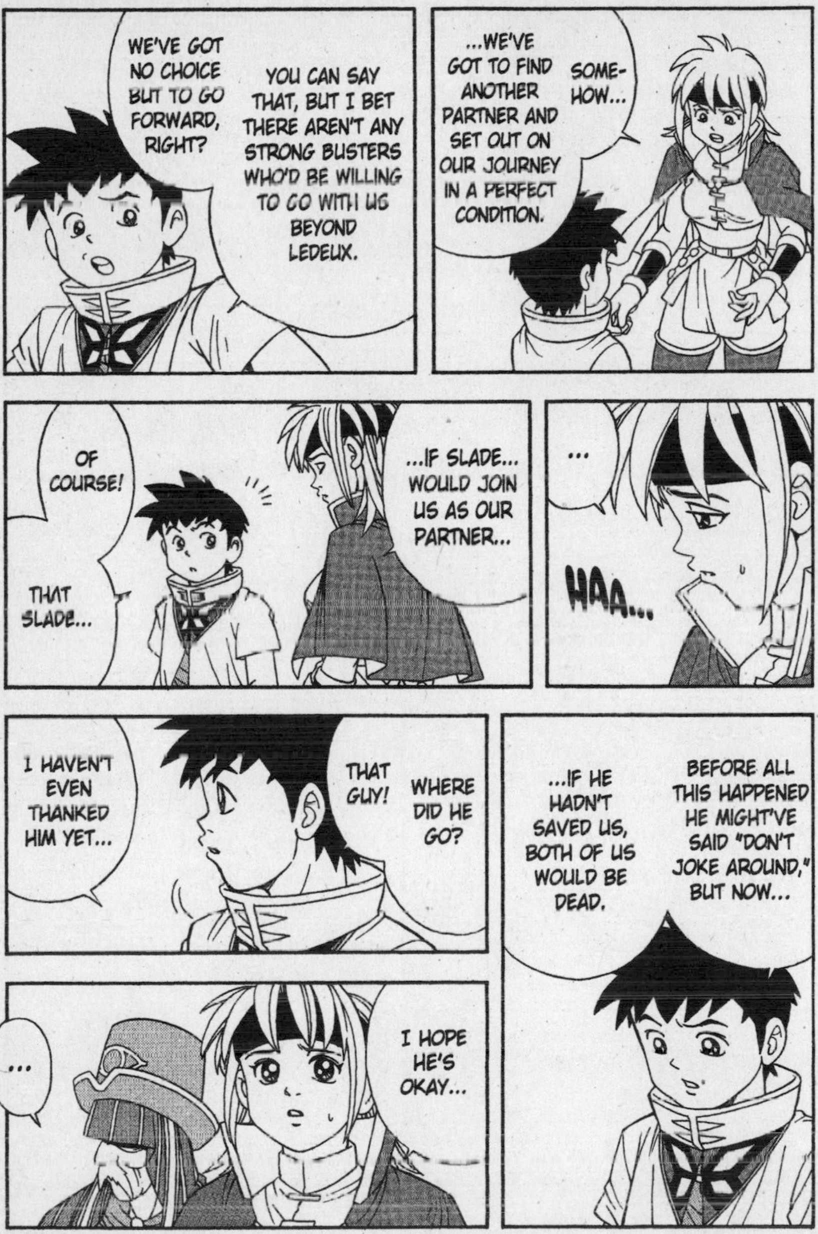
SOME-HOW...
...WE'VE GOT TO FIND ANOTHER PARTNER AND SET OUT ON OUR JOURNEY IN A PERFECT CONDITION.
YOU CAN SAY THAT, BUT I BET THERE AREN'T ANY STRONG BUSTERS WHO'D BE WILLING TO GO WITH US BEYOND LEDEUX.
WE'VE GOT NO CHOICE BUT TO GO FORWARD, RIGHT?
...
HAA...
...IF SLADE... WOULD JOIN US AS OUR PARTNER...
OF COURSE!
THAT SLADE...
BEFORE ALL THIS HAPPENED HE MIGHT'VE SAID "DON'T JOKE AROUND," BUT NOW...
...IF HE HADN'T SAVED US, BOTH OF US WOULD BE DEAD.
WHERE DID HE GO?
THAT GUY!
I HAVEN'T EVEN THANKED HIM YET...
I HOPE HE'S OKAY...
...

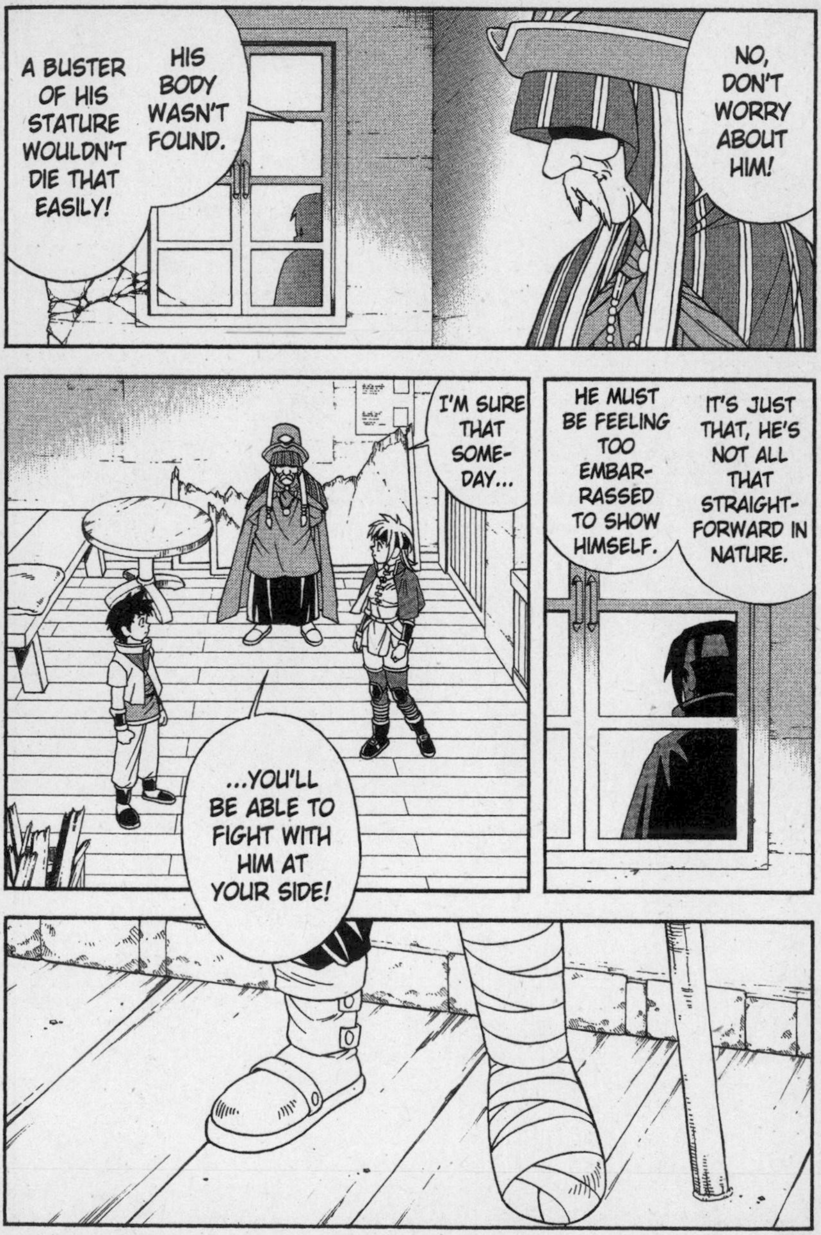
NO, DON'T WORRY ABOUT HIM!
HIS BODY WASN'T FOUND.
A BUSTER OF HIS STATURE WOULDN'T DIE THAT EASILY!
IT'S JUST THAT, HE'S NOT ALL THAT STRAIGHT-FORWARD IN NATURE.
HE MUST BE FEELING TOO EMBAR-RASSED TO SHOW HIMSELF.
I'M SURE THAT SOME-DAY...
...YOU'LL BE ABLE TO FIGHT WITH HIM AT YOUR SIDE!

READ THIS WAY

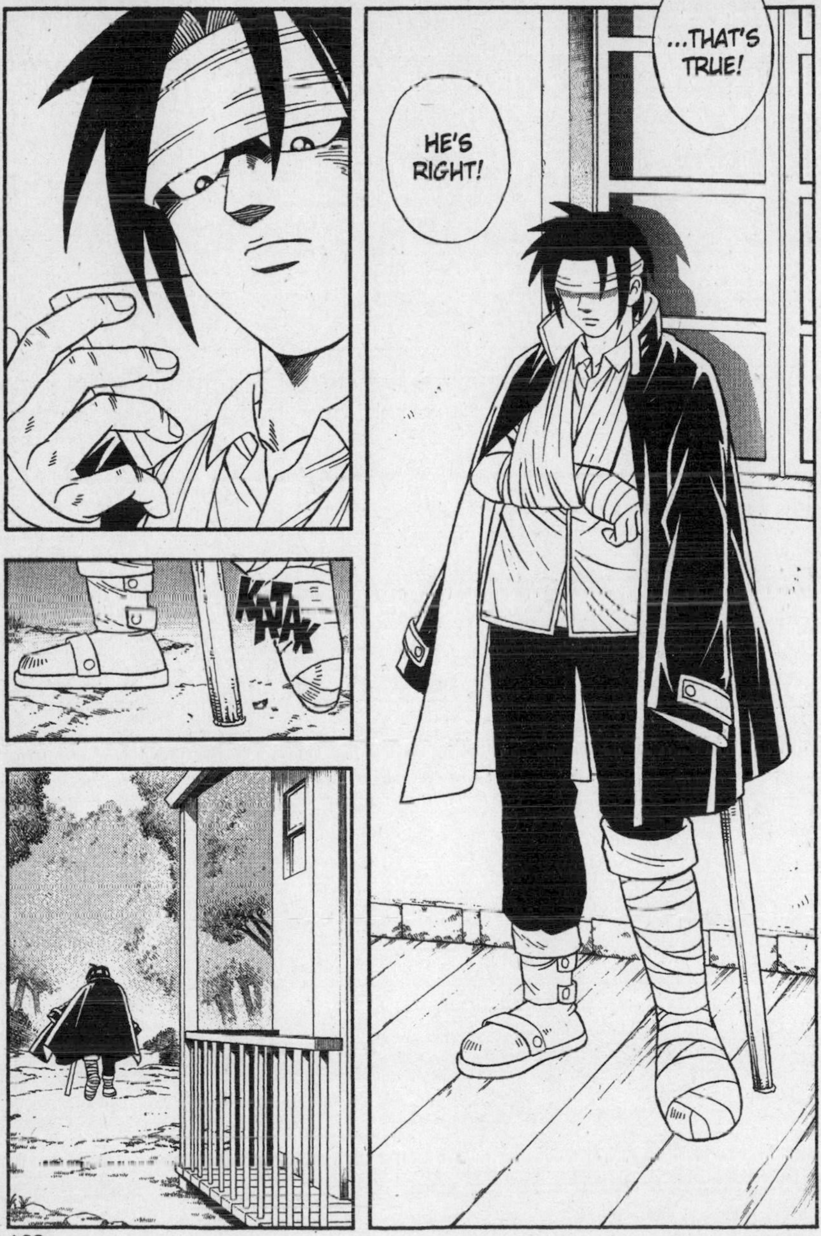
...THAT'S TRUE!
HE'S RIGHT!
KATAK

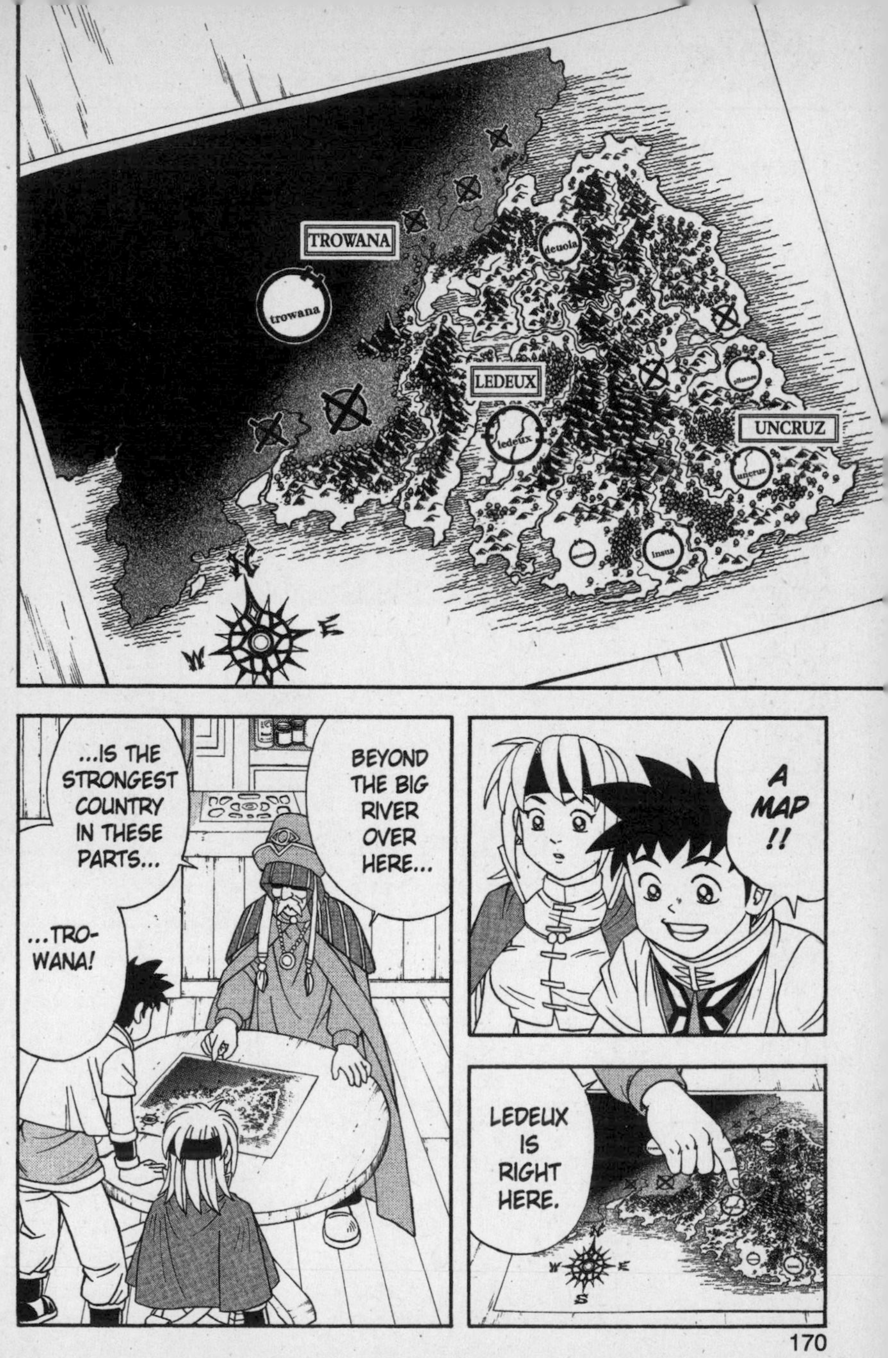
TROWANA
trowana
deuola
LEDEUX
ledeux
UNCRUZ
uncruz
insua
N
E
W
A MAP !!
LEDEUX IS RIGHT HERE.
N
W
E
S
BEYOND THE BIG RIVER OVER HERE...
...IS THE STRONGEST COUNTRY IN THESE PARTS...
...TRO-WANA!

READ THIS WAY

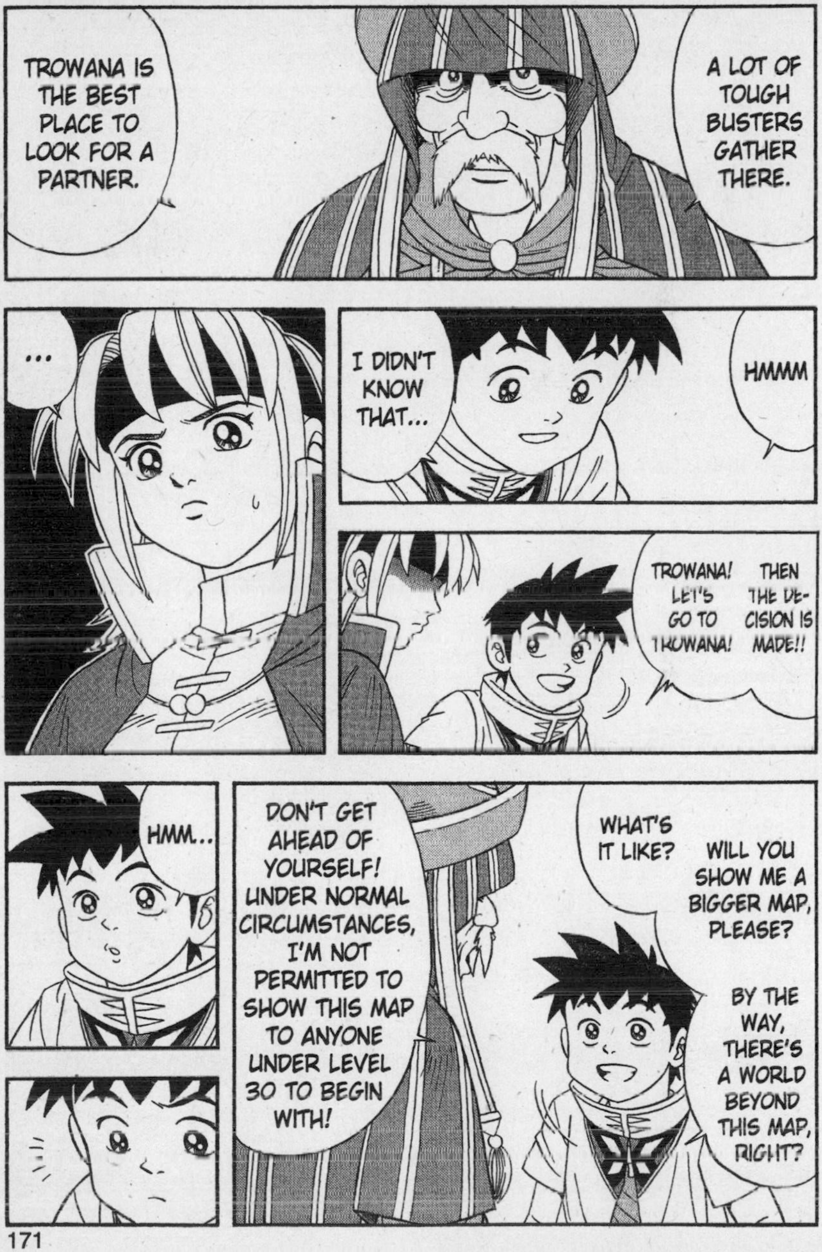
A LOT OF TOUGH BUSTERS GATHER THERE.
TROWANA IS THE BEST PLACE TO LOOK FOR A PARTNER.
HMMM
I DIDN'T KNOW THAT...
THEN THE DECISION IS MADE!!
TROWANA! LET'S GO TO TROWANA!
...
BY THE WAY, THERE'S A WORLD BEYOND THIS MAP, RIGHT?
WHAT'S IT LIKE?
WILL YOU SHOW ME A BIGGER MAP, PLEASE?
DON'T GET AHEAD OF YOURSELF! UNDER NORMAL CIRCUMSTANCES, I'M NOT PERMITTED TO SHOW THIS MAP TO ANYONE UNDER LEVEL 30 TO BEGIN WITH!
HMM...

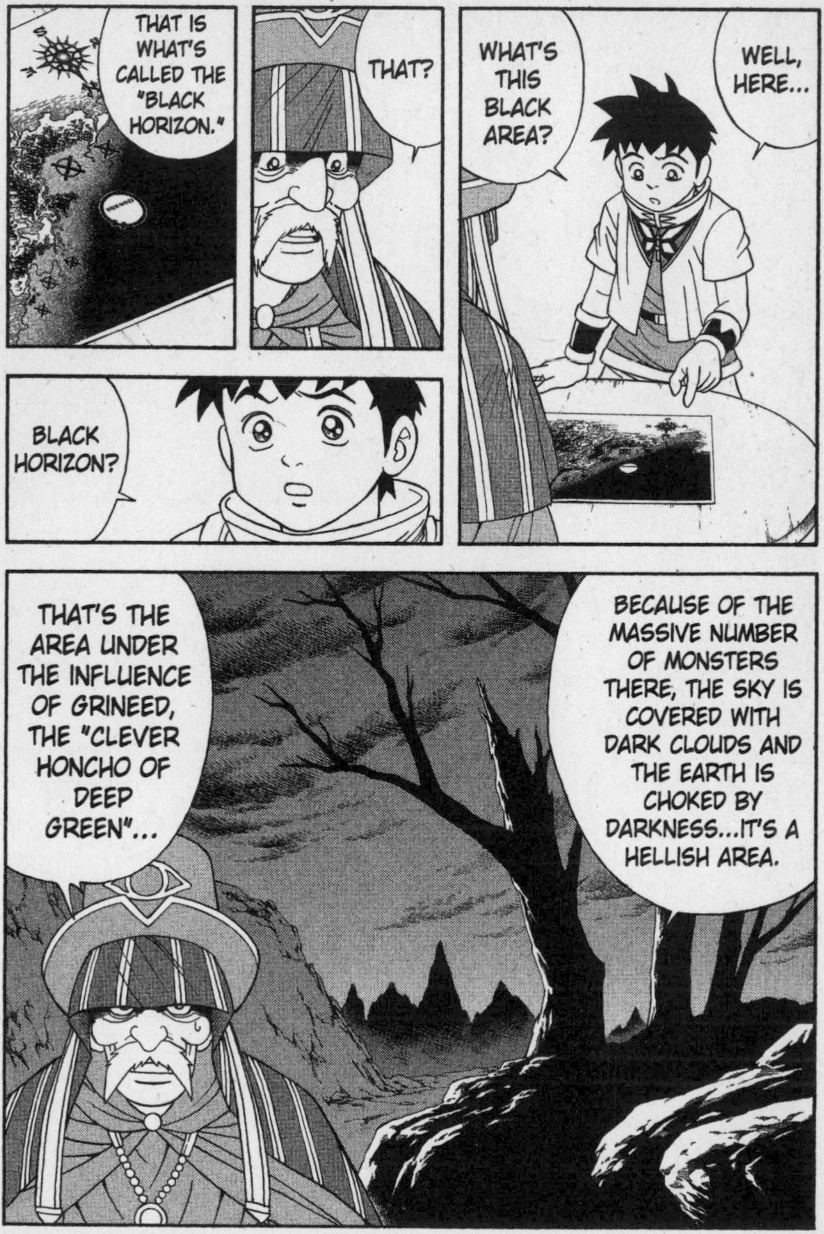
WELL, HERE...
WHAT'S THIS BLACK AREA?
THAT?
THAT IS WHAT'S CALLED THE "BLACK HORIZON."
BLACK HORIZON?
BECAUSE OF THE MASSIVE NUMBER OF MONSTERS THERE, THE SKY IS COVERED WITH DARK CLOUDS AND THE EARTH IS CHOKED BY DARKNESS...IT'S A HELLISH AREA.
THAT'S THE AREA UNDER THE INFLUENCE OF GRINEED, THE "CLEVER HONCHO OF DEEP GREEN"...

READ THIS WAY

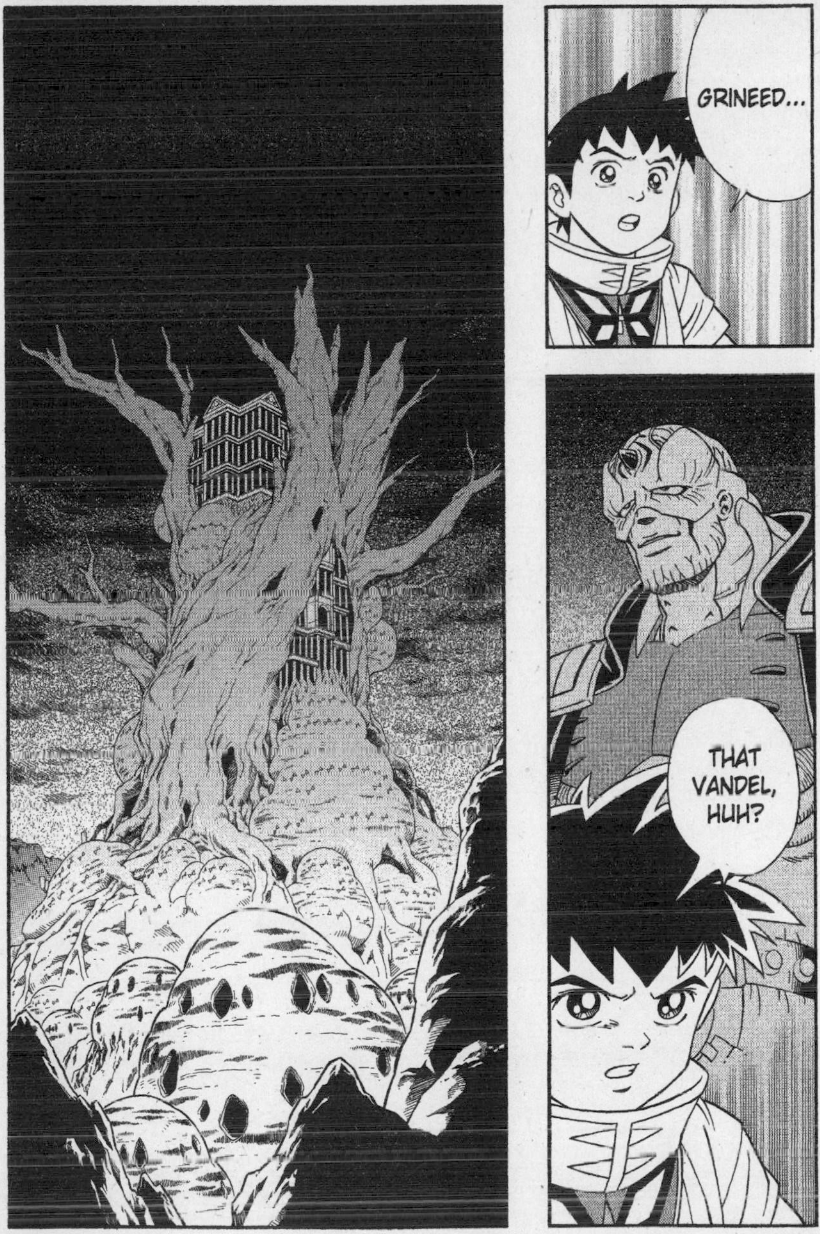
GRINEED...
THAT VANDEL, HUH?

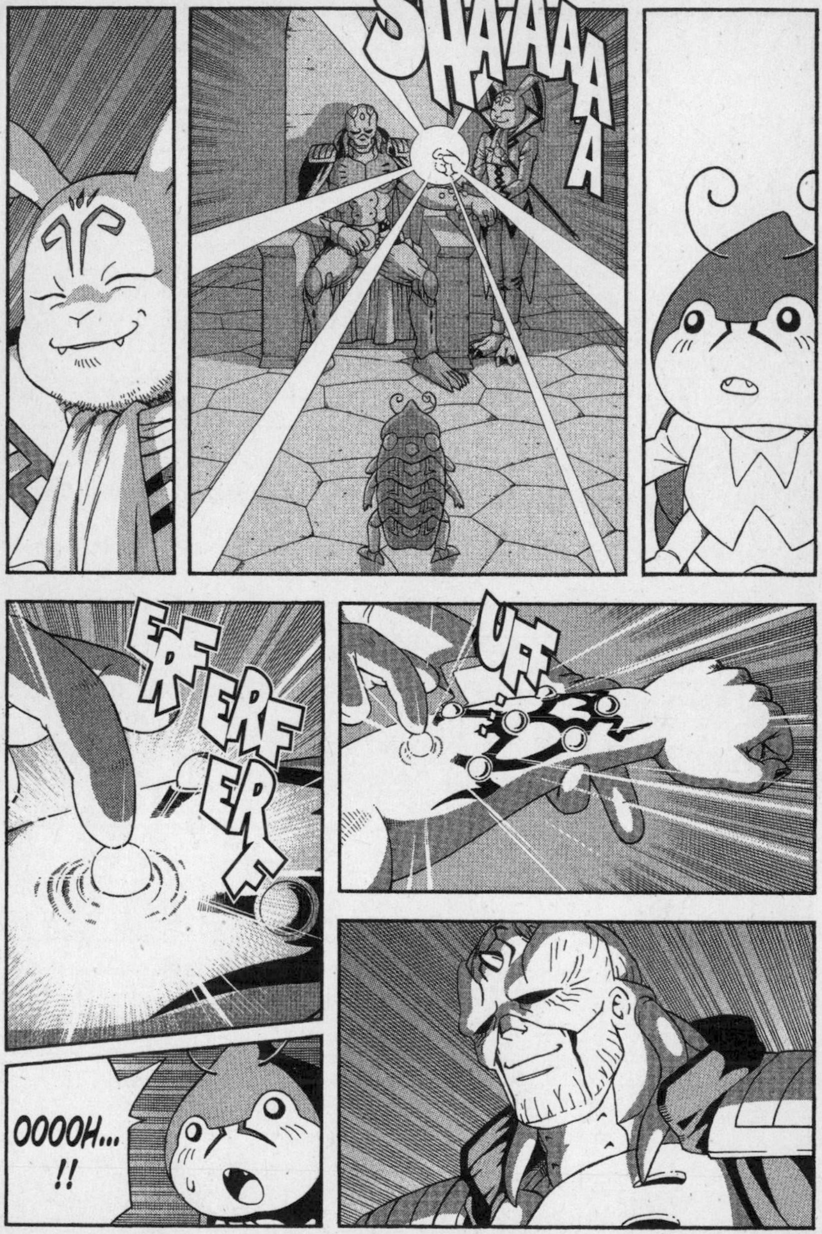
SHAAAAAA
UFF
ERF ERF ER F
OOOOH... !!

READ THIS WAY

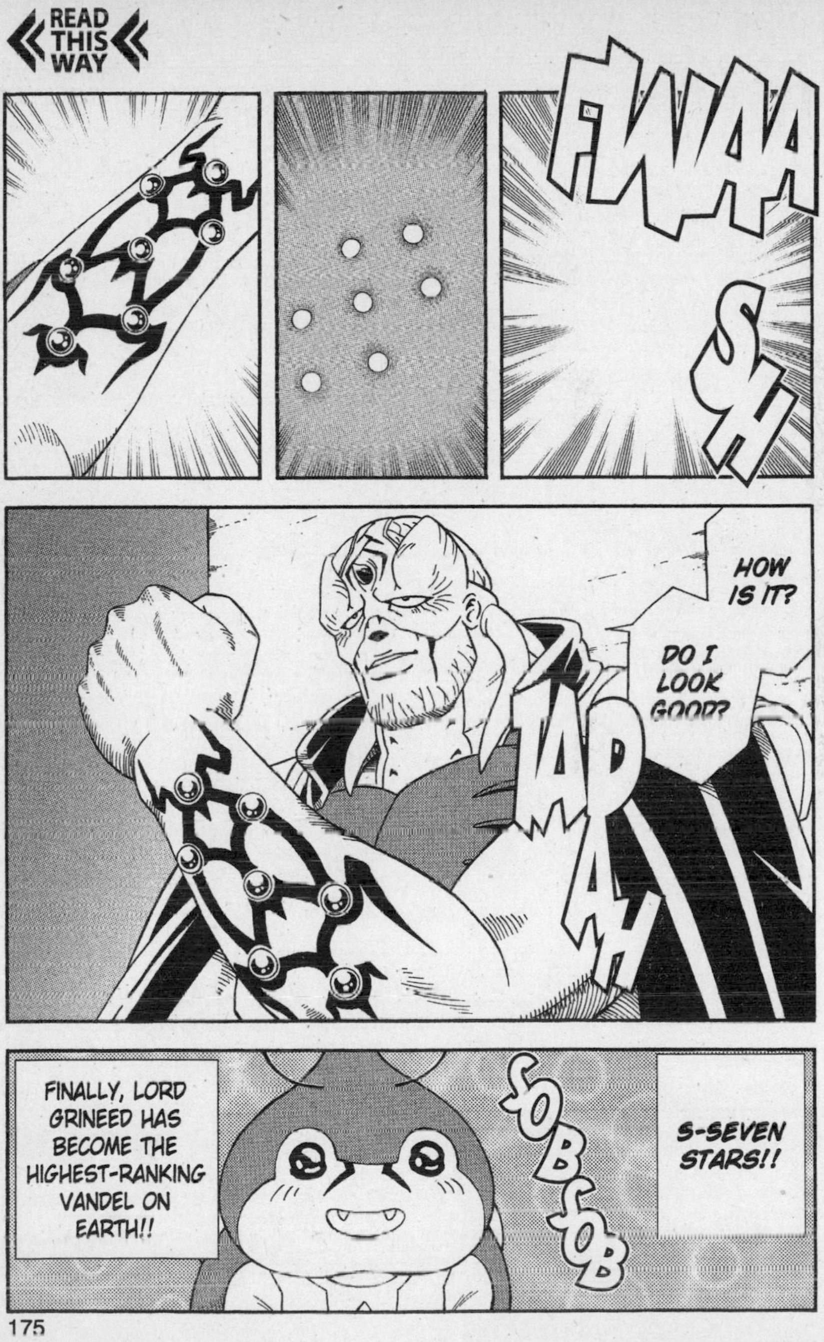

FWAASH
HOW IS IT?
DO I LOOK GOOD?
TADAH
S-SEVEN STARS!!
SOBSOB
FINALLY, LORD GRINEED HAS BECOME THE HIGHEST-RANKING VANDEL ON EARTH!!

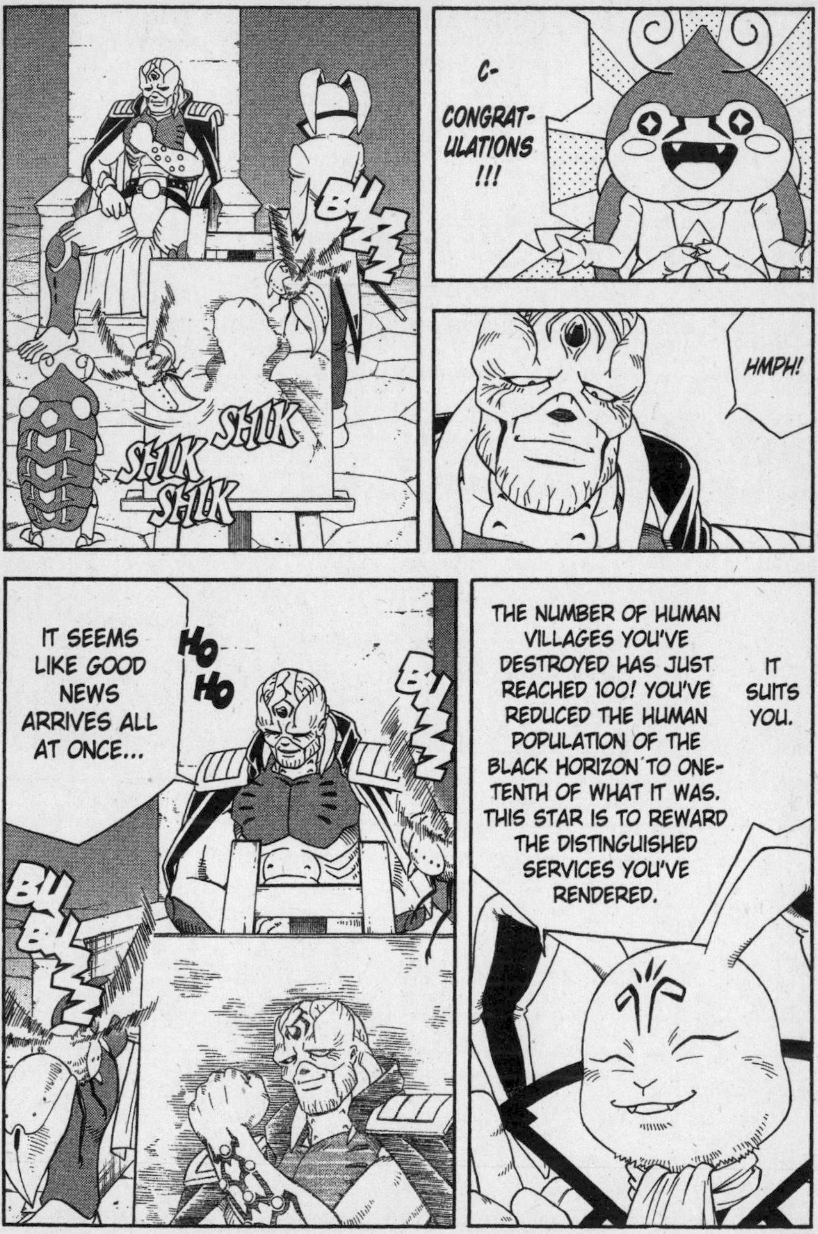
C-
CONGRAT-ULATIONS !!!
HMPH!
BUZZZ
SHIK
SHIK
SHIK
IT SUITS YOU.
THE NUMBER OF HUMAN VILLAGES YOU'VE DESTROYED HAS JUST REACHED 100! YOU'VE REDUCED THE HUMAN POPULATION OF THE BLACK HORIZON TO ONE-TENTH OF WHAT IT WAS. THIS STAR IS TO REWARD THE DISTINGUISHED SERVICES YOU'VE RENDERED.
HO HO
BUZZZ
IT SEEMS LIKE GOOD NEWS ARRIVES ALL AT ONCE...
BUBUZZZ

READ THIS WAY

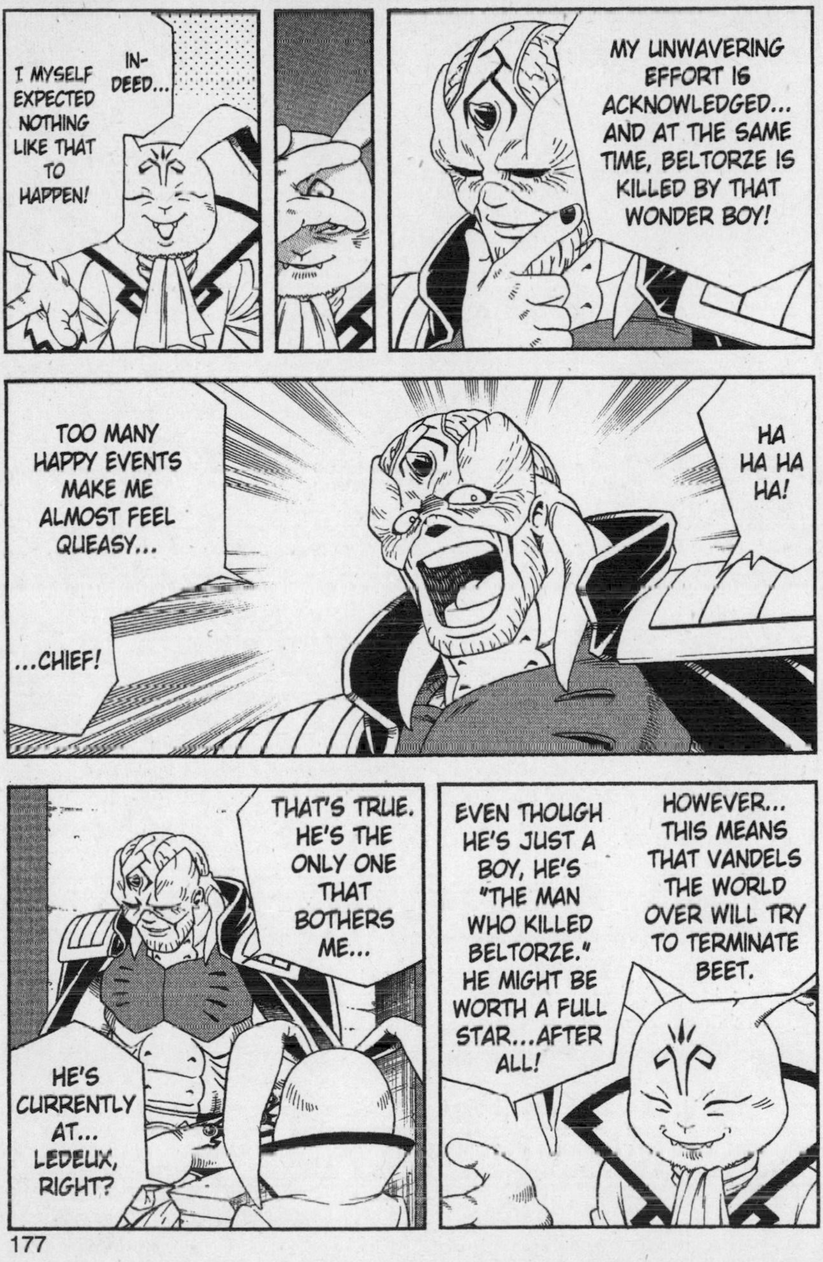
MY UNWAVERING EFFORT IS ACKNOWLEDGED... AND AT THE SAME TIME, BELTORZE IS KILLED BY THAT WONDER BOY!
IN-DEED...
I MYSELF EXPECTED NOTHING LIKE THAT TO HAPPEN!
HA HA HA HA!
TOO MANY HAPPY EVENTS MAKE ME ALMOST FEEL QUEASY...
...CHIEF!
HOWEVER... THIS MEANS THAT VANDELS THE WORLD OVER WILL TRY TO TERMINATE BEET.
EVEN THOUGH HE'S JUST A BOY, HE'S "THE MAN WHO KILLED BELTORZE." HE MIGHT BE WORTH A FULL STAR...AFTER ALL!
THAT'S TRUE. HE'S THE ONLY ONE THAT BOTHERS ME...
HE'S CURRENTLY AT... LEDEUX, RIGHT?

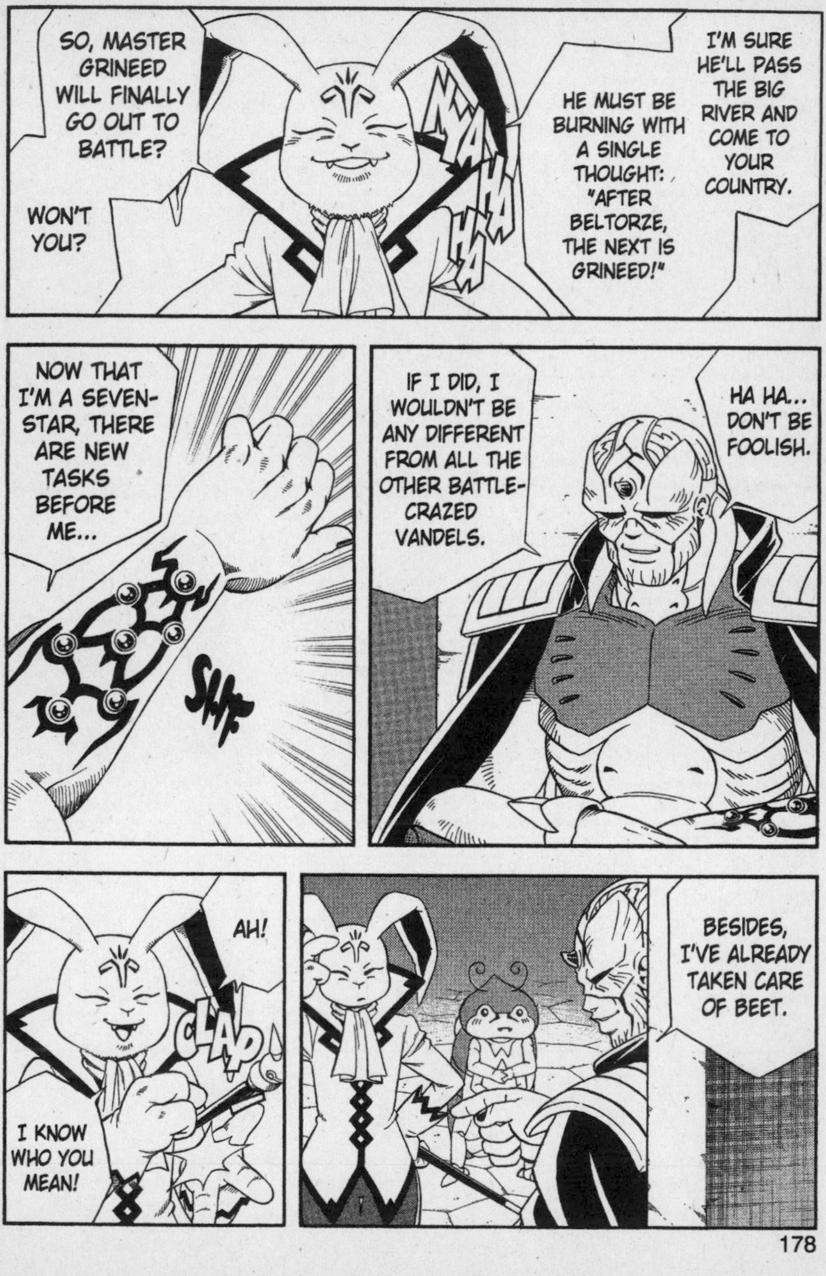
I'M SURE HE'LL PASS THE BIG RIVER AND COME TO YOUR COUNTRY.
HE MUST BE BURNING WITH A SINGLE THOUGHT: "AFTER BELTORZE, THE NEXT IS GRINEED!"
NYAHAHA
SO, MASTER GRINEED WILL FINALLY GO OUT TO BATTLE?
WON'T YOU?
HA HA... DON'T BE FOOLISH.
IF I DID, I WOULDN'T BE ANY DIFFERENT FROM ALL THE OTHER BATTLE-CRAZED VANDELS.
NOW THAT I'M A SEVEN-STAR, THERE ARE NEW TASKS BEFORE ME...
SHF
BESIDES, I'VE ALREADY TAKEN CARE OF BEET.
AH!
CLAP
I KNOW WHO YOU MEAN!

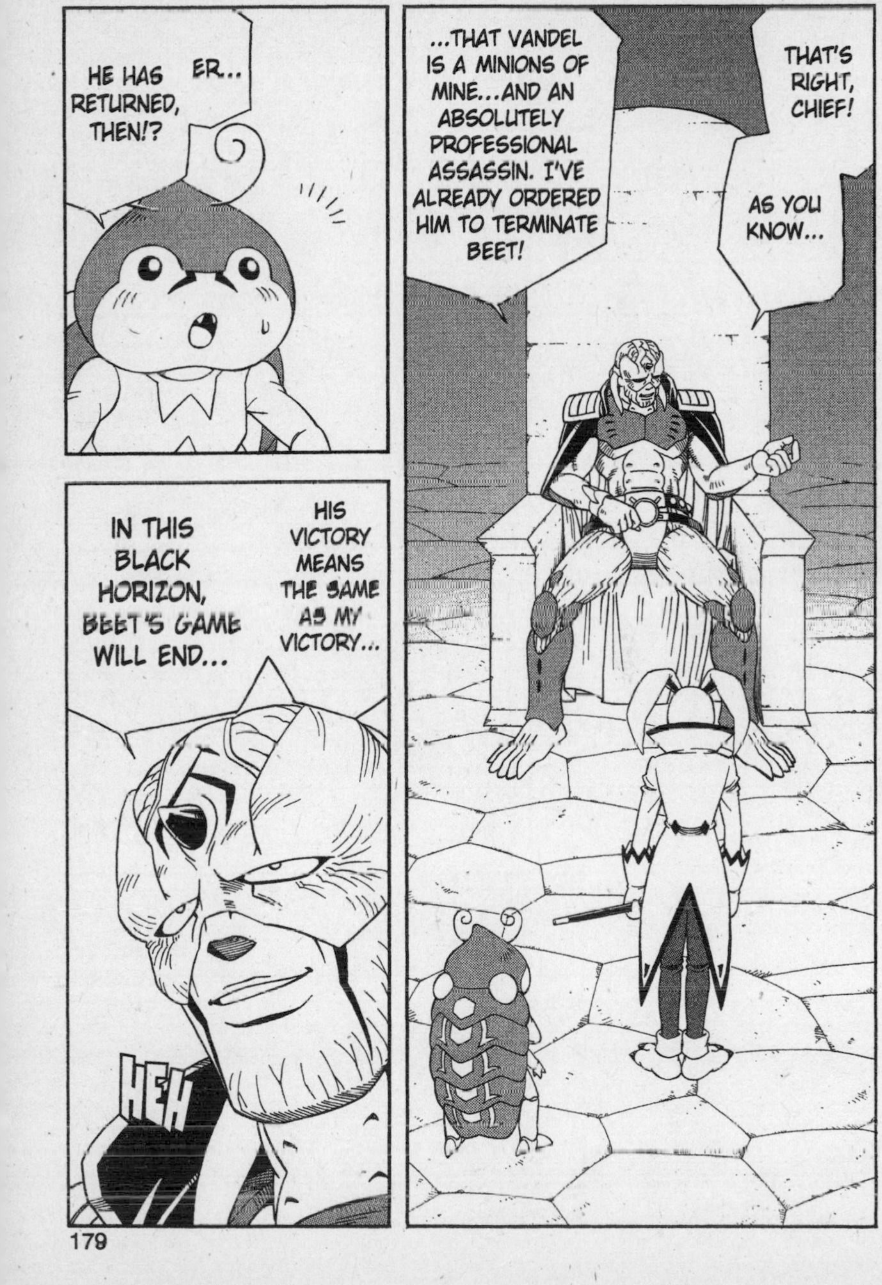
THAT'S RIGHT, CHIEF!
AS YOU KNOW...
...THAT VANDEL IS A MINIONS OF MINE...AND AN ABSOLUTELY PROFESSIONAL ASSASSIN. I'VE ALREADY ORDERED HIM TO TERMINATE BEET!
ER...
HE HAS RETURNED, THEN!?
HIS VICTORY MEANS THE SAME AS MY VICTORY...
IN THIS BLACK HORIZON, BEET'S GAME WILL END...
HEH

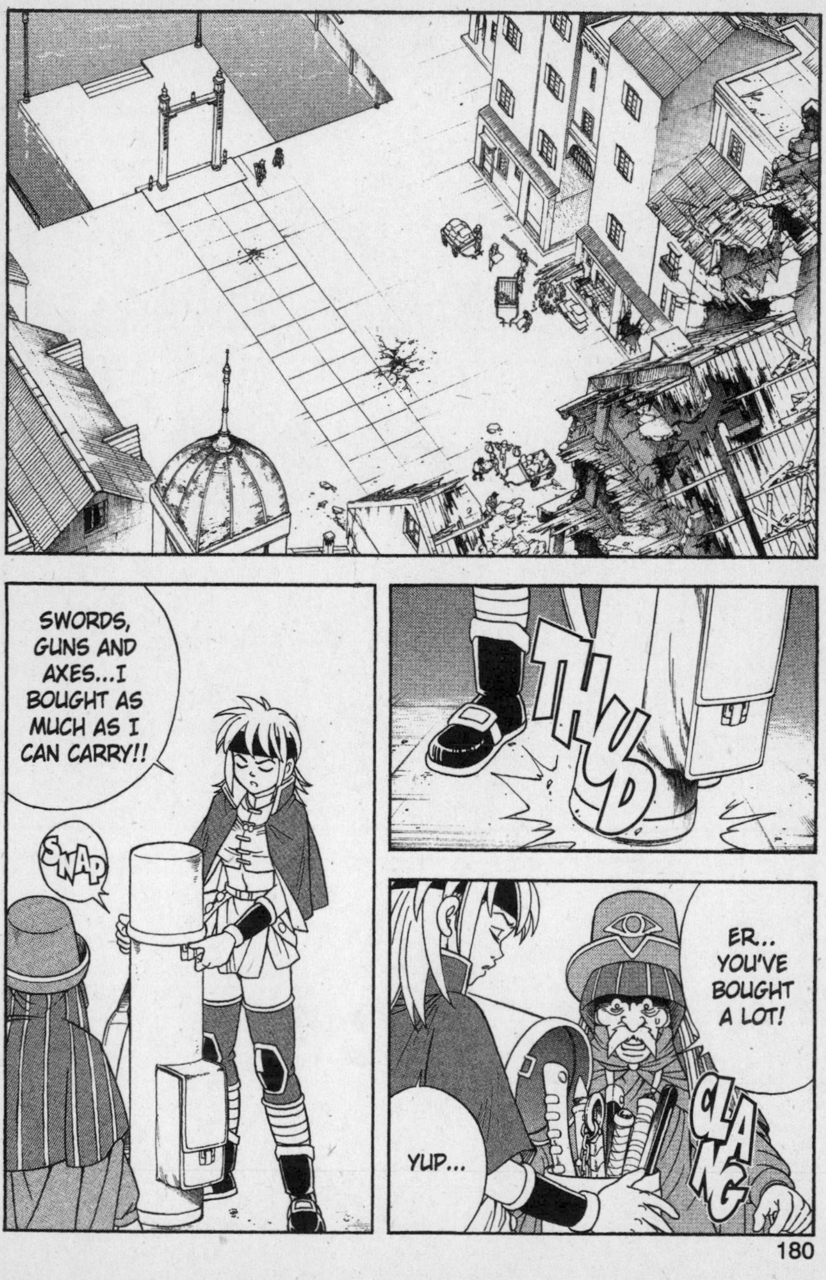
THUD
ER... YOU'VE BOUGHT A LOT!
CLANG
YUP...
SWORDS, GUNS AND AXES...I BOUGHT AS MUCH AS I CAN CARRY!!
SNAP

READ THIS WAY

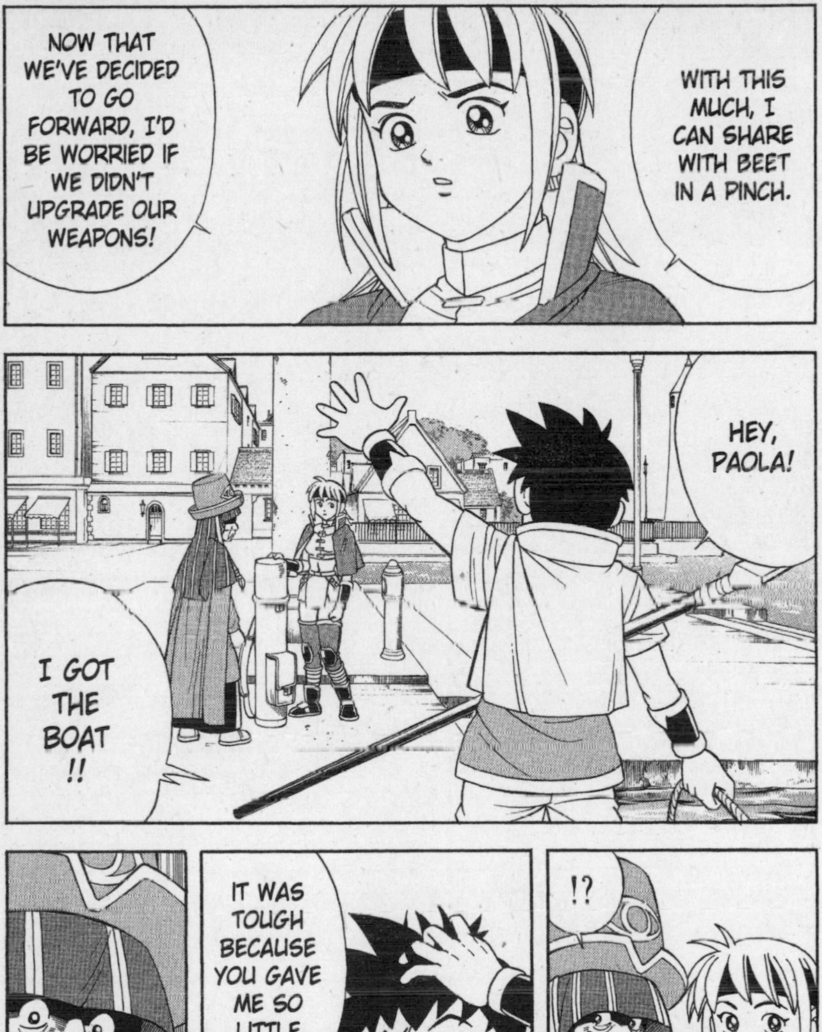

WITH THIS MUCH, I CAN SHARE WITH BEET IN A PINCH.
NOW THAT WE'VE DECIDED TO GO FORWARD, I'D BE WORRIED IF WE DIDN'T UPGRADE OUR WEAPONS!
HEY, PAOLA!
I GOT THE BOAT !!
!?
IT WAS TOUGH BECAUSE YOU GAVE ME SO LITTLE MONEY.

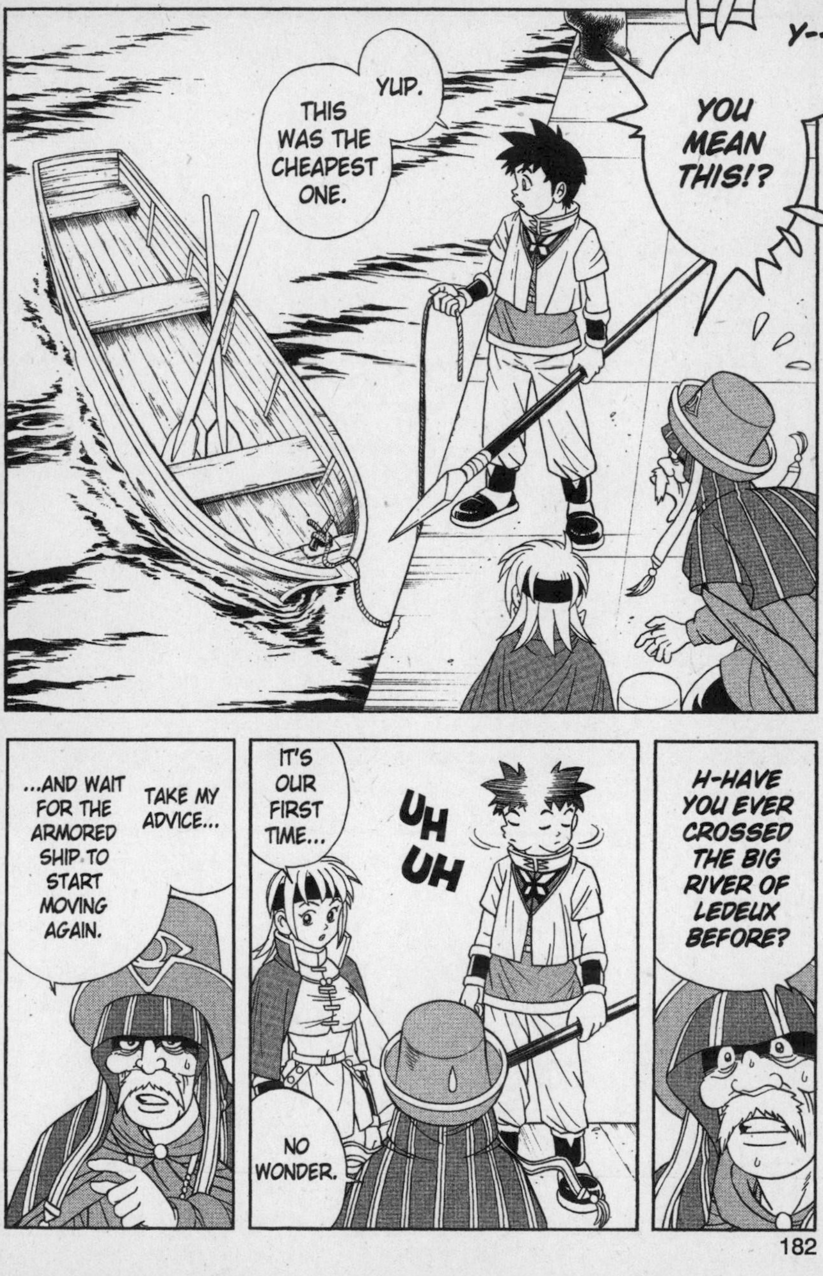

Y--
YOU MEAN THIS!?
YUP.
THIS WAS THE CHEAPEST ONE.
H-HAVE YOU EVER CROSSED THE BIG RIVER OF LEDEUX BEFORE?
UH UH
IT'S OUR FIRST TIME...
NO WONDER.
TAKE MY ADVICE...
...AND WAIT FOR THE ARMORED SHIP TO START MOVING AGAIN.

READ THIS WAY

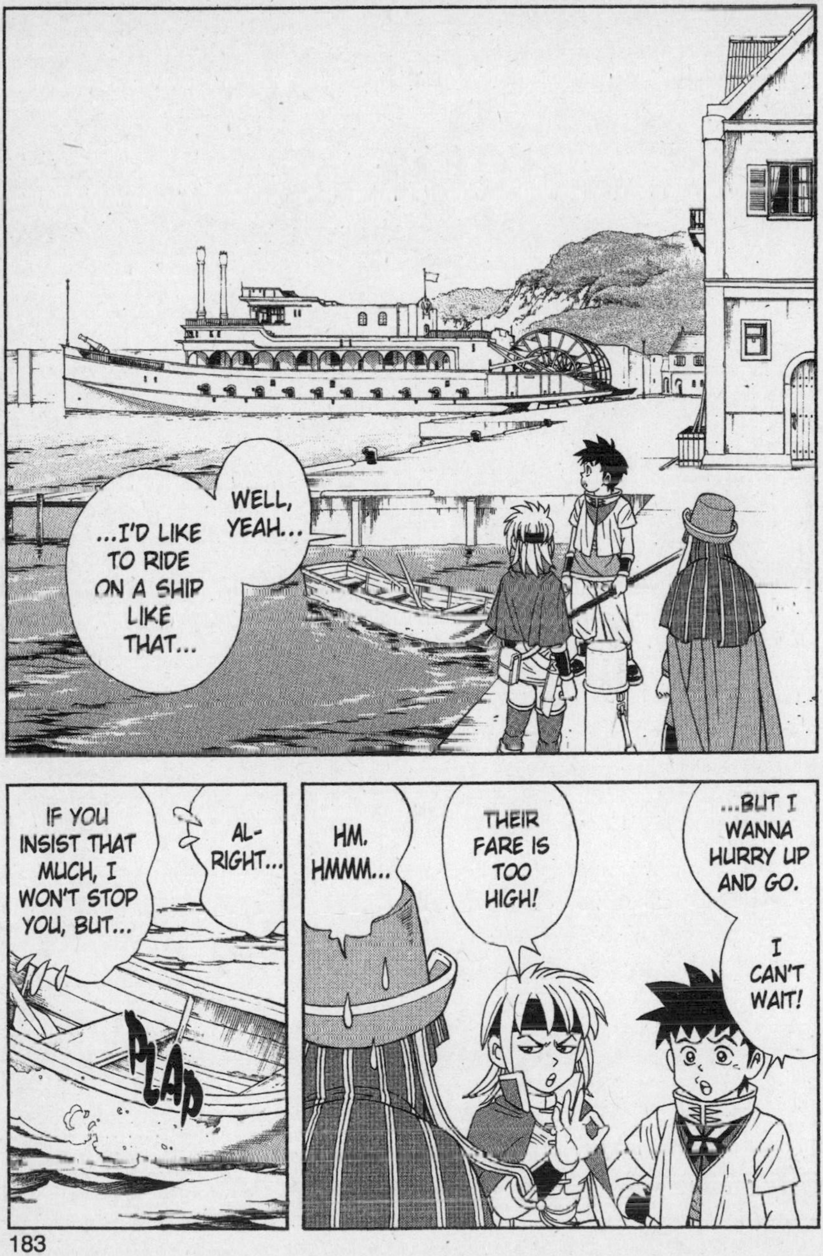
WELL, YEAH...
...I'D LIKE TO RIDE ON A SHIP LIKE THAT...
...BUT I WANNA HURRY UP AND GO.
I CAN'T WAIT!
THEIR FARE IS TOO HIGH!
HM. HMMM...
AL-RIGHT...
IF YOU INSIST THAT MUCH, I WON'T STOP YOU, BUT...
PLAP

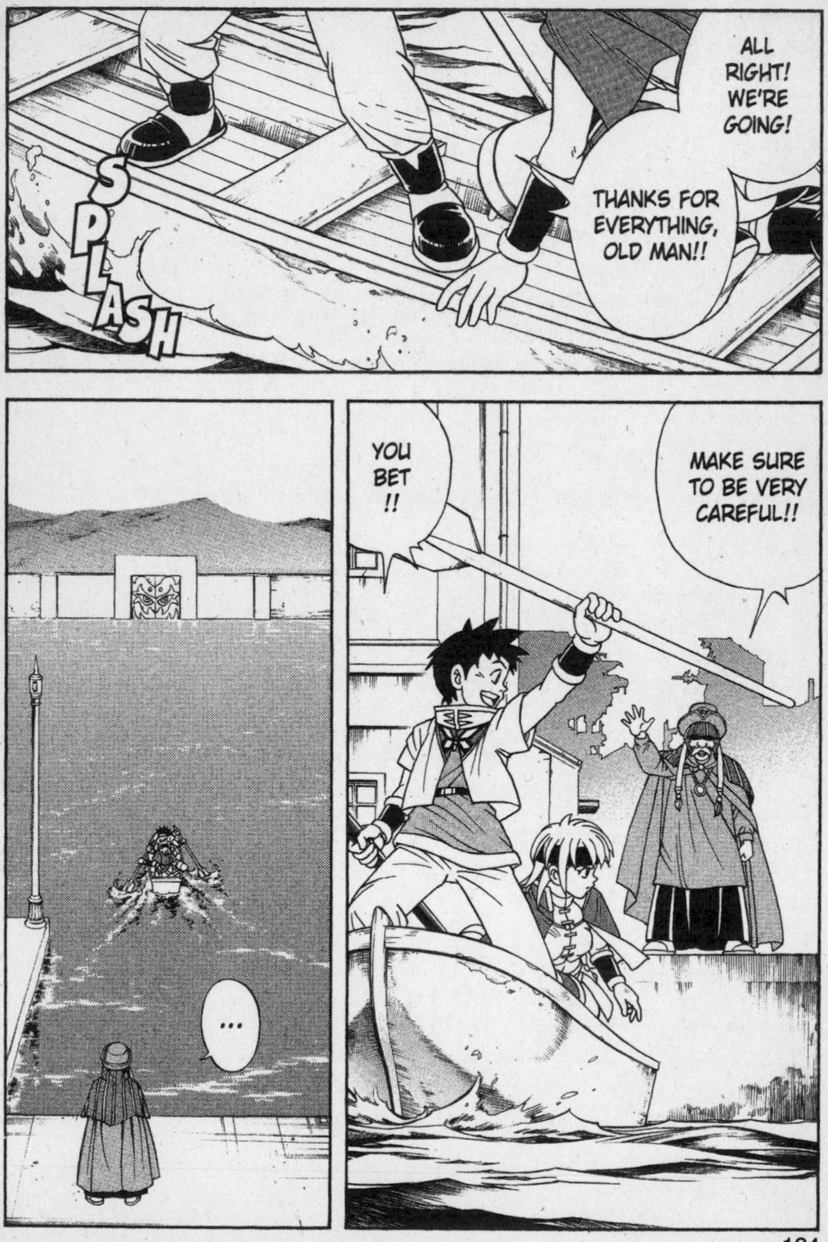
ALL RIGHT! WE'RE GOING!
THANKS FOR EVERYTHING, OLD MAN!!
SPLASH
MAKE SURE TO BE VERY CAREFUL!!
YOU BET!!
...

READ THIS WAY

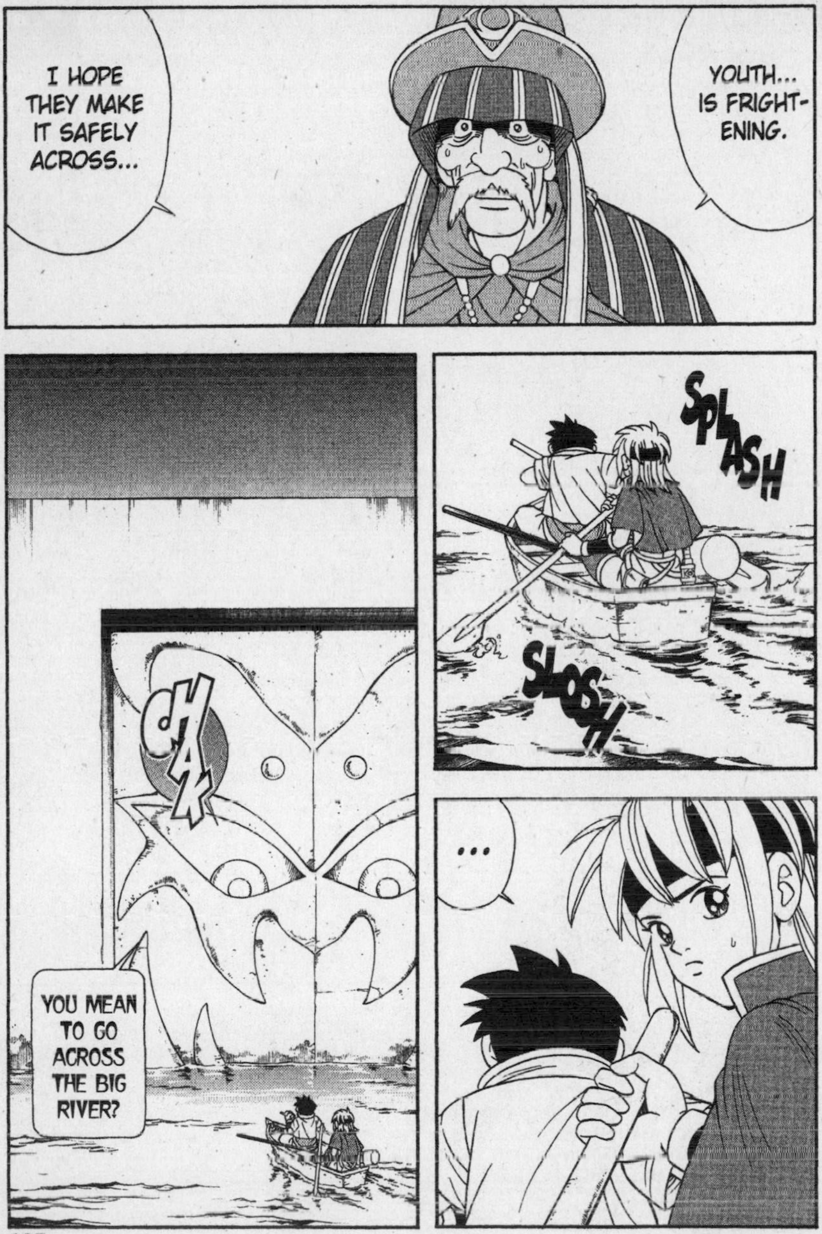
YOUTH... IS FRIGHT-ENING.
I HOPE THEY MAKE IT SAFELY ACROSS...
SPLASH
SLOSH
...
CHAK
YOU MEAN TO GO ACROSS THE BIG RIVER?

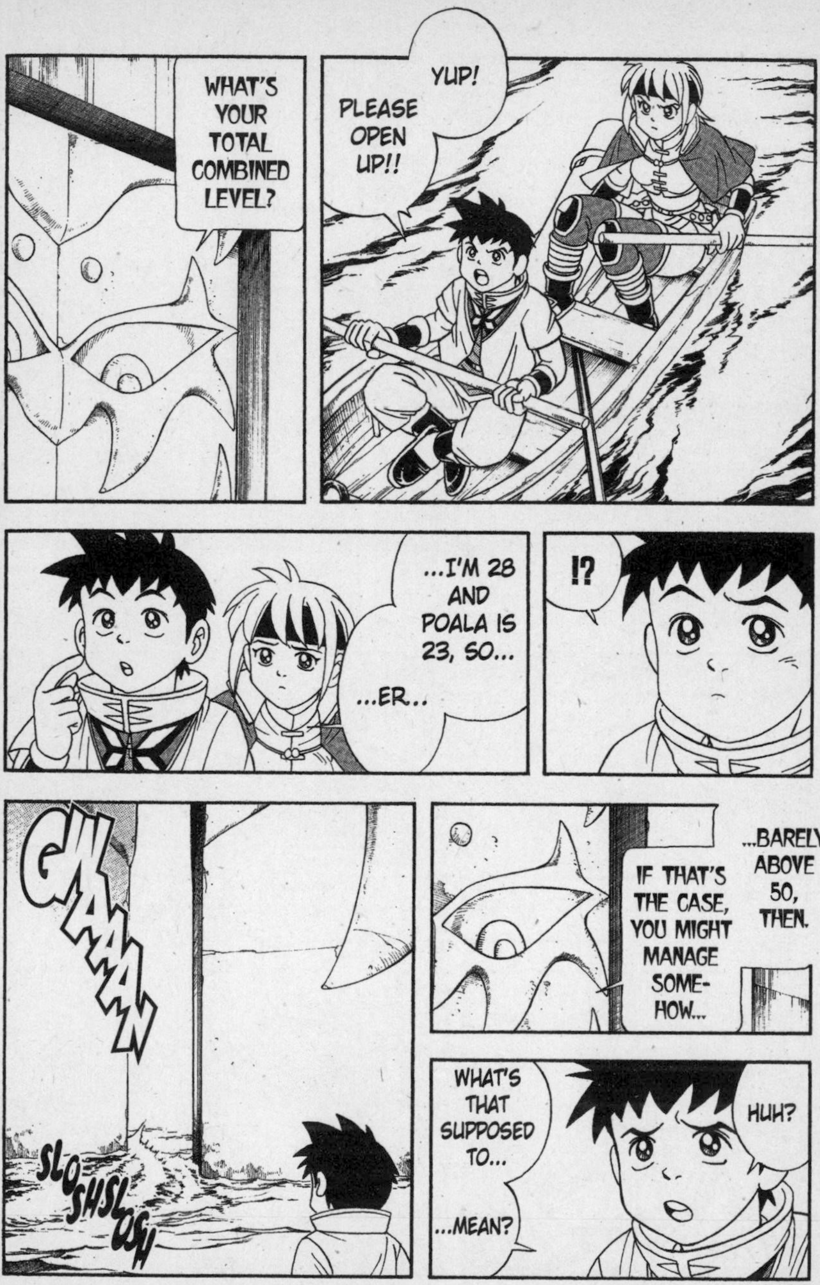
YUP!
PLEASE OPEN UP!!
WHAT'S YOUR TOTAL COMBINED LEVEL?
!?
...I'M 28 AND POALA IS 23, SO...
...ER...
...BARELY ABOVE 50, THEN.
IF THAT'S THE CASE, YOU MIGHT MANAGE SOME-HOW...
HUH?
WHAT'S THAT SUPPOSED TO...
...MEAN?
GWAAAN
SLOSHSLOSH

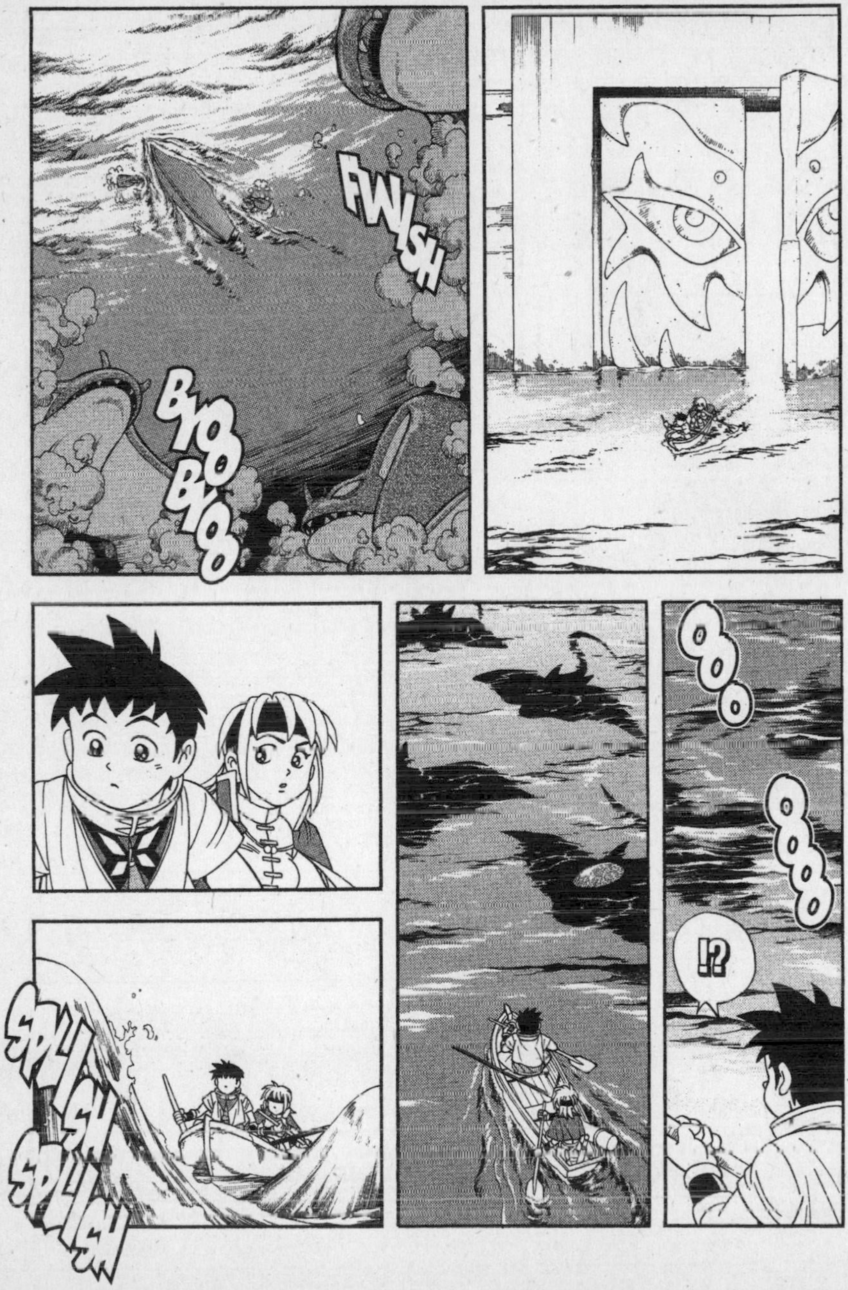
FWISH
BYOO BYOO
OOO
OOOO
!?
SPLISH SPLISH

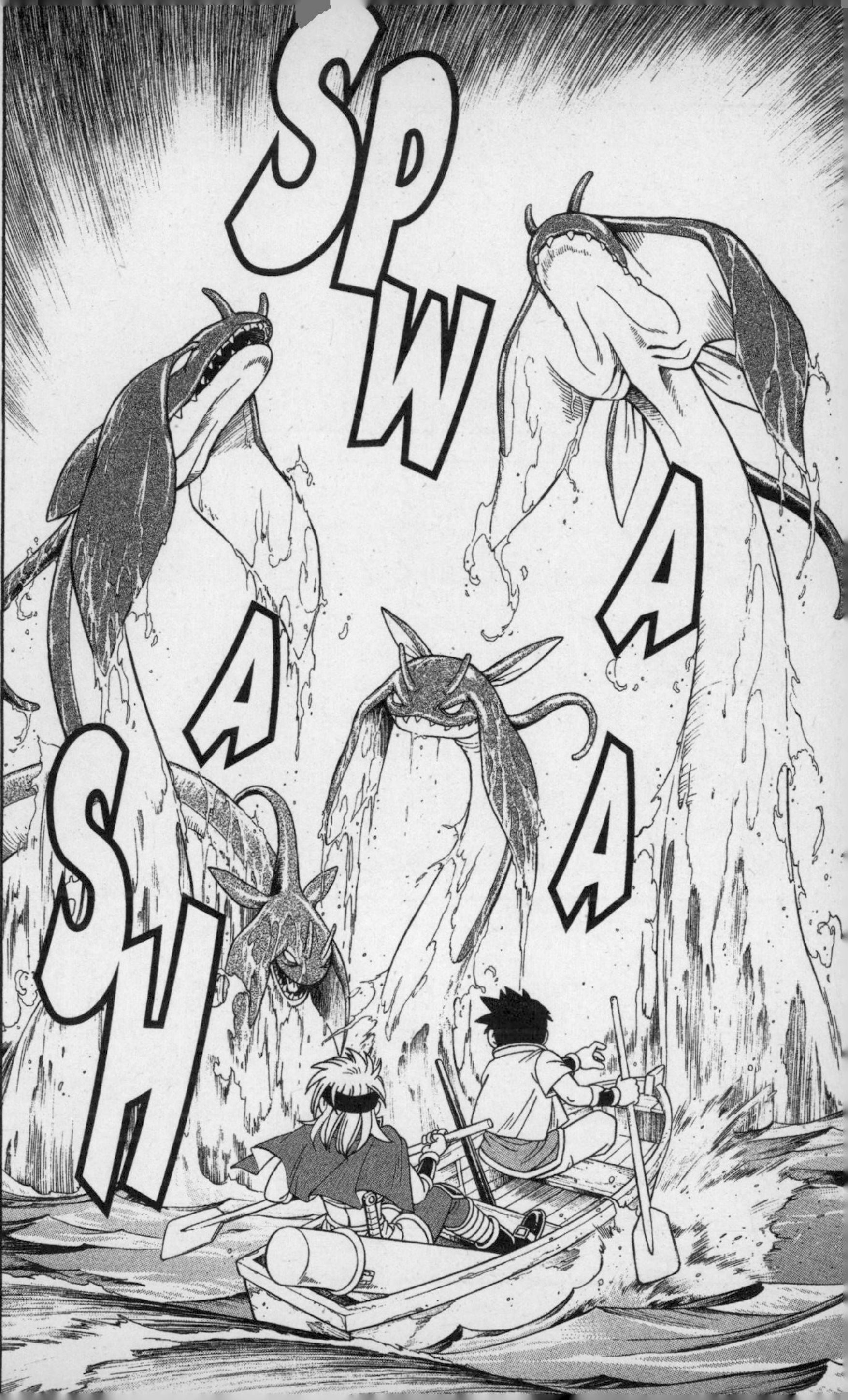
SPWAA
SHA

READ THIS WAY

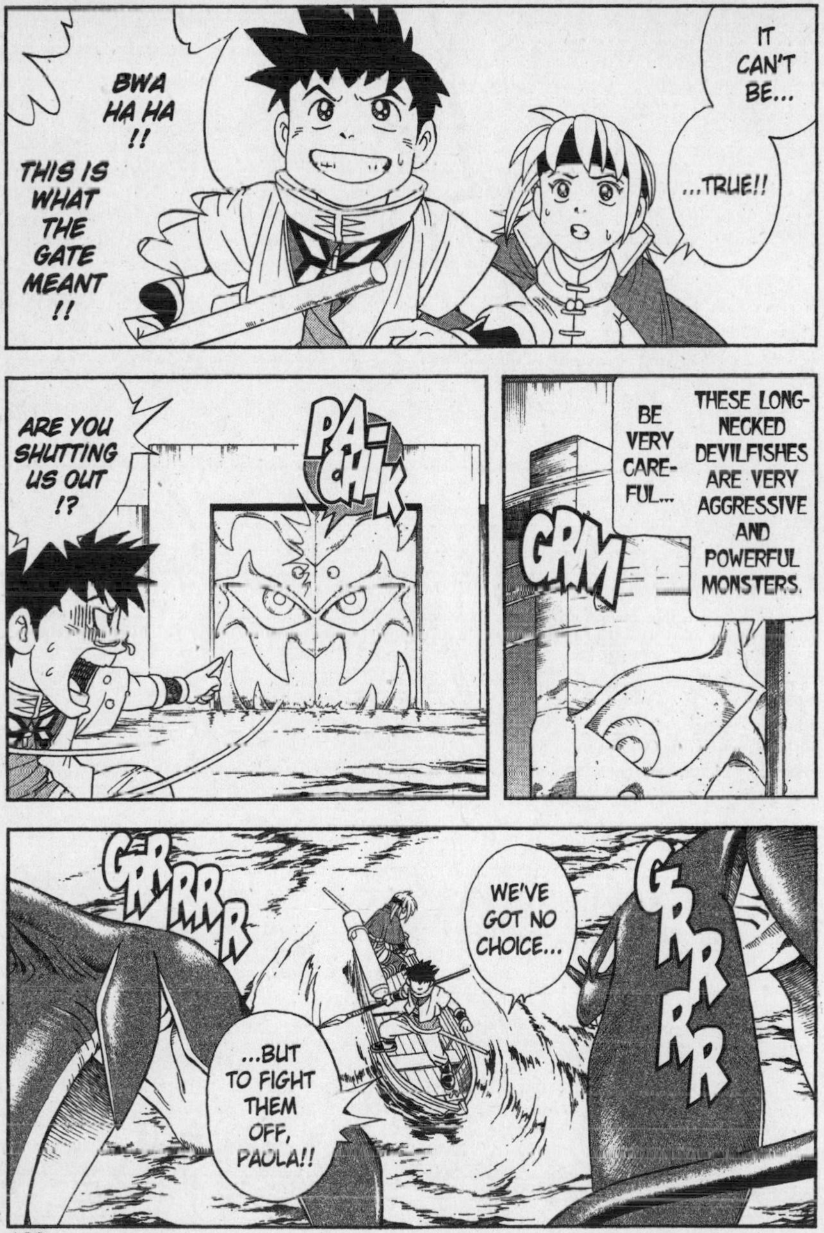

IT CAN'T BE... ...TRUE!!
BWA HA HA!!
THIS IS WHAT THE GATE MEANT!!
THESE LONG-NECKED DEVILFISHES ARE VERY AGGRESSIVE AND POWERFUL MONSTERS.
BE VERY CAREFUL...
GRM
PA-CHIK
ARE YOU SHUTTING US OUT!?
GRRRR
WE'VE GOT NO CHOICE...
...BUT TO FIGHT THEM OFF, PAOLA!!
GRRRRR

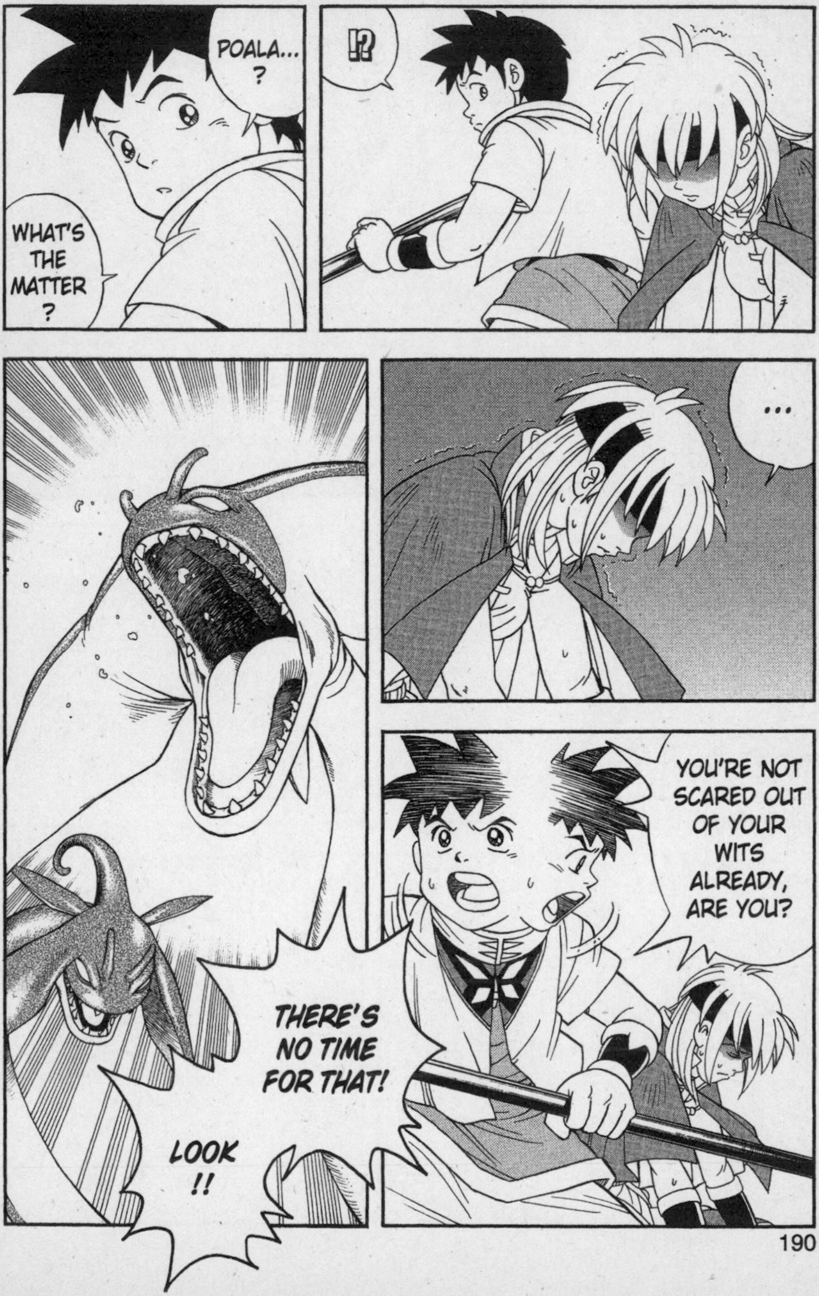

!?
POALA... ?
WHAT'S THE MATTER ?
...
YOU'RE NOT SCARED OUT OF YOUR WITS ALREADY, ARE YOU?
THERE'S NO TIME FOR THAT!
LOOK !!

READ THIS WAY

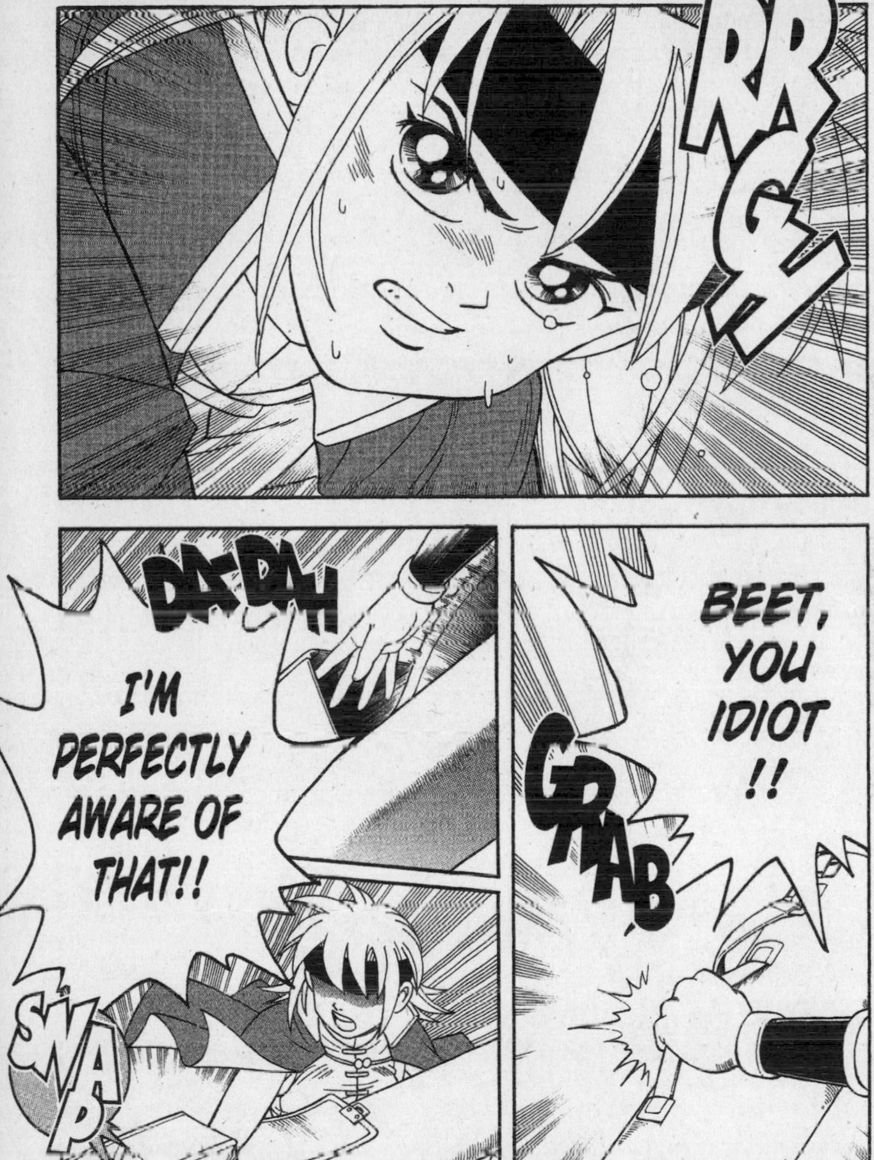
RRGH
BEET, YOU IDIOT!!
GRAB
I'M PERFECTLY AWARE OF THAT!!
SNAP

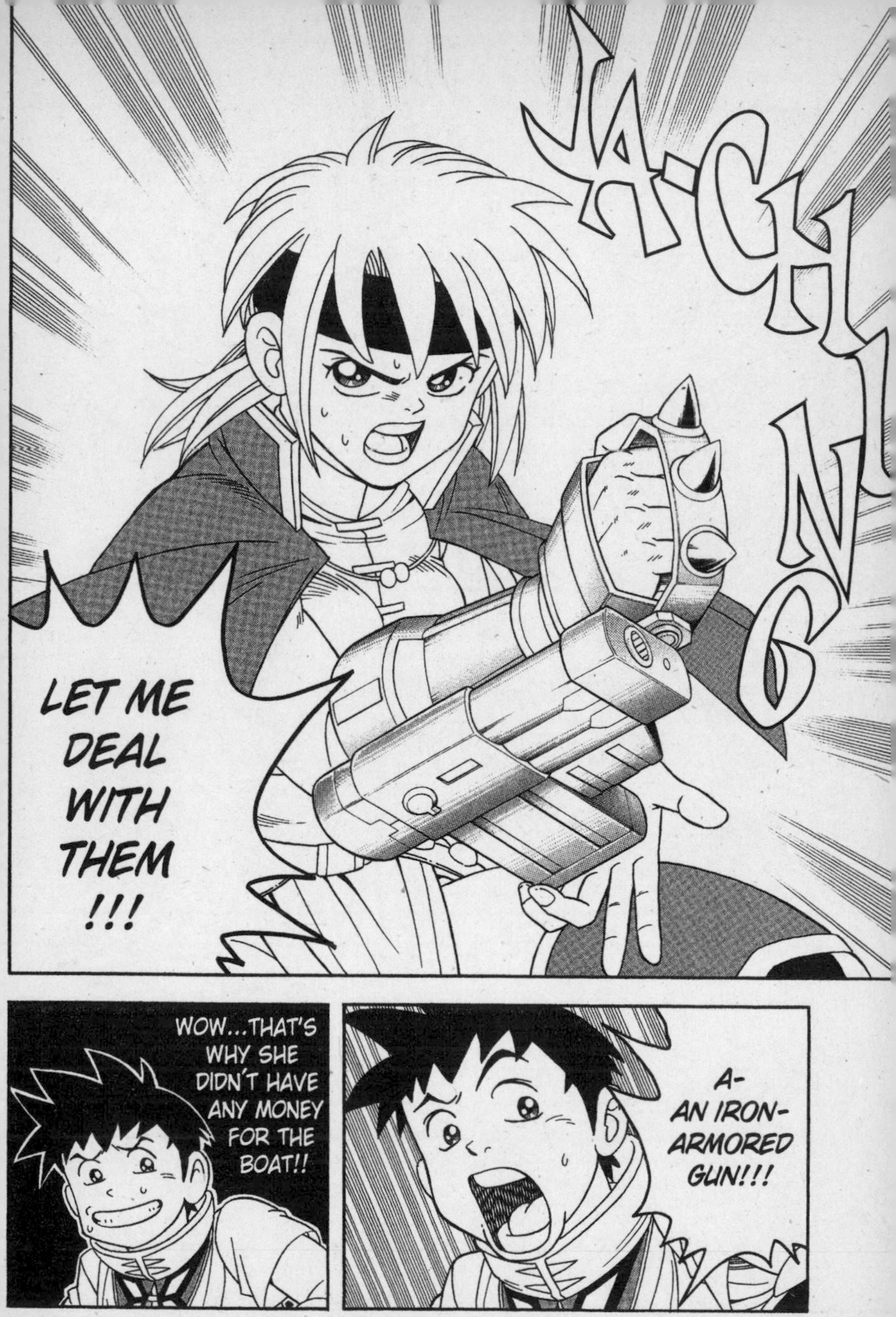
JA-CHING
LET ME DEAL WITH THEM !!!
A- AN IRON-ARMORED GUN!!!
WOW...THAT'S WHY SHE DIDN'T HAVE ANY MONEY FOR THE BOAT!!

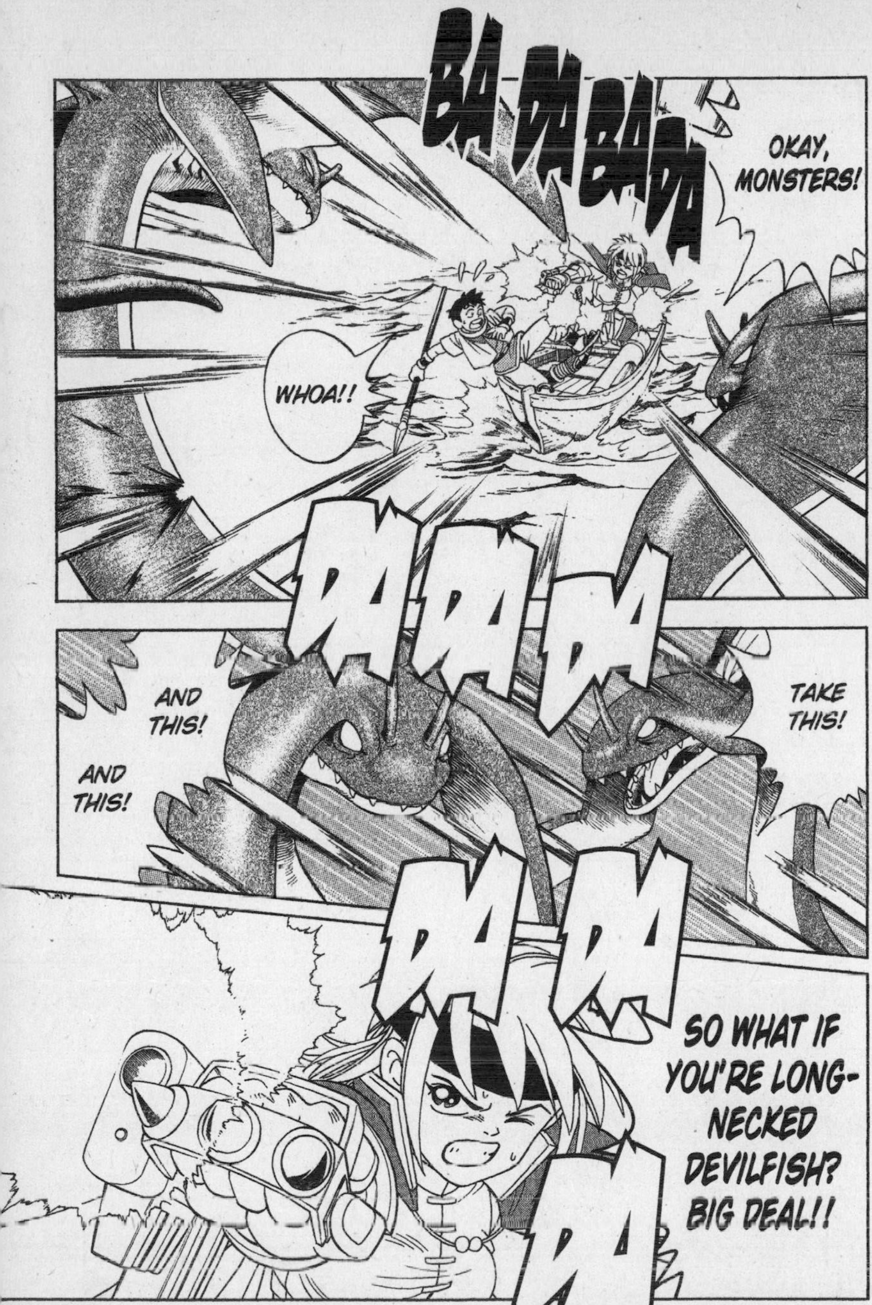
BA-DA BA-DA
OKAY, MONSTERS!
WHOA!!
DA-DA-DA
TAKE THIS!
AND THIS!
AND THIS!
DA DA
SO WHAT IF YOU'RE LONG-NECKED DEVILFISH? BIG DEAL!!
DA

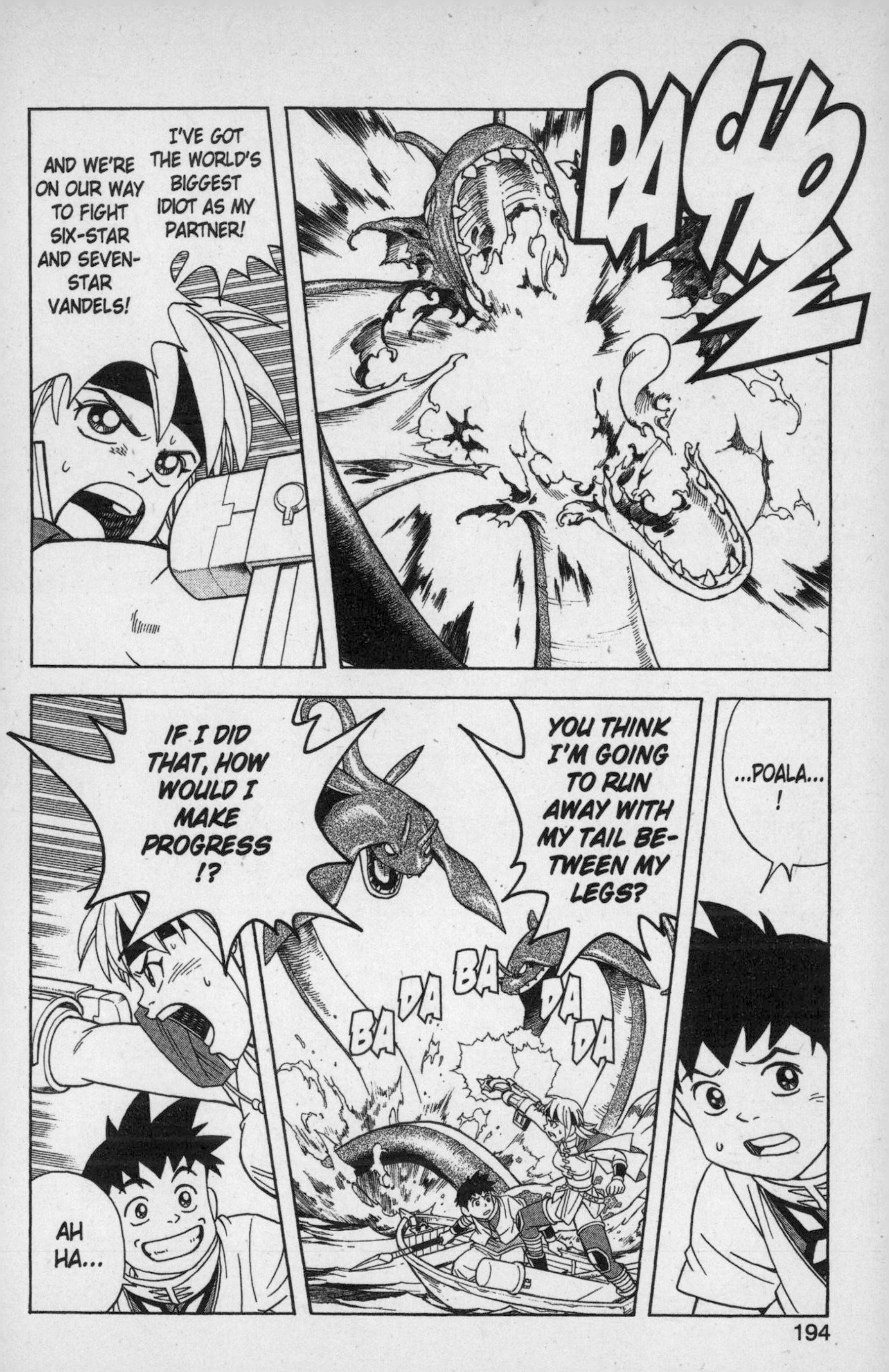
PACHOM
I'VE GOT THE WORLD'S BIGGEST IDIOT AS MY PARTNER!
AND WE'RE ON OUR WAY TO FIGHT SIX-STAR AND SEVEN-STAR VANDELS!
...POALA...!
YOU THINK I'M GOING TO RUN AWAY WITH MY TAIL BE-TWEEN MY LEGS?
BA DA BA DA DA
IF I DID THAT, HOW WOULD I MAKE PROGRESS !?
AH HA...

READ THIS WAY

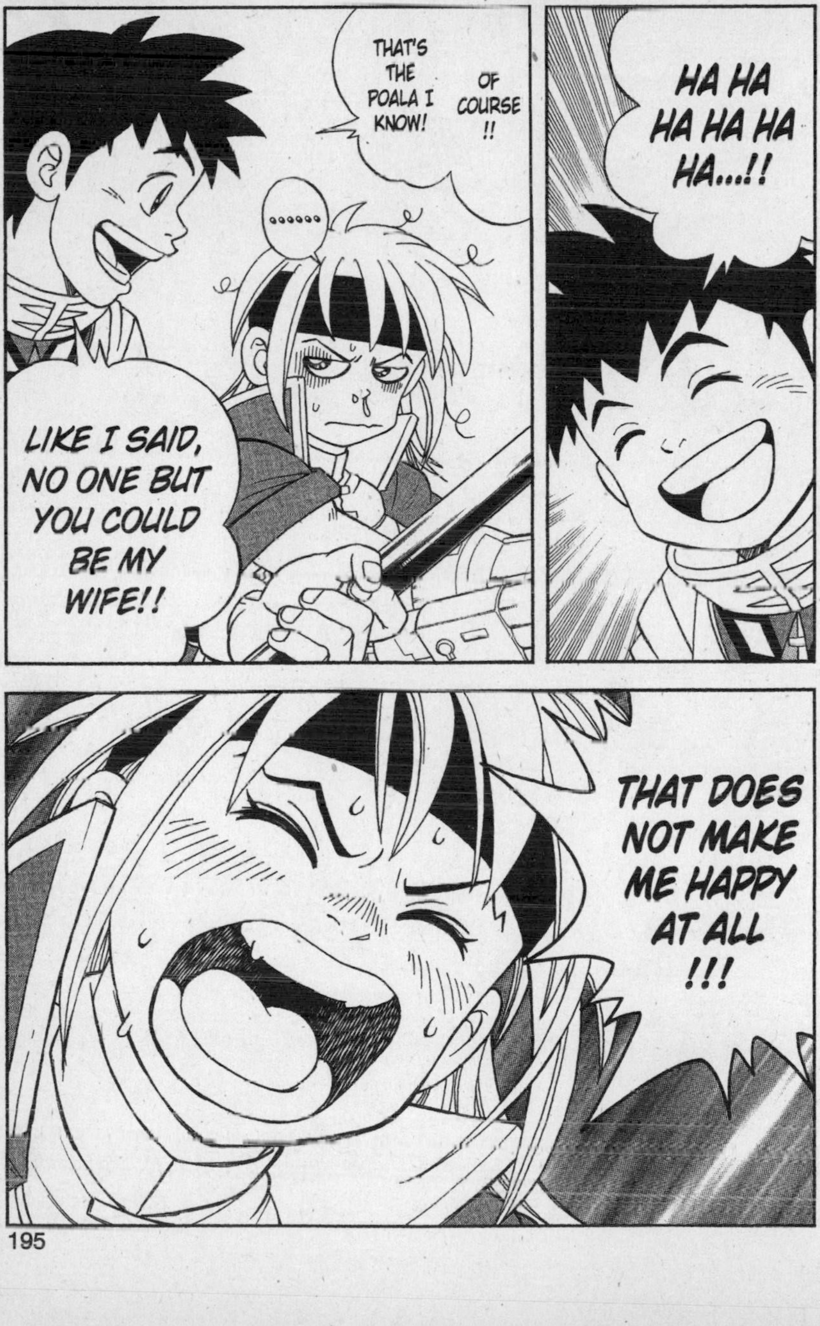
HA HA HA HA HA HA...!!
OF COURSE !!
THAT'S THE POALA I KNOW!
......
LIKE I SAID, NO ONE BUT YOU COULD BE MY WIFE!!
THAT DOES NOT MAKE ME HAPPY AT ALL !!!

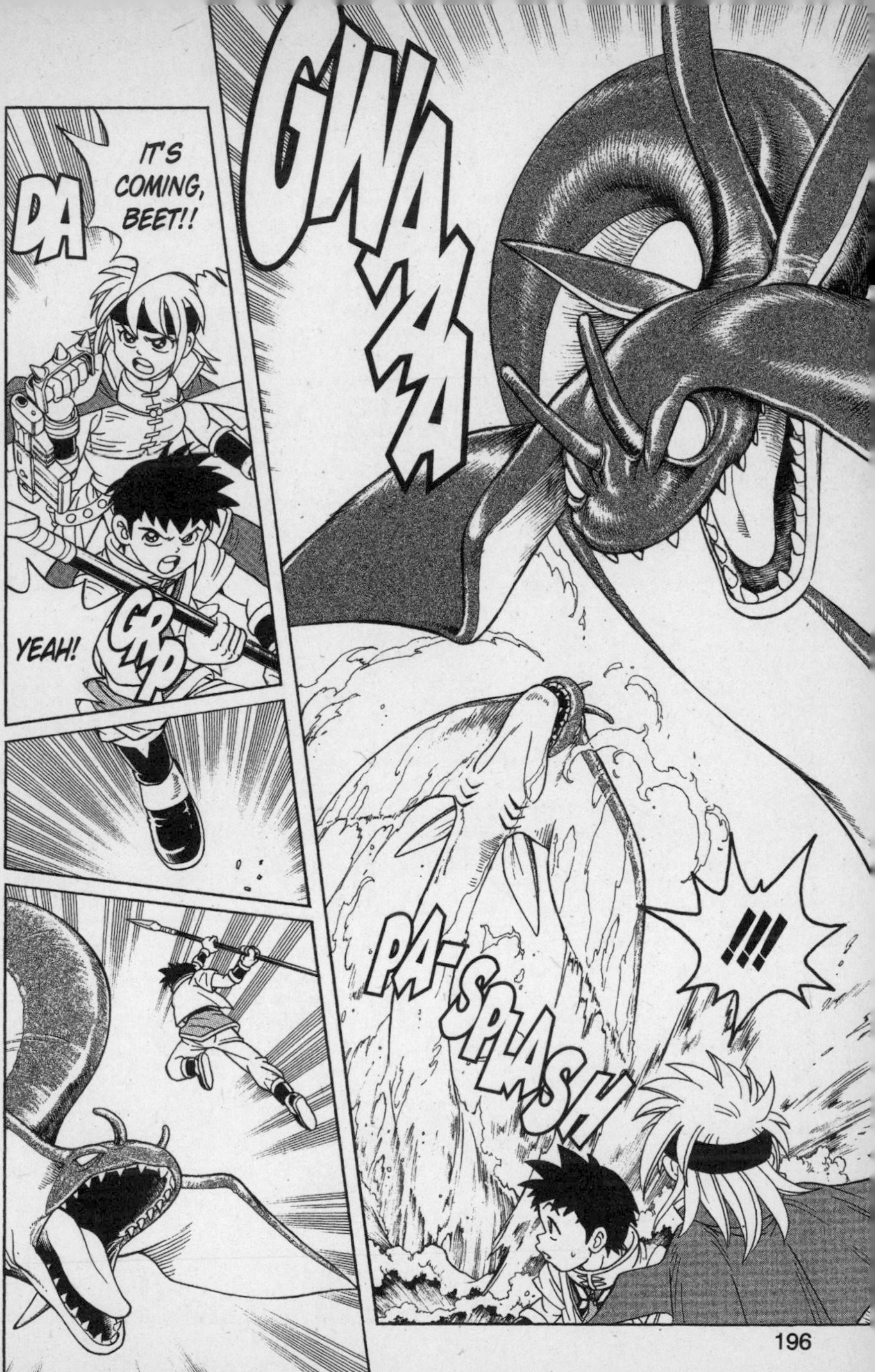
GWAAA
!!!
PA-SPLASH
DA
IT'S COMING, BEET!!
YEAH!
GRP

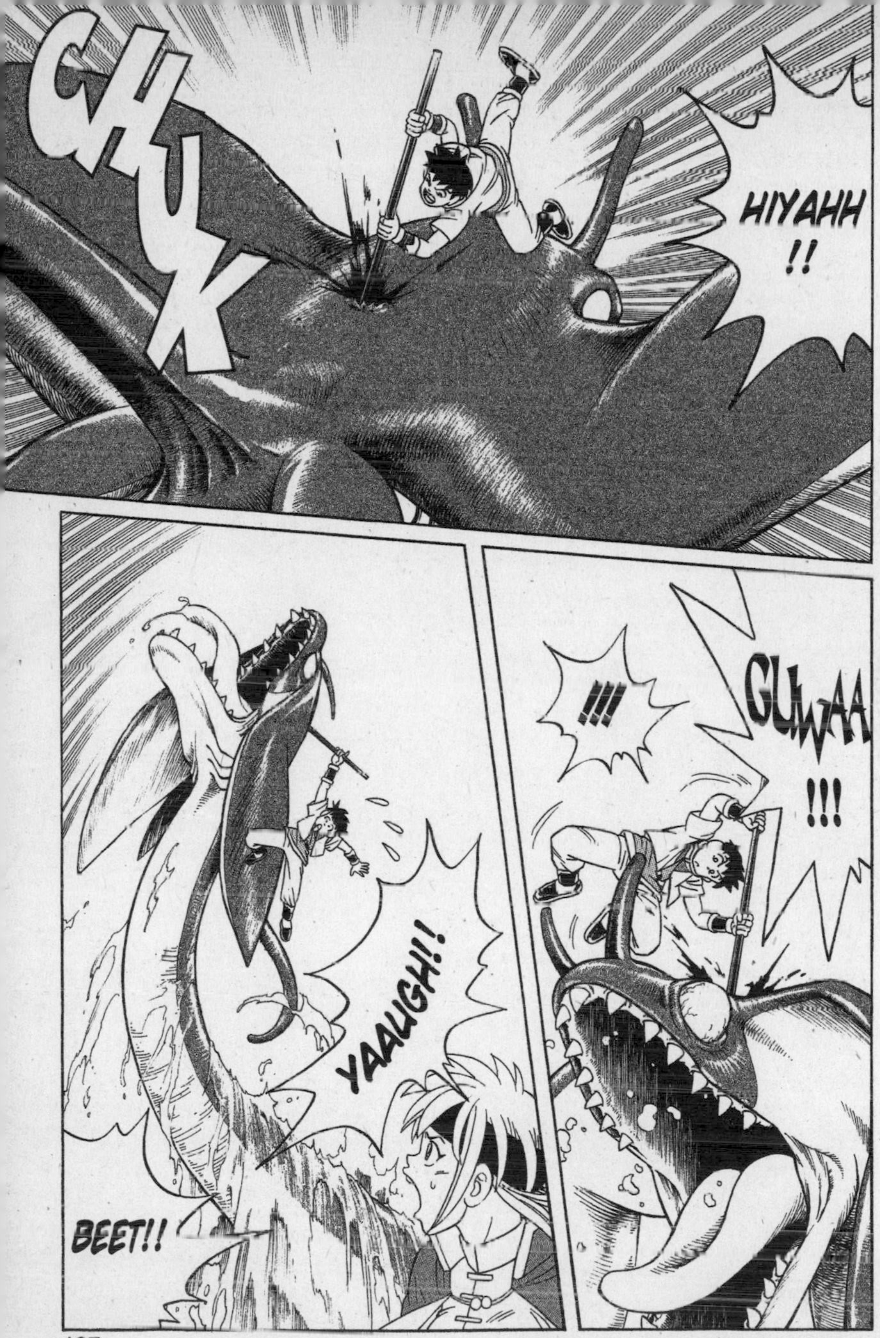
HIYAHH!!
CHUK
GUWAA!!!
!!!
YAAUGH!!
BEET!!

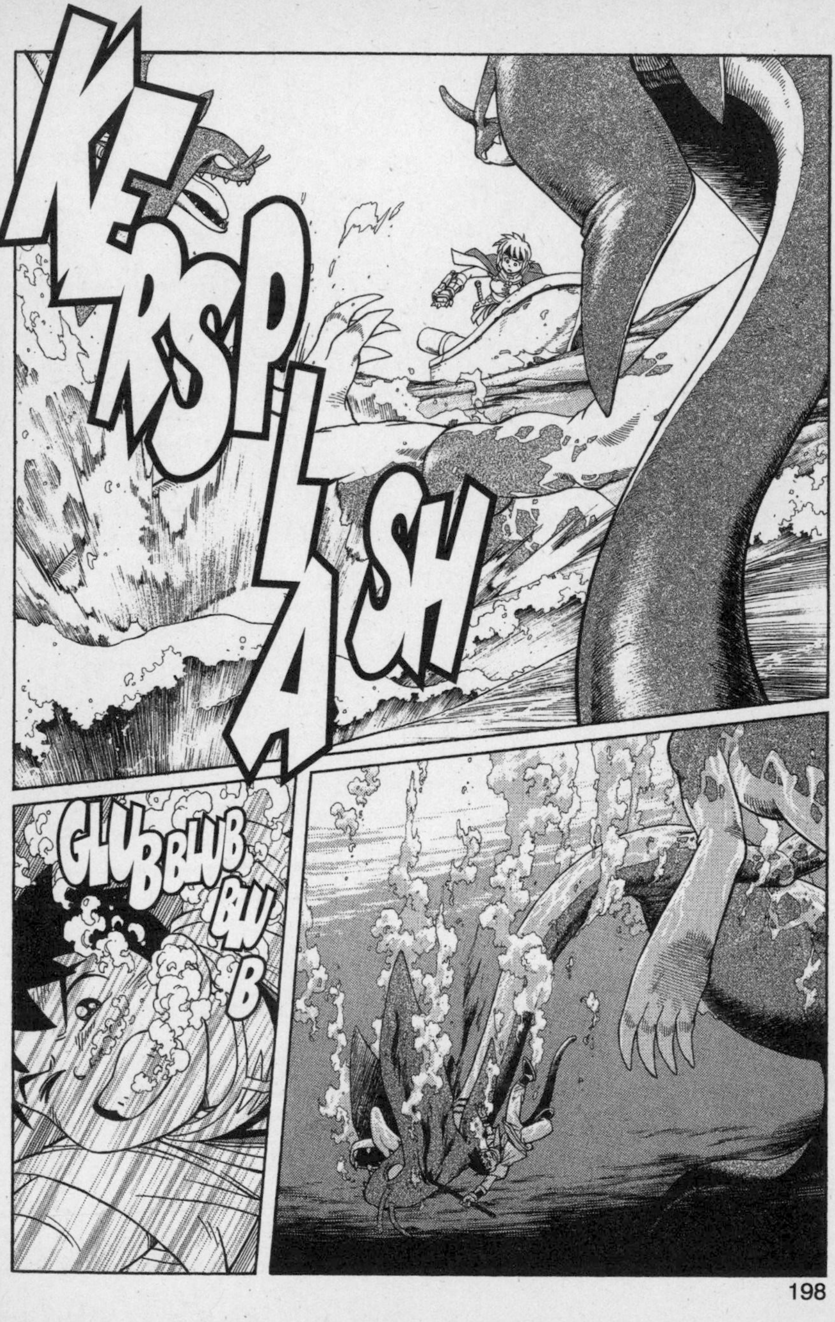
KERSPLASH
GLUB BLUB BLUB

READ THIS WAY

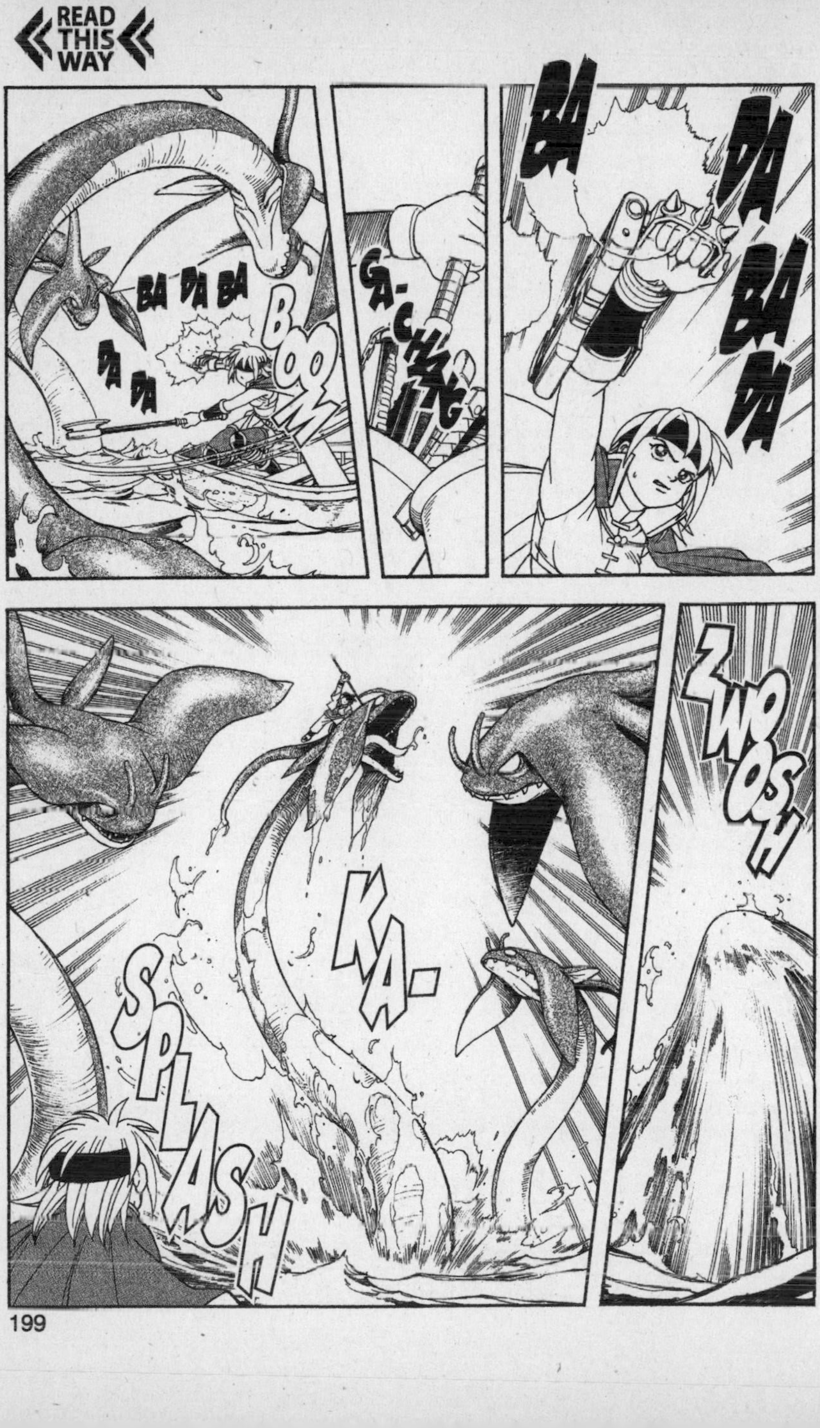
BA
DA BA DA
GA-CHANG
BA DA BA
DA DA
BOOM
ZWOOSH
KA-
SPLASH

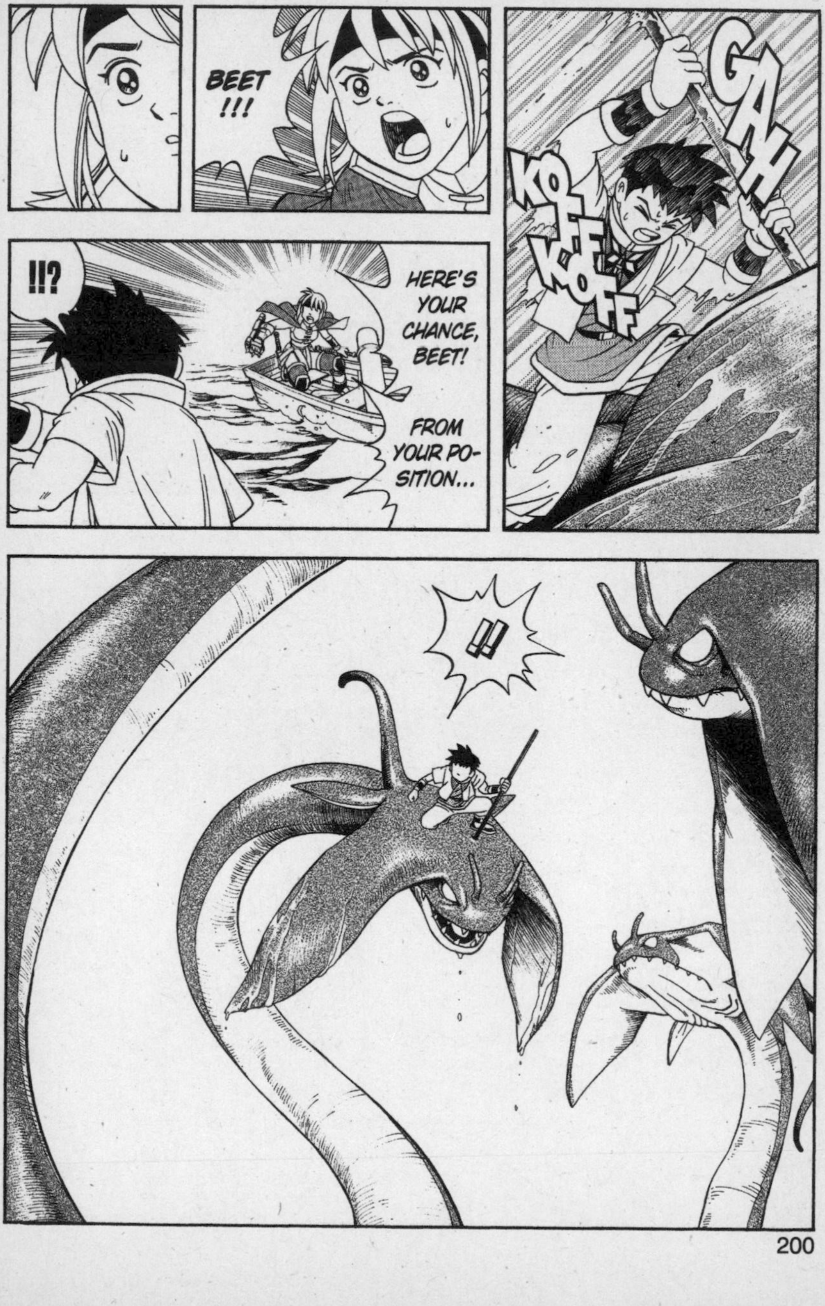
GAH
KOFF KOFF KOFF
BEET !!!
HERE'S YOUR CHANCE, BEET!
FROM YOUR PO-SITION...
!!?
!!

READ THIS WAY

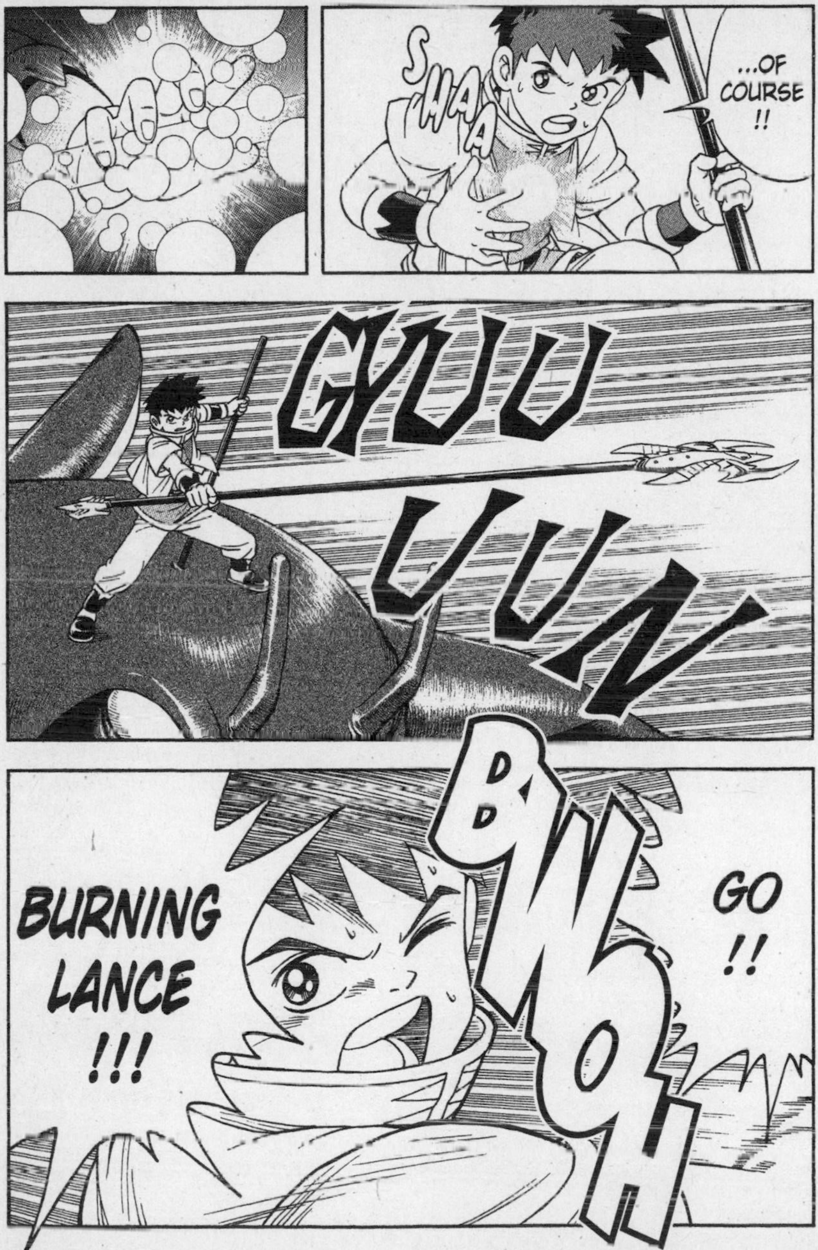
SHAA
...OF COURSE !!
GYUUUUN
GO !!
BWOH
BURNING LANCE !!!

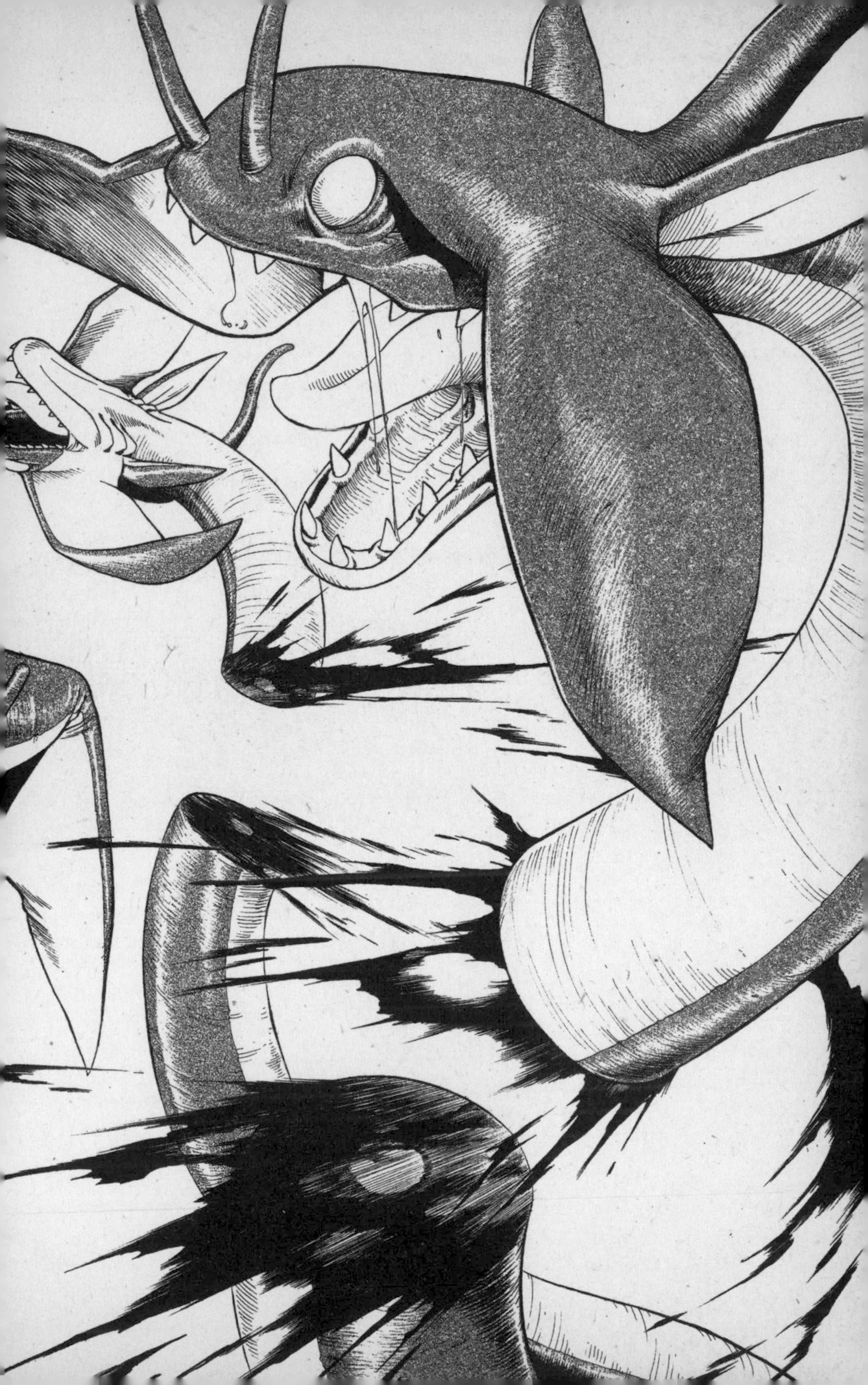

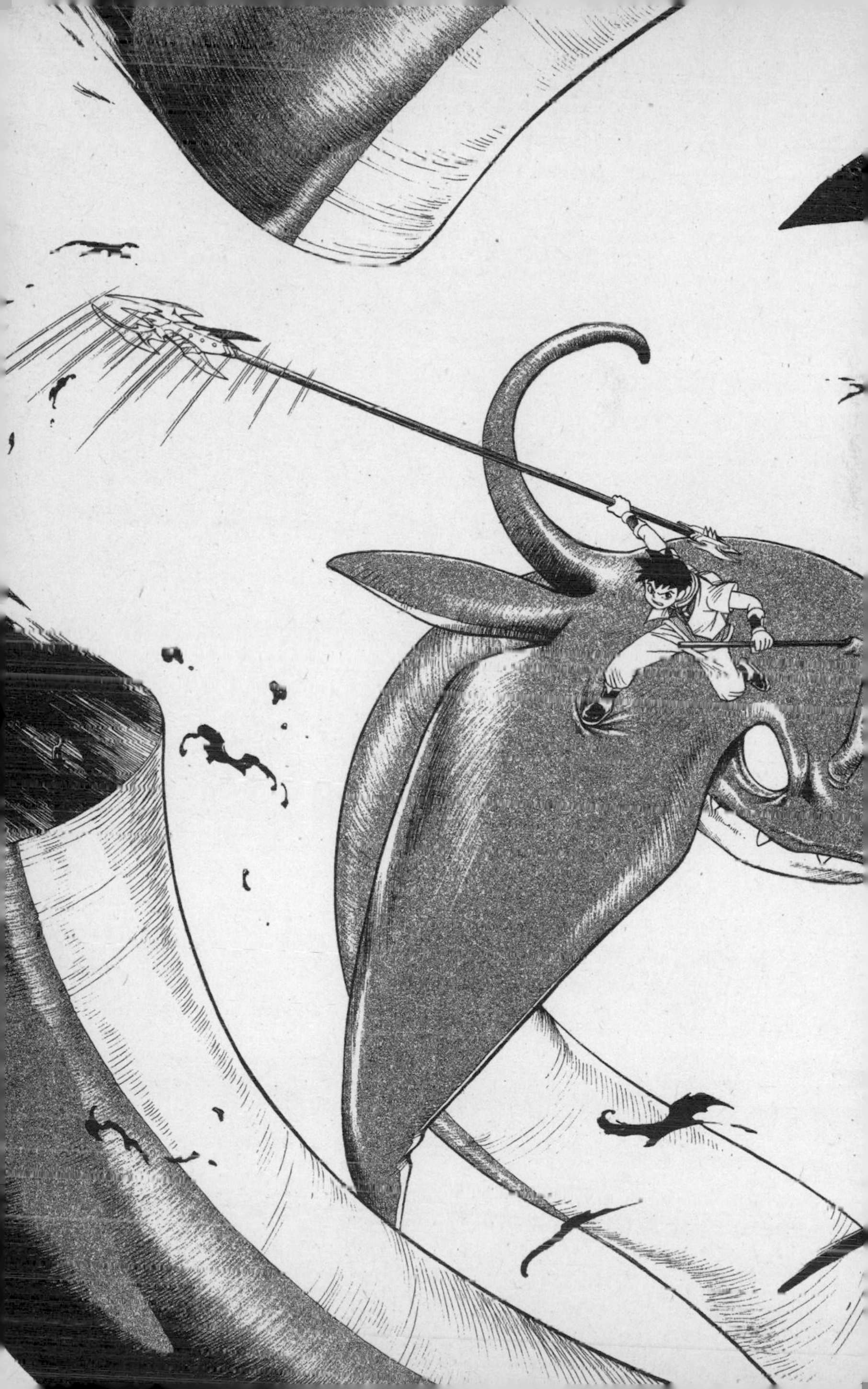

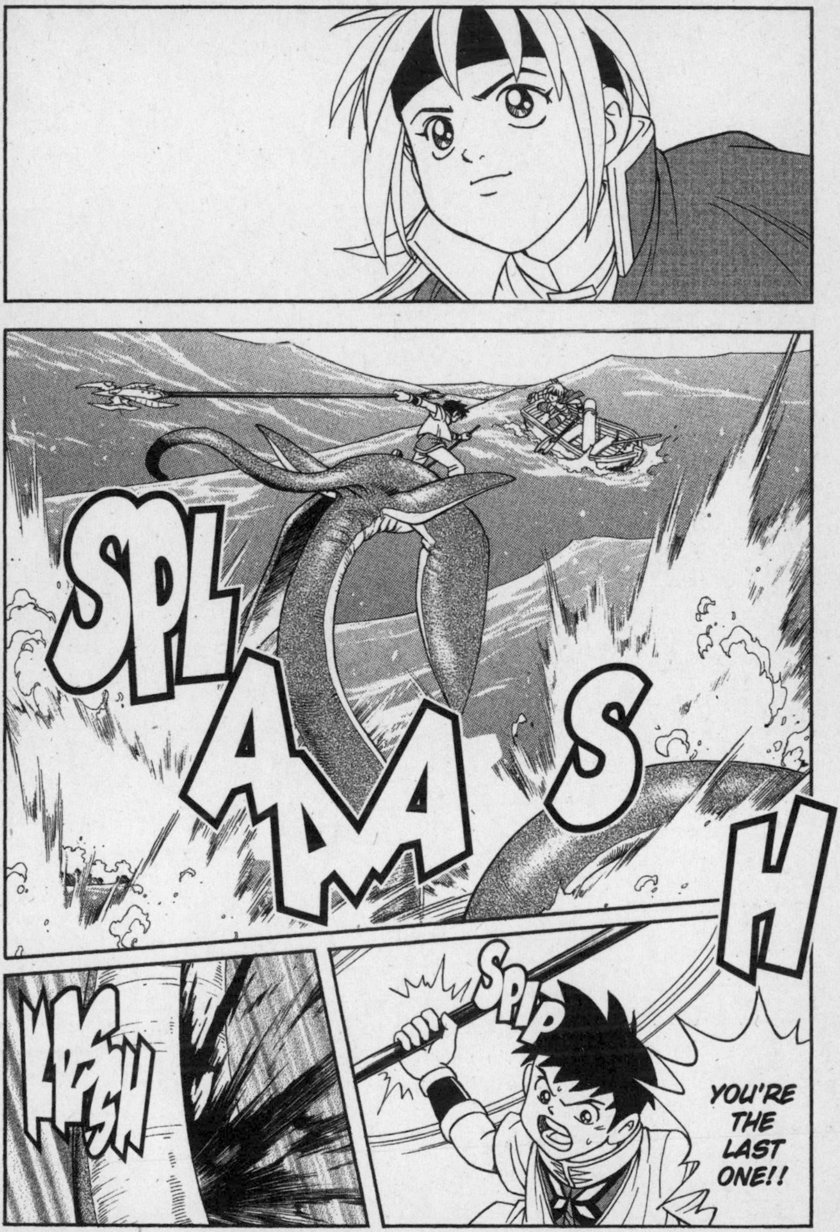
SPLAASH
SPIP
YOU'RE THE LAST ONE!!

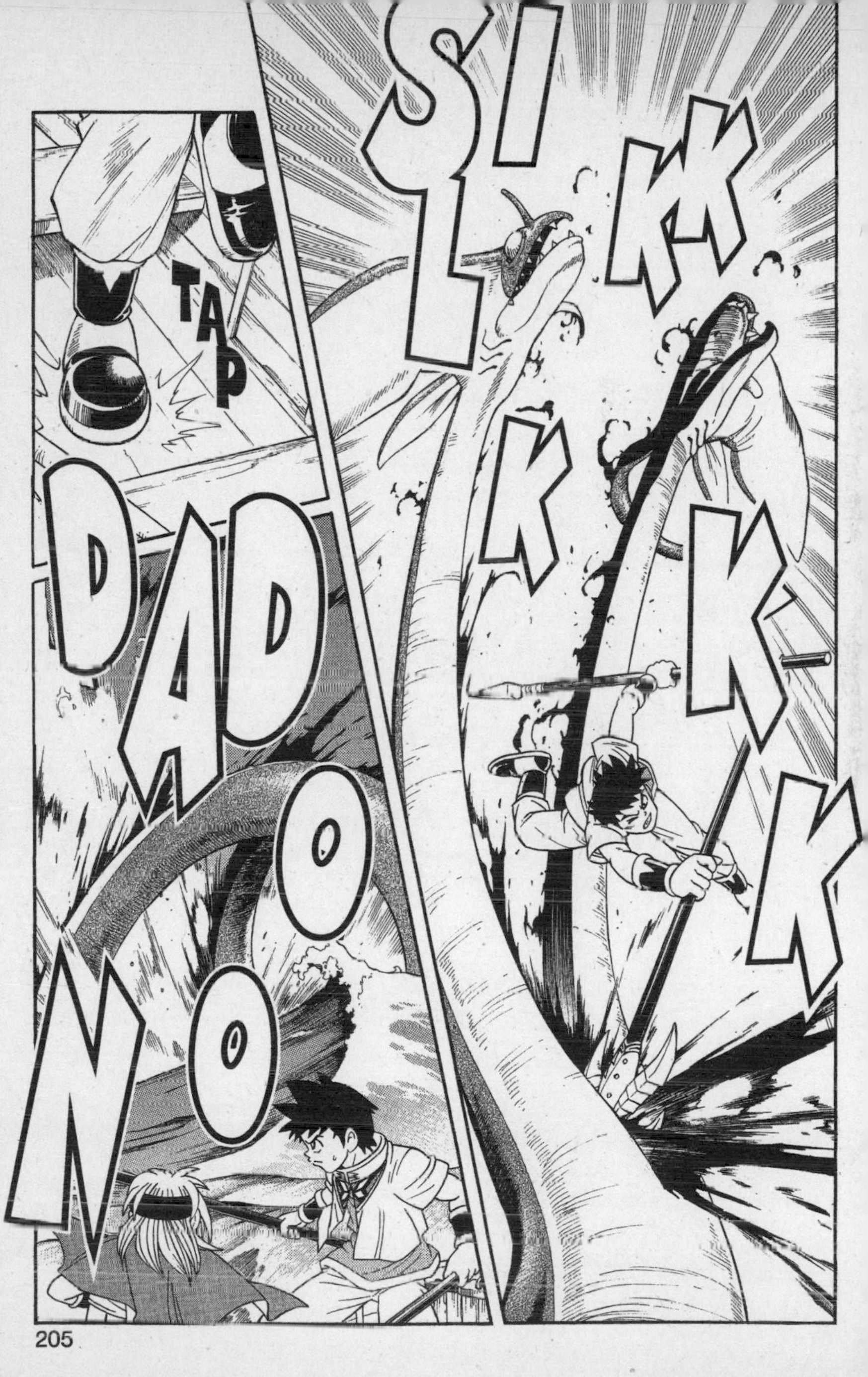
SLIKKKK
TAP
DADOON

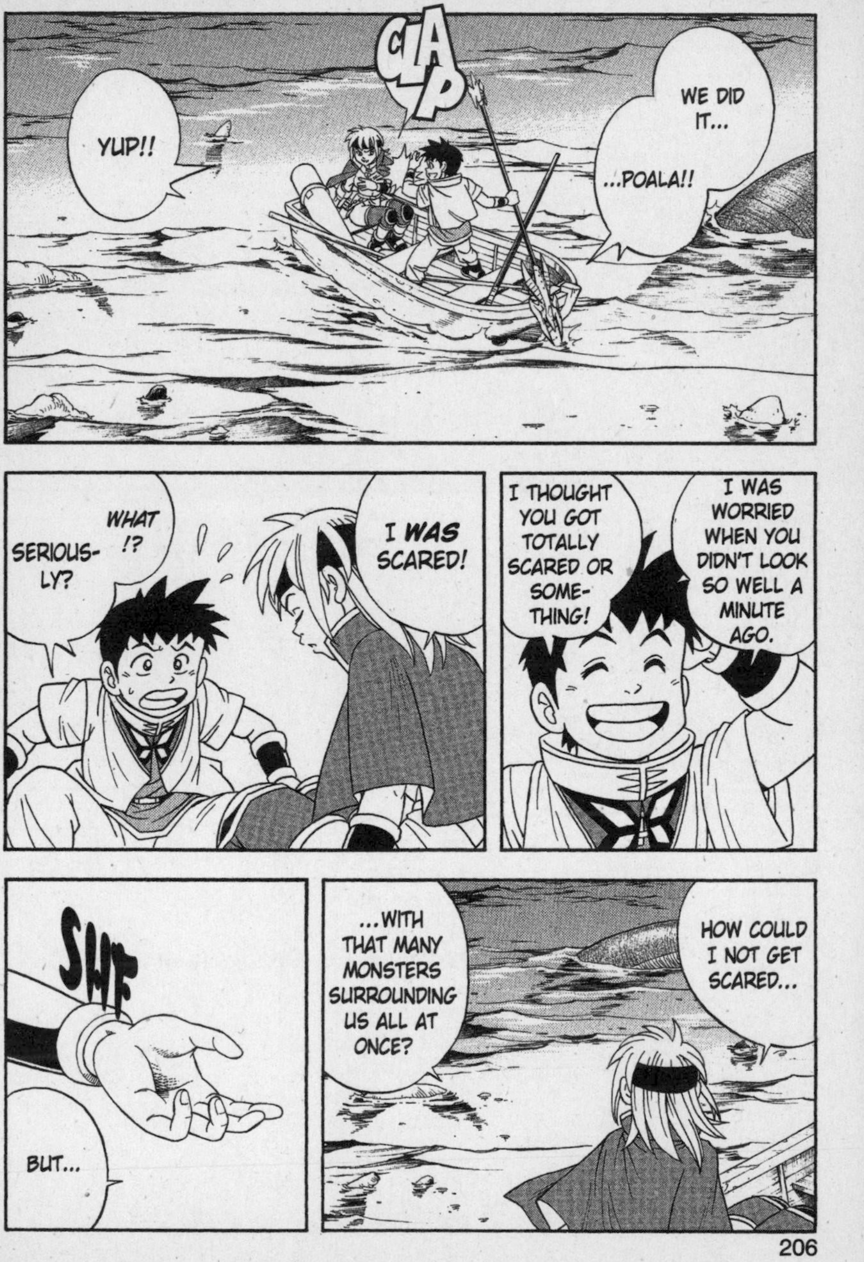
WE DID IT...
...POALA!!
CLAP
YUP!!
I WAS WORRIED WHEN YOU DIDN'T LOOK SO WELL A MINUTE AGO.
I THOUGHT YOU GOT TOTALLY SCARED OR SOME-THING!
I *WAS* SCARED!
WHAT !?
SERIOUS-LY?
HOW COULD I NOT GET SCARED...
...WITH THAT MANY MONSTERS SURROUNDING US ALL AT ONCE?
SHF
BUT...

READ THIS WAY

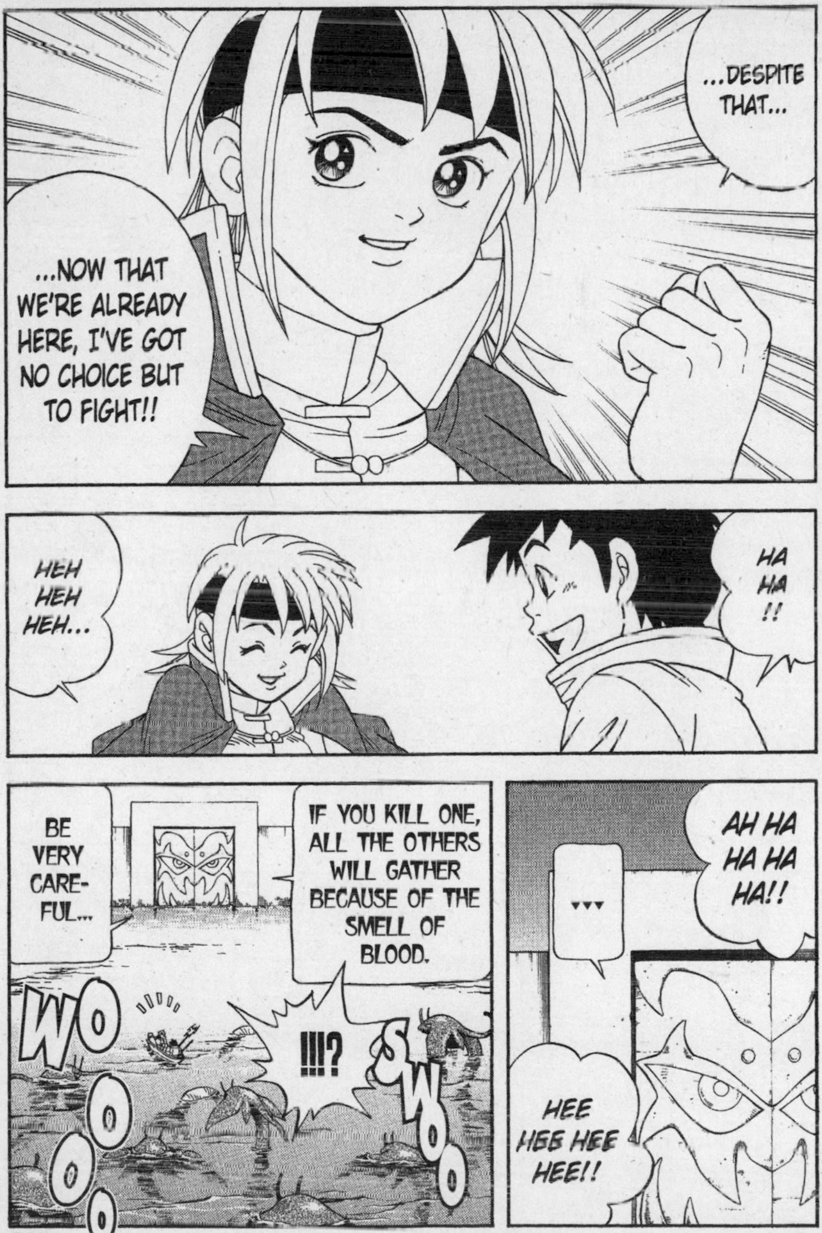
...DESPITE THAT...
...NOW THAT WE'RE ALREADY HERE, I'VE GOT NO CHOICE BUT TO FIGHT!!
HA HA !!
HEH HEH HEH...
AH HA HA HA HA!!
...
HEE HEE HEE HEE!!
IF YOU KILL ONE, ALL THE OTHERS WILL GATHER BECAUSE OF THE SMELL OF BLOOD.
BE VERY CARE-FUL...
!!!?
SWOOO
WOOOOO

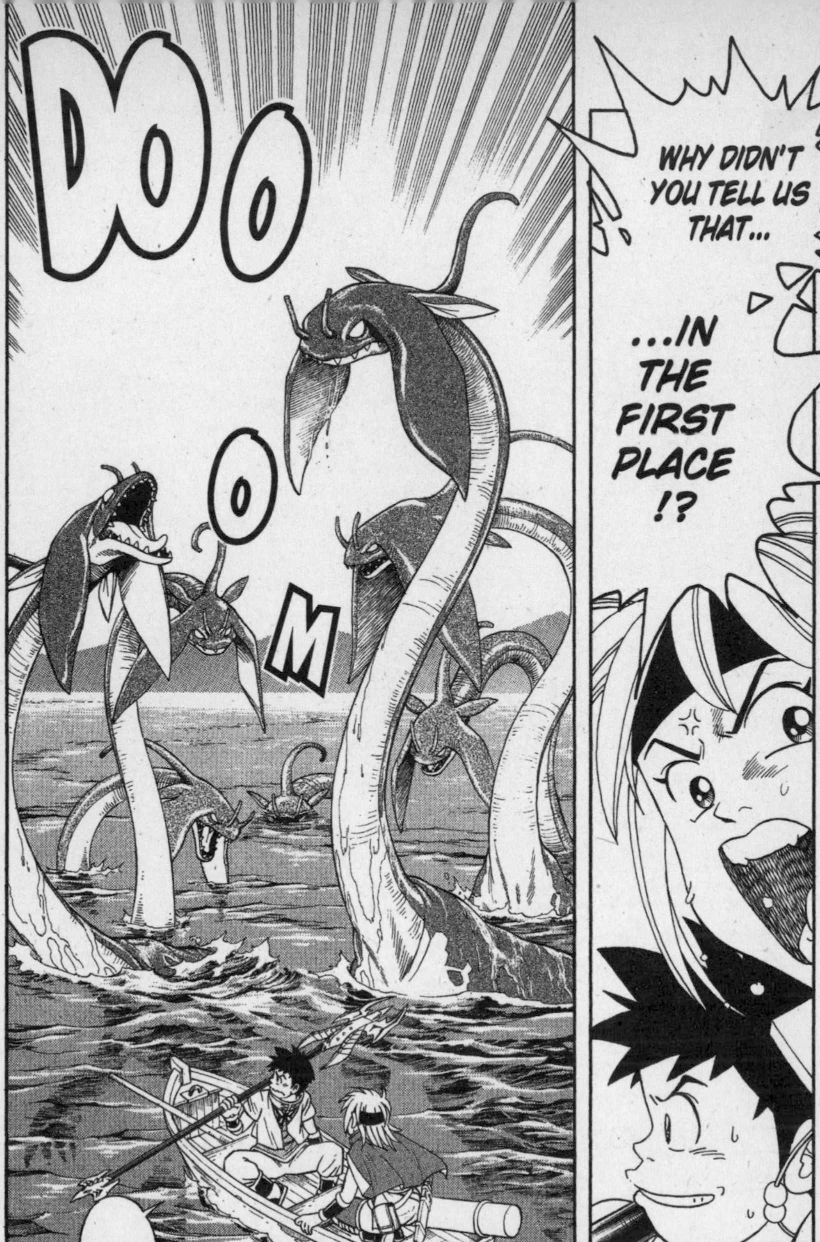
WHY DIDN'T YOU TELL US THAT...
...IN THE FIRST PLACE!?
DOOOM
....

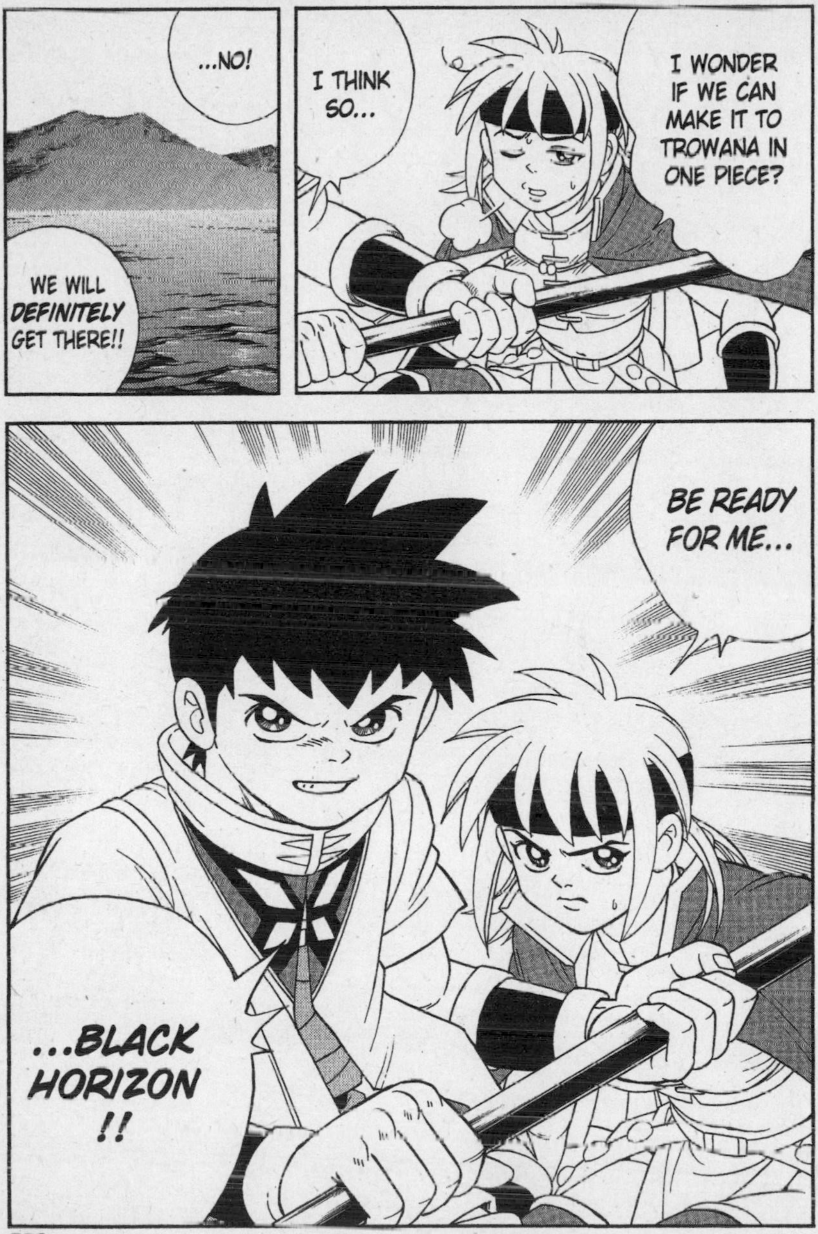
I WONDER IF WE CAN MAKE IT TO TROWANA IN ONE PIECE?
I THINK SO...
...NO!
WE WILL DEFINITELY GET THERE!!
BE READY FOR ME...
...BLACK HORIZON !!

Coming Next Volume...

Beet and Poala thought that Beltorze was bad, but that
was before they wandered into "Black Horizon," a sinister
land ruled by the Vandel Grineed. While fighting Grineed's
most terrifying monsters, Beet runs into his old Buster
friend, Kissu. With this new ally, Beet and Poala get ready
to take on Grineed's minions. But is Kissu still Beet's
friend, or is he in league with darker forces...?

Available in April 2005!

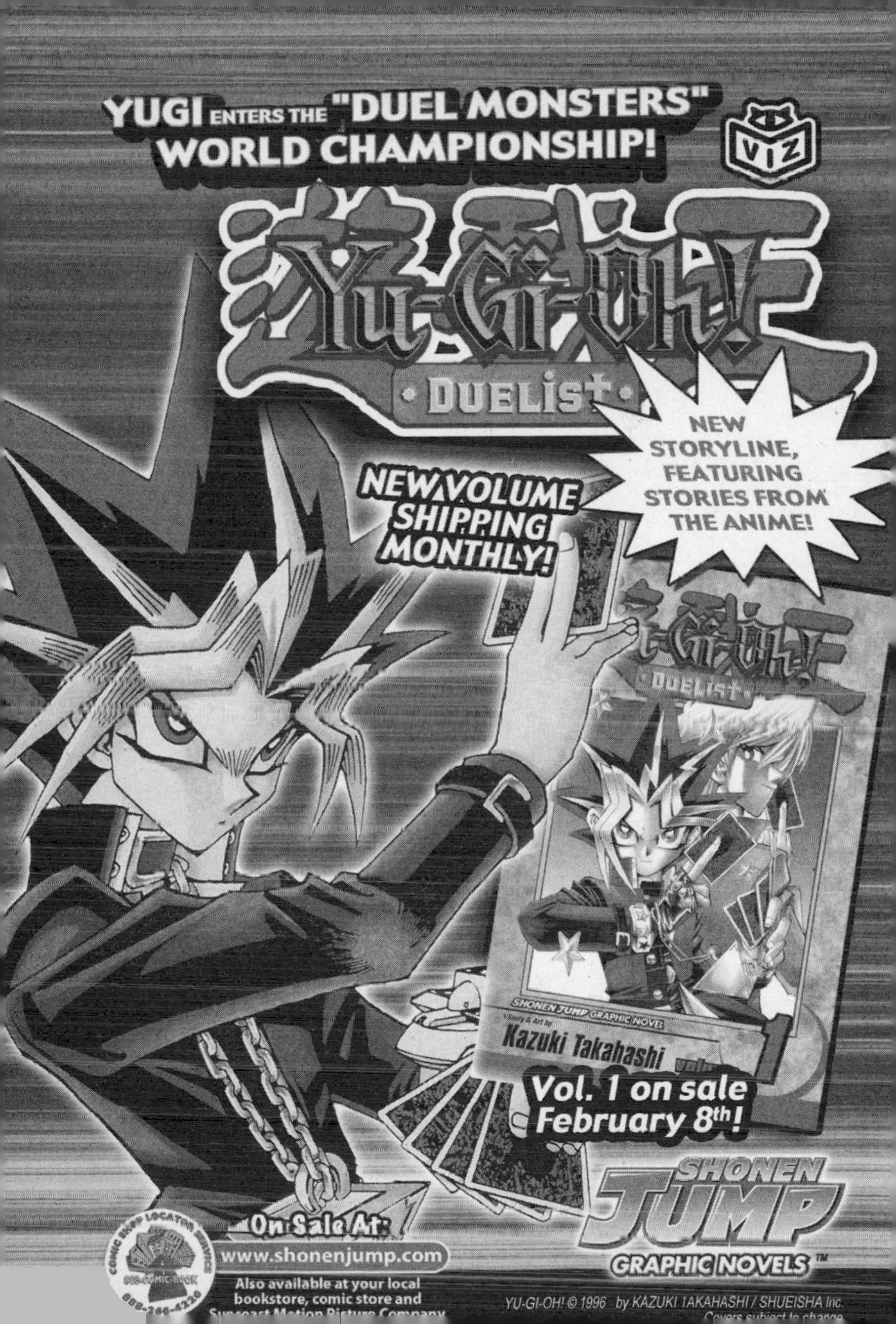
YUGI ENTERS THE "DUEL MONSTERS" WORLD CHAMPIONSHIP!
VIZ
YU-GI-OH!
DUELIST
NEW STORYLINE, FEATURING STORIES FROM THE ANIME!
NEW VOLUME SHIPPING MONTHLY!
YU-GI-OH! DUELIST
SHONEN JUMP GRAPHIC NOVEL
Kazuki Takahashi
Vol. 1 on sale February 8th!
SHONEN JUMP GRAPHIC NOVELS ™
On Sale At:
www.shonenjump.com
Also available at your local
bookstore, comic store and
YU-GI-OH! © 1996 by KAZUKI TAKAHASHI / SHUEISHA Inc.

DRAGON BALL ©1984 by BIRD STUDIO / SHUEISHA Inc.
Cover Art Subject to Change.

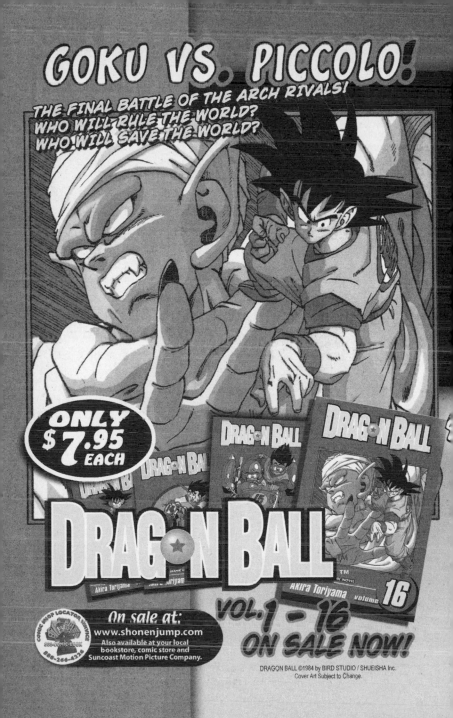
DRAGON BALL ©1984 by BIRD STUDIO / SHUEISHA Inc.
Cover Art Subject to Change.

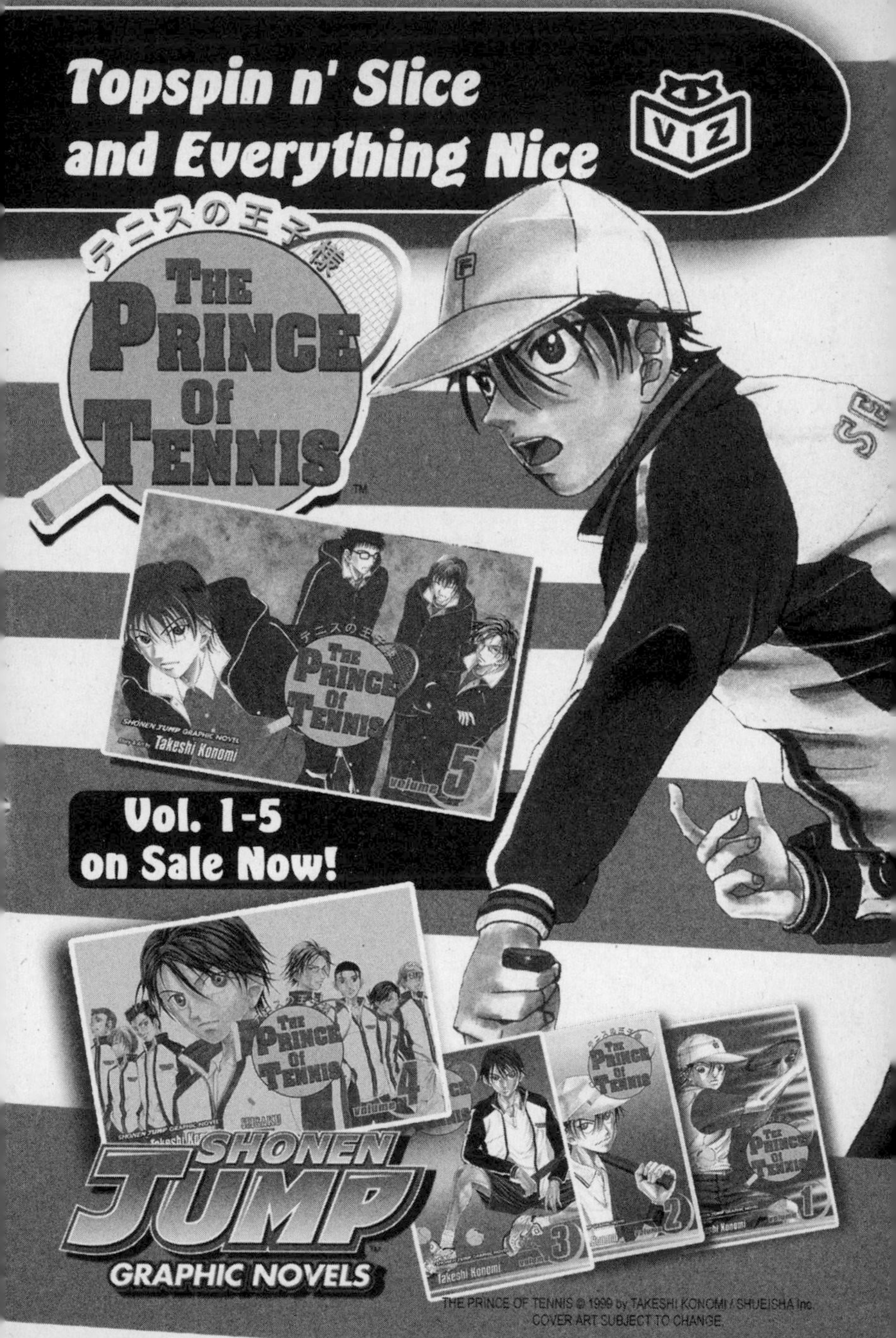
Topspin n' Slice and Everything Nice
VIZ
テニスの王子様
THE PRINCE OF TENNIS™
Vol. 1-5 on Sale Now!
SHONEN JUMP GRAPHIC NOVELS
THE PRINCE OF TENNIS © 1999 by TAKESHI KONOMI / SHUEISHA Inc.
COVER ART SUBJECT TO CHANGE.

Victory is just one goal away!

WHISTLE! volume 3

Vol. 1-3 On Sale Now!

All Books $7⁹⁹ and Under

WHISTLE!

WHISTLE! volume 2
Daisuke Higuchi

WHISTLE! volume 1
KAZA
Daisuke Higuchi

On sale at:
www.shonenjump.com
Also available at your local bookstore, comic store and Suncoast Motion Picture Company.

COMIC SHOP LOCATOR SERVICE
888-266-4226

WHISTLE! © 1998 by DAISUKE HIGUCHI / SHUEISHA Inc.

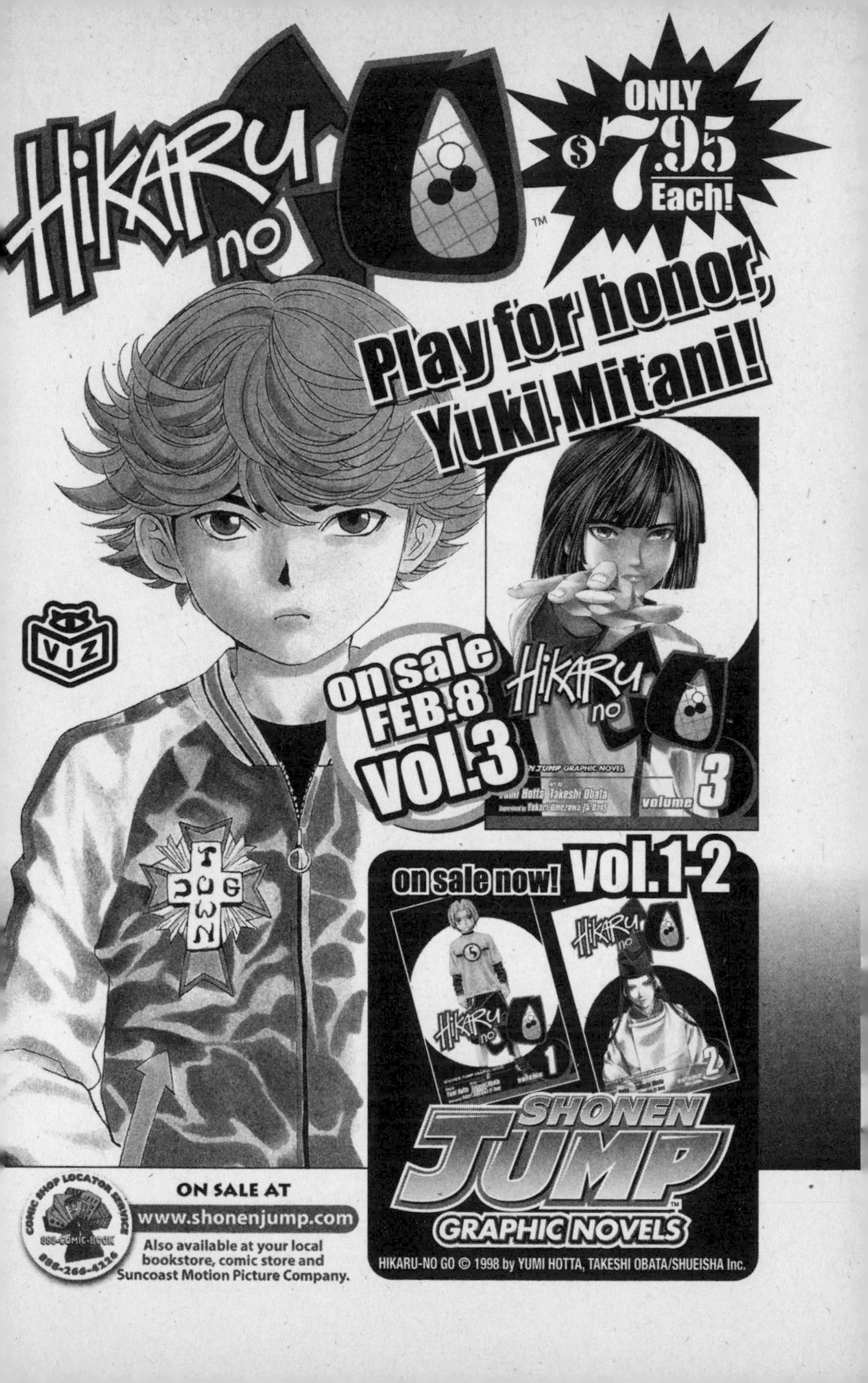

HIKARU no GO™
ONLY $7.95 Each!
Play for honor, Yuki Mitani!
on sale FEB.8 vol.3
HIKARU no GO
SHONEN JUMP GRAPHIC NOVEL
volume 3
on sale now! vol.1-2
SHONEN JUMP™ GRAPHIC NOVELS
ON SALE AT
www.shonenjump.com
Also available at your local bookstore, comic store and Suncoast Motion Picture Company.
COMIC SHOP LOCATOR SERVICE
888-COMIC-BOOK
888-266-4226
HIKARU-NO GO © 1998 by YUMI HOTTA, TAKESHI OBATA/SHUEISHA Inc.

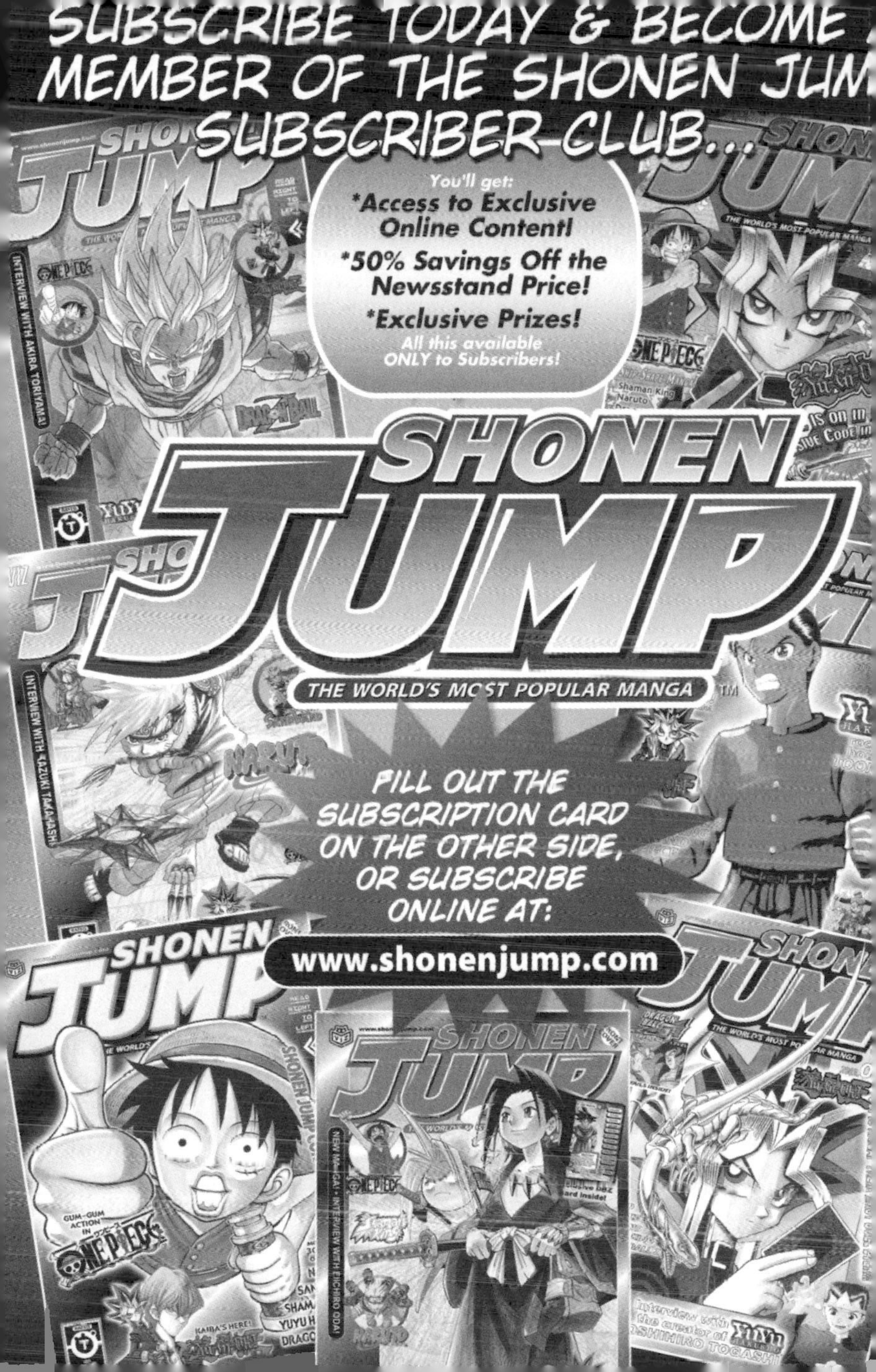
SUBSCRIBE TODAY & BECOME A MEMBER OF THE SHONEN JUMP SUBSCRIBER CLUB...
You'll get:
*Access to Exclusive Online Content!
*50% Savings Off the Newsstand Price!
*Exclusive Prizes!
All this available ONLY to Subscribers!
SHONEN JUMP
THE WORLD'S MOST POPULAR MANGA
FILL OUT THE SUBSCRIPTION CARD ON THE OTHER SIDE, OR SUBSCRIBE ONLINE AT:
www.shonenjump.com

Save 50% off the newsstand price!

THE WORLD'S MOST POPULAR MANGA

**Subscribe today and save
50% OFF the cover price, PLUS enjoy
all the benefits of the SHONEN JUMP
SUBSCRIBER CLUB, exclusive online
content & special prizes.
ONLY AVAILABLE to SUBSCRIBERS!**

☑**YES!** Please enter my 1 year subscription
(12 issues) to *SHONEN JUMP* at the INCREDIBLY
LOW SUBSCRIPTION RATE of $29.95, and sign me
up for the Shonen Jump Subscriber Club.

$29⁹⁵

NAME

ADDRESS

CITY   STATE   ZIP

E-MAIL ADDRESS

☐ **MY CHECK IS ENCLOSED**   ☐ **BILL ME LATER**

CREDIT CARD: ☐ **VISA**   ☐ **MASTERCARD**

ACCOUNT #   EXP. DATE

SIGNATURE

CLIP AND MAIL TO ➤   SHONEN JUMP
                            Subscriptions Service Dept.
                            P.O. Box 515
                            Mount Morris, IL 61054-0515

Make checks payable to: **SHONEN JUMP.**
Canada add US $12. No foreign orders. Allow 6-8 weeks for delivery.

P5SJGN   YU-GI-OH! © 1996 by KAZUKI TAKAHASHI / SHUEISHA Inc.